DRYDEN: THE POETICS OF TRANSLATION

Judith Sloman argues that the collections of translations that Dryden produced or contributed to are unified works of literature, not just miscellaneous collections. Through his selection of passages, through his use of language, and through changes and new emphases in the passages he translated Dryden could express his personality and convictions. In this book the author is therefore concerned in part with the connection between personality and art and in part with the political, religious, and literary context in which Dryden worked. Although *Fables* receives most emphasis, *Ovid's Epistles*, *Miscellany Poems*, *Sylvae*, *Examen Poeticum*, and the *Aeneis* are also examined in some detail.

Dryden has a re-creative approach to translation, integrating groups of short poems into a whole with epic force. Just as multiplicity and complexity were facts of Dryden's character and situation, they are characteristic of his composite poems, which create a unified and integrated whole out of a multiplicity of parts. *Fables* is thus not a unique entity in Dryden's canon but the conclusion of a pattern that can be traced through his entire career as translator and poet.

JUDITH SLOMAN was a member of the Department of English, University of Calgary, from 1968 until her death in 1980.
ANNE MCWHIR, Department of English, University of Calgary, prepared Professor Sloman's manuscript for publication.

JUDITH SLOMAN

Dryden: The Poetics of Translation

Prepared for publication by Anne McWhir

UNIVERSITY OF TORONTO PRESS
Toronto Buffalo London

Toronto Buffalo London
Printed in Canada
ISBN 0-8020-5642-3

Canadian Cataloguing in Publication Data

Sloman, Judith.
Dryden: the poetics of translation
Includes bibliographical references and index.
ISBN 0-8020-5642-3
1. Dryden, John, 1631–1700 – Criticism and interpretation. 2. English poetry – Translations from foreign languages – History and criticism. I. McWhir, Anne Ruth, 1947– II. Title.
PR3427.T73S43 1985 821'.4 C85-098037-2

Publication of this book has been made possible by grants from the Canadian Federation for the Humanities, using funds provided by the Social Sciences and Humanities Research Council of Canada, from the Endowment Fund of the University of Calgary, and from the Publications Fund of the University of Toronto Press.

Contents

FOREWORD by Anne McWhir vii

PREFACE by Patricia Brückmann ix

1
The Poetics of Translation: Beyond Metaphrase, Paraphrase, and Imitation 3

2
Translation and Personal Identity 26

3
Collective Translations 51

4
Sylvae and Epicurean Art 77

5
Examen Poeticum: Dryden against His Age 108

6
Dryden's *Aeneis* and *Fables* 125

7
Fables Ancient and Modern 147

8
Dryden's Theological Poets 174

9
The Use of Hieroglyphs in *Fables* 207

EPILOGUE 220

NOTES 223

GENERAL INDEX 251

INDEX OF DRYDEN'S WORKS 262

Foreword

In the last month of her life Judith Sloman asked me as a friend and a colleague to see her book on Dryden through the press. Without any special knowledge of Dryden I undertook simply to check the manuscript for mechanical errors and slips in quotations and notes and to write on Judy's behalf to the University of Toronto Press, which had already expressed interest in seeing the manuscript. Perhaps my lack of specialized knowledge has been an advantage: the book remains Judy's alone, and where I have had to change phrases or clarify arguments, I have tried throughout to do so unobtrusively.

Most of the manuscript had been typed from a pencilled draft by the time of Judy's death but had not yet been checked and proofread. A few sections still needed to be typed from the rough version. The checking process was more laborious for me than it would have been for Judy, because I had to retrace her steps, going through her books and files to complete the rather sketchy documentation in some of her notes. Her concluding statement, still very much a draft, turned up in the course of the search, and I have included it in its rough state as an epilogue because it clearly belongs with the rest of the book.

In completing this project I have had the advantage of help and advice from many friends and colleagues. Joyce Kee patiently and efficiently retyped the whole manuscript, incorporating new material along with my changes and corrections: without her help my task would have been almost impossible. For encouragement and practical assistance I should also like to thank James Black, Patricia Brückmann, John LeBlanc, Jay Macpherson, Earl Miner, David Oakleaf, and Neil Querengesser. The final version of the book has benefited from the criticisms and suggestions of readers for the University of Toronto Press and of its editors, Prudence Tracy and Joan

Bulger. Some of the ideas in chapter 1 were published in different form in 'An Interpretation of Dryden's *Fables*,' *Eighteenth-Century Studies*, 4 (1970–1), 199–211, and they appear in this book with the permission of the editors. In her notes Judy makes some acknowledgments of her own; I should like to acknowledge my debt to the staffs of the William Andrew Clark Memorial Library, Los Angeles, of the University of Calgary Library, and of Research Services, University of Calgary.

ANNE McWHIR
University of Calgary
October 1984

Preface

That Dryden's late translations are not simply random selections from ancient and modern authors is not a wholly new critical discovery. In 1968, as Judith Sloman finished her University of Minnesota dissertation on the structure of the *Fables* under the direction of Samuel Holt Monk, Earl Miner, in his *Dryden's Poetry* (published in 1967), was arguing that this collection of translations did not show a decrease of poetic power, reflected in a need for the groundwork of an original, but was rather a reinvention of particular ancients and moderns for a seventeenth-century occasion. That occasion in turn both re-created and shared the borrowed origin and, in combination with the contexts chosen, made a new poem.

This technique is not really at odds with Dryden's usual practice. *Absalom and Achitophel* 'translates' biblical and Miltonic story and depends on the reader's response to Dryden's placing seventeenth-century events within the biblical experience of David's political crisis and then within Milton's larger biblical story. Both these contexts, in very different ways, also reassert and redefine doctrines of kingship, the state, and the role of those other members of the body politic who, if they no longer subscribe to earlier views about what the waters of the rough rude sea might do to an anointed king, are at least agreed that there is virtue to unity, not least for poetry. Dryden's only anxiety would be that this influence might go unrecognized, for, without this recognition, his poem would be merely propaganda. If his immediate design in *Absalom and Achitophel* was to hang Shaftesbury, that, as we know, failed. To argue, as Miner and Sloman do, that *Fables* and other 'collective translations' are deliberate choices from the tradition, which resonate and give the grandeur of generality to Dryden's immediate experience, is really only to reverse the process we can see easily in *Absalom and Achitophel.* The usual body of allusion forms the foreground of the main story and Dryden's own experience acts as if it were biblical or Miltonic echo. The effect is the same. If the earlier satire is not merely propagandistic because it lives in a larger tradition, then the later poems are not merely translations because they have been given new life in a quite literal way. They are no longer just themselves for they have a new context which gives them different valence and, in addition to the altering neighbourhood of other poems, they also have the career of their translator as a ground for this new figure.

Our reading of Dryden has generally been too partial, as Jean Hagstrum's *Sex and Sensibility* with its emphasis on the more sensual passages in the plays and in the less read poems tells us, and the effect has been, through a concentration on the most famous satires and places in the prose, to lose sight of the complex wholeness of that writer who moved from lyric to play to satire to essay to translation, not necessarily in sequence. If we read him only in this limited way, we lose his ground and hence his figure. Part of Judith Sloman's concern for Dryden is her sense of the wholeness of the career and the appearance of the man who signs, she says in an early page, every line of his work; the direction we know from *Absalom* of *poeta loquitur* might be everywhere. Her account of these later poems as 'collective translations' is meant primarily to establish their integrity as poems in the way I have suggested above in my analogy with the allusive procedures of the early satires. She also wants to highlight a preoccupation that dominated his career, his fear of the disintegration of language and the consequent fragmentation of literary experience. Writing from an exceptional command of the canon, her allusions to works earlier than the translations suggest a poet (not unlike contemporaries who wrote about language) with what Sloman calls 'a near existential fear of the power of language' as this power might menace the state. Even as the plays with their array of split selves show, the days of real heroes were over, and with them, in her phrase, 'the spurious finality of epic.' If we see this point, then, it is easier also to read the *Religio*, a poem centred quite literally on Henry Dickinson, the only one who is not torturing a text or reaching, as he does so, for spurious finality. The loose form of the *Religio* and the fabular character of *The Hind and the Panther* are but conscious contrasts with those epic gestures Dryden had made in the early poems on Cromwell and Charles as he tried to create *anni mirabili*, with anointed kings to activate and to people them. His conversion, Sloman argues early, contributed to his interest, expressed in the lives of his heroes in the later plays, in examinations of consciences. Given his own Catholicism, Dryden would also be aware of the necessity of both a personal examination of conscience and of a depersonalization of self. In these terms he would look to the past not simply to ask with Chaucer's Parson (part of the *Fables*) which were the old ways, that he might walk in them and find refreshment for his soul, but to find out how these old ways might illuminate the new. And as Sloman notes, he not only finds himself in the old; his translation depersonalizes the old as well. Indeed, everywhere in the canon, not just in the 'collective translations,' overactive, personalized characters are the most dangerous, for all, from the 'various' Zimri to the agitators in the *Fables*, have not only forgone common quiet but are also active disturbers of the peace whose chief aim is to invent noisy and spurious heroism. As such, they are obstacles to Dryden's ideal of the philosopher-king and his personal and correlative aspiration to a status above satire.

In addition to giving us a volume which asks for a different reading of the later Dryden, Sloman also sends us back to other places in his work and asks us to see them differently. Perhaps most critically, she tells us that we cannot read him in part, although the forms of his work, not just those of the later period but those of the earlier as well, have perhaps led us to assume that we can. Her careful study of the late poems, which often involves sharply pinpointing a particular political allusion, leads us not simply to appreciate these poems as sequential wholes (and to establish that sequence and whole are not mutually exclusive) but to go back, sometimes with helpful hints, sometimes because we now know that we must look, to the early career for instances of the same technique. Her argument, then, is not just for the late 'collective translations.' It is also for the collective Dryden, and it will, I hope, open fresh discussion of the late poems and some of the strategies of the earlier career that the technique of these late poems invites.

Had Sloman lived to make her own final draft, she would doubtless have made a variety of changes, but none, I think, to the main argument of her book. She might, for example, have reduced some places where there seems too much evidence adduced to establish the argument. Her style at its best is energetic and witty; more of the prose would have exhibited these qualities. She would also have wished to thank other scholars, notably Earl Miner, for help and perhaps especially for helpful disagreements.

Without one scholar's work the book would not exist. Anne McWhir of the University of Calgary, who came to know Judith Sloman well only two months before her death, accepted the task of seeing the manuscript through to publication. Perhaps aware of the need for haste, Sloman had written the text (some of her work had, of course, been published as articles and could be incorporated with changes) in a year's time. Some of the chapters were typed; other parts were handwritten in examination books. Some of the argument read well; other parts were clear but fragmentary, and final corrections had not been made. A pencilled conclusion was found in a filing cabinet. Professor McWhir has published in the eighteenth century, but her chief research interest is later and she was much aware of this factor as she edited the manuscript. She edited the prose with care and, once the version she sent to the University of Toronto Press had been forwarded to readers, worked to respond to their comments, especially to their objections, but only as these emerged from ambiguities in the prose. Even had she been a Dryden scholar, any further change would have been an interference in the author's intention. She also checked all the quotations and put the notes in order. Some of these were sketchily set down and thus hard to find in her own library and those to which she was obliged to travel. In addition, then, to editing the text, as she found it and as she incorporated the readers' comments, Professor McWhir had the considerable task of putting time-consuming finishing touches to the manuscript. She has also prepared the index. If the book makes, as I believe it does, a substantial contribution to our study of Dryden by restoring these later works to the centrality of his canon, we have Professor McWhir to thank. It is admirable that a young scholar should be generous enough to take time from her own work to make this study possible. I use that 'generous,' of course, in its full eighteenth-century sense.

PATRICIA BRÜCKMANN
Trinity College, University of Toronto
October 1984

DRYDEN: THE POETICS OF TRANSLATION

1

The Poetics of Translation: Beyond Metaphrase, Paraphrase, and Imitation

Some great poems demand essentially new approaches on the reader's part, although the poems evoke instantaneous admiration. One wants to account for the pleasure and give due respect to the complexity of the poet's art, and not just declare one's pleasure in discovering a new masterpiece. This platitude takes on new force when speaking of a translation, which is a kind of poem that has ostensibly been written by someone other than the poet one is reading. How can one discuss 'Virgil by Dryden' or 'Dryden's "The Wife of Bath Her Tale"'? One or two obvious approaches would keep the translator, no matter how brilliant, firmly in his dependent role. The reader may, for instance, compare the translation to its original to see how well the new version measures up; this approach inevitably ends in a value judgment, even if it also manages to define the distinctive qualities of the translation, and it wholly fails to do justice to a translation that clearly has an integrity of its own.[1] A critic can also make detailed comparisons to isolate the translator's linguistic shifts and thus manage to underline his stylistic mannerisms. This too, however, ignores the new meanings inherent in the truly re-creative translation and fails to account for its wholeness as a poem, the qualities that aroused our admiration in the first place.

Dryden's poetic translations are so re-creative that it is tempting to ignore their moorings in their originals and to discuss them as 'poems by Dryden,' a tactic that seems rewarding enough to justify itself. Unfortunately, one has to arrive at some balance between these extremes, because Dryden himself had much to say about the nature of translation, and he remained aware (sometimes guiltily or with irritation) of the difference between translation or adaptation (a related matter) and original composition. In the Preface to *Fables* he accorded Homer supremacy among the great poets because Homer invented: he found his own material and made up his own stories, so far as we know. My compromise is related to a strategy of Dryden's own. More often than translating complete works, he translated fragments and arranged them to achieve a distinctive kind of composite poem. He produced two masterpieces in this genre, *Sylvae* (1685) and *Fables Ancient and Modern* (1700); both are almost entirely made up of translations, taken from long works like the *Aeneid* and the *Iliad*, and from still other collections like the *Decameron*, the *Canterbury Tales*, and Horace's *Odes* (an integrated book of short poems).[2] Ovid's *Metamorphoses*, the work from which Dryden took more pieces for *Fables* than from any other, is itself somewhere between a collection and an integrated work: Earl Miner has thus felt that the *Metamorphoses* was Dryden's primary model for *Fables*.[3] 'Collective translations' in turn can be studied in two ways at least. One can detach pieces taken from one original from the whole, as Norman Austin did with the Lucretius selections in *Sylvae*. Austin's article is a fine example of this method, for it is more than an enumeration of Dryden's changes and a value judgment on his accuracy, but rather an exploration of Dryden's response to Lucretius and of Lucretius's relationship to Dryden's thought.[4] Austin's study is not, however, nor does it try to be, an examination of *Sylvae* as an integrated poem.

I am interested in the nature of these integrated poems. They belong, I think, to a genre which requires some appreciation, or at least the recognition that it is a genre. *Sylvae* and *Fables* are long works: *Sylvae* about 2,200 lines and *Fables* of epic magnitude, over 11,300 lines. *Sylvae* includes selections from the *Aeneid*, *De rerum natura*, Horace's *Odes*, and Theocritus's *Idylls*, as well as two songs by Dryden himself. *Fables* includes selections from the *Metamorphoses*, the *Decameron*, and *Canterbury Tales*, as well as Book I of the *Iliad*, two original panegyrics, an elegy, and 'Alexander's Feast,' originally written in 1697 but included in the collection with striking thematic relevance. Dryden had published the complete *Aeneis* in 1697 and could no longer fragment it. I assume that the reader's experience of the books that Dryden himself made is of some importance. When as a graduate student I first studied *Fables*, I responded to the thematic coherence that emerged when I read the poems in their proper order, and I assumed that my experience of wholeness meant that it was really there. This coherence is lost or suppressed if one isolates selections from a given original from the rest, though many readers have preferred Dryden's translations from one writer to those from others, as Wordsworth (who hated Dryden because of his own sense of belatedness) preferred Dryden's Boccaccio to his versions of Chaucer.[5] From the fact that, until the years of my first study of the poem, no one had published an interpretation of *Fables* like mine, I conclude only that readers are put off by long works or influenced by the great names of Dryden's originals to make their selections before they begin to read. *Fables* and *Sylvae* have thus been treated as anthologies, not as coherent poems where the reader begins at the beginning and moves continuously through the whole, the procedure that one generally tries to follow with works such as *Paradise Lost*, *Tom Jones*, or even Dryden's *Aeneis*.

Because of the lengths of these collections a study emphasizing versification, diction, or imagery in all of them could not be complete. When one compares each poem to its original, however, one necessarily observes a number of small changes that contribute to a new meaning. Dryden's changes are not always subtle or obscure, and they are certainly numerous. The California editions of Dryden's translations have already demonstrated the extent and frequency of his additions, whether they be satiric reflections on the pagan gods, allusions to his own misfortunes, turns of phrase recalling his other writings, or topical allusions. The sarcasm on William the Conqueror is one of Dryden's signatures, and it reminds us of his presence in the poem as much as it contributes to a political point. Even a cursory study of these details reveals some consistency in subject-matter and tone. Dryden's attitudes, as revealed in his translations, can be studied by a kind of subtraction process, focusing on the most obvious changes from the original. One has a solid base for looking not just at 'Dryden the translator' but at Dryden on materialism, standing armies, old age, or some other fairly conspicuous theme. One learns in this way much about the creative process of translation, and I have tried to base my arguments about Dryden's ideas on the results of this kind of comparison (using alternative translations in the case of the Greek). Thus, I experience Dryden's translations as if I were monolingual, but I try to verify my intuitions. I can often spot a Dryden addition before I check it out: he is very consistent, very assertive; he signs his name on practically every page.

There have already been some attempts to generalize from the small changes. In 1932 Wolfgang Jünemann compared passages in some of Dryden's *Fables* to their originals, stressing 'baroque' effects like pictorialism, a sense of motion, and a tension between thesis and antithesis.[6] Despite his tendency to equate Dryden's attitudes with those of his age, Jünemann is interesting and his perceptions about style still seem valid. However, he discusses only the five Chaucer poems (including 'The Flower and the Leaf,' which Speght included in his edition of Chaucer) and for some reason adds a brief chapter on 'Sigismonda and Guiscardo,' one of the Boccaccio selections. Logically Jünemann need not have limited himself to Chaucer; he must have simply preferred Chaucer, or English literature, or been interested in Dryden's response to medieval literature.

In his early book on Dryden and translation William Frost has combined some considerations on translation itself with a close analysis of Dryden's style and made the essential point that a mass of local effects can undergo a quantum leap to become a new imagistic structure. Frost has emphasized the coherence of rhythm and imagery which enabled Dryden to be interesting and he refers at least briefly to virtually everyone whom Dryden translated. However, Frost's closest analyses are of 'Palamon and Arcite' ('The Knight's Tale') and the *Aeneis* because he is interested in Dryden's treatment of heroic literature in an age that was 'ambivalent' towards heroism.[7] Virtually every student of Dryden's *Aeneis* or of *Fables* has been and remains interested in that question. Dryden said much about his desire to write an epic, and his translations from 1685 on draw upon epic (and reveal his affinity to the modern heroic poets Spenser and Milton); yet he deflected that impulse into satire, translation, and two prefaces of epic length, the 'Discourse of Satire' (1693) and the dedication of the *Aeneis* (1697). Frost does not go quite so far as to say that *Fables* just might be Dryden's epic, but he certainly treats it as the place where we might discover Dryden's attitudes to epic.

Except for my own earlier work, only Earl Miner has treated *Fables* as an integrated collection. Miner emphasizes the various meanings of 'fable' and Dryden's interior links, as well as outlining several important topics, such as the role of myth and the theme of human relationships. Indeed Miner indicates half a dozen directions in which a subsequent critic could go and accomplishes what one has to agree is the main point, bringing a collective translation under the rubric of 'Dryden's poetry.' I disagree with Miner's treatment of Ovid as Dryden's primary model. Dryden's most lasting personal affinity may have been with Ovid, but Chaucer and Boccaccio provided other elements in his structure, besides being Christian models to offset the Roman model.[8] However, this is a relatively small matter in comparison to the main issue, the sense of Dryden's *Fables* as one of his major literary achievements.

My reading of Dryden's collective translations has led me to expand rather than qualify my original ideas about the wholeness of *Fables.* In my doctoral dissertation I considered the work unique and was mainly concerned to demonstrate the reality of its structure and the thematic analogies to Dryden's original works. However, eventually I saw that Dryden integrated other collective translations as well, even when they were printed in a miscellany with other poets and even when his translations were not printed consecutively. Enthusiastic about a new hypothesis, I saw that I could present *Fables* as the conclusion of a trend in Dryden's career as a translator and not as a unique entity. *Fables* stands out because Dryden produced the whole book, and *Sylvae* stands out almost as much because Dryden's translations (though not his two songs) are grouped together at the beginning of the volume, which includes works by various others. Nevertheless, his three contributions to *Ovid's Epistles* (1680) are linked, even though they were distributed throughout the collection. The translations for *Miscellany Poems* (1684) – five selections – are also linked, though again they were not printed as a group 'by Dryden.' Dryden apparently found a congenial mode of dealing with translation in these two earlier works; he chose and arranged his selections as if they were parts of a totality, or perhaps he just let the associative process have its way, without regard for the conditions of publication which made it unlikely that his readers would grasp his accomplishment. The emphasis on his authorship in *Sylvae* suggests that by 1685 he or his editor did care. The three Ovid pieces in *Examen Poeticum* (1693) are also connected, as their modern editor, Frost, points out.[9]

Yet Dryden was so obviously the important figure in the earlier miscellanies, the writer who lent credibility to everyone else, that one cannot assume that he got buried under the mass; similarly, his interpolations in *The Second Part of Absalom and Achitophel* are unlikely to be confused with the work of Nahum Tate by any reader who is half awake. In both cases a reader was as likely to have read Dryden and skimmed the rest as to have extracted Dryden's Chaucer from the whole *Fables* and left the Ovid for another day. It seems to me that during the early 1680s Dryden developed a characteristic approach to the fragments that he selected to translate, beginning in the five-year period between *Religio Laici* and *The Hind and the Panther*, which is sometimes treated as a void in Dryden's life.[10] In fact, both his poetics and his ideas developed significantly. For various reasons, which I shall explore in the next chapter, Dryden needed a literary form through which he could reveal and conceal himself at the same time, and creative translation provided one answer. After 1688, when Dryden's conversion and James II's abdication left Dryden with a readership of which he was even more apprehensive than it was of him, the need for a form of oblique self-expression became pressing for other reasons. Dryden never really gave up his impulse to comment on public affairs, but he was sometimes unsure how directly to comment, not just out of fear for his own safety, but out of fear that he would be misunderstood, and out of some sense that direct speech from anyone might be considered the height of arrogance. Fortunately for us Dryden's poetic impulse and his confidence in his own powers always won and he continued to write – deviously, if necessary – and ultimately to accept himself as a devious man, the Proteus of his age. On one level, then, this book concerns Dryden's sense of himself as he grew old, in the relatively neglected period between 1685 and 1700.

Dryden's own comments on translation do little enough to explain his practice in his collective translations, or indeed in any of them. His most famous statement, the distinction between metaphrase, paraphrase, and imitation that occurs in the preface to *Ovid's Epistles*, Dryden's first published translations, may lead only to pointless questions about whether an exceptionally independent version is a paraphrase or an imitation, and one must conclude that the two concepts were essentially flexible, both for Dryden and for others. As T.R. Steiner has indicated, Dryden's 1680 statement was just a point of departure, not a programmatic statement which he intended to abide by for the rest of his life;[11] it was an attempt to sum up a century-long tradition of free translation and to clarify the relationship between literal and more creative modes of translation. Free translation had been a rallying cry for decades, and my own readings of earlier versions of the *Aeneid* have revealed instances of 'creative' omissions, skewings, and fragmentation (but not of collage) that make Dryden seem a model of respect for his sources. By distinguishing metaphrase from all kinds of free translation and adaptation, however, Dryden could reject it for himself and show his preference for the variety of modes available in the broad range between paraphrase and imitation.

The 1680s and 1690s were a period of unusual diversity and experimentation in the various forms of paraphrase and imitation.[12] The most influential models both of 'translational imitation' (which only modernizes details) and of 'creative imitation' (which not only modernizes details but differs significantly from the original in structure or meaning) were written just before and during this period.[13] As Howard Weinbrot says, however, the minimal distinction between imitation of any sort and paraphrase is that the first modernizes names and allusions while the second repeats them.[14] Oldham uses English details in his version of Juvenal's third satire and Rochester also changes some of the ideas in 'An Allusion to Horace,' but, despite differences in the extent of variation, both poets replace one set of cultural particulars with another taken from their own culture, to produce the witty, sometimes ironic analogies that may be the ultimate pleasure to be derived from imitation. Imitation more than paraphrase, as Weinbrot says, demands our familiarity with the original. Dryden's work is already harder to categorize. We can look at his version of Juvenal's tenth satire, 'The Vanity of Human Wishes,' published in a volume containing all of Juvenal and all of Persius, and hence not the sort of collection *mingling* several writers that I am mainly concerned with. In Dryden's poem the Roman proper names are not modernized, but at some telling moments the political vocabulary is:

> Adorn your Doors with Laurels; and a Bull
> Milk white and large, lead to the Capitol;
> *Sejanus* with a Rope, is drag'd along;
> The Sport and Laughter of the giddy Throng!
> Good Lord, they Cry, what *Ethiop* Lips he has,
> How foul a Snout, and what a hanging Face!
> By Heav'n I never cou'd endure his sight;
> But say, how came his Monstrous Crimes to Light?
> What is the Charge, and who the Evidence
> (The Saviour of the Nation and the Prince?)
> Nothing of this; but our Old *Cæsar* sent
> A Noisie Letter to his Parliament;
> Nay Sirs, if *Cæsar* writ, I ask no more;
> He's Guilty; and the Question's out of Door.
> How goes the Mob, (for that's a Mighty thing?)
> When the King's Trump, the Mob are for the King:
> They follow Fortune, and the Common Cry
> Is still against the Rogue Condemn'd to Dye.[15] (98–115)

It is therefore impossible to pinpoint the cultural environment of these lines. The proper nouns and the references to historical events preserve the original Roman setting, in contrast to Samuel Johnson's anglicization of such details in his version of the same poem (Johnson describes Cardinal Wolsey's fall instead of Sejanus's and changes praetors to mayors). Nevertheless, Dryden's up-to-date political vocabulary – 'Parliament,' 'Mob,' 'the Mob are for the King' – produces a second context in terms of which the passage must be read, a kind of double exposure, the feeling that a new layer has been imposed on what could have been a smooth surface, unengaged with modern life. This second exposure happens to remind us that Dryden was hostile to William III and, inevitably, ensures that the translator's implacable personality will not be rendered invisible. Yet, Dryden's overlay is not equally present throughout, and this is characteristic of his translations generally: he underscored what he could make provocative. One thus floats uneasily between two frames of reference, waiting for Dryden to spark a connection for which a prior knowledge of his personal discontents has perhaps put one on the alert. Dryden's terminology is inadequate for this particular effect, which happens to work quite well in communicating the Juvenalian grotesque. 'Imitation' is probably better than 'paraphrase,' but one does not find the consistency in feeling and cultural reference that one finds in Johnson.

The distinction between paraphrase and imitation strikes me as limited in helpfulness and it has absolutely nothing to say about collective poems. But Dryden does discuss his personal involvement in translation, and the peculiar suppression of identity it demands from the translator. Dryden both wants and does not want to remain himself while he translates; he feels both equal to and inadequate to the task of translating his great originals, though his certainty of outclassing other translators of a given poem usually gives him the needed encouragement. A translator can choose which of two fields he wants to compete in. Johnson was competing with Dryden, and, in a sense, Juvenal was the field of contest as well as another competitor.

Over the years Dryden became both less anxious and more self-conscious. Even if he wished to suppress his identity, he was probably not able to do so. As early as the preface to 'Annus Mirabilis' (1667), Dryden described his effort to replicate Virgil's style: 'my Images are many of them copied from him, and the rest are imitations of him. My expressions also are as near as the Idioms of the two Languages would admit of in translation' (I, 55). Here, 'translation' borders on what we call 'allusion' and the word 'imitations' has its conventional meaning; it is not the mode of translation that Dryden defined in 1680. Interestingly, Dryden also notes in this preface that Virgil's Dido is inferior to 'the *Myrrha*, the *Biblis*, the *Althæa*, of *Ovid*,' for 'if I see not more of their Souls then I see of *Dido*'s, at least I have a greater concernment for them: and that convinces me that *Ovid* has touch'd those tender strokes more delicately then *Virgil* could' (I, 54). Already Dryden has become interested in Dido as a normative heroine and picked out two of the heroines of *Fables*, Althea and Myrrha, telling us that his selections were not all chosen at the last minute, as the preface to *Fables* might imply, but in some cases were favourites that may have been translating themselves in his mind for years. Dryden may have rejected Byblis because John Dennis translated 'The Passion of Byblis' in 1692 or more likely because Byblis loved her brother and *Fables* mentions only father-daughter incest. Audiences seemed to like multiple translations of the same work, as the presence of various duplicated translations in the miscellanies will show. Irrelevancy of subject-matter seems to me a better reason for rejecting Byblis.

In 1667 Dryden reveals a willingness to be challenged by his great precursors, but at the same time he shows what would become a useful strategy, the comparison of *two* great poets to each other, instead of one to Dryden himself. Ovid is not strictly relevant to the plan for 'Annus Mirabilis'; Virgil is Dryden's model. The technique of comparison reveals inevitable limits in each of the figures being compared, as here it keeps Virgil from becoming the universal poet and protects Dryden from the status of timid ephebe. One can only admire the way Dryden subordinates Homer in *Fables* by translating just one book of the *Iliad*, less than from any other original, placing it next to 'The Cock and the Fox' from Chaucer, and including Chaucer's complete, three-part epic, 'Palamon and Arcite.' This is not even subtle. Yet Dryden could genuinely claim that he was not trying to disparage anyone, that it was all a game, as 'the contention between our three Poets' (Horace, Juvenal, and Persius) in the 'Discourse concerning the Original and Progress of Satire' (IV, 75) is like the race in the *Aeneis* where everyone got a prize. The real losers are those who do not even get a chance to compete.

However, Dryden inevitably enters the realm of comparisons. In the preface to *Ovid's Epistles* he starts to explore the fact that a translator becomes *more* aware of his individuality, instead of losing his self-awareness, because he must recognize the differences between himself and the writer he is translating:

> No man is capable of Translating Poetry, who besides a Genius to that Art, is not a Master both of his Authours Language, and of his own: Nor must we understand the Language only of the Poet, but his particular turn of Thoughts, and of Expression, which are the Characters that distinguish, and as it were individuate him from all other writers. When we are come thus far, 'tis time to look into our selves, to conform our Genius to his, to give his thought either the same turn if our tongue will bear it, or if not, to vary but the dress, not to alter or destroy the substance. (I, 118)

Dryden feels somewhat constrained at this point because he cannot improve upon his original, even when he recognizes such limits as Ovid's witty excesses (I, 112). By 1685, however, in the preface to *Sylvae*, Dryden's self-awareness becomes a source of pride, as he announces 'a secret of which few Translatours have sufficiently thought': 'I have already hinted a word or two concerning it; that is, the maintaining the Character of an Author, which distinguishes him from all others, and makes him appear that individual Poet whom you wou'd interpret' (III, 5). The words 'distinguish' and 'distinction' occur everywhere in this preface, which consists mostly of a comparison, or at least a series of descriptions, of the four poets of *Sylvae* – Virgil, Lucretius, Horace, and Theocritus. The process of becoming another writer places restrictions on Dryden's own nature, for he has to be unnaturally concise in translating Virgil, 'a succinct and grave Majestick Writer' (III, 6), and unnaturally dogmatic in translating Lucretius. There is no sense that either Lucretius or Virgil could be an *alter ego*, though in the dedication to the *Aeneis* Dryden partially identified himself with Virgil on the basis of their similar political situations. Lucretius's atheism is so central to his thought that Dryden presumably found the difference between them inescapable: 'And accordingly I lay'd by my natural Diffidence and Scepticism for a while, to take up that Dogmatical way of his, which as I said, is so much his Character, as to make him that individual Poet' (III, 11). Both Virgil and Lucretius come across as stiff and unyielding in character, while Dryden, already flexible, is encouraged by his role as translator of four different poets to be even more so.

Dryden seems less involved with Theocritus: 'I direct this part of my Translations to our Ladies'; he may have worked on Theocritus only because he was part of the communal mind of the miscellanies. Horace was more fun and Dryden tried to imitate his good humour: 'his other Excellencies, I confess are above my Imitation' (III, 15, 16). Dryden's versions of both poets are better than one would ever guess from the preface, though his disclaimers may also account for his extreme freedom in recreating them. Generally he tried to find a personal link with each of his originals, even if it was based on opposition or difference, to help his genius conform to theirs. On the whole Dryden is proud of his versatility, sufficient to make up for the need to control some parts of himself; bad translators always sound the same, revealing nothing but themselves:

> In such Translatours I can easily distinguish the hand which perform'd the Work, but I cannot distinguish their Poet from another. Suppose two Authors are equally sweet, yet there is a great distinction to be made in sweetness, as in that of Sugar, and that of Honey. (III, 6)

Dryden's superiority comes out, paradoxically, in his success in the role of protean translator.

A more traditional form of assertiveness is expressed in the 'Discourse of Satire,' where Dryden revives an image used by earlier defenders of free translation:[16]

> We have follow'd our Authors, at greater distance; tho' not Step by Step, as they [Holiday and Stapylton] have done ... A Noble Authour wou'd not be persu'd too

close by a Translator. We lose his Spirit, when we think to take his Body. The grosser Part remains with us, but the Soul is flown away, in some Noble Expression or some delicate turn of Words, or Thought. (IV, 87–8)

However, Dryden's editorial treatment of the satires is more intriguing, for it shows how he refuses to fade into invisibility. His commentaries almost dominate the poems. Sometimes he deliberately draws attention to himself, as in the argument to Persius's fifth satire, with its tribute to Doctor Busby, his old schoolmaster. The argument of Juvenal's sixth satire (against women) denies at some length, whether seriously or not, that the translator shares his author's opinions: '*Let the Poet therefore bear the blame of his own Invention; and let me satisfie the World, that I am not of his Opinion. Whatever his* Roman *Ladies were, the* English *are free from all his Imputations*' (IV, 146).[17] Dryden is admitting the possibility of translational schizophrenia, even if in fact this particular case entertained him: '*The whole World must allow this to be the wittiest of* [Juvenal's] *Satyrs*' (IV, 145). If Dryden felt an inadmissible enthusiasm for the subject, he could hide his own delight behind the mask of his original.

A variation of this schizophrenia, a genuine conflict between his own identity and that of his original, appears in the dedication of the *Georgics* (1697), where Dryden claims that his advanced age (sixty-six) puts him out of touch with the poems that Virgil wrote in his thirties, '*in the full strength and vigour of his Age, when his Judgment was at the height, and before his Fancy was declining*.'[18] In the case of the third Georgic Dryden adopts the strategy of comically drawing attention to himself, abandoning the pretence of invisibility and taking advantage of the circumstances of publication to exploit his pretended shame at being no longer thirty-five. This poem was completed early, by the end of 1693, and published in Tonson's fourth miscellany to announce the larger project to come, the translation of Virgil's complete works.[19] Thus, 'Dryden's Virgil' and not just 'Virgil' or even 'Dryden' was being advertised. The poem opens with a rousing statement of Virgil's poetic ambition, which becomes truly interesting if it is read as the utterance of Dryden himself:

New ways I must attempt, my groveling Name
To raise aloft, and wing my flight to Fame.
  I, first of *Romans*, shall in Triumph come
From conquer'd *Greece*, and bring her Trophies home:
With Foreign Spoils adorn my native place;
And with *Idume*'s Palms, my *Mantua* grace. (13–18)

If we keep the translator's identity in mind, this becomes almost a parody of Virgil's 'youthful' ambition (false modesty concealing real pride). However, Dryden's name was anything but 'groveling' at this time and the image of conquest, which is in the original, suggests a parallel between William III's military activities and Dryden's literary activities. (As William's heroism figured prominently in the miscellanies of this time, I do not think this reading is forced.) The third Georgic, moreover, is about sexual love in the animal world, influenced by Lucretius's treatment of love. When this is taken into account, the poem may recall Dryden's translation of that part of Lucretius, which had been included in *Sylvae*. The third Georgic thus advertises Dryden's progress as a translator, makes a claim for some continuity in his career, and mimics the historical progress from Lucretius to Virgil. One can quite genuinely read some parts of the poem as if Dryden and not Virgil (certainly not an anonymous 'I') had personally written it.

Much in Virgil's poem involves a contrast between youth and age, or generally between different stages of life. Virgil's sympathies, to judge from his treatment of animal sex, appear to be with the young. Dryden, however, so conspicuously expands his lines on an old stallion turned out to pasture that once again we think of the translator. If Dryden had suppressed himself, we might have been embarrassed; as it is, we may find ourselves laughing with him:

But worn with Years, when dire Diseases come,
Then hide his not Ignoble Age, at Home:
In peace t'enjoy his former Palms and Pains;
And gratefully be kind to his Remains.
For when his Blood no Youthful Spirits move,
He languishes and labours in his Love.
And when the sprightly Seed shou'd swiftly come,
Dribling he drudges, and defrauds the Womb.
In vain he burns, like hasty stubble fires;
And in himself his former self requires. (151–60)

In effect, Dryden undercuts Virgil's injunction *not* to feel pity for the old stallion.[20] Dryden may be laughing at himself or even inviting the reader's pity at a time when England seemed to have turned *him* out to pasture; but, most important, he is calling attention to himself and his own continued vitality, and at the same time demonstrating the distance between himself and Virgil, perhaps even showing a limit in Virgil's sympathies. In brief, Dryden chose to advertise his project by way of a device that presents the translator as being as forceful and varied as the writer he translated and even suggests the translator's eternal youth. Dryden's aggressively self-referential 'I' might be a joke to a deconstructionist, but it is more than likely that Dryden would have laughed in return.

In the preface to *Fables* the movement at first seems to be in the opposite direction, towards relaxed submission. Poems come to Dryden (or so he describes his experience in finding material) by a process of wise passiveness. 'The Speeches of Ajax and Ulysses' just happens to lie in his way, Chaucer comes into his mind as he finishes with Ovid, and serendipity itself seems to be his ruling principle:

> When I had clos'd *Chaucer*, I return'd to *Ovid*, and translated some more of his Fables; and by this time had so far forgotten the Wife of *Bath*'s Tale, that when I took up *Boccace*, unawares I fell on the same Argument of preferring Virtue to Nobility of Blood, and Titles, in the Story of *Sigismonda*; which I had certainly avoided for the Resemblance of the two Discourses, if my Memory had not fail'd me. (K, IV, 1460)

Dryden writes as if his favourite authors' minds were mirror reflections of his own and confidently reconstructs a Chaucer who resembles nothing so much as the assured man who built a house when he intended but a lodge. Dryden's certainty that Chaucer was a kindred spirit permits him to take liberties in translation that he had earlier sacrificed:

> An Author is not to write all he can, but only all he ought. Having observ'd this Redundancy in *Chaucer* ... I have not ty'd my self to a Literal Translation; but have often omitted what I judg'd unnecessary, or not of Dignity enough to appear in the Company of better Thoughts. I have presum'd farther in some Places, and added somewhat of my own where I thought my Author was deficient, and had not given his Thoughts their true Lustre, for want of Words in the Beginning of our Language. (K, IV, 1457)

There is no indication that Dryden felt inferior to Chaucer, Ovid, and Boccaccio, though he did feel his age when he tried to contend with Homer's energy. However, inferiority is not the main issue in this preface, at least on the surface; the question of essential likeness is. If Dryden can read his authors' minds, he can reshape their poems or rearrange parts of their poems to serve his own purpose. How could they object if members of the community of great writers all think alike?

Dryden now uses his translated fragments to project the shape of his mind upon the past and to insinuate that the history of European literature might plausibly be said to culminate in his book. This is an undeniable implication of his linking the original poems with the translations; even his emphasis on the workings of his own mind contributes to it. Dryden claims that his limitations work to his advantage, like the memory failure that helped him find a Boccaccio story to set beside the Wife of Bath's tale and the problem of sustaining Homer's 'Vehemence' (K, IV, 449), which excuses his postponing twenty-three books of the *Iliad* to some indefinite date in the future. Dryden's writers become extensions of himself. He seems to relive Chaucer's experience when he writes: 'There is such a Variety of Game springing up before me, that I am distracted in my Choice, and know not which to follow' (K, IV, 1455). He is also convinced that Homer and Virgil have each 'follow'd his own natural Inclination, as well in Forming the Design, as in the Execution of it. The very *Heroes* shew their Authors' (K, IV, 1449). The problem of self-suppression can hardly arise if on some level all authors are joined.

As so often with Dryden, we find a noticeable element of strategic redefinition. He discusses translation, original creation, and literary borrowing as if they were all more or less the same. When he tells us that '*Milton* was the Poetical Son of *Spencer*, and Mr. *Waller* of *Fairfax*; for we have our Lineal Descents and Clans, as well as other Families,' Dryden includes Fairfax, the translator of Ariosto, with three poets noted for their original work. Chaucer is later called 'our *English* Translatour' because several of his greatest poems, including one that Dryden translated, 'The Knight's Tale,' were borrowed from the Italians (K, IV, 1445, 1450). This extension of the meaning of 'translation' seems to be justified by the fact that poets inevitably borrow from each other because they all draw on a shared body of material, a communal literary past. Dryden's imagery is Platonic; he believes that all true poets are inspired by the same soul, that they are linked in poetic families by their ability to respond to and re-create images that have a permanent existence in the realm of spirit.[21] In the opening lines of 'To Her Grace the Dutchess of Ormond' (K, IV, 1463) he thus connects himself to Chaucer by way of their shared admiration for an idealized woman from the Plantagenet line:

If *Chaucer* by the best Idea wrought,
And Poets can divine each others Thought,
The fairest Nymph before his Eyes he set;
And then the fairest was *Plantagenet*;
...

O true *Plantagenet*, O Race Divine,
(For Beauty still is fatal to the Line,)
Had *Chaucer* liv'd that Angel-Face to view,
Sure he had drawn his *Emily* from You. (11–14, 30–3)

Dryden has a *logos* theory of translation, at least in the realm of secular literature. All poetry involves translating ideas from the realm of ideas or archetypes into whatever human language the translator works in, and translation between two poets is mediated through these ideas.

Thus, poetic translation gains authenticity as a creative act if the translator is good enough to enable the *logos* to invigorate his poem. There is a subtle but important difference between Dryden's version of the spirit metaphor as used here and Denham's use of it in 1656. Denham was scientific, consciously trying to make the translator sound modern and imagining him as a sort of chemist in a laboratory pouring liquid from one container to another; when 'spirit' in this somewhat materialistic sense evaporates from the first (since the very process of experimentation affects what it works upon), the translator is perforce required to replace it with his own and of necessity becomes creative. Denham requires no *logos*, therefore; just two spirited individuals. Dryden was never so materialistic. His first allusion to Denham's metaphor, which occurs in the preface to 'Annus Mirabilis,' imagines Virgil's spirit as a kind of great soul unifying his *Aeneid*: 'We see the Soul of the Poet, like that universal one of which he speaks, informing and moving through all his Pictures' (1, 54). In the preface to *Fables* Dryden apparently distinguishes levels of participation in the realm of spirit when he separates the line of Chaucer, Spenser, and Milton from the inferior one of Fairfax and Waller. Dryden's poetic community seems to be modelled on Dante's hierarchically ordered circles of the blessed in paradise. There are unequal degrees of poetic intensity, although every poet revolves in heaven.

Dryden's views on language made him see translation as an essentially reconstructive activity, and this has much bearing on his interest in *collective* translations, where the last stage in his art is the arrangement of fragments into a new, though tentative, whole. The myth of Babel was still current in his time and exerted considerable influence on the development of some aspects of language theory, such as the possibilities of a universal language. The destruction of the tower of Babel had been seen as a quasi-fall which led to the fragmentation of human society into different linguistic groups. Some language theorists, such as Comenius, saw a political and humanistic purpose in overcoming language differences, and John Wilkins, the major

English writer on universal languages, was an Anglican bishop who treated linguistic unity as an aspect of religious unity. His most important work, published in 1668, gained some of its impact from the recent civil war. Dryden's awareness of these language theories and of the relevance of Babel to language theory scarcely needs demonstration,[22] but the importance of these matters for his own work certainly does require comment, because it involves more than a conflict between concrete and abstract words or 'meaningless' words and referential ones. Linguistic goals were almost millenarian, though their aim was the relatively modest one of reconstructing a whole, not the impossible goal of reviving conditions before Babel. Language theorists wanted to approach, as closely as human abilities permitted, a new, if provisional, unity. The project was essentially Baconian. For instance, Richard Simon's project for a collaborative translation of the Old Testament, which occupies the entire third book of his *Critical History*, was designed to be a synthesis of the best efforts of all available translations up to his time, Jewish, Protestant, and Catholic. Simon vigorously dismissed the possibility of reproducing the original Hebrew text, since it was forever inaccessible.[23]

The Hind and the Panther (III.119–200) is Dryden's most important poem about language and possibly reflects Simon's influence much more than *Religio Laici*, in which Dryden actually responds to a translation of the *Critical History.* A sense of the fragmentation of modern language underlies everything Dryden says about the tortured text in *The Hind and the Panther*, although *print* has been responsible for the fragmentation. The invention of print is Dryden's Babel and he virtually locates the second fall at the time of the Reformation and the advent of a climate of religious controversy under the Tudors. He wittily uses the image of *pointing*, or punctuating, time (*The Hind and the Panther*, II.606–7), as if to say that memorable events break up the seamless flow of history just as commas, which are necessary only on the page, break up the flow of vocal sound. 'Points' are also the marks denoting vowel sounds in written Hebrew, which were often omitted from older texts, thus causing problems and ambiguities in interpretation. Here, too, print creates a problem that does not exist with the spoken word. However, *The Hind and the Panther* goes back even further, to an image of primal man, a mythic figure who antedates all history and appears in the middle of the first part after Dryden has described the various Protestant beasts. Primal man is shown with his arms extended in a gesture of love for all creatures; he can thus be understood in terms of the Renaissance emblem of human perfection in which the head and the four limbs become a five-pointed star whose points are located on the circumference of a circle. There were no words before the fall, just the universal language of gesture, through which human being and animal could find a shared level of communication, though obviously it is one far too simple for social life as we know it. The allegorical beasts, however, are mute, not only because of their natures, but because they are *muzzled*; that is, they are living under conditions of enforced silence because of the lack of toleration for the various Protestant sects. As Dryden characterizes them, they communicate frustrations and hostilities through awkward but readily understandable gestures and facial expressions. Feelings can be understood directly, though a shared human language is necessary for anything more. Dryden saw the grotesque results of enforced silence even before he had to undergo the experience and in spite of his dislike for the sects themselves.

Dryden's primal man is not called 'Adam,' because no names existed in the state of innocence. Instead, Dryden links the act of naming, which was conventionally credited to Adam, with his own futile efforts at allegory:

> These are the chief; to number o'er the rest,
> And stand, like *Adam*, naming ev'ry beast,
> Were weary work (I.308–10)

Dryden actually identifies the 'fall' which was responsible for the origin of speech, not in the Babel episode, but in the vocal cries that followed hard upon the first acts of violence (I.15, 280). Such cries may consist of demands for forgiveness of one's enemies, like those uttered by the Hind's sons, or cries for yet more violence; speech in either case is a response to fragmentation, but it can take two opposite forms, being either violent or redemptive, according to the speaker's nature. However, it is always the symptom of a fallen state. In fact, Dryden's two central beasts begin their dialogue under pressure; after several false starts, recapitulating the failure of Dryden's personal confession at the beginning and the failure of his beast allegory, the Hind and the Panther learn to speak a common language. Neither of Dryden's opening styles was likely to be appreciated by a hostile audience and he was in fact attacked for the false naïvety of such statements as 'Can I my reason to my faith compell, / And shall my sight, and touch, and taste rebell?' (I.85–6). The steady but discontinuous progress of this long poem enacts Dryden's own attempt to find a language that he could share with other Englishmen, even if it failed to communicate his idealism as a convert. From this point of view the Hind's glorious vision of the True Church in Part II is just another failure in communication, since the Hind effectively silences the Panther and turns her inward upon herself. Their common language turns out to be the language of fable, a mode of discourse initiated by the Panther and taken up by the Hind in Part III. Dryden thus justifies fables in the traditional way, by analogy to parables, as a mode of accommodating one's discourse to ordinary people. Nevertheless, the Hind outdoes the Panther at satire and historical allegory, the two beasts arrive at an uneasy truce, and each manages to change the other in the interval between the fables (III.669, 756–8). Dryden is, broadly speaking, in the tradition of Comenius, though less idealistic. Still, he envisions a limited degree of tolerance and understanding, sufficient to avoid outright violence and disruption so far as this is possible within the framework of religious and political controversy.[24]

Biblical criticism in the 1680s and 1690s tended to fragment not only the text but also the identity of the first author, hitherto assumed to be Moses (not God). Jean Leclerc, a friend of John Locke, accepted Simon's demonstration of the lack of textual unity in the Bible but felt called upon to defend Mosaic authorshiop of the Pentateuch. However, Leclerc treated Moses less as an original author than as one who received and integrated traditional material into written form.[25] Moses' work was itself a reconstruction, comparable to Chaucer's stance with relation to European literature, as Dryden presented it. Analogies were current between biblical authorship and that of secular texts whose origins are lost in the distant past, and speculations about religious and literary texts could be used to support each other. Leclerc thus compares the problem of Moses' identity to questions about Homer's existence and the true authorship of the 'Homeric' poems: Homer existed, he feels, and wrote the poems attributed to him, even if the poems include some lines that are not authentic. There was resistance to the deconstructive spirit. An author's identity is not shattered just because his text is flawed.

It was important to prove the integrity of an author's life – that is, to show that a poem had an author who was an individual person – because the absence of an author deprived writing of its authenticity, as if a book's 'integrity' in the sense of its 'worth' or 'truth' depended on its integrity in the sense of its wholeness, in turn dependent on the presence throughout of a single authorial voice like the one to which Dryden responded in the *Aeneid*. Against this background one can see how important are the biographical sections of Dryden's dedication of the *Aeneis*, with their emphasis on Virgil's presumed behaviour in his historical setting, because, whatever we think of Virgil's motives, Dryden can show us, first, that at least one of the two great epic poets had a discoverable identity and, second, that our knowledge of 'Virgil the man' makes his poem more comprehensible. In contrast, Pope's far more speculative life of Homer, written in 1715, tackles another problem, that of restoring what had been given up by scholars like Leclerc – the reader's sense of Homer as a person. Pope is inevitably concerned with separating the more or less plausible traditions from the myths and thereby achieving a *probable* biography:

> Being therefore to write something concerning a Life, which there is little Prospect of our knowing, after it has been the fruitless Enquiry of so many Ages, and which has however been thus differently treated by Historians, I shall endeavour to speak of it, not as a Certainty, but as the Tradition, Opinion, or Collection of Authors, who have been suppos'd to write of *Homer* in these four preceding Methods, to which we also shall add some farther Conjectures of our own. After his Life has been thus rather invented than written, I shall consider him Historically as an Author, with regard to those Works which he has left behind him.[26]

Biography was of necessity invention, but Pope, like Dryden, rests his case upon one poet's intuitive response to the greatness of another. Longinus is called upon to answer Bentley. Nevertheless, Dryden and Pope share the feeling that an author's biography is suspect if it reads like a fable or myth; it should not resemble in style or structure the works that he composed.

However, the attacks on the identities of the ancient authors were potent enough to create a vacuum which the modern author, editor, or translator had to fill somehow, perhaps by drawing attention to himself in such a way that we do not miss the original author, or by creating a composite figure in which original and modern author are fused or in which the modern author pretends to *be* the original. Such might be the rationale for the composite Dryden/Chaucer of the preface to *Fables*. By implication, just because Dryden was translating 'fables' and because of current interest in the subject, Aesop is also an element in Dryden's synthetic 'author.' Aesop's character was thoroughly dismantled in the course of the controversy between the Ancients and the Moderns. The traditional life of Aesop, attributed to a Byzantine monk, Planudes, and prefixed to most collections of Aesop's fables in the seventeenth century, suspiciously resembled a series of moral anecdotes, an imitation of the Aesopic style. Roger L'Estrange, himself a collector of fables, responded to the doubts cast on Planudes' life and to the higher criticism aimed at distinguishing the truly Aesopic from the spurious fables. L'Estrange included Planudes' life in his 1692 collection, but recast it with enough parenthetical remarks to dissociate himself from his unenlightened source:

> ÆSOP (according to *Planudes*, *Camerarius* and Others) was by birth, of *Ammorius* a Towne in the *Greater Phrygia*; (though some will have him to be a *Thracian*, others a *Samian*) ... the Excellency of his Mind might otherwise [were it not for a speech impediment] have Attoned in some Measure, for the Uncouth Appearance of his Person (at least if That Part of his History may pass for Current.) There goes a Tradition, that he had the good hap to Relieve certain Priests that were Hungry, and out of their way, and to set them Right again, and that for that good Office, he was, upon their Prayers, brought to the Use of his Tongue: But *Camerarius* whom I shall Principally follow, has no Faith in the Miracle.[27]

During the Phalaris controversy Richard Bentley went so far as to ask if Aesop had written anything at all, or even if he had existed. The response of Charles Boyle is essentially a defence of oral tradition: once again an attack on a literary figure endangers the foundations of faith. According to Boyle, later Earl of Orrery, in some sense a mediator like Leclerc, Aesop's existence does not depend on whether or not he wrote down his fables: 'By the same way of Deduction [as Bentley's] will I prove, that we have not a *Written Creed* now, nor ever had one: for have not all People from the Rise of Christianity down to this Time learnt it, without the help of a Book?'[28] One can see that Dryden might have found both Aesop and the fable form relevant, since an essential aspect of Catholicism was its preference for oral tradition over the frozen, written word.[29]

By the late 1690s 'Aesop the man' became a joke for many, a shadow for all his readers. The notable symptom of his fragmentation was the proliferation of Grub-Street Aesops after 1698 in the wake of the Phalaris controversy.[30] These involved collections of verse fables, political satires revolving around Charles Montagu's policies, with titles like *Aesop at Tunbridge*, *Aesop at Bathe*, and *Aesop at Epsom*. The earliest ones referred to English watering places, but Aesop could also be found at Westminster and in Amsterdam, and a few years later in Paris and Spain as well. The joke was, that if every Greek town claimed to be Homer's birthplace, every English watering place could claim to be Aesop's.[31] Moreover, each Aesop had a different political identity whose precise nature has some bearing on Dryden's persona in *Fables* as well. I shall return to the Aesops later but meanwhile suggest that Dryden had good reason to emphasize the wholeness of his own identity in *Fables*, in part in response to the attacks on the identities of a range of traditional authors. Dryden had a large space to fill, and he exploited the opportunity.

Though several other themes (political, amatory, ethical) are obviously important in Dryden's collective translations, the notion of tentative unity itself is fundamental to their structure: this interest surfaces in the 1690s. Dryden's principle of selection explicitly argues for the unity of a truth that had been dispersed in the course of history among a variety of characters in works by many great writers, who in turn project themselves into their characters. In *Fables* a character's experience of revelation is one of the dominant themes. The content of these passages varies in detail, but their exalted tone and their cosmological emphasis link them to each other, so that *Fables* displays a range of fragmentary perceptions that, taken together, suggest the complex wholeness of truth. The very form of the poem is an image of the permanence and occasional accessibility of truth, even if it comes to each individual in limited form.

Collective poems or arranged books are still current today, and a modern collective translation which bears comparison to Dryden's is Robert Lowell's *Imitations.* Lowell's book has also been misunderstood, that is, it has been read as a failure at adequate paraphrase instead of as a creative reintegration of past literature, and it has been pushed to the side of the Lowell canon. One sympathetic reader, Stephen Yenser, points out the need 'to recognize the nature of the volume and its unity. *Imitations* is primarily neither a collection of translations nor a collection of original poems based on others, but rather a carefully organized *book*, the thematic center of which is the continuity of life and art for the poet.'[32] Lowell makes a direct reference to Dryden in his introduction, from which I conclude, not only that Dryden was Lowell's model for free translation, but that Lowell understood the aim of Dryden's collections.[33] Lowell's range of selections is entirely different from Dryden's. He takes lyric rather than fable as his normative form and he is even more explicitly concerned with the character of the artist. Nevertheless, he and Dryden duplicate each other at one point, since both include the invocation to the Muse from the beginning of the *Iliad* – seven lines in Lowell, eight in Dryden's couplets. Lowell's fragment heads the volume as a whole; it is followed by an ellipsis and then by Achilles' slaughter of Lycaon from Book XXI, which displays Achilles' violence at its most chilling and provides an immediate justification for rejecting the ideal of military valour. Dryden translated all of Book I, but he reduced Homer from his primal position at the fountain of European literature by placing him in the middle of *Fables*. Thus, both Lowell and Dryden replace military heroism with the ideal of poetic endeavour, but by entirely different poetic means. There are no verbal parallels between Lowell's and Dryden's invocations, for Lowell, even more than Dryden, is concerned with establishing a personal voice. His position is one of second- or maybe even third-order belatedness, requiring him to distinguish himself from a poet who was in turn an imitator and whose originals were, as Dryden demonstrated in his preface, themselves collectors of already available material.

The fragmentary form in both Lowell and Dryden tends to break down distinctions between genre. Both poets, in effect, 'fashion retrospectively a tradition for [their] accomplishment,'[34] and their works have a 'progressive or incremental structure.'[35] In each the words of the original writer are assimilated to the translator's personal voice, whose nature we deduce from its continuity throughout the total poem.

Lowell's implied commentary on Dryden is persuasive as to the meaning of Dryden's design, but I find Jorge Luis Borges's story 'Pierre Menard, Author of the *Quixote*' irresistible in its implications. I read this story before I began work on Dryden, and it affected my response and increased my pleasure. Pierre Menard is (or was?) a fictitious writer of the early twentieth century, a contemporary of Mallarmé and Valéry, who succeeded in writing 'word for word and line for line' two fragments of *Don Quixote* containing the essence of Cervantes's book. Borges's phrase 'word for word' identifies Menard as a translator aiming at the impossible goal of metaphrase[36] and Borges's distinction between Menard's *visible* and *invisible* works, of which the *Quixote* is one, draws ironic attention to our usual practice of extracting a writer's original works from the totality of his canon, behaving as if his translated works were not there. Borges's irony is especially relevant since Menard's visible works are at least as contingent as his *Quixote*, being themselves responses to other writers or works, often to critics, sometimes to an individual who functions as a muse. Thus Borges, like Dryden, assimilates original composition to translation, reducing the space occupied by original works to virtually nothing.

Borges presents Menard's *Quixote* as more subtle than Cervantes's, since our awareness of each writer's historical situation makes us marvel at Menard's struggle to write a few pages identical to those that Cervantes wrote in a natural style. Our knowledge of Menard adds a level of complexity to the reader's response. We cannot help reading the *Quixote* of Menard differently from the identical *Quixote* of Cervantes, because the fact of changed authorship provides a new context and also because the writer of two carefully chosen fragments claims to have captured the essence of the original work, far more diffuse in Cervantes's version. To follow Borges, we should not only read Dryden's *Fables* as a construct by Dryden, but read his translation of Virgil's *Aeneid* as if it were *Virgil's Aeneis* by John Dryden – which in fact Dryden encourages us to do because of his imposition of his own personality on the translation. Dryden made no effort to suppress his identity (though at first he felt that the translator should) or to deflect his readers' awareness of it; in fact he wrote endlessly about himself either directly or by implication. His very heroes show their author. He stressed his personhood all the more when his work took forms that threatened him with invisibility and when the general tendency of scholars was to treat all authors as shadows. Doubles, twin figures, and rivals appear everywhere in *Fables* and in other late works, with a variety of meanings. One of their meanings is to suggest the character of the translator, who is and is not the author of his poem, and the translator's dispersion of identity when he allies himself not with one primal author but with several.

2

Translation and Personal Identity

COMPETITION, INDEPENDENCE, AND ADVANCING AGE

Obviously there was a considerable element of choice and personal expression in Dryden's translations, even though he wrote them to support himself. Not all literature that is written to make money, translated or otherwise, is bad, or trivial, on that account, and from Dryden's point of view the fact that he could live by negotiating with a bookseller instead of depending on the court actually increased his feelings of independence, particularly after 1688. Dryden chose to consider himself a free-born subject,[1] a man who could make contracts, and this put him in the same league as the politicians who failed to appreciate him. His defiant but not entirely successful posturing in the letters to Tonson concerning accurate payment for translating Virgil shows him adopting that stance. Tonson had a lot to put up with:

> Some kind of intercourse must be carryed on betwixt us, while I am translateing Virgil. Therefore I give you notice, that I have done the seaventh Eneid in the Country: and intend some few days hence, to go upon the Eigth: when that is finishd, I expect fifty pounds, in good silver; not such as I have had formerly. I am not obligd to take gold, neither will I; not stay for it beyond four & twenty houres after it is due.[2]

This, and his several references to clipped money and to the unstable value of pounds and guineas,[3] show Dryden setting his personal affairs in the context of current economic issues, especially the problems involved in recoinage.[4] As a man who could use a political vocabulary to discuss his own literary activities, Dryden rather ostentatiously suggests his ability to talk the language of a member of parliament, and hence his continued interest in and his ability to concern himself with affairs of state. In the 'Life of

Lucian,' written in 1696, Dryden blamed the commercialism of English booksellers for the relative failures of translation in England, again relating translation to the character of the free-born subject; it is 'so very useful to an enquiring people, and for the improvement and spreading of knowledge, which is none of the worst preservatives against slavery.'[5]

Translation may have helped Dryden to preserve his economic self-respect and to outdo the republicans at their own mythmaking, while the oblique mode of self-expression that it necessarily imposed on him made him all the more assertive in business relationships. Translation for Dryden led to over-compensation and to an increased concern with the integrity of the writer's self. One can readily agree that Dryden was the sort of translator described by Renato Poggioli, not offering 'an empty vessel which he fills with a liquor he could not distill by himself,' but moved by 'an elective affinity: the attraction of a content so appealing that he can identify it with a content of his own.'[6] However, even this sort of translator still has to overpower another voice which must be as forceful as his own or it would not be worth translating. It is interesting, though, that Dryden's concern with the competition of voices dates back to *Religio Laici* (1682; II, 97–122), where the dangerously overpowering voice was that of God himself, not revealed directly, but in the translated Bible. Dryden's very point is that God's voice survives the limits of the various flawed translations and defective texts through which we know that voice. God is unique, for the very structure of *Religio Laici* is designed to show the relative weakness of the human voice even at its best. The exceptional beauty of Dryden's exordium ('Dim, as the borrow'd beams of Moon and Stars') at last yields to the plain style and self-disparaging tone of the conclusion:

> Thus have I made my own Opinions clear:
> Yet neither Praise expect, nor Censure fear:
> And this unpolish'd, rugged Verse, I chose;
> As fittest for Discourse, and nearest Prose:
> For, while from *Sacred Truth* I do not swerve,
> *Tom Sternhold*'s or *Tom Sha---ll*'s *Rhimes* will serve. (451–6)

Dryden, following his own logic, must question the metaphors of the opening lines because they are based on a complex set of analogies between divine truth and truth as the human mind perceives it, and analogies between the finite mind and infinity must collapse. He cannot entirely justify borrowing or trying to simulate God's voice. God's voice overwhelms him, even in the imperfect form in which the sacred text reveals it to him.

But the *Logos* does not silence him. *Religio Laici* could have become a self-consuming artefact, like George Herbert's poem 'The Collar,' in which the poet argues himself into silence,[7] but Dryden ends instead by allying himself with the unpolished style of two poets he despised. This conclusion is distinctly uneasy. Dryden has not decided to give up his art; he has only shown that he cannot readily justify writing beautiful poetry in his own voice. He cannot for very long have contemplated (if he ever did) sinking to Shadwell's level, as shown by the angry lines on Doeg and Og which he contributed to *The Second Part of Absalom and Achitophel* (II, 61–96). Bad poetry is an offence; it is tantamount to treason and blasphemy:

> ... Treason botcht in Rhime will be thy bane;
> Rhime is the Rock on which thou art to wreck,
> 'Tis fatal to thy Fame and to thy Neck:
> Why shoud thy Metre good King *David* blast?
> A Psalm of his will Surely be thy last.
> Dar'st thou presume in verse to meet thy foes,
> Thou whom the Penny Pamphlet foil'd in prose? (485–91)

Who can read the eleven hundred lines of this otherwise innocuous poem without knowing exactly where Dryden's contribution begins and ends? Dryden goes out of his way to draw attention to himself by intensifying his poetic superiority to Naham Tate, his collaborator (and friend), as well as to his satiric enemies (Tate and Dryden would remain friends until the 1688 revolution). Dryden has lost the competition with God, but his superiority to other human poets provided rapid consolation and even stimulus. This consolation was not available to Herbert, who wrote in isolation.

In *Religio Laici*, too, prose translation is shown as one way that a modest man can stay alive as a writer. At its structural centre (224–51) is a eulogy to Henry Dickinson, the youthful translator of Richard Simon's *Critical History of the Old Testament*. Probably Dryden had no personal interest in Dickinson himself,[8] but in his symbolic role as translator of a secular text, not of God's word, Dickinson becomes the only man in the poem who does not contribute to the multiplication of error. Simon himself, misrepresented as a crabbed old man (in truth he was eight years younger than Dryden), has only provided some easy learning for the benefit of lazy priests:

> A Treasure, which if *Country-Curates* buy,
> They *Junius*, and *Tremellius* may defy:
> Save pains in various readings, and Translations;
> And without *Hebrew* make most learn'd quotations. (240–3)

Translation, however, shows a commitment to 'the severe Delights of Truth' (233), analogous to the 'unpolish'd, rugged Verse' Dryden later says he has accepted.

The address to Dickinson is also interesting as Dryden's first effort to praise a younger writer, in part because of envy for the young writer who uses time well, in part because advanced age does not necessarily bring superior wisdom or talent. Dryden's mistake concerning Simon's age may be unconscious evidence of this tendency to link old age with the misuse of wisdom. He assumes that Simon was isolated in an ivory tower, 'in the Sifting Care / Of *Rabbins* old Sophisticated Ware / From Gold Divine' (236–8), and expresses near contempt for Arius, a 'good old Man' (221) but also a well-meaning crackpot who found it easy to consign his enemies to hell. Old men, it seems, can fall into Laputan isolation, losing touch with the worldly implications of their work, while young men are intellectually responsible. At the critical age of fifty-two Dryden tries to dissociate himself from old age and to identify with youth, at least in finding youthful qualities more admirable than those of old men and in suggesting that a young man might be a superior model. One cannot escape the feeling, evident more obviously in 'To Mr. Oldham' (1684), that Dryden felt guilty about his own late start as a writer. In 'To Mrs. Anne Killigrew' (1685; III, 109–15), another poem to a poet who died too soon, guilt is further suggested in Dryden's contrast between Anne Killigrew's purity and the inevitable degradation of poets who have prostituted their muse. Those critics who think that Dryden's praise of Mrs Killigrew was intended ironically should keep in mind the fact that, if Dryden had died at her age, he would have left even fewer poems than she did for us to remember him by. Only in the poem addressed to Congreve in 1693 does Dryden seem to have reconciled the complementary roles of youthful and aged poets, but during the 1680s he was feeling guilty about his past and anxious about his future as a poet. These tendencies showed before his conversion and long before the political 'exile,' in part self-imposed, of the 1690s, which at least provided him with a new identity as an angry and independent man.

Dryden probably feared aging, like everyone else, and thus in the years between 1682 and 1685 he may have needed to construct a radically new identity as a poet. It is not surprising to discover that he had a mid-life crisis, which must have been exacerbated by the atmosphere of controversy that made it hard to write anything that was not political. A mood of pessimism is evident in the writings of other poets and dramatists of this time. I do not interpret these self-exploratory passages in Dryden as a prelude to religious conversion, though the decisive action of conversion might have generated a new sense of purpose.

More light on Dryden's feelings about age can be shed by 'To the Memory of Mr. Oldham,' a poem pervaded by allusions to Shakespeare and Virgil, both of whom died, coincidentally, at the same age, fifty-two, precisely when Dryden began questioning himself in his public poetry. It is tempting to read this poem as an implied elegy to Shakespeare and Virgil and then ask: 'What could advancing Age' have added to *their* achievement? Dryden had already outlived these two great poets when he wrote the Oldham poem and he may have been afraid that he would die before he could express himself fully, or do so in a way that would grant him self-respect. His most important original poems in this period, besides the elegies on poets who died young, were a 'Funeral-Pindarique,' 'Threnodia Augustalis,' on Charles II's death in 1685 (III, 91–107) and a poem on translation, 'To the Earl of Roscomon', written in 1684 (II, 172–4). Charles II was only one year older than Dryden when *he* died, so that when Dryden turns from Charles to James II in 'Threnodia Augustalis,' one can sense his interest in his own rebirth:

> Heroes, in Heaven's peculiar Mold are cast,
> They and their Poets are not form'd in hast;
> Man was the first in God's design, and Man was made the last. (432–4)

Dryden looks to his own future in elevating James, and not necessarily in a self-aggrandizing way. If his old self had died with Charles, a fulfilment or extension of his powers might be possible under the new reign. However cynically one reads a passage that on one level may be a bid for royal attention, Dryden apparently hoped that he had a phoenix-like power of self-renewal, ultimately a kind of adaptability, a capacity to revise his earlier ideals,that enabled him to survive as a poet. His various experiments at new identities, like the mock-defiance of Tonson, are a kind of creative role-playing that carried him through the transitional stages in his life. The engagement with translation in the years 1684 and 1685 gave him added vitality as a poet without requiring him to step forward as a person.

APELLES AND HIS STATUE: THE CONCEALED AUTHOR

Far more than an original poet, a translator is concealed behind his work, but Dryden sometimes treats even original works of literature as indirect modes of self-revelation for their authors. For example, he sees Aeneas and Achilles as embodiments of contrasting modes of energy, yet as similar in that each hero reveals the 'natural Inclination' of the poet who created him:

'The very *Heroes* shew their Authors: *Achilles* is hot, impatient, revengeful ... *Æneas* patient, considerate, careful of his People, and merciful to his Enemies; ever submissive to the Will of Heaven' (K, IV, 1449). This part of the preface to *Fables* is ultimately Longinian, for it is concerned with the reader's engagement with a poem: the reader comes to share a specific quality of mind with a given poet through the medium of a hero whom the author has consciously or unconsciously created in his own image. Dryden assumes that the poet wants to be known and will inevitably be known if, like Homer and Virgil, he has the power to recreate himself.

Dryden's most extended treatment of the concealed author occurs in the dedication of the *Aeneis*, but a related theme emerges in his lives of the three Greek writers Plutarch, Polybius, and Lucian, who are scarcely known at all except through their works. The contrast between Greek and Roman, as Dryden presented it, is itself of prime importance. Whereas the Roman Virgil had to express himself indirectly, because he was constantly under the eye of his ruler, Augustus, the three Greeks embodied the simplicity and unity of truth. They are what Dryden might have liked to be, whereas Virgil is what he had to be because of his own political situation. The Greeks also seem congenial with Dryden's Catholicism in its commitment to absolutes, as expressed in a letter to Mrs Steward, written late in Dryden's life: 'May God be pleasd to open your Eyes, as he has opend mine: Truth is but one, & they who have once heard of it, can plead no Excuse, if they do not embrace it.'[9] The three Greek writers – a biographer, a historian, and a writer of satiric dialogues – all embody the conviction that truth is a value to be defended without equivocation. For instance, Polybius could describe his own father's incompetence without any sign of partiality: 'It is true, Lycortas in all probability was dead when Polybius wrote this history; but had he been then living, we may safely think that his son would have assumed the same liberty, and not feared to have offended him in behalf of truth.'[10] Polybius explodes superstition (from which Catholics in Dryden's time were equally anxious to dissociate themselves) and risks displeasing superficial readers by accepting only natural causes as evidence. He 'commends nothing but plainness, sincerity, and the common good, undisguised, and set in a true light before the people.'[11] Though Polybius was not religious at all, as a pagan exemplar of integrity and in the search for truth he is a proto-Catholic.

That Dryden associated these values with the Greek spirit and not with Polybius alone may be seen in his similar treatment of Plutarch and Lucian. Lucian might have been a Christian, though Dryden thinks it unlikely; however, *if* he ever was one, he surely never 'became a renegade to our belief.'[12] One senses that Dryden is using his self-knowledge to reconstruct an image of Lucian, on the basis of fragmentary and perhaps apocryphal evidence; Lucian becomes to some degree an *alter ego*, since Dryden has to discover an affinity between himself and his subject in order to make any sort of informed judgment about him. The point of contact in this case is that Lucian, like Dryden, lived in a 'knowing' and hence a 'sceptical' age. Dryden concludes, in the absence of any definitive information about Lucian's beliefs, that Lucian was a sceptic, entertaining each of several philosophies for as long as it interested him or was useful in his writing: 'And indeed this last opinion [that he was a sceptic, not an eclectic] is the more probable of the two, if we consider the genius of the man, whose image we may clearly see in the glass which he holds before us of his writings, which reflects him to our sight.'[13]

Robert Hume has suggested that Dryden in his later years began to read literature with an increasing interest in detecting the author's character.[14] To a large extent this is so, but in the essays on the Greeks Dryden is involved with biography itself and especially with the problem of writing about men who have been dead for centuries and about whom few trustworthy records remain, other than their own writings. Although his subjects were not so ready to disintegrate as Aesop or Homer, they were not absolutely secure from oblivion. As I said in chapter 1, Dryden and his contemporaries could recognize a legend masquerading as life history (and so Dryden rejects a tale that Lucian was eaten by dogs as punishment for his apostasy),[15] but a sort of biography of a man's mind, based on his writings, was still possible and was, in its way, more reliable than conjectures based on pseudo-facts from other sources. At least an author's writings emerge from his mind and whatever they tell us about his character is definitive on that level.

In the 'Life of Plutarch' (1683), the earliest of these three essays, Dryden developed a theory of inference based on Plutarch himself and related to his own technique of collective translations. Plutarch, by his own account, based his works on 'Forreign observations and the scatter'd writings of various Authours';[16] Dryden in turn becomes a collector of fragments of knowledge about Plutarch: 'we are forc'd to glean from *Plutarch*, what he has scatter'd in his Writings, concerning himself and his Original: Which (excepting that little memorial, that *Suidas*, and some few others, have left concerning him) is all we can collect, relating to this great Philosopher and Historian' (XVII, 239). The image of the truth-seeker reconstructing a whole from the scattered fragments of truth can be found in Plutarch's *Isis and Osiris*, in which the myth of Isis piecing together the fragments of Osiris's body becomes an allegory for the philosopher's search for the unity of truth.

Dryden based his reference to the myth on a secondary source and may not have read Plutarch's essay – did he remember Milton's use of the myth of dismembered Osiris or Truth in *Areopagitica*?[17] Still, as the myth parallels Dryden's activity in collective translations, and as Isis herself is the focal character in his first translations from the *Metamorphoses*, one may wonder if this myth did not have some attraction for him. Dryden glorifies Plutarch, imagining him as 'a Soul insatiable of knowledge' (XVII, 247) who, in Pythagorean style, sought Egyptian wisdom. Wanting Plutarch to be like himself, Dryden speculates on whether he anticipated Christian belief:

> I have ever thought, that the Wise-men in all Ages, have not much differ'd in their opinions of Religion; I mean as it is grounded on human Reason: For Reason, as far as it is right, must be the same in all Men; and Truth being but one, they must consequently think in the same Train. Thus it is not to be doubted, but the Religion of *Socrates*, *Plato*, and *Plutarch* was not different in the main: Who doubtless beleiv'd the identity of one Supream Intellectual Being, which we call GOD. (XVII, 250)

In 1683 Dryden thus sought for heroes among the ancients, who were unsullied by the factionalism of English Protestantism, apparently praising them with less qualification than in *Religio Laici*. Dedication in the search for truth had gained precedence over the Christian's false security in his knowledge of the gospels.

Dryden clearly admires Plutarch's ability to rest content with a tentative or a probable truth which enabled him to find values even without an infallible guide to belief. Although Plutarch extended probability to religious matters, Dryden uses it to define a historical method. It provides a middle ground between complete certainty and the opposite dogma of Pyrrhonism: 'there is a kind of positiveness in granting nothing to be more likely on one part than on another' (XVII, 249). Dryden's own essay is filled with confessions of ignorance and with analyses of anecdotes that might or might not be true, leading him repeatedly to use expressions like these, as if he were absorbing Plutarch's spirit in the very act of writing about him:

> Tis then most probable, that he pass'd his days at *Rome* ...
> Now 'tis my particular guess (for I have not read it any where) ...
>
> When he was first made known to *Trajan* is like the rest uncertain, or by what means, whether by *Senecio*, or any other, he was introduc'd to his acquaintance: But 'tis most likely, that *Trajan*, then a private Man, was one of his Auditors, amongst others of the Nobility of *Rome*. (XVII, 264–5)

In sum, the historian's search for causes should 'be drawn at least from the most probable circumstances' (XVII, 272). It is interesting that Dryden finds the intellectual honesty implied by the acceptance of probable truth among several Greeks who would in another age have been Christians, or even Catholics. Without arguing that Dryden was preparing himself for conversion, I suggest that something was going on in his mind between 1682 and 1685, a dissatisfaction with his own times and with himself, that found an outlet in an admiration for Plutarch, the first of several Greeks whom he saw as dedicated and honest in their search for truth. Plutarch in effect provided an interim philosophy, and his view of the historian's reconstitutive role is a striking commentary on Dryden's method at this time in *Miscellany Poems* and in *Sylvae*.

The Roman Virgil of 1697 is entirely different and parallels an altogether different aspect of Dryden's sense of self. For all Virgil's personal integrity, he is shown as always holding something back. Dryden does not blame Virgil, who was constantly accused of being a time-server, because he was more closely implicated in a particular society than the Greeks, even though he did not entirely identify with it. Dryden's Greeks were cosmopolitans, professional travellers, conveniently detached from any given culture, a choice not available to everyone. If the Greeks stand for an ideal of cosmopolitanism, Virgil represents the social reality that poets born into a powerful nation-state must come to terms with; his deviousness, which is more serious than game-playing yet less serious than Machiavellian calculation, is that form of accommodation. It involves compromise; that is, Virgil concealed his republicanism from Augustus, but the involutions of his artistic intentions seem to make up for it and to suggest that calculation can provide its own sort of literary interest.

Dryden's pleasure in unravelling the clues to a writer's mind is apparent in his response to an 'Essay on Poetry' written by John, Marquis of Normanby, Earl of Mulgrave, to whom Dryden dedicated the *Aeneis*. Mulgrave's essay had been published anonymously:

> But to come *Anonymous* upon me, and force me to commend you against my interest, was not altogether so fair, give me leave to say, as it was Politick. For by concealing your Quality, you might clearly understand how your Work succeeded; and that the general approbation was given to your Merit not your Titles. Thus like *Apelles* you stood unseen behind your own *Venus*, and receiv'd the praises of the passing Multitude: the Work was commended, not the Author: And I doubt not this was one of the most pleasing Adventures of your Life. (The dedication of the *Æneis*, K, III, 1009)

In this response Dryden anticipates the various eighteenth-century writers who were to experience all kinds of titillation from anonymous publication,[18] and also suggests his feelings about the ambiguous kind of concealment that writing itself affords an author. The image of Apelles and his statue has general significance, for in some sense all works of art simultaneously conceal and reveal their creators, and the artist who thinks he wants to conceal himself may in fact be incapable of sacrificing the chance to let the public know the truth. Poets and sculptors are real beings and the 'life' of a work of art may really consist in a game of hide and seek whereby artist and reader or viewer try to catch each other. On this level it may not matter precisely why the artist chooses to conceal himself or herself. Mulgrave's reason for anonymity (a disarming combination of modesty and proper pride) would not be precisely duplicated in Dryden or Virgil, who both had serious reasons for caution; yet it shows that a writer could be politic without being despicable – 'it is possible for a Courtier not to be a Knave' (K, III, 1016) – and that the politic aspects of self-concealment may be converted into fun. Dryden himself emerges as relatively open in character, even though he too has to conceal some of his opinions. He gives himself no special credit for outspokenness; it is simply his good fortune to have been born English: 'I shall continue still to speak my Thoughts like a free-born Subject as I am; though such things, perhaps, as no *Dutch* Commentator cou'd, and I am sure no *French*-man durst' (K, III, 1016).

Virgil's admitted deviousness, therefore, is thoroughly bound up with his accomplishment as a poet – after all, we admire the poet who is calculating in his art. Dryden credits Virgil with almost sublime address both in ordering the *Aeneid* and in foreseeing its effect upon Augustus.[19] Virgil had 'secret Reasons' and 'Motives' for everything, and the planning that is inevitable in constructing an epic poem flows naturally into his ability to foresee its political impact. We come to understand his reasons, both aesthetic and political, for including the Dido episode, for making Dido and Aeneas contemporaries, and for assuring us that the forsaken Dido had really married Aeneas. Augustus had recently divorced his wife: Virgil 'drew this dimple in the Cheek of *Æneas*' to suggest an analogy between Augustus and Aeneas (K, III, 1032). Dryden's defence of Virgil against various charges of servility and inconsistency thus takes the form of making us see how the court poet's heightened self-consciousness is essentially another facet of the qualities that we respect in his art.

Dryden imagines Augustus as a potentially 'Arbitrary Master' who nevertheless had redeeming qualities that caused him to restrain his power. Dryden thus lacks the overt anti-Augustanism that Howard Weinbrot has found elsewhere in the eighteenth century, nor does he attribute it to Virgil. However, Dryden takes it for granted that a subject's feelings of resistance will usually be futile, so that the true problem is having to accept the inevitable without abandoning self-respect. Dryden is sympathetic with Virgil's presumed inner conflict, impressed with his performance, and anxious to suggest that his own situation has not forced him into Virgilian extremes of deviousness; he insists on his own character as a free-born subject, a stance which is not only of a piece with the letter to Tonson but also an attempt to assuage his own potential enemies. Virgil was not a time-server, as Dryden reads him, but a man who accepted the need for a strong ruler after a long period of decay in the Roman republic, interrupted by only two or three false reformations. He knew that the commonwealth was dead, that the Romans had already experienced slavery, and that, if a despot had to arise at that point, Augustus was not the worst imaginable. Virgil saw no use in expressing his true thoughts, which Dryden reconstructs as follows: 'Yet I may safely affirm for our great Author (as Men of good Sense are generally Honest) that he was still of Republican Principles in his Heart' (K, III, 1014).

Dryden's conviction that Virgil was in part a kindred spirit, whose concealed motives he could safely deduce, suggests that in 1697 Virgil was a device to analyse his own situation as a writer forced to live under an alien, but not hopelessly oppressive, government. Another model for political quietism is Montaigne, who believed that 'an Honest Man ought to be contented with that Form of Government, and with those Fundamental Constitutions of it, which he receiv'd from his Ancestors, and under which he himself was Born' (K, III, 1014). 'Honesty' is thus consistent with a degree of secretiveness, and one notes that Montaigne's principles require loyalty not to the current *monarch* but rather to enduring political principles or to an ancient constitution, either of which might be said to precede that monarch both historically and logically. Montaigne provides Dryden with an excuse for treating William as essentially irrelevant to his underlying loyalty to England.

Dryden's version of honesty lets a writer adopt oblique modes of expression to avoid the twin evils of crass flattery and dangerous plain speech. He is very sensitive to obliqueness in others, taking for granted the presence of political allegory and topical allusion in the *Aeneid*. The several flawed kings in that poem are assumed to be foils for Aeneas/Augustus, especially the tyrant Mezentius, who has been expelled for his cruelty and who is at once a warning to Augustus and a reminder to the Romans that they could be infinitely worse off. Dryden's really negative image of arbitrary government, which puts both England and Augustan Rome in perspective, is the French monarchy which inhibited both Montaigne and Segrais, Dryden's main source of material in the dedication (K, III, 1014, 1020). Dryden and Virgil, unlike the French authors, have the dubious privilege of expressing themselves as long as they do so obliquely. Augustus is always in Virgil's eye, as Dryden puts it; and Dryden is relatively safe under the reign of William III because the existence of an ancient constitution and perhaps the forthright English character itself are possible safeguards against Williamite tyranny. Dryden never makes Virgil's ultimate concession – turning the hero of his poem into a mask for the king.

SPLIT IDENTITY IN THE LATE PLAYS

After 1680 Dryden returned to writing plays, again for financial reasons, until his project for translating Virgil enabled him to stop in 1694, with *Love Triumphant*. His late plays have been unjustly neglected, perhaps because of their lack of continuity with the heroic drama of the 1660s and 1670s, though at least two, *Don Sebastian* and *Amphitryon*, are excellent on their own account. *Cleomenes* anticipates the stoic ideals of Addison's *Cato* and thus might be regarded as a new sort of political problem play, and *Love Triumphant* reflects Dryden's changing attitudes towards the self. All the late plays treat the theme of split identity, and two of them, *Amphitryon* and *Love Triumphant*, bear upon Dryden's sense of his role as a translator, who is a poet with a split identity.

The theme has a political application. Two of Dryden's heroes, Don Sebastian and Cleomenes, find themselves leaders without a following and thus without a function. The leader's sense of his own identity has been so bound up with his public role that he is forced to become a new self, and the plays are really about this process of self-examination and inner recognition. Political activities – empire-seeking, heroic love, rebellions – are pushed to the side in these plays and sometimes treated as theatrical jokes, though Dryden does not quite banish them offstage. Heroic self-examination is not the same as a conversion experience, but Dryden's own conversion must have contributed to his interest in his heroes' inner lives. His conversion must have become an unpleasantly extended process, and not a sudden illumination solving all problems forever, since William's accession had forced him into new relationships to the government and to society at large, and the idealism of the Greek lives (and of *Cleomenes*) had to co-exist with Dryden's natural flexibility and the pleasure he took in accommodation as a test of himself. I do not think that Dryden became cynical, but that the process of time worked certain kinds of personal changes, one of which was towards acceptance of the inevitable. Dryden's plays are effective because the heroes are intermittent allegories both for himself – Don Sebastian has 'died' and been reborn before the play begins; Amphitryon and his servant Sosia have their identities stolen – and also for a recognizable monarch: James II had been exiled from his country like Don Sebastian and Cleomenes, while William III was a military man, like the slightly ridiculous Amphitryon. A play, like a translated poem, is a literary work in which the author appears, if he does so at all, indirectly, but the recurrence of some patterns is undeniable.

Earl Miner has pointed out that Dryden's prologue to *Don Sebastian*, drawing attention to his religion, was a courageous statement 'at a time when men were being arrested for high treason only on the suspicion of adhering to that religion.'[20] The play itself concerns the question of speaking out, of being oneself, and asks whether direct self-exposure through speech accomplishes much more than a futile exhibition of the speaker's integrity. The importance of the theme in this excellent play suggests that Dryden could not silence himself and once again had to justify the literary impulse which was so obviously the equivalent of his own sense of self.

Don Sebastian is a historical figure, but history is silent about his actions during the part of his life that is covered by the play; almost certainly the real Don Sebastian died in the battle with Muley-Moloch that precedes the play, as Dryden constructs the action. Dryden imagines him and his sister/mistress, Almeyda (a recent convert to Christianity), as surviving and being captured: '*As for the story or plot of the Tragedy, 'tis purely fiction; for I take it up where the History has laid it down*' (XV, 67). Don Sebastian and Almeyda marry and sleep together before they learn the truth about their relationship. Because Sebastian's body was never found, the Portuguese cherished a belief that he might reappear, and in fact several impostors did, thus making Sebastian an obvious parallel to the myths of Arthurian rebirth that Dryden mentions. The story has some relevance to England because of the parallel to Arthur, but there is nothing for which Dryden could have been condemned, even though Sebastian is a sympathetic character. If Dryden cherished fantasies of a Jacobite return, extending the Arthurian parallel to a desire that James might return as well, the play is an attempt to exorcise them by treating Sebastian/Arthur/James as dead to the public world, whatever he might be in Dryden's imagination.

If we speculate that Sebastian really did survive the battle, the silence of history demonstrates a self-abnegation on his part that might be said to approach saintliness. However, Dryden clearly felt that saintliness had to be earned; on the two occasions when he associates his hero with saintliness, he is ironic. In his preface he apologizes for Sebastian's innocent incest:

This being presuppos'd, that he was Religious, the horror of his incest, tho innocently committed, was the best reason which the Stage cou'd give for hind'ring his return. 'Tis true I have no right to blast his Memory, with such a crime: but declaring it to be fiction, I desire my Audience to think it no longer true, than while they are seeing it represented: For that once ended, he may be a Saint for ought I know; and we have reason to presume he is. (xv, 68)

In the first act Sebastian himself uses an image – 'Let fortune empty her whole Quiver on me' (I.i.352) – that links him to the traditional iconography associated with Sebastian, who was martyred by being shot with arrows, though it also suggests the long-suffering Hamlet, another hero who lived on the boundary between existence and nothingness. However, the bravado of Sebastian's language in the first act is really that of the false heroic, even to its clever pun: 'where one Atome / Of mine shall light; know there *Sebastian* Reigns' (I.i.366–7). He apparently believes that he is indestructible and that he will retain the power of a natural force after his death. In other words, Sebastian is least saintly at the point where he claims to be so, and achieves some semblance of saintliness only after he has recognized his human fallibility and even sunk so low as to consider suicide, '*transported from* [piety] *by the violence of a sudden passion*' (xv, 68). Saintliness involves a genuine acceptance of absolute exile and privacy, 'Unvex'd with noise, and undisturb'd with fears' (V.i.654), the willingness to be silent and sacrifice a public role forever.

Thus, a failure in saintly commitment is linked to loudness and verbosity. Almeyda outdoes Sebastian in this respect and she is slower to accept the futility of speech. By the second act Sebastian learns that his words misfire after he has tried to persuade the Emperor not to kill Almeyda and has only succeeded in making him love her:

> Let me be dumb for ever, all I plead,
> Like Wild-fire thrown against the Wind, returns
> With double force to burn me. (II.i.431–3)

By Act III, when the Emperor has discovered Sebastian's and Almeyda's marriage, Sebastian finds his soul able to 'shut out Life as calmly / As it does words' (III.i.217–18). He refuses to plead for his own life or for Almeyda's, though she attacks him for behaving like 'a dumb Sacrifice' (III.i.236). On one level, of course, Sebastian's conflict concerns the question of whether life is worth anything at all to him at this point, but on another it raises the possibility that words have no meaning that two people can share. Even worse, words often do have consequences in the play, but those consequences are dangerously unpredictable. Most of the play expresses a near existential fear of the power of language.

Almeyda hastens to fill the vacuum left by Sebastian's silence and by the linguistic confusions of the rabble, the captain of the rabble, and the Mufti, an embodiment of the state church. Though she is a fictitious character, with sources only in romance, Dryden links her to a Portuguese family '*which was very instrumental in the Restoration of Don* John de Braganza, *Father to the most Illustrious and most Pious Princess, our Queen* Dowager,' that is, Charles II's widow (XV, 69).[21] Almeyda is thus characterized as a sort of Jacobite, anxious that she and Sebastian be restored to the power that she feels they deserve; her failure to effect this restoration suggests Dryden's pessimism about such attempts, even at this early date, only a year or two after James's abdication. Almeyda talks too much and far too aggressively for a woman. She tricks Benducar, the ambitious favourite, by challenging the people directly: 'Why shou'd I fear to speak, who am your Queen?' (IV.iii.213). If we are pleased with Benducar's downfall, her demagoguery should arouse our suspicions:

> *Almeyda to the People.* No, let me rather dye your sacrifice
> Than live his Tryumph;
> I throw my self into my Peoples armes;
> As you are Men, compassionate my wrongs,
> And as good men, Protect me. (IV.iii.267–71)

It works, and the political plot is effectively over in Act IV. But this is a false ending, for Almeyda has misjudged the certainties in her personal relationships and behaved with dangerous assurance in ignoring her mother's warning not to marry. The speech of *others* is meaningless to her. The banality of the ending of Act IV, which *we* may misread as a true reconciliation, looks ahead to disaster.

In Act V the aged Alvarez reveals the incestuous relationship, not knowing that the couple are already married. His revelation is the most obvious example in the play of the dangers of honest but foolhardy speech. At first Alvarez simply refuses to be quiet, despite accusations of senility, malice, and incoherence. When he tries to reveal the truth 'in whispers,' Almeyda virtually trumpets her wish for public speech (v.i.257–60). She and Sebastian are at last convinced by the 'dumb Evidence' of a handwritten letter (v.i.383), which Almeyda cannot silence by tearing to shreds; the fact is as indestructible as Sebastian's atoms. Alvarez regrets his persistence once he knows the truth (v.i.426–30). One character after another thus loses confidence in his own speech as soon as he comes to see how foolhardy were his own intentions. Nevertheless, Dryden provides one more reversal: Sebastian's friend Dorax succeeds in saving him through the device of a lie, a 'pious fraud' (v.i.531), in which he urges Sebastian to commit suicide, knowing that his argument will have precisely the reverse effect because it will terrify Sebastian with images of hell. Dorax is the only character who learns to manipulate the abyss between intention and consequence in public speech that defeats Sebastian. And Almeyda decides that women's language is wrong and leaves for her own exile without saying farewell to Sebastian:

> I will not speak; but think a thousand thousand.
> And be thou silent too, my last [sic] *Sebastian*. (v.i.710–11)

She and her lover have had considerable difficulty, but at last they silence themselves.

Dryden's own inability or refusal to accept silence might be illustrated by the extreme length of the play itself, which had to be cut by twelve hundred lines for performance. However, Dryden restored the omissions when he published the play, and he informed his readers that he was doing so. From his standpoint the real choice in the play lies between Alvarez's timid and ill-considered direct utterance and Dorax's clever lies. It is Dorax, the malcontent who once disgraced himself by talking back to his king, who turns out to be indestructible, and the confused old man, a stereotypical worrier, who is wrong. Once again Dryden rejects old age with pitying contempt and provides a justification, however circuitous, for a continued dialogue with his audience.

Amphitryon is a fascinating comedy about loss of identity. Jupiter turns himself into Amphitryon's double in order to seduce Alcmena, his wife, and Mercury becomes the double of Amphitryon's servant Sosia in order to keep the real Amphitryon, away at the wars, from entering his house at an inconvenient time. The real Amphitryon and Sosia are thus compelled to decide how they know who they are and how they can demonstrate their true identities to the world, while Alcmena (in Dryden's version only) must decide how she knows her true husband from the impostor. She chooses the kinder husband, rejecting 'the Cholerick *Amphitryon*' (v.i.190), who has weakened his case by displaying all too human frustration. Anger again destroys an individual's credibility as Dorax and Almeyda, in two different ways, seem suspect. Alcmena says to Jupiter:

> Th' Impostour has thy Features, not thy Mind;
> The Face might have deceiv'd me in my choice;
> Thy kindness is a Guide that cannot err. (v.i.270–2)

Her reference to an unerring guide suggests that this crisis has religious overtones that did not exist in Dryden's sources. (In the versions of Plautus and Molière Alcmena is not even present at the *dénouement.*) Despite the absurdity of her personal problem Alcmena is like any human being who has to transcend or even ignore the evidence of her senses in order to know the truth. She makes the wrong choice; her god is a party to the deception.

Man and woman might as well be on their own, and the existence or non-existence of the gods makes no real difference in the nature of their problem. When Amphitryon attacks Jupiter, he declares that he will trust in the gods. The judge, Gripus, an original character in Dryden's version, weighs the merits of the two Amphitryons in a scene that parodies the judgment of Solomon (v.i.181ff), but human justice revolves around physical evidence like scars and bags of money, the usual paraphernalia of romantic plots, including that of *Don Sebastian*. Human instinct inclines to the man with more money; thus Phaedra, another new character, inclines to the false Sosia, who has given her a gold goblet (IV.i.413–14). She is no more capable than Alcmena of believing in the absurd. Dryden uses the scenes involving Phaedra and Gripus to suggest analogies to the English political order. The object of his satire is interesting when we consider that it was virtually impossible for him to attack the government. Phaedra says to the judge (a local agent of administration and potentially a stabilizing force):

> Thou Seller of other People: thou Weather-cock of Government: that when the Wind blows for the Subject, point'st to Priviledge; and when it changes for the Soveraign, veers to Prerogative. (v.i.13–16)

Dryden satirizes neither Williamites nor Jacobites but the passive, shifting man of no stable commitments. Country justice here is like the state church of *Don Sebastian*, for both 'stand in the main question dumb.' Thus Dryden found an outlet for his satire which did not require him to attack William, but rather the men who could have resisted William and who could yet make William irrelevant.

However, the character in *Amphitryon* who represents Dryden's point of view, and the one who most strongly represents personhood, is Sosia, as is also the case in Plautus's and Molière's versions.[22] In all three versions, moreover, Sosia has a noticeable poetic streak, which enables him to give vivid form to his dismay when he finds that Mercury has stolen his perceptible identity. When Sosia is going to tell Alcmena the news of Amphitryon's victory over the Teleboians and of his imminent return home, he rehearses the manner in which he will address her. First, he puts down his lantern and pretends that it is Alcmena. Then he becomes so involved in his narration, which is really a dialogue with himself, that for a few moments he forgets who he is. In Plautus's version he starts acting out the battle. In Molière's Sosia actually conducts a dialogue with the lantern, adopting a new voice for his imagined address to Alcmena and imitating her responses in a third voice. Molière's version, even more than Plautus's, portrays Sosia as naturally prone to splitting himself because he has the imagination of a dramatist. Mercury's deception only forces him to recognize his own inner divisions.

Dryden's version follows Molière in that Sosia carries on a dialogue with the lantern and imitates Alcmena's voice. Now, however, Mercury is already on stage when Act II begins, 'in Sosia's *shape*' but unnoticed, to make some pointed asides on the effect of Sosia's 'Oration,' reminding the audience that he, Mercury, is among other things the 'God of Eloquence' (II.i.41–2). In Molière's version Sosia pauses to commend his own effectiveness, but in Dryden's play Mercury judges Sosia's oratory, calling him, for instance, a 'Midnight Ballad-singer' (II.i.87). One of these asides – 'When *Thebes* is an University, thou deservest to be their Orator' (II.i.61–2) – sounds like a reference to Dryden's world, because, as Saintsbury has pointed out, Dryden had associated Cambridge with Thebes in his 'Prologue to the University of Oxford' (1676).[23] Saintsbury thinks that Sosia may represent someone else; perhaps he is a reference to Dryden himself. Dryden's Sosia is a sympathetic character, not a Shadwell, but a man who gets carried away only when he is alone. He can become several fictitious people in rapid succession, but, quickly deflated by Mercury's condescension, he has trouble defending his right to his own name. Without pushing this reference too far, one must note that it comes up in a play whose subject was so often reworked that any new version necessarily involves some literary theft; the whole project of dramatic adaptation resembles translation. In his dedication Dryden claims to be uneasy at the thought of his predecessors: 'As for *Plautus* and *Moliere*, they are dangerous People; and I am too weak a Gamester to put my self into their Form of Play.' If his play had been *no more than* a translation, he might have feared less: 'But I am affraid, for my own Interest, the World will too easily discover, that more than half of it is mine; and that the rest is rather a lame Imitation of their Excellencies, than a just Translation' (xv, 225). Dryden thus betrays more nervousness about the problems of literary competitiveness when he is neither translating nor creating an entirely new work, yet he appears to have added so much of his own to avoid being judged by the standards of 'their Form of Play.'

The production of *Cleomenes* was almost stopped because of the blatant parallel between the Spartan hero's exile in Egypt and James II's exile in France.[24] Though Dryden claimed that he had become interested in Cleomenes seven or eight years before, presumably when he was involved with Plutarch's lives, he did not say why he chose Cleomenes from the 'many subjects that [he] had thought on for the stage' (SS, VIII, 219), and it seems more pertinent to ask what Dryden did with the parallel than to wonder if it is there. In fact, though Dryden expresses sympathy for his hero in exile, that sympathy is qualified in important ways. Cleomenes cannot justify himself by pointing to his superior leadership, for his enemy Antigonus has enacted a bloodless invasion of Sparta. Cleomenes waits rather too hopefully for the tales 'of sacrilege and murders, / And fires, and rapes on matrons and on maids' (II.i; SS, VIII, 281), but Antigonus if anything has renewed the land:

think some king,
Who loved his people, took a peaceful progress
To some far distant place of his dominions;
Smiled on his subjects, as he rode in triumph,
And strewed his plenty, wheresoe'er he passed.
Nay, raise your thoughts yet higher; – think some deity,
Some better Ceres, drawn along the sky
By gentle dragons, scattered as she flew
Her fruitful grains upon the teeming ground,
And bade new harvests rise. (I.i; SS, VIII, 284)

The soldiers act as if they are on holy ground, 'peace and liberty' are proclaimed, trade continues, laws and customs remain as they were. By chance Antigonus dies in battle soon afterwards, but if he had not died, Cleomenes would have had no hope of reconquering Sparta by gaining the support of his countrymen and the play could have ended with the first act.

Antigonus's peaceful conquest resembles William's conquest, leaving Cleomenes a superfluous man. If this parallel was noted in 1690, it could only offend, because of its apparent effort to make Englishmen feel guilty for their failure to support their rightful king. Dryden must have felt the curious irrelevancy of the man at the top when subjects can rely on the persistence of everyday values and institutions no matter who rules. Yet, he does not idealize the character and the values of the common man, since the common man's inertia contributes to the failure of heroism itself. In Act v Cleomenes makes a last effort to regain his own freedom by appealing to the Egyptians' presumed desire for liberty: Egypt thus stands for St Germains at some points in the play, for England at others. There follows a strikingly flabby and underpopulated rabble scene, which is appropriate to satirize the Egyptians' lack of commitment:[25]

> *Cleom[enes].* ... The cowards whisper liberty so softly,
> As if they were afraid the gods would hear it,
> And take them at their word.
> *1 Egypt[ian].* No, friend: we vulgar never fear the gods; but we whisper, for fear our overthwart neighbours should hear us cry Liberty, and betray us to the government. (v.ii; ss, VIII, 353)

Cleomenes is again about the futility of heroism, or at least of those kinds which require either action or public display, or indeed aggressive, self-trumpeting speech. Dryden even changed the ending, as his readers could note, since Plutarch's life of Cleomenes was printed with the play. In Plutarch, Cleomenes, his family, his friend Pantheus, and Pantheus's wife are executed in public, the women especially demonstrating Spartan courage. In Dryden's play, however, Cleomenes and his family are left to starve in a cell, a slow death that gives them time to perceive the decay of the self while they are still alive. Spartan stamina, the identity on which the whole family has prided itself, is destroyed by physical frailty. Cleomenes' brief escape from prison only saves him from that kind of personal degradation, as if private heroism, the preservation of self-respect, were the only kind left.

To some extent Cleomenes seems to represent Dryden's own idealized self; like Don Sebastian, he gains power from that double reference in which king and poet can be embodied in the same character. Dryden was still trying to exorcise James. He quickly saw the pointlessness of expecting James to return and may have early begun to wonder if James were capable of organizing a return invasion or if Englishmen (other than Catholics) would benefit significantly enough to care.[26] The play salvages James as an object of personal admiration and loyalty while admitting the virtual impossibility of seeing him as a focus of concrete political action. The satire in *Cleomenes*, as in *Amphitryon*, is directed against the weathercocks who were incapable of any sort of permanent loyalty at all.

Love Triumphant (1694), Dryden's last play, makes a direct reference to his work which suggests another line of introspection. It also returns to the incest theme. Alphonso and Victoria, who in the early part of the play think that they are siblings, discover their love for each other while reading a book, in the manner of Dante's Paolo and Francesca, who had been placed in one of the earlier circles of hell for their illicit love (*Inferno*, Canto v). Paolo and Francesca were aroused by the story of Lancelot; Dryden's couple read, of all things, the story of 'Canace and Macareus,' an incestuous brother and sister in one of the three Ovidian epistles that Dryden had translated in 1680.[27] In order to arouse Victoria, Alphonso reads some passages – from Dryden's own translation – carefully selecting and rearranging his lines to suit his purpose: he perverts Dryden's own technique! But Victoria is shocked:

> Incendiary book, polluted flame,
> Dare not to tempt the chaste Victoria's fame!
> I love, perhaps, more than a sister should;
> And nature prompts, but heaven restrains my blood. (II.i; SS, VIII, 403)

This is a judgment not only on Ovid, 'the soft philosopher of love,' but on Dryden himself, who had helped to popularize Ovid and done nothing to mitigate the attractions of his image of love. *Love Triumphant* thus contains a recantation in which Dryden takes personal responsibility for a translated poem. Oddly enough, he implies that the poem was as much his as Ovid's, or at least that the fact of its being a translation provides no excuse for him to dissociate himself from it.

Nevertheless, Dryden returned to the incest theme in *Fables*. I think that *Fables* represents yet another new direction on the subject; like *Love Triumphant* it differs from 'Canace,' where incest does in fact seem to be treated for its own sake. Alphonso and Victoria, like Sebastian and Almeyda, are brother and sister, and Dryden sees brother-sister incest as a drastic kind of rebellion against authority, unless the couple are so elevated that there is no one to rebel against. Absalom's 'warm excesses, which the Law forbore' included a possessiveness towards his sister Tamar, which led to the murder of Amnon in revenge for Amnon's incest/rape of Tamar. Dryden clearly presents both the sexual excess and the murder as activities that were possible only because David did not trouble himself to exert parental authority.

Sebastian and Almeyda have the arrogance of assuming that no superior being exists to control their impulses. Juno and Jupiter, who appear in *Fables*, are brother and sister and their incest is part of their characters as gods, although Homer, Ovid, and Dryden all satirize them.

Alphonso persistently rebels against the authority of his father, the king, and in particular resents Veramond's efforts to arrange a marriage for Victoria. He initiates a rebellion to save Victoria 'from a father's tyranny' (IV.i; SS, VIII, 442), but Victoria, understandably, refuses to exchange one form of captivity for another. She is intelligent enough to use women's condition to affirm her own moral independence:

> A slave I am; but nature made me so,
> Slave to my father, not my father's foe:
> Since, then, you have declared me free, this hour
> I put myself within a parent's power. (IV.i; SS, VIII, 443)

In the conciliatory mood of this play, however, the power of love, even of physical love, is linked to the power of goodness. Ximena, the queen, explains the trick by which she had replaced her dead child with Alphonso, really her sister's child: Ximena was terrified of Veramond's anger if he found that his own son was dead (III.i; SS, VIII, 425). The sexual insecurity evident in Veramond (much like that of Leontes in *The Winter's Tale*) is a blot upon his character as a ruler, and the patriarch is persuaded to respect the humanity of other people. However, Alphonso's rebellion is futile and immoral. Veramond's eventual acceptance of Ximena's pious fraud is paralleled in the subplot, where Sancho agrees to marry Dalinda, knowing that she has had two bastards by another man. On both levels of the play women are allowed to have authority in matters pertaining to love and sexuality.

The suggestions of incest in *Fables* (K, vol IV) sometimes involve figures like Juno and Jupiter or Chantecleer and Partlet, who do not have to obey human rules. These two pairs are comic characters. The other cases of incest involve the more disturbing relationship between father and daughter, disturbing because each of Dryden's fathers is a patriarch combining political and familial power, whose daughter cannot protect herself or her husband and may even desire the pleasures of intimacy with the most powerful man she knows.[28] In 'Sigismonda and Guiscardo' Tancred, who is consistently presented as a tyrant, prevents his daughter from remarrying and kills the husband she eventually chooses on her own. In 'Ceyx and Alcyone' the central couple are king and queen, but Alcyone's father is Aeolus, god of the winds (and also the father of Canace and Macareus, as it happens). Alcyone warns Ceyx not to journey by sea, aware that Aeolus 'sits precarious on the Throne' (44) because the winds are uncontrollable and Aeolus is as likely to release them as to hold them back. Her fears are justified; Ceyx drowns, with Aeolus's acquiescence. In both poems a father's real or apparent hatred of a son-in-law becomes a shocking symbol for the evils of tyranny.

'Cinyras and Myrrha' is the only poem in *Fables* where father-daughter incest is overt and consummated. Here the daughter loves her father and, though tormented by inner conflict and the awareness of sin, she allows her nurse to arrange a secret meeting. In spite of the fact that Myrrha initiates the action, she is still a more sympathetic character than her father. Cinyras, whose wife is still alive, is willing to sleep with a woman his daughter's age (253); he gets drunk before the act, and perhaps enjoys a quasi-paternal relationship with the young girl (300–3). If Myrrha behaves sinfully, she appeals to urges that her father secretly experiences. On recognizing Myrrha, Cinyras reverts to the character of a tyrant:

> the Revealer, Light,
> Expos'd both Crime, and Criminal to Sight:
> Grief, Rage, Amazement, cou'd no Speech afford,
> But from the Sheath he drew th' avenging Sword;
> The Guilty fled. (310–14)

In other words, incest in *Fables* is a metaphor for the sickness of the tyrant-subject relationship. The fact that a daughter-subject can seek intimacy with her father instead of the reverse does not alter this fact, since he has confined her in a world where she can respond to no other man, a situation most apparent in 'Sigismonda.'

The subplot of *Love Triumphant* contains a little parody of the Amphitryon story, in the second scene of Act III. Dalinda's two suitors, Carlos and Sancho, act independently of each other to disguise themselves as the hunchbacked Don Alonzo, Dalinda's long-time lover and the father of her two children. Alonzo is the equivalent of Amphitryon, now away at war, while Carlos and Sancho are both equivalents of Jupiter. However, the two impostors approach Lopez, Dalinda's father, at the same time and fail to produce a believable story. When a messenger appears to announce Don Alonzo's death in battle, he is believed immediately, things being simpler in this play, and the two counterfeits are forced to reveal themselves. Dryden's self-parody carries the original joke yet further. Jupiter and Mercury lowered themselves by taking on human disguise; Sancho and Carlos are ultimately more acceptable in their own persons (a fool and a penniless wit) than in disguise as a titled hunchback. Disguise is burdensome and the multiplication of impostors defeats the very purpose of disguise; it is also not very convincing, as we see by the fact that Lopez suspects a plot even before the messenger arrives. Dryden thus demystifies a situation that produced existential crises for his characters in the earlier play. Perhaps Dryden repeated the *Amphitryon* story to show that he could take an alternative view of his earlier work, much as he took a new view of 'Canace and Macareus.' Human identity might not be so readily threatened as had appeared in 1690; the happy marriage of Sancho and Dalinda and Lopez's acceptance of his daughter's misbehaviour – Dalinda freely and guiltlessly multiplies *her* self – attest to a saving flexibility in human nature.

Another parallel between *Cleomenes* and *Love Triumphant* is that each contains an episode modelled on Dante's *Inferno.* I have mentioned the scene in *Love Triumphant* that is based on Paolo and Francesca, and even Dryden's title recalls 'the love that moves the sun and the other stars,' although his subtitle, 'nature will prevail,' also suggests a more physical kind of love. Ximena's pious fraud includes both kinds of love, and the marriage of Christian and Jew in the subplot evokes the religious values of charity and patience (v.i; ss, VIII, 461) not to mention a toleration absent in another of Dryden's models for this action, the story of Shylock in *The Merchant of Venice.*[29] In *Cleomenes* the hero and his family are locked up to starve together, recalling Dante's story of Ugolino in Canto xxxiii. Ugolino is one of the most horrible figures in the *Inferno*, for he managed to survive temporarily by eating the dead bodies of his sons, so that Cleomenes becomes his moral superior, a virtuous pagan. Since Dryden never discussed Dante, it is interesting to see that he occasionally used images from Dante's work. He twice alludes to Dante's image of 'the great Devil's Mouth,' once at the end of *The Hind and the Panther*, where King Buzzard becomes a feast for the 'Tyrant' in hell (III.1288), and once in the dedication of the *Aeneis*, where he mentions the fate of Brutus, Cassius, and Judas, who were eaten by the three-faced devil. Myrrha, incidentally, appears near the bottom of Dante's hell (Canto xxx), though not in connection with cannibalism.

Dryden apparently became interested in Dante at a time when he would naturally have sought Catholic models for large-scale literary works. Theologically at least Dante should have been better than the Puritan Milton as a model, but on the whole the experiment with Dante contributed little beyond the two scenes in the late plays, neither of which provides a guiding pattern for the play in which it appears. Only the cannibalism theme – terrifying and insistent at the end of the *Inferno* – is truly important, because it could suggest either damnation or a negative version of the Eucharist in which Christ's body, as Catholics insist, is really, unequivocally, present. A Catholic imagination thus informs Dryden's images of death and damnation. The worst satiric curse that he can think of is, following Dante, to tell an enemy that he will be devoured in hell: one recalls his insistence that Lucian *could not* have been eaten by dogs. Cannibalism is important in *Fables*, and I shall return to it, since there it is combined with positive images of the Eucharist to generate a central theme.

Dryden's relative failure with Dante might be explained by the private nature of an interest which he could not have shared with many of his readers. For inclusion in *Fables* he chose two other medieval authors, Chaucer and Boccaccio, whose appeal is far broader and less dependent on their Catholicism than Dante's. But the Dante experiment is important because it exists and thereby shows that Dryden wanted to write as a Catholic poet. He also wanted, for a time, to throw his Catholicism in his enemies' teeth, perhaps even to threaten them with being eaten alive. This phase extended through the prologues to *Don Sebastian*, *The Prophetess*, and *Amphitryon*, which unambiguously state Dryden's wish to write satire and his frustration at being inhibited, until it became clear that life under William III did not mean the end of all things good. Dryden's late plays enable us to trace the various divisions in his character as an English Catholic, a Jacobite losing confidence in his hero, and an original, inventive writer constantly performing in the modes of translation, adaptation, reconciliation of contradictory models, and even self-revision. In all these 'dependent' literary modes Dryden peers around the edge and announces his presence, and in the last of his plays he seems to have accepted inner multiplicity as a fact of life.

3

Collective Translations

COLLECTIVE POEMS

Fables (1700) is the only one of Dryden's collective poems in which he translated or wrote the whole book. However, his contributions to *Ovid's Epistles* (1680), *Miscellany Poems* (1684), *Sylvae* (1685), and *Examen Poeticum* (1693) give the impression that Dryden linked his translations even when, as in the published collections of *Ovid's Epistles* and *Miscellany Poems*, they would not be placed next to each other. The fact that Dryden's three translations are distributed throughout *Ovid's Epistles* may be explained simply by the editor's desire to avoid placing all the strong contributions together. However, basic principles of contrast and continuity, still current in literary journals today, affected the arrangement of the miscellanies. There is sometimes a guiding theme or at least enough evidence of planning to suggest that Dryden could readily have extended the principle to his own work.[1]

Dryden may have felt that his readers would be interested enough in his work to detach it from the whole and read it as a book within a book, or he may not have cared at first whether his principles of arrangement were understood and just have allowed the process of composition to help him make his selections and discover links between them. The preface to *Fables* shows Dryden eventually relying on personal association to integrate a group of short works, indeed to discover the works he liked. At that late stage Dryden obviously wanted his readers to know how his mind worked. He not only told them about it but urged them to find connections between the poems or at least to make comparisons between them:

For these Reasons of Time, and Resemblance of Genius, in *Chaucer* and *Boccace*, I resolv'd to join them in my present Work; to which I have added some Original

Papers of my own; which whether they are equal or inferiour to my other Poems, an Author is the most improper Judge; and therefore I leave them wholly to the Mercy of the Reader. (K, IV, 1446)

The reader thus recapitulates the author's experience, though with a distinctly greater emphasis on judging. Making comparisons is the first step in discovering connections; if the morals of the poems 'leap foremost into sight,' we know at least that the poems have meanings and that we are expected to react to them. Dryden also provides one instance of an idea repeated in two poems: 'Sigismonda' and 'The Wife of Bath Her Tale' both have passages on true nobility of soul. The preface hardly begins to explicate *Fables*, but it is a guide on how to read them; it certainly makes provision for the reader's response.

But Dryden did not in 1700 suddenly discover the idea of an integrated book; it had been developing for some time. *Ovid's Epistles*, of course, provides its own unity, but *Miscellany Poems* – to speak of the whole book and not just Dryden's contributions – is itself pleasingly integrated through its arrangement according to author; it could have been a model for a composite work in which Dryden provided all the material. Possibly Dryden arranged *Miscellany Poems* himself, but that may not have been the case; a collection of Dryden's poems published a year after his death is also arranged with some care according to the poems' length, genre, and tone.

The preface to *Sylvae* anticipates the idea of arrangement by natural association. In 1685 Dryden chose to translate what he liked and perceived the impulse to translate as almost as natural as bodily feeling, though prose translation bored him. Dryden was no Henry Dickinson:

For this last half Year I have been toubled with the disease (as I may call it) of Translation; the cold Prose fits of it, (which are always the most tedious with me) were spent in the History of the League; the hot, (which succeeded them) in this Volume of Verse Miscellanies. The truth is, I fancied to my self a kind of ease in the change of the Paroxism; never suspecting but that the humour wou'd have wasted it self in two or three Pastorals of *Theocritus*, and as many Odes of *Horace*. But finding, or at least thinking I found, something that was more pleasing in them, than my ordinary productions, I encourag'd my self to renew my old acquaintance with *Lucretius* and *Virgil*; and immediately fix'd upon some parts of them which had most affected me in the reading. These were my natural Impulses for the undertaking. (III, 3)[2]

Sylvae goes beyond *Miscellany Poems*, for Dryden contributed much more poetry to it, almost half the total book. Moreover, his translations are all placed together at the beginning of the volume, so that one immediately reacts to Dryden; the translator is not submerged by an emphasis on the original poet. One can without difficulty read Dryden's part of *Sylvae* as a sequence, whereas the links in *Ovid's Epistles* and *Miscellany Poems* may have been evident to the author alone.

The very concept of such sequences hardly exists in our critical terminology, although contemporary poets often publish integrated books or books where a major section is designed as a sequence. Modern critics of the Greek and Latin poets whom Dryden translated often assume that some kind of structure and conscious arrangement are present, but they do not always assume the presence of a meaningful structure. Analyses of mathematical symmetry are not what I mean by meaningful structure, although one poem in *Sylvae*, 'The Speech of Venus and Vulcan,' actually has the word 'triumph' in the twenty-seventh of its fifty-four lines – at the central point – and thus illustrates one kind of mathematical symmetry, probably for ironic purposes.[3] I am convinced that Dryden often sought symmetry of the centre, since his endings are often relatively weak or unclearly marked. But there are more obvious kinds of balance, like contrasts between consecutive poems, or of structure, like verbal or thematic connections between poems tying the whole together. These devices exist in some of the classical works that Dryden presumably used as his models and certainly knew well.

N.E. Collinge uses the term 'structure of structures' to describe a book of Horace's odes.[4] Collinge wants to modify the new critics' tendency to isolate a short poem from its context. Though the single poem may indeed be densely structured, it acquires much more poetic resonance in the links and cross-references if it is related to the rest of the book: 'the Odes are a corpus wherein the interrelation of units may possibly be as important as their own unity, and to understand one poem (however complete) at a time may be to understand less than the poet has achieved.'[5] Enough has been written about Virgil's *Eclogues*, Ovid's *Heroides*, and Theocritus's *Idylls* to show that these poets planned their collections with an eye towards gaining effects of balance, alternating moods, and recurrence in theme. Frequently the total effect simply transcends aesthetic complication: 'Theocritus apparently felt that he could say what he wanted to say only by grouping together a number of poems. He has more to express about man and the world than he could encompass in one brief poem.'[6] A specific kind of meaning emerges in a 'structure of structures,' since the individual poem may read one way when considered alone but have entirely different implications when it is compared to others in the collection. One can therefore discuss 'structure' either on a small scale, concerning oneself with one poem only or with a part of a poem, or on a larger scale, discussing patterns that take the whole collection into account. I think of Dryden's collections as 'sequences' because they have a cumulative effect if read from beginning to end and because the sense of development contributes to their meaning. Each poem functions almost as a stage in an argument or in a thought process.

The phrase 'collective poem' sometimes implies a more static or spatial type of arrangement,[7] like figures on a vase or murals composed of several parts, the pictorial analogies to which classicists are often drawn. In a spatial arrangement the centre is the main focal point (and so Virgil's fifth eclogue might be more important than his tenth) and symmetries radiate outwards in both directions. Dryden sometimes does focus on the centre, as in *Miscellany Poems*, where the song 'The Tears of Amynta, for the Death of Damon' is the third of his five selections. His endings are without doubt less resolved than one would expect if one's preconceptions derived from epic unity, but his collections have a progressive movement as well. He may even have been pointing to the irony implied by the use of spatial form in showing that art cannot in fact impose a static order on the flux of history.

Spatial form, emphasizing the part over the whole, can lead to important shifts of emphasis in traditional material, like the rejection of extended narrative for the sake of close analysis of carefully selected moments, which would have been slighted in an epic. For instance, Ovid's *Heroides* focuses on the emotions of rejected women, not the goals of the heroes who abandoned them. And Brooks Otis says of Catullus's *Peleus and Thetis*: 'There is only the illusion, not the reality of narrative; the centre of the Ariadne episode is occupied by a long declamatory lament, a lament which reiterates a single sensation and idea and actually stops the action. We find the same asymmetry in the *Attis*: an (expanded) moment of religious frenzy followed by a similar moment of repentance.'[8] Short pieces like this are pseudo-narratives in which the reader, not the poet, supplies much of the knowledge of the story. Such was the material for the miscellanies of the 1680s. Despite Dryden's proclaimed admiration for epic in the dedication of the *Aeneis*,[9] he imitated a form developed by the Hellenistic poets – one that could parody epic material, underline what epic leaves out, show that the epic vision of life is not the most inclusive, and reduce epic to the level of a song by giving an epic fragment and a song equivalent structural significance. Hellenistic collective works are marked by a breakdown of genre or by the blending of several genres in the whole,[10] just as Dryden's collective works are.[11] The epic material in his collections appears in fragmentary form and in a context that discourages us from taking it as the final version of experience.

Greek and Latin poetry generates a disposition to see the interconnectedness of literary works, whether by the same or by different writers, because of the constant reuse of the same material from myth and traditional story. Whether Theseus or Helen appear as central characters or as minor characters, whether they are simply alluded to or are used in a metaphor, they are never far from our consciousness and we expect them to appear eventually, in some new context. Certain images from nature and epic similes work in the same way. The classical poets' awareness of each other is a major fact in our reading of their works, though one need scarcely regard those works as only poems about other poems. Virgil's *Aeneid* is in part a response to Lucretius (as well as to Homer). Ovid's *Metamorphoses* reworks Virgil; moreover, it subordinates both the *Aeneid* and the *Iliad* within a frame so broad that they become interludes in a far more inclusive view of experience. This sort of literature leads one to expect multiple perspectives. No version of life is conclusive, epic least of all. Indeed, the spurious finality of epic seems to demand a revision.

Perhaps one function of the collective work is to search for the ultimate frame, the perspective that can include everything, or at least that can allow for new perspectives. Whether sequential or not, collective poems imply an exploratory and sceptical view of life in which the poet creates his own order out of the materials available to him. This probably explains the appeal of collective poems for Dryden. While the epic poet tries to understand the cosmic order in a unified way, the sequence poet is aware of a variety of plausible options and may not even want to produce a final arrangement. In the preface to *Sylvae* Dryden said that Lucretian dogmatism was untenable and slightly absurd,[12] and his own selections reverberate upon each other in ways that undercut their own finality. His sequences, particularly *Sylvae* and *Fables*, demonstrate the mutual relativity of a number of different beliefs and views about human life. The poems are not meaningless because their inner ordering and their variations on traditional material – not to speak of the changes Dryden made in translation – permit one, indeed encourage one, to interpret them; but the comparative subtlety of the links and the fragility of Dryden's frames, which consist of short poems, brief prefaces, and inconclusive endings, bear out the exploratory nature of his form.

OVID'S EPISTLES

Dryden's three contributions to *Ovid's Epistles* are 'Canace to Macareus,' written by a woman whose incest with her brother has just been discovered;

'Helen to Paris,' written to urge Paris to elope; and 'Dido to Aeneas,' written after Aeneas has left Dido to pursue his journey to Italy.[13] There is little sequential effect in the 1680 volume, which seems generally to aim at achieving a communal style in sentimental heroic couplets. All the translators but Dryden evoke the hypnotic mood that was considered appropriate to Ovid's 'feminine' world, a style recalling the pathetic tragedies of the 1670s. The other contributors include the dramatists Nathaniel Lee and Thomas Otway and also Aphra Behn, who made no claims to expertise in Latin and paraphrased 'Oenone to Paris,' but whose participation was justified to the world by her knowledge of the female mind.

The female mind, as Ovid and his male admirers understood it (Behn prudently went along), was marked by extreme, really claustrophobic subtlety and inwardness and by a striking repetitiveness of experience, borne out by the fact that almost all the epistles are variations on one idea: a woman is separated from her lover or husband and because of this separation is also shut off from external reality. *He* can travel and make history; *she* can worry, or commit suicide, or perhaps write a letter in an effort to bridge the inner and outer worlds.[14] The themes are the same, whether the poem has a mythic setting or is set in the world of historical time, or whether the woman's traditional character is fundamentally good or evil. Probably Helen was justified in wanting adventure; certainly Dido was justified in resenting Aeneas, at least from the Ovidian perspective. It is interesting that Behn's Oenone, a simple country girl, is much less ambiguous than the three heroines of Dryden's poems; it was risky enough to appear in print in the company of men without assuming a persona like Helen as well. In the last poem in the collection, 'Sappho to Phaon,' the character of woman merges into the character of the poet, who may be of either sex. Through this device the restricted female experience is generalized to become an aspect of human experience, and the male poet's interest in women is accounted for.

The historical perspective is hardly the most striking theme of the 1680 collection, but it is apparent in Dryden's three poems once we extract them from the rest. They provide a condensed version of human history, which seems hardly to develop at all, though the poems seem ever more modern. 'Canace to Macareus' is prehistoric or mythic in setting; 'Helen to Paris' takes place before the Trojan war (which Helen's action helped to cause); and 'Dido to Aeneas' takes place after the Trojan war and looks ahead to the founding of Rome. The worlds of the three poems, as Dryden renders them, progress in time, but the similarities between them counterbalance the sense of historical progression to suggest the repetitiveness of the characters' experience. Dryden concerns himself with this ironic fact. As so often in his translations he has only to exaggerate a device in the original poems or give a slightly different cast to their vocabulary to convince us that he is writing about his own world.

Canace is the most innocent and the most isolated of the three heroines, an almost abstract example of female passivity, who scarcely understands even her own physical experiences: 'Not knowing 'twas my Labour, I complain / Of sudden shootings, and of grinding pain' (53–4). When her father, Aeolus, discovers her child, born of a relationship with her brother, Macareus, he sends Canace a sword with a command to kill herself. This family romance, in which a mortal woman has 'Kindred Gods' (17), involves a mythic condensation of relationships – Aeolus is at once a father, king, god, and natural force, a tyrant on all possible levels. Dryden emphasizes his patriarchal role in several passages, such as this:

Jove justly plac'd him on a stormy Throne,
His Peoples temper is so like his own.
The *North* and *South*, and each contending blast
Are underneath his wide Dominion cast:
Those he can rule; but his tempestuous mind
Is, like his airy Kingdom, unconfin'd. ('Canace to Macareus,' 11–16)

Aeolus's perverse use of his power against his own daughter can thus be read as an indictment of patriarchy. Canace, who seems to have spent her entire life at the back of a cave, could hardly have found anyone but her brother to love: her unborn child, 'secure in his dark Cell' (49), is doubly imprisoned. Aeolus's attack on her and the child is clearly based on instinctual jealousy, not on law. In Aeolus's kingdom members of the family are prisoners.

Through most of the poem Canace presents herself as inarticulate; she is unable or afraid to use language, and stifles even her groans for fear of being discovered. Indeed, her crime is discovered because her baby cries just as the nurse is carrying him outside. The use of one's voice is the prerogative of power; Aeolus is no more verbal than his daughter or his grandchild, but he does make noise:

Swift as a Whirl-wind to the Nurse he flyes;
And deafs his stormy Subjects with his cries.
With one fierce puff, he blows the leaves away:
Expos'd, the self-discover'd Infant lay.
The noise reach'd me, and my presaging mind
Too soon its own approaching woes divin'd. (85–90)

The 'cruel Father' becomes a 'loud Father' (6, 93). Everyone here belongs to a prearticulate society. Even the letter form, as Canace uses it, reflects this, because it is written in secrecy and may never be read (if the page is covered with the writer's blood), and especially because it makes no noise. No one in this poem can talk openly; even the messenger who brings the sword trembles as he speaks.

This theme is implicit in Ovid's poem, but he and Dryden treat it differently. Ovid's genius is his power as a ventriloquist; he can imitate the voice of every imaginable speaker and, even better, give a sense of a character's voice in the process of transition, as the speaker's very being changes. In Ovid's poetry voice constitutes personal identity and is close to the essence of life. Thus, as Canace moves from the tearful baby-talk of her opening lines to a declamatory style worthy of her father, one asks if she is acquiring selfhood:

> Siqua tamen caecis errabunt scripta lituris,
> oblitus a dominae caede libellus erit. (XI.1–2)

> his mea muneribus, genitor, conubia donas?
> hac tua dote, pater, filia dives erit?
> tolle procul, decepte, faces, Hymenaee, maritas
> et fuge turbato tecta nefanda pede!
> ferte faces in me quas fertis, Erinyes atrae,
> et meus ex isto luceat igne rogus! (XI.99–104)

LOEB TRANSLATION If aught of what I write is yet blotted deep and escapes your eye, 'twill be because the little roll has been stained by its mistress' blood ...

Is it presents like this, O my sire, you give me on my marriage? With this dowry from you, O father, shall your daughter be made rich? Take away afar, deluded Hymenaeus, thy wedding-torches, and fly with frightened foot from these nefarious halls! Bring for me the torches ye bear, Erinyes dark, and let my funeral pyre blaze bright from the fires ye give![15]

Perhaps Canace's display of a new personal identity is ironic, for she has not so much found her own voice as learned to mimic Aeolus's and her indictment is presented in the clichés of outraged womanhood. Though she becomes conscious of her father's injustice, she fails to gain, and has no imaginable way to gain, psychic independence from him.

Dryden loses much of this effect. He either could not or did not want to reproduce Ovid's multiple voices; instead he adopts a personal voice that is capable of an immense range of variation. As a result his Canace does not seem to transcend herself. Nevertheless, Dryden insists that words have power, as Macareus's words return Canace to life: 'Such pow'r have words, when spoke by those we love' (70); and he virtually equates speech with freedom: 'Out went the King; my voice its freedom found' (107). Dryden's treatment of the theme of speech has chilling political implications when we recall how early it occurs in his career. Canace cannot talk while her father is present. The presence of a father/king inhibits freedom, free speech, and the growth of personal identity, since all are bound up together. Dryden's poem exhibits a slight air of political resentment, but because it is expressed in a translation whose main character is female, one hesitates before attributing this attitude to Dryden himself.

Helen shows a sceptical detachment from Canace's inarticulate mythic world. Though she makes much of her divine parentage – Jupiter was her father, who raped Leda, her mother – she tends to regard the whole story as a pleasing legend:

Fair *Leda*'s Story seems at first to be
A fit example ready found for me,
But she was Cousen'd by a borrow'd shape,
And under harmless Feathers felt a Rape. ('Helen to Paris,' 45–8)

Leda appears to have been fooled by a gentleman in masquerade. Paris also has a mythic background; of the three goddesses' competition for his favour, which Venus won by promising Helen to him, Helen remarks that 'Miracles are not believ'd with ease' (130). This is enough to make the poem seem contemporary. Helen thus stands outside the legends of her own past and of Paris's, and the present moment described by the poem becomes purely human, the careful building up to a sexual encounter. Helen's language domesticates both legend and the world of epic:

But if I e're offend great *Juno*'s Laws,
Your self shall be the Dear, the only Cause. (67–8)

You bid me use th' occasion while I can,
Put in our hands by the good easie man. (172–3)

A bland perspective on Canace's world is suggested by the 'Propitious winds' (160) that have carried Menelaus away. Helen represents a leap into modernity without the moral responsibility that might make life in an age of disbelief possible.

Helen, however, represents the high point of control among the three women, for we know that her letter will reach its object and what its effect will be. Helen perceives letters as active sexual agents:

When loose Epistles violate Chast Eyes,
She half Consents, who silently denies. (1–2)

Though she accuses Paris, it is Helen herself who uses a letter seductively, attacking Paris, describing the kisses she has given to other men, and finally admitting that a pleasing rape would not come amiss (182–3). Helen is disingenuous when she calls her letter 'th' Essay of my unpractis'd pen' (140), a remark that could not fool anyone but Paris, but even here inexperience in writing implies inexperience in sexual relationships. Helen's manipulation of her art suggests that she is in control of events, yet the end of the poem foreshadows a new period of uncertainty. Helen admits to a superstitious belief in omens forecasting the fall of Troy – 'Your teeming Mother dreamt a flaming Brand / Sprung from her Womb consum'd the *Trojan* Land' (230–1) – and she recognizes that 'gentle Winds' may become 'loud Tempests' (228–9). Ironic references to time, which Dryden has added, increase the sense of pressure (250–5), so that at last Helen may be the victim of fate that she says she is, although she herself uses the term offhandedly, as a cliché.

Ovid's poem is filled with legalistic and religious terminology, as if Helen were presenting a case for herself in an ecclesiastical court – a novel sidelight on one's image of the fatal beauty. Dryden does not convey precisely that aspect of the poem; Helen is instead the central panel in a triptych that taken as a whole becomes an ironic cycle beginning and ending in unconsciousness. The last of the three poems is the most conspicuously Drydenian, containing turns of phrase recalling his original poems. Once we are enabled to move outward in this way, from Ovid to Restoration England, translation does become a form of personal expression.

'Dido to Aeneas' is clearly linked to the two previous poems. Dido recalls Leda when she compares her letter to the 'Elegie' of a 'mournful *Swan*' (1–2) and her comparison of the pen to the sword recalls 'Canace': like Canace, Dido will kill herself as soon as she has finished writing:

One hand the Sword, and one the Pen employs,
And in my lap the ready paper lyes. ('Canace to Macareus,' 3–4)

Death holds my pen, and dictates what I say,
While cross my lap thy *Trojan* Sword I lay. ('Dido to Aeneas,' 197–8)

Ultimately these links are Ovid's. But if their presence in Dryden's version fails to show his originality, they do show his understanding of the workings of an integrated volume and his tendency to go his own way in a collection by various translators, most of whom understood their author differently.

Dryden's triptych appears ironic because Dido is at once another rejected Canace and a sophisticate whose verbal powers outdo even Helen's. She compulsively plays on words. Though Dryden said that Ovid 'often writ too pointedly for his Subject, and made his persons speak more Eloquently than the violence of their Passion would admit: so that he is frequently witty out of season' (I, 112), Dryden imitates his author, as in playing on words like 'lost,' 'loose,' 'life,' and 'love' in the opening lines. Dido's unseasonable wit in fact brings out the conflict between her role as a modern woman and her equally real primitive isolation. Dryden's Dido is more sarcastic, less relentlessly hypnotic in cadence, than Ovid's. In the original Dido seems incapable of expressing anger, even when she attacks Aeneas directly (recall Canace's attack):

Fallor, et ista mihi falso iactatur imago;
matris ab ingenio dissidet ille suae.
te lapis et montes innataque rupibus altis
robora, te saevae progenuere ferae,
aut mare, quale vides agitari nunc quoque ventis,
quo tamen adversis fluctibus ire paras. (VII.35–40)

LOEB TRANSLATION Ah, vain delusion! the fancy that flits before my mind is not the truth; far different his heart from his mother's. Of rocks and mountains were you begotten, and of the oak sprung from the lofty cliff, of savage wild beasts, or of the sea – such a sea as even now you look upon, tossed by the winds, on which you are none the less making ready to sail, despite the threatening floods.

Dryden translates this passage of invective, reproducing the tone of Nourmahal in *Aureng-Zebe*:

I rave: nor canst thou *Venus'* offspring be,
Love's Mother cou'd not bear a Son like Thee.
From harden'd Oak, or from a Rocks cold womb,

At least thou art from some fierce *Tygress* come,
Or, on rough Seas, from their foundation torn,
Got by the winds, and in a Tempest born. ('Dido to Aeneas,' 35–40)

Much of the interest of this passage lies in the overlay of personalities which we may distinguish from each other – Dryden's, Ovid's, Dido's, and possibly Virgil's as well, for Ovid is imitating Virgil here. Dryden's method is almost the opposite of Ovid's submergence of himself in the speaker's personality.

The lines just quoted show the return of the Aeolus myth in 'Dido to Aeneas.' Dido refers to the 'loud winds,' an 'avenging storm,' and 'Northern Blasts' (52, 67, 185), and she mentions the cave where she and Aeneas found 'common shelter' (96), a link to the cave of Aeolus. Nature is malevolent enough to make her superstitious: her world-view retreats to the past, and when she says that Venus could not be Aeneas's mother, it is not because divine parentage is incredible but because Aeneas is unable to love. 'Dido to Aeneas' is also the only one of the three poems in which the two sides of the male character – lover and punitive authority figure – are united in one person, making Dido's world seem even more enclosed than Canace's, more absolutely oppressive.

Yet, in another sense, her world is more open, for Dryden's Dido has a political awareness that the other two heroines lack. Her poem is not confined by her personal fantasies. She is a queen, aware of being surrounded by enemies and aware of Aeneas's role in the Trojan war; she thus exists within a historical and social environment absent in the mythic world of the first two poems. Dryden must have perceived Dido as a political commentator, for he recasts two of her couplets in *Absalom and Achitophel.* Dido asks,

Know'st thou not yet what dangers Ships sustain,
So often wrack'd, how darst thou tempt the Main? (55–56)

anticipating an image in the character of Achitophel, who

sought the Storms; but for a Calm unfit,
Would Steer too nigh the Sands, to boast his Wit. (161–2)

The second couplet from 'Dido to Aeneas,'

Æneas is my thoughts perpetual Theme:
Their daily longing, and their nightly dream, (27–8)

reappeared in Achitophel's first speech to Absalom:

The Peoples Prayer, the glad Deviners Theam,
The Young-mens Vision, and the Old mens Dream! (238–9)

If Dryden could use Aeneas's character as a basis for Achitophel's, he must have shared Dido's attitude towards the hero who seemed compelled to unnecessary adventure. Dido's world blends into that of English politics. She wants Aeneas's 'weary Men' to enjoy their 'ease' in Carthage (189) and attacks the very foundation of Aeneas's journey:

Suppose you Landed where your wish design'd,
Think what Reception Forreiners would find.
What People is so void of common sence,
To Vote Succession from a Native Prince? (15–18)

This is obviously conceived against the background of the exclusion crisis, but that is not important merely for underlining Dryden's allusive compulsions. His concrete topical references appear in the third poem, not scattered at random among the three. The three poems thus give a sense of false progress, in which Dido, but not Canace or Helen, seems to be a contemporary. This mode of imitation has a structural purpose, creating an image of history in which human consciousness grows in awareness without freeing the individual from the prison of his or her emotions. History is at once progressive and cyclical. The 'feminine' attack on history could be universalized.

MISCELLANY POEMS

Miscellany Poems is unique among the later Tonson miscellanies in that the editor took care to achieve a pleasing arrangement by contrasting various kinds of short poems. Whether elegy, eclogue, or prologue, all seem to belong together or are contrasted in a meaningful way, and the overall effect has a point: the world of satiric controversy is contrasted with, perhaps even supplanted by, the world of pastoral or scholarly retreat, which is ultimately symbolized by translation itself, and here implies an escape to Greek or Latin poetry. The volume begins by reprinting three Dryden satires, *Absalom and Achitophel*, *The Medall*, and *MacFlecknoe*, and includes five new poems by Dryden, which are again scattered throughout the volume: 'Ovid's Elegies, Book II. Elegy the Nineteenth,' 'Amaryllis, or the Third Idyllium of Theocritus, Paraphras'd,' 'The Tears of Amynta, for the Death of Damon. Song,' 'Virgil's 'Fourth Eclogue. Pollio,' and his 'Ninth Eclogue.'[16] The song is original and the four translations are grouped with other translations from the same authors. However, despite the impulse towards retreat which is embodied in the volume as a whole, Dryden does not want to retreat entirely. As is the case with *Ovid's Epistles*, his themes transcend and may even deviate from their context.

In this collection Dryden is the only modern poet to get a section to himself, a clear indication that his contemporaries were willing or even anxious to set him beside the classical writers, including the Virgil of the *Eclogues*. Whether he is considered as a translator or as an original poet, Dryden transcended his time. When in *Fables* he equates himself with Ovid, Boccaccio, and Chaucer, it is not for the first time; ultimately it is not his own arrogance that supplied him with the idea. Dryden's satires lead into the love poetry in a surprisingly natural way, since *Absalom and Achitophel* ends with David's silencing the rebels in an image suggesting sexual conquest – 'And willing Nations knew their Lawfull Lord' (1031) – while *The Medall* even more strongly advises peace, using a similar image of passive sexuality:

> Thus inborn Broyles the Factions wou'd ingage,
> Or Wars of Exil'd Heirs, or Foreign Rage,
> Till halting Vengeance overtook our Age:
> And our wild Labours, wearied into Rest,
> Reclin'd us on a rightfull Monarch's Breast. (318–22)

The retreat to love in Ovid's elegies thus comes very naturally[17] and makes the conclusions of the satires seem more like transitional images. Satire and elegy are presented as alternative poetic outlets in a faction-ridden society; elegy, for all its apparent limitations, appears as a private response to life and therefore is preferable to sustaining a controversial mood.

Five elegies are included from Ovid's first book, nine from the second (one is translated twice), and five from the third (one of these also appears in two versions). Dryden's poem 'Elegy the Nineteenth' is the last of the second group, so that it is relatively well placed for climactic effect. Dryden's fellow translators seem cheerfully unaware that the world of elegy has any limitations at all. Some of their poems are pleasant experiments in a colloquial style, or experiments in englishing a classical mode, like the following by Thomas Rymer, from 'Book 3, Elegy the Sixth,' in which the speaker attacks a river which bars him from his mistress:

> Not my Love-tales can make thee stay thy course,
> Thou – Zounds, thow art a – River for a horse.

Thou hadst no Fountain, but from Bears wer't pist,
From Snows and Thaws, or *Scotch* unsavoury mist.
Thou crawlst along, in Winter foul and poor,
In Summer puddl'd like a Common-shore.
In all thy days when did'st a courtesie?
Dry Traveller ne'er lay'd a lip to thee.[18]

In spite of their colloquialism and sexual frankness the elegists are not so much nasty as unreflective and enthusiastic, as in this passage by Thomas Creech which Pope imitated in *The Rape of the Lock*:

Triumphant Laurels round my Temples twine,
I'm *Victor* now, my dear *Corinna*'s mine.
As she was hard to get, a carefull spy,
A Door well barr'd, and jealous Husband's Eye
Long time preserv'd her troublesome Chastity.
Now I deserve a Crown, I briskly woo'd,
And won my Prey without a drop of Bloud:
'Twas not a petty Town with Gates and Bars,
(Those little Trophies of our meaner Wars;)
No 'twas a Whore, a lovely Whore I took,
I won her by a Song, and by a Look.[19]

These poets seem to have taken Dryden's advice to ignore public issues, but, as we shall see later, Dryden did not follow that direction himself and he certainly did not share the flippancy of his collaborators.

Elegies are followed by the Eurydice section of Virgil's fourth Georgic (the fragment becoming a poem about lost love), and a few random pieces, including two in praise of *Religio Laici*, which itself is not reprinted. Oddly enough, Dryden's religious poem would have been too controversial for *Miscellany Poems*, since it raises problems for the thoughtful individual instead of seeking to dismiss them. There are ten poems, mostly odes, translated from Horace, a few miscellaneous pieces, and then a Theocritus section, of which Dryden's poem is the first, again well placed for emphasis. The translators continue to avoid politics. Even Creech's translation of the politically charged story of Lucrece from Ovid's *Fasti* emphasizes only the heroine's emotions, in striking contrast to the contemporary play by Nathaniel Lee.

The various ungrouped poems sometimes work as transitions or sum up the implications of a group by a single poet, like the following lines from Petronius Arbiter. This is what passes for a reflective poem, a comment on the limits of sexual pleasure:

'Tis but a Short, but a filthy Pleasure,
And we soon nauseate the enjoy'd treasure;
Let not us then as lustfull Beasts do,
Slovenly, abruptly, blindly fall to:
Lest we put out Love's gentle fire,
And he droop, and languish in impotent desire:
But thus we'll lye, and thus we'll kiss,
Thus, thus, improve the lasting bliss![20]

Another transitional poem is a Christian heroical epistle, spoken by the wife of St Alexias, whose husband has left her because of dedication to his religious ideal. The saint's wife plans to follow him, instead of trying to draw him back, like Ovid's heroines. The epistle is followed, with some ironic effect, by Dryden's 'Amaryllis,' spoken by a shepherd who contemplates suicide because his lover has rejected him. Richard Duke's poem at the end of the section, a pastoral on the death of the Duchess of Southampton, resembles Dryden's 'Tears of Amynta.' It may be that Dryden composed his song with another part of the collection in mind, since the song does help to integrate the parts.

The Theocritus section is followed by a large group of prologues and epilogues, all but one by Dryden, who thus dominates the volume even more than a list of his new contributions would imply. One may conclude as well that in the 1680s the prologue or epilogue was considered roughly equivalent to the elegy or idyll. The prologues and epilogues seem to be a thematic advance, since they introduce the theme of scholarly retreat instead of sexual escape. One of the Oxford poems, the prologue to *The Silent Woman* of 1673, anticipates a revival of Greek learning which the Theocritus translations included in this very collection seem actually to be.[21] Another prologue refers to the 'Discord, and Plots which have undone our Age,' and an epilogue dating back to 1674 includes the famous lines about Oxford:

Oft has our Poet wisht, this happy Seat
Might prove his fading Muses last retreat.[22]

Thus, at least in these earlier poems, Dryden is presented as sharing his collaborators' desire for quiet, but he imagines a superior means of obtaining it – learning, not the loss of self in sexual indulgence. His prologues and epilogues, written over a period of more than a decade, now seem prophetic, as they are collected in a volume that apparently fulfils their prediction, so that the miscellany in its modest way is organized around a typological sense of history.

Some of the prologues and epilogues concern the opening of a new theatre or the rebuilding of an old one, in either case treating the theatre as a kind of second temple. Dryden was to express this idea again in his imagery of Doric and Corinthian columns in his poem to William Congreve, 'On His Comedy, call'd *The Double Dealer*,' but one finds that the conceit was fairly common. Richard Duke's prologue uses the same idea, in an address to the queen, asking her to help construct a new building at Cambridge University:

> Soon now, since Blest by your Auspicious Eyes,
> To full Perfection shall our Fabrick rise.
> Less powerful Charms than Yours of old could call,
> The willing Stones into the *Theban* Wall,
> And Ours which Now its rise to You shall owe,
> More fam'd than that by Your great Name shall grow.[23]

Obviously the prologues and epilogues were selected to emphasize a serious purpose in literature, showing absolutely nothing of the 'playwright as prostitute' theme or other frivolous motifs that one would expect to find in a randomly selected group of such poems.

The miscellany ends with Virgil's *Eclogues*, including two versions each of the second, fourth, and tenth, as if the prime object were to demonstrate the plenitude of capable translators in Restoration England and not just to produce a complete set of *Eclogues*. These poems are, among other things, concerned with the poet's social role. *Miscellany Poems* in general urges that learning be substituted both for factionalism and for sexual indulgence, and the whole book makes a greater impact than its individual parts. The editor/arranger, whoever he was, can take credit for this; if someone other than Dryden was responsible, he has as much sensitivity as Dryden to the possible impact of an integrated book of short poems. It is not clear that the various translators were fully aware of the theme to which they perforce contributed, though some were scholars themselves, and translation, even of poems about sex, may have seemed a nobler activity than engaging in political controversy.

Dryden's five poems, however, are a coherent group in themselves. They demonstrate less certainty about the retreat from politics, and treat sexual escapism with a scarcely disguised contempt, preparing us for the more serious treatment of Epicureanism that was to come in *Sylvae* the next year. Dryden already is drawing back from the easier Epicureanism of his fellow translators, in part because of his sense of himself as an older man. The first poem, 'Book II. Elegy the Nineteenth,' exposes the 'Fantastick humour' (9) of a young man who prefers the obstacles to enjoyment more than enjoyment itself. The speaker addresses part of the poem to his mistress – 'Thou whom I now adore be edify'd, / Take care that I may often be deny'd' (19–20) – but then turns to her 'dull Husband' (37), whose failure to guard his wife is already causing the lover to lose interest. The speaker's logic is extraordinarily devious. If the husband takes his cue from the lover and leaves his wife unguarded, hoping thus to get rid of him, he will in effect be aiding the lover to see his wife. Ovid's speaker is neither simple enough to be unaware of this nor clever enough to manipulate the confusions that he has made for himself. He is essentially a perversely complicated man who enjoys the unnecessary tangle and who would rather blame his mistress and her husband than himself for the failure of his love affair.

Creech or Rymer would have made this laughable, for Dryden's speaker is not in the original poem any different from their speakers. However, Dryden turns Ovid's immature youth into an older, seedier rake, who is altogether jaded about his feelings and therefore repellent. Ovid's diction is somewhere between the two styles of translation, unpleasantly narcissistic without being completely obscene, as in the food imagery, which one may compare to Dryden's version:

pinguis amor nimiumque patens in taedia nobis
vertitur et, stomacho dulcis ut esca, nocet. (*Amores*, II.xix.25–6)

Gross easie Love does like gross diet, pall,
In squeasie Stomachs Honey turns to Gall. (25–6)

One can only admire Dryden's inventiveness in diction, but that very tone makes his speaker at once pathetic and contemptible:

I'll be no Drudge to any Wittall living
...
Damn him who loves to lead so dull a life.
Now I can neither sigh, nor whine, nor pray,
All those occasions thou hast ta'ne away.
Why art thou so incorrigibly Civil?
Doe somewhat I may wish thee at the Devil.
For shame be no Accomplice in my Treason,
A Pimping Husband is too much in reason. (48, 54–60)

What has Dryden accomplished by creating a new kind of Ovidian rake? I doubt that he is exposing Ovid's shallowness by making his character worse;

rather he reveals an aspect of sexual relationships that was latent in Ovid's poem and that his own contemporaries failed to see or were unable to suggest in their poetry. As with Virgil's *Georgics*, Dryden recast a 'youthful' poem from the viewpoint of a middle-aged man, in this way revealing the limits of the young man's perspective on life. Sexual energy may be diminished, but poetic energy and insight continue to grow and may be advertised as proof of sustained vigour.

Dryden's style recalls Rochester's cynicism, and on a more general level the world of city comedy and even the Nicky-Nacky scenes in *Venice Preserved*. Though Dryden's speaker in 'Elegy the Nineteenth' is imprisoned by his own feelings, his moral emptiness is not limited to himself but is part of the confusions of his society. For example, he is determined to commit 'Treason,' if only in a love affair. He addresses his mistress in language recalling Anchises' advice to Aeneas, not to mention Fleckno's advice to Shadwell, in which Dryden had imitated the Anchises passage:

> Forget the promis'd hour, or feign some fright,
> Make me lye rough on Bulks each other Night.
> These are the Arts that best secure thy reign ... (21–3)

These traces of political awareness remind us of what *Miscellany Poems* has elsewhere left out. Its self-imposed limits do not account for the frustration of Dryden's energetic rake-hero who has not really changed by giving up politics for love.

The speaker of 'Amaryllis' is nicer, but he also suffers from an obsession with 'the force of Love' (32). His knowledge that his desires are unreal adds to his sense of imprisonment:

> I would not ask to live another Day,
> Might I but sweetly Kiss my Soul away!
> Ah, why am I from empty Joys debar'd,
> For Kisses are but empty, when Compar'd! (45–8)

The speaker is even more disturbed at knowing that no one hears him (53); his raving becomes a 'raging fit' (49) and his antagonism towards his mistress – which he cannot act out – turns into an impulse to suicide. Theocritus's shepherd thus displays a hostility that is related to that of Ovid's rake, though it takes a subtler form, since it is directed against himself.

Dryden's style prevents too much sympathetic involvement with the shepherd. For example, he treats the shepherd's religion, which is really superstition, sardonically:

I try'd th' infallible Prophetique way,
A Poppy leaf upon my palm to lay;
I struck, and yet no lucky crack did follow,
Yet I struck hard, and yet the leaf lay hollow. (63–6)

I wept for Woe, the testy Beldame swore,
And foaming with her God, foretold my Fate;
That I was doom'd to Love, and you to Hate. (77–9)

The shepherd cannot turn to religion either for consolation or for an alternative world-view that might provide a way out of his despair. His notion of God is indefinite – 'Some God transform me by his Heavenly power' (28) – and he calls upon religion only to support his fantasies of love. The shepherd's lack of certainty in religion makes his self-enclosure complete and ultimately supports his impulse to suicide. However, nothing in the poem implies that Dryden was complacent about the shepherd's limitations or that he disparaged him as a simple pagan in contrast to the Christian sophisticate. He seems rather to have been asking: what are the consequences of religious uncertainty and of turning inward? Religious uncertainty was a fact of life for Dryden as well, since he had no evidence or reliable authority for his belief and it is evident that Christianity does not solve all the problems of faith. The relationship between pagan and Christian is not a simple contrast but an apparent contrast in sophistication concealing an underlying similarity, which consists of the persistence of certain emotional needs. Dryden's treatment of religion in 'Amaryllis' is consistent with his more extended treatment of the same uncertainties in *Sylvae*.

'Amaryllis' ends with the conventional *double entendre* on the meaning of death – 'For Love has made me Carrion e'er I dye' (127) – but 'The Tears of Amynta' revolves almost entirely around it. Since Amynta's lover has really died, her unhappiness and self-involvement seem more defensible than those of the two male speakers, yet the song sustains the theme of the separation of lovers and their resulting disconnection from objective reality. The poem creates no sense of pastoral landscape or social environment (although some of Dryden's songs, like Sylvia's in *Sylvae*, do), and it leaves Amynta entirely in the world of ambiguous feeling:

Never shall we both ly dying
Nature failing, Love supplying
All the Joyes he drain'd before. (22–4)

Though 'Nature' here seems to be a sexual euphemism, Amynta actually perceives Damon as a nature spirit or life force, 'the Pride of Nature' (13):

> Hope is banish'd
> Joys are vanish'd;
> *Damon*, my belov'd is gone! (7–9)

Amynta's elevation of Damon into an absolute suggests a decline in religious depth from 'Amaryllis,' while both poems lack the social texture that characterizes 'Elegy the Nineteenth.' The three poems as a sequence progress away from the various kinds of external reality; Amynta's life, without the prospect of sexual pleasure, seems a blank. However, her reference to time, 'Time, I dare thee to discover / Such a Youth, and such a Lover' (10–17), looks ahead to 'Pollio' and suggests that the psychic curve is as yet incomplete.

Against this background Dryden's two Virgilian eclogues appear as a kind of psychic resurrection. In meaningful contrast to the first three poems they present new values and a quality of mind that once again opens itself to reality, including some definite notions about the poet's relation to society. 'The Fourth Eclogue. Pollio' and 'The Ninth Eclogue' also balance each other, setting a visionary reconstruction of nature against a commentary on things as they are, where a poet is menaced by social conditions that in some ways recall 'Elegy the Nineteenth.' The poems thus become a cycle, returning to the role of the poet at the end instead of leaving him invisible, detached from his subject-matter, as he was at first.

Dryden's 'Fourth Eclogue' scarcely recognizes the traditional Christian reading of this poem, although his headnote does say that '*Many of the Verses are translated from one of the Sybils, who prophesie of our Saviour's Birth*' (II, 165). The headnote seems to have no bearing on the poem and, though Dryden evidently shared the general view that the poem was 'messianic,' the poem is more comprehensible if it is read as a deviation from that view. Dryden's 'Fourth Eclogue' displays a rebirth in nature, but not the rebirth of a saviour, unless we are determined to misread what is plainly stated on the page. There would be less distortion in secularizing it altogether and reading it as the poet's response to his own ability to create illusions and thereby persuade himself and his readers of a rebirth in nature, never quite admitting his capacity for self-deception. Some modern critics have seen this as Virgil's own meaning.[24] Dryden was apparently able to ignore the accumulated interpretations of his culture and respond to the poem directly:

The Goats with strutting Duggs shall homeward speed,
And lowing Herds, secure from Lyons feed.
His Cradle shall with rising flow'rs be crown'd;
The Serpents Brood shall die: the sacred ground
Shall Weeds and pois'nous Plants refuse to bear,
Each common Bush shall *Syrian* Roses wear. (25–30)

However, a rebirth *has* occurred on an altogether different level, because the speaker of this poem has broken through the mental enclosures revealed in the earlier three poems. If we see Dryden's poems as a sequence analogous to Virgil's eclogues, we can recognize a level of meaning in which the significant imagery parallels the poet's sense of his own development. For example, nature's labour is in process as the poem is being uttered (Dryden uses the word 'Unlabour'd' once, 'labouring' twice), reflecting the birth pangs of the child's mother; and the new age, when labour will be unnecessary, will come about when the child can respond to 'Heroick Verse' (31). In effect, the poet projects his own struggle to achieve into the development of nature and of the child.

Dryden's emphasis on the physical – 'Beneath his pompous Fleece shall proudly sweat' (55) – connects this poem to the seemingly incongruous 'Elegy the Nineteenth.' But divinity becomes important near the end when the poet asks for 'Spirits' (66) to enable him to compete with Orpheus and Linus, his poetic ancestors, who in turn have heavenly parents themselves (69). The poet's new sense of his divine ancestry creates another analogy between his self and that of the child who might be a saviour. Dryden's inverted word order succeeds in imitating Virgil, and implies that the child could inspire his parent/muse as well as the reverse. In this case successful translation implies an original comprehension of the poem and a capacity to ignore traditional misreadings:

Not *Thracian Orpheus* should transcend my Layes,
Nor *Linus* crown'd with never-fading Bayes:
Though each his Heav'nly Parent shou'd inspire;
The Muse instruct the Voice, and *Phoebus* tune the Lyre. (67–70)

The speaker urging 'Incipe, parve puer, risu cognoscere matrem' (60) or addressing the 'auspicious Boy,' as Dryden says, is essentially addressing an urgent message to his own newly created self, and the child's acknowledgment of his mother becomes the speaker's recognition and acceptance of his own future.[25]

Dryden thus succeeded in finding poetic equivalents for Virgil's complicated turn of meaning at the end. His slow-moving lines, for instance – several are six feet in length, and one is seven – imitate the theme of slow, introspective, psychic labour, as well as of childbirth. However, Dryden's conclusion reverses Virgil's meaning. Virgil's speaker asks the child to smile at his mother, and one feels that he will smile, although he has not yet done so. As one critic says,

With its juxtaposition of lofty aims and slender beginnings, this final image confirms the tentative nature of the poem. Both the child and his poet are incomplete, full of a promise whose meanings and specific applications are unknown. The prophecy is no more than a poetic experiment: an attempt to portray the world of experience in images belonging to the world of innocence.[26]

Virgil does leave an opening for a pessimistic conclusion, but one's essential feeling at the end is positive. However, Dryden is not tentative. There can be no doubt about the fact that his child decides to frown:

Begin, auspicious Boy, to cast about
Thy Infant Eyes, and with a smile, thy Mother single out;
Thy Mother well deserves that short delight,
The nauseous Qualms of ten long Months and Travail to requite.
Then smile; the frowning Infants Doom is read,
No God shall crown the Board, nor Goddess bless the Bed. (73–8)

Dryden's nobility of tone thus disguises his stated meaning by creating an illusion of promise which the last two lines destroy. This technique will be repeated in *Sylvae* – a blatant contradiction between the realm of art, which can persuade us of anything, and the realm of fact, where disillusionment still operates and nothing essential has been changed. Even here the phrase 'nauseous Qualms' is an unpleasant recollection of 'Elegy the Nineteenth': 'What comes with ease we nauseously receive' (3). Dryden's 'Pollio' thus begins to imagine an age when the higher flights of poetry will be appropriate, but at last it retreats to 'The Ninth Eclogue,' which dramatizes the poet's situation in a world indifferent to poetry.

Dryden's headnote to 'The Ninth Eclogue' indicates that he read the poem biographically:

When Virgil *by the Favour of* Augustus *had recover'd his Patrimony near* Mantua, *and went in hope to take possession, he was in danger to be slain by* Arius *the*

> Centurion, *to whom those Lands were assign'd by the Emperour in reward of his Service against* Brutus *and* Cassius. *This Eclogue therefore is fill'd with complaints of his hard Usage; and the persons introduc'd, are the Bayliff of* Virgil, *and his Friend.* (II, 167–8)

One cannot say that Dryden's translation, by analogy, represents his own experiences in any literal way, but the headnote brings us back to thoughts of authorship and suggests that 'The Ninth Eclogue' expresses Dryden's feelings about the poet's situation in society in 1684 and not just in Virgil's time. The poem shows Dryden taking an interest in the theme of the outcast poet four years before he had solid reasons for considering himself as one, but it does recall the end of *Religio Laici*, and Moeris's hoarse voice (73) can be compared to the 'rugged Verse' to which Dryden decided to commit himself, as the proper style for responding to an unappreciative age. Menalcas (possibly Virgil himself) never appears in this poem. The poet with whose fate we are concerned is Virgil's bailiff, Moeris, who tries to recall fragments of Menalcas's songs to console himself and his friend Lycidas but finds even this power disappearing, 'for Cares and Time / Change all things, and untune my soul to rhime' (69–70). Though even Menalcas needs 'a friend at Court' (94), the second-order poet, who derives his own limited power from Menalcas, is inevitably far more endangered.

As Dryden presents him, Moeris adopts the voice of his enemy, the man who evicted him, whose 'surly tone' recalls the style of 'Elegy the Nineteenth':

> O *Lycidas* at last
> The time is come, I never thought to see,
> (Strange revolution for my Farm and me)
> When the grim Captain in a surly tone
> Cries out, pack up ye Rascals and be gone.
> Kick'd out, we set the best face on 't we cou'd,
> And these two Kids, to'appease his angry Mood
> I bear, of which the Devil give him good. (2–9)

Moeris's experiences provide an adequate reason for a satiric voice, at least from Dryden's viewpoint. In Virgil's poem Moeris is simple but not satiric or surly: surliness is the Drydenian tone given not only to contemptible individuals but ironically to men who have lost their self-respect because they have been treated with contempt. The 'revolution' Moeris has experienced – Dryden's word, not Virgil's, though each has a similar parenthesis –

has brought him to 'hard iron times' (15), an ironic descent from the changes expected in 'The Fourth Eclogue.'

Moeris and Lycidas quote fragments of Menalcas's poetry, which come to seem like memories of a lost ideal world when contrasted to Moeris's normative voice. The most interesting fragment is the one from 'Amaryllis' itself, for it creates a link within Dryden's set of translations. Moeris refers to

> that heavenly lay,
> That shorten'd as we went, our tedious way;
> 'O *Tityrus*, tend my herd and see them fed;
> To Morning pastures, Evening waters led:
> And 'ware the *Libyan* Ridgils butting head.' (26–30)

If 'Amaryllis' is now set in the irrecoverable past, the sequence even more emphatically than before comes to represent a temporal process, each poem reflecting a progressively later stage in some kind of psychological or historical evolution, which is in part only spurious, for the hostility of the rake-hero persists in those figures like the grim captain who embody political power and in the exile's resentment.

Dryden's use of the 'Amaryllis' quotation also complicates the historical relationship between his poets without actually contradicting Virgil's sense of poetic influence. Since the author of the quoted fragment was really Theocritus, Moeris himself can almost be taken as Virgil, who responded to Theocritus and wanted to recreate him, and Dryden can be recognized as yet another poet who, in unpropitious circumstances, tried to sustain the imaginative conceptions of his predecessors. Another literary allusion brings Dryden's poem up to his own time – his phrase 'the grim Captain in a surly tone,' which recalls in its very accent the 'grim wolf with privy paw' in Milton's *Lycidas*, where the poet played briefly with the notion of sporting with Amaryllis, that is, of writing Theocritan pastorals. All of the post-Theocritan poets use Theocritus to stand for the ineffectiveness of pastoral in an age when the poet is forced to be aware of social ills and of their impact on himself. 'The Ninth Eclogue' indicates no definite direction for the poet, but it does show that an awareness of social reality will impinge upon his work and complicate his struggle to find a personal voice: pastoral is thereby expanded to include a satiric comment on the age.

Dryden's contributions to *Miscellany Poems* can be read as a critique of the lighter style that satisfied his fellow translators, or they can be read without reference to their aims at all. One certainly detects some reference to Dryden himself which substantiates the doubts about the nature of poetry that can be found in *Religio Laici*: a beautiful style has no point except to construct an illusion, while a harsh style, which can be justified, is ugly. In 1684 Dryden appeared to be marking time with these admittedly slight translations, but the following year he used in *Sylvae* an essentially similar style to produce a major work balancing the attractions of art against the claims of fact. Dryden does not seem to have regretted his failure to attain to Henry Dickinson's humility.

4

Sylvae and Epicurean Art

LUCRETIUS

The varieties of Epicureanism soon became a fashion in the miscellanies, with form and content eminently suited to each other: the effort to remain uninvolved with life (or the pretence of lack of involvement) implied short poems, by no means invariably on lightweight themes, but often rather sentimental in their treatment of love and death. The sense of triviality really comes from the lack of political substance in these poems, not that politics is the only imaginable theme of real importance, but in this period silence on politics implies almost as much as commentary itself. Probably no one feared reprisals, but there was a sense of the pointlessness of taking a political stand or of engaging in social satire. Dryden's accomplishment in *Sylvae* (1685) is to raise the Epicurean response to a higher level by including translations of Lucretius and Virgil, as well as of two poets who worked in short forms, Theocritus and Horace; Dryden thus suggests a far broader range of implications in the Epicurean stance than any of his contemporaries. Moreover, some of his individual selections, especially those from Horace, are astonishingly beautiful as poetry. If beautiful poetry needs justification (and in *Religio Laici* Dryden implied that it did), it can be found here, in a sequence largely concerned with the conflicts between art and life. The Horatian poems are the freest of Dryden's translations in *Sylvae* and in a way they attest to a new confidence that great poetry provides its own justification.

About 140 pages of *Sylvae*, a little less than half,[1] consists of Dryden's poems. His songs are detached from his translated work, but they are placed quite close to the end of the book, in a climactic position, immediately after a Latin poem by Dryden's son, Charles. One of Dryden's songs, 'Sylvia the fair,' is about a girl who seems, because of her name, intended to personify the spirit of *Sylvae* itself[2] and, because of her youth, to be a quasi-daughter, offsetting the contribution of Dryden's son. The rest of the book consists mainly of other poets' translations from Horace, Theocritus, Ovid's elegies, Catullus, and Tibullus, who is represented by one elegy only. There are also two fragments of poems by Virgil, the Orpheus section of the fourth Georgic and 'The Episode of the Death of *Camilla*' from Book XI of the *Aeneid*, translated by Mr Stafford. This is the last selection in the book; it recalls in more pathetic vein one of Dryden's fragments from the *Aeneid*, 'The Entire Episode of Mezentius and Lausus,' as both poems portray a 'disdainful' soul leaving its body. A '*Person of Quality*' translated 'Of Natures Changes' from Book V of *De rerum natura*, progressing from an image of elemental strife to one of the ultimate dissolution of the universe.[3] Just before the end of the collection (between Dryden's songs and 'Camilla') are two poems, one on Oldham's death and another 'On the Kings-House Now Building at Winchester,' which recalls the temple-building theme emphasized in *Miscellany Poems*.[4]

Virtually all of the translators are anonymous, a notable change from *Ovid's Epistles* and *Miscellany Poems*. 'Mr. Stafford,' William Bowles, and Charles Dryden are the only names besides John Dryden's to appear. One poem celebrates Dickinson's translation of Simon's *Critical History* on the grounds that both author and translator have partly repaired the damage of Babel.[5] There are few inner links outside of Dryden's work, but *Sylvae* is still fairly well unified in tone and theme. *Sylvae* is more languishing or meditative than *Miscellany Poems*, frequently returning to the subjects of isolation, imminent death, and separation. The various poems provide a range of Epicurean responses to the contemplation of the void, responses which are in general uneasy and conscious of some degree of cosmic isolation. The well-known passage from Catullus sums it up:

> The Suns may rise again that once are set,
> Their usual Labour, and old Course repeat,
> But when our Day's once turn'd have lost their Light,
> We must sleep on one long Eternal Night.[6]

This poet soon turns to sex but only after analysing his emotional need for it. The vision of sexual escape as a solution to anxiety constitutes one kind of Epicureanism, but the Epicureanism of Dryden's work is on another plane altogether – probably higher, in the sense of being more morally serious, and certainly suitable to an older man. Dryden's poetry is a suitable introduction to the volume, though perhaps unintentionally it shows the limits to the kind of Epicureanism that is readily accepted.

Lucretius is the normative poet of *Sylvae*, as Ovid the elegist was in *Miscellany Poems*, but when we read 'Lucretius' we must to some extent think of Hobbes. Once we recognize the importance of Hobbes, at least to Dryden, we can see that materialism represented a genuine threat to the writers' cosmic security; it was no longer mere toying with antiquity. Dryden virtually identified Hobbes and Lucretius, implying that the current interest in Lucretius was really a displaced interest in Hobbes, but he made one essential distinction:

> From his time to ours, I know none so like him, as our Poet and Philosopher of *Malmsbury*. This is that perpetual Dictatorship, which is exercis'd by *Lucretius*; who though often in the wrong, yet seems to deal *bonâ fide* with his Reader, and tells him nothing but what he thinks; in which plain sincerity, I believe he differs from our *Hobbs*, who cou'd not but be convinc'd, or at least doubt of some eternal Truths which he has oppos'd.[7]

Paradoxically Hobbes, a Christian underneath his materialism, is *less* forthright than Lucretius, as if Christianity complicates problems of belief before it resolves them! However, the awareness of Hobbes helps to explain the anxiety of the various translators' responses to Lucretius, and there is little, if any, Christian consolation either in Dryden's part of *Sylvae* or elsewhere. The absence of a balancing Christian viewpoint, enough to outweigh the Lucretian presence, suggests a real anxiety and should be taken into account in interpreting Dryden's poems.

According to Norman Austin, Dryden followed his friend Thomas Creech, who had recently translated all of *De rerum natura* (in 1682), in intensifying the negative aspects of Epicureanism. Epicureanism thus betrays its limits and becomes its own critique; it is nasty and brutish, since the escape to sex is disgusting, while it fails to provide the consolation and moral guidance available in Christianity. The reader will be impelled to Christianity as the obvious alternative to a message which Austin paraphrases thus:

> All human existence is pain, and Epicureanism is an absurdity because pursuit of pleasure is a doomed attempt to evade the human curse. Gratification of pleasure can lead only to intensification of pain. This is the consolation that Dryden's Lucretius has to offer his fellow men. We who read Dryden's translation hear in Lucretius' lament on human existence the swan song of paganism.[8]

Austin implies that the speaker of the Lucretius poems must be thought of as distinct from Dryden himself, a created persona whose viewpoint will be rejected with disgust, like that of the speaker of 'Elegy the Nineteenth.'

I have already quoted Dryden's comment on Hobbes's inability not to believe, which surely testifies to Dryden's own steadfast if questioning Christian belief. But if Dryden in 1685 had no doubts about the ultimate truth of Christianity, he may still have experienced religious doubts of his own about the connection between Christian belief and the material world, which science takes as its object of study. Christianity does not make materialism untrue, but materialism casts doubt on – indeed it may destroy – the conviction that God is responsible for the cosmic harmony apparent to the human observer. Evidence from the senses may conflict with faith; the individual may be forced to accept a kind of double truth in which two kinds of evidence yield different answers, each appropriate only on one level and providing no help in relating matter and spirit to each other.

Dryden's uncertainties at this time are borne out by his attraction to Plutarch, which I have discussed in chapter 2, and by some aspects of his religious imagery in 'To ... Mrs. Anne Killigrew' (III, 109–15). In this poem images of the dead woman in heaven are cast in the form of speculation (What ever happy Region is thy place'), and they should be read as fantasies which the poet first invents to console himself and then discards. No evidence about supernatural regions is available now. At the end of the poem genuine evidence for faith is displaced forward in time to the last judgment: the definite, not interrogative 'when' in the last stanza replaces the more uncertain 'whether' in the first. The intervening stanzas of the poem work out a basis for accepting Anne as a quasi-divine artist, one who is able to create a second nature. However, Anne is not a creator perceived in God's image, a fact which explains the diversity and freedom with which she creates. Anne resembles God mainly in her penchant for the grotesque:

> What Nature, Art, bold Fiction e're durst frame,
> Her forming Hand gave Feature to the Name.
> So strange a Concourse ne're was seen before,
> But when the peopl'd Ark the whole Creation bore. (123–6)[9]

Anne's smallpox itself exemplifies God's tolerance of the grotesque in real life, as does the image near the end of 'ratling Bones' (184), which is not supposed to be pretty or dignified in tone. God's imagery may violate the standards of human aesthetics.

The idea that an aesthetic order may, somewhat uneasily, replace the unknowable divine order reappears in Dryden's part of *Sylvae*. But I think that Austin has overstated the consolations available in Christianity. Also, the pessimism of Dryden's Lucretius is partly an attempt to compensate for Creech's limits, at least to demonstrate a kind of poetry that he had neglected. Creech's translation of Horace's *Odes, Satires, and Epistles* (1684) was dedicated to Dryden, and he translated Theocritus in the same year, thus anticipating three of Dryden's four poets.[10] Creech was popular (a third edition of his Lucretius was published by 1685), but his translation encouraged a hedonistic misreading of Lucretius, who was quickly taken as a spokesman for sexual liberation. Nahum Tate's complimentary poem, praising Creech as a sexual conqueror, is typical of several:

> 'Twas bold for Youth Lucretius Heights to storm,
> But Youth alone had Vigour to perform.[11]

Aphra Behn's point is essentially the same, though she also makes the feminist point that Creech has made an ancient poet available to women:

> The Godlike Virgil, and great Homer's Muse
> Like Divine Mysteries are conceal'd from us,
> We are forbid all grateful Themes,
> No ravishing Thoughts approach our Ear.[12]

These reactions are based on a natural desire to find a model who was not authoritarian, and I think that people then as now find their models where they can. Yet the 'youthful' readings are based on as important a distortion as Dryden's distortion in the other direction.

The contrast is glaringly obvious in the fourth of Dryden's Lucretius fragments in *Sylvae*, 'Concerning the Nature of Love.' In the Lucretian original, sexual intercourse is an image for the collision of bodies, which can neither unite completely nor destroy each other, though they may wear each other out. Lucretius's abstract diction turns human bodies into images of bodies in general:

> nequiquam, quoniam nil inde abradere possunt
> nec penetrare et abire in corpus corpore toto. (IV.1110–11)[13]

Even when his sound effects are 'too lively, and alluring,' as Dryden puts it (III, 12), the action itself is described in a clinical fashion because Lucretius is reducing sexuality to an image of his world-view. A reader might be aroused by this passage, but only if he fails to see that the body is a clumsy and hopelessly material object.

Creech is euphemistic in diction, yet he brings out the melancholy inherent in the fact that complete intercourse is forever unattainable. He translates the two lines quoted above thus:

> In vain! Fond Fools, they can not mix their Souls,
> Altho' they seem to try, in am'rous Rouls;
> So strictly twin'd, till all their Pow'rs decay,
> And the loose airy PLEASURE slips away.[14]

But Lucretian man and woman do not have souls to mix (unless Creech is using the word ironically), while 'powers' and 'loose airy pleasure' soften the effect of Lucretius's technical terms. Dryden seems far closer to the controlled distaste of the original:

> In vain; they only cruze about the coast,
> For bodies cannot pierce, nor be in bodies lost.
>
> ('Concerning the Nature of Love,' 77–8)

Creech's failure in accurate translation is surely the result of awkwardness with a graphic description of sexuality; he solved the problem by bowdlerizing, omitting Lucretius's account of male orgasm, the comparison of human to animal intercourse, the list of sexual positions, and the erosion metaphor at the end of the book. Dryden in all cases expands and elaborates. He could well have had Creech in mind when he added a phrase on those who 'veil with some extenuating name' (144) and when he wrote in his preface:

> If to mince [Lucretius's] meaning, which I am satisfi'd was honest and instructive, I had either omitted some part of what he said, or taken from the strength of his expression, I certainly had wrong'd him; and that freeness of thought and words, being thus cashier'd in my hands, he had no longer been *Lucretius*. (III, 12)

If Creech's translation was dishonest, the other poets' understanding of Lucretius was simply wrong and the conclusions they drew had no basis. Lucretius was not a poet of sexual liberation or of human freedom generally. His philosophy was determinist. Dryden ignored Lucretius on 'swerve,' a justification of free will within the context of atomism, but then so did everyone else; they were interested in his open descriptions of sexuality. Dryden probably regarded this response as immature. Possibly he was interested in showing that old age may be more capable than youth, if only because the older poet has no reason to glorify sex. His translation reacts to at least three Lucretiuses at once – the writer of *De rerum natura* itself, the flattering Lucretius imagined by Dryden's contemporaries, and the shadow man, who was essentially a mask for Hobbes.

EPIC AND LYRIC IN *SYLVAE*

Dryden's part of *Sylvae* includes four selections from the *Aeneid*, five from *De rerum natura*, three Theocritan idylls,and four Horatian poems (three odes and an epode). The two original songs appear later in the volume. Dryden's emphasis on epic and on the philosophical poem differentiates him from the other contributors to the miscellany, but the fragments from Virgil are rearranged while those from Lucretius are kept in their original order. Dryden thereby gives Lucretius a slightly greater emphasis, translating a passage from each book except the sixth. Lucretius's philosophy tends to become normative because his book seems the least transformed. At the same time Dryden's poets appear in descending order according to the nobility of the forms in which they wrote, an arrangement which gives the effect of a disintegrating consciousness, gradually playing itself out and accepting ever greater limits in its aspirations. The critique of materialism is pervasive. Virtually all the poems, as Dryden's changes emphasize, are concerned with the materiality of the perceptible world, the rule of chance or fortune, and the ironic fact that physical contact still provides the most reliable knowledge. Human beings are literally battered by nature and by each other and there are many images of enclosure; ultimately men and women are locked within their own bodies and can know only through their bodies.

Instead of the various perspectives one might expect in a collective work, Dryden repeats the same perspective on a gradually diminishing scale. His selections within each group by the same poet diminish as well. Each group starts with an heroic, almost godlike, image of human endeavours and ends with an image of human powerlessness or self-deception. Yet each conclusion involves a striking dichotomy between content and style; there is a sense of poetic closure in each case, with a pleasing, spacious image that may be totally unrelated to the action. This is the aesthetic detachment of Epicurean art, what happens when the artist puts Lucretius's advice into practice:

> Tis pleasant, safely to behold from shore
> The rowling Ship; and hear the Tempest roar:
> Not that anothers pain is our delight;
> But pains unfelt produce the pleasing sight.
> ('Lucretius: The beginning of the Second Book,' 1–4)

This passage could be the basis for a theory of tragedy.[15] However, in this context detachment seems inauthentic, for Dryden's speaker has not overcome 'These bugbears of the mind, this inward Hell' (64), as we see by the end of the selection. The illusory nature of Epicurean art is revealed throughout. Poetically Dryden's collection is ordered and resolved, while emotionally it is inconclusive.

Dryden's choice and arrangement of selections illustrate the breakdown of genre that we have just discussed; despite the progression from epic to song, epic and song can also be equivalent forms. The *Aeneid* is so fragmented that it can no longer be read as epic narrative, while *De rerum natura* seems to retain its original coherence (in fact it does not). Dryden links Virgil and Lucretius by placing Virgil's 'The Speech of Venus to Vulcan,' in which Venus seduces Vulcan into making armour for Aeneas, just before Lucretius's invocation to Venus. Lucretius's passage influenced Virgil. Dryden, who could play games with his ancestors' literary thefts, reverses the order, giving Virgil apparent priority and making the two poets somehow equivalent in spite of the differences between their total poems. Poetic matter is dissolved and reconstructed. In addition, epic material overflows into the other poems. Lucretius's 'Against the Fear of Death' alludes to fallen heroes; the first Theocritus idyll is 'The Epithalamium of Helen and Menelaus'; the speaker of the second idyll, 'The Despairing Lover,' recalls Dido attacking Aeneas – 'Ah Nymph more cruel than of humane Race, / Thy Tygress heart belies thy Angel Face' (35–6); and the third, 'Daphnis,' opens with an allusion to Paris's abduction of Helen, recalling the first of the three idylls as well as the *Iliad* itself. Dryden's version of Horace's 'Ode 3. Lib. I' is addressed to Roscommon; the original was addressed to Virgil. Epic is absorbed into a new context.[16]

Song-like or even dance-like passages also appear throughout, in the manner of Theocritus. The 'Epithalamium' addressed by the Spartan maidens to Helen and Menelaus is a song that one could imagine in performance: 'For this their artful hands instruct the Lute to sound, / Their feet assist their hands and justly beat the ground' (10–11); the poem contains references to song, dance, races, and sexuality, physical activities that seem related to each other and provide a bodily base for poetic rhythm. In 'Idyllium the 23rd. The Despairing Lover' the cruel nymph goes to a dance and her rejected lover hangs himself: 'The bounce burst ope the door; the Scornful Fair / Relentless lookt, and saw him beat his quivering feet in Air' (96–7). In 'Idyll. 27' Daphnis's 'naughty Pipe' (23) is also an image for sexuality. The physical impulses of dance and song are thus associated with bodily impulses in general, which in turn are treated as a force pervading all of life; indeed, the rejected lover continues to dance even after he is dead. In Dryden's Theocritus the body in all its unreflectiveness, though in its pleasure as well, becomes the ground for art and for a perspective of life.

The Virgil and Lucretius selections at some points approach the lyrical norm, both in content and style. The first Virgil passage, on Nisus and Euryalus's role in the funeral games in Book v, contains a rising and falling pattern which has a dance-like symmetry:

His heels flew up, and on the grassy floor,
He fell besmear'd with filth and holy gore.
Nor mindless then *Euryalus* of thee,
Nor of the sacred bonds of amity,
He strove th' immediate Rival to oppose,
And caught the foot of *Salius* as he rose. (59–64)

'Rise' or 'rose' is used as a rhyme word three times and 'race' is used twice in a passage only 102 lines long. In general, Dryden's repetition of rhyme words or near-rhymes and his frequent use of triplets and alexandrines work against the narrative style of unvaried heroic couplets; Dryden's variations slow down the progressive forward movement and give his poetry a patterned effect like that of stanzas, although not so rigid in form. The second part of the Nisus and Euryalus episode contains eight triplets in 386 lines, as well as a reference to the lyrical *carpe diem* motif (103). In 'Mezentius and Lausus' the word 'wound' is a rhyme word four times, in three cases with 'ground,' and there are four alexandrines and ten triplets in only 241 lines. Dryden mentions the freedom he took in translating this passage (III, 8). His freedom took other forms as well, but one of them is the extensive use of metre and rhyme to make death seem melancholy, not a narrative event.

'The Speech of Venus to Vulcan' and its companion piece, the invocation to Venus from *De rerum natura*, have so many words rhyming with 'ire' (like 'fire' and 'inspire') that the device becomes one of the most important poetic facts about both selections, creating a sense of continuity between the two and suggesting that Venus's power cannot be contained within one poem or by one human poet. Lucretius's invocation, fifty-seven lines long, contains four triplets, five alexandrines, two heptameters, and so many repeated rhymes and near-rhymes that one comes to expect recurrence; in fact, eighteen out of a possible twenty-seven rhyme words occur more than once. Not every reader might count words like 'drest' and 'express' as rhymes, but Dryden himself rhymes 'War' and 'care,' and uses the near-rhymes 'bear/appear' and the rhymes 'inspire/fire' in two consecutive couplets (30–3). The flexibility of his rhymes suggests the intangible powers of Venus, who is the source of poetic inspiration.

'Lucretius: The beginning of the Second Book' treats a naval battle as a show. In 'Against the Fear of Death' Dryden added an image comparing the seeming random movement of atoms to a dance:

> Nay, tho' our Atoms shou'd revolve by chance,
> And matter leape into the former dance ... (19–20)[17]

Human dancing thus imitates, or enacts, the movements of nature, as in another image that Dryden adds in 'Against the Fear of Death':

> Besides we tread but a perpetual round,
> We ne're strike out; but beat the former ground
> And the same Maukish joyes in the same track are found. (305–7)

These additions create thematic links within the collection. The 'Shaking Fit' which 'hangs' upon the man bored with life (290) also parallels the Theocritan lover who hangs himself. These dance images are ironic because they reduce human beings to whatever force keeps them in perpetual motion, although motion can take attractive forms. The conflict between what is pleasing to contemplate and what we know is produced by matter in motion generates a characteristic melancholy which is Dryden's closest link to the other poets in *Sylvae*. 'Against the Fear of Death' contains this lament:

> Mean time, when thoughts of death disturb thy head;
> Consider, *Ancus* great and good is dead;
> *Ancus* thy better far, was born to die,
> And thou, dost thou bewail mortality? (236–9)

The much later poem 'Alexander's Feast' (1697) has a similar line: 'He sung *Darius* Great and Good' (75). The image has become bathetic, with melancholy as pleasing as an after-dinner liqueur. Even in *Sylvae* the tone of Epicurean lament is rendered as a characteristic form of sentimentality, as contemplation of the void leads to a whole range of posturing that just borders on self-indulgence.

'Concerning the Nature of Love' contains sexual 'leapings' (274), and the brief selection from Book v, on a shipwrecked babe imagined as isolated in a state of nature, emphasizes the child's need to soothe itself with one sort of rattle or another. All forms of dancing and leaping can be traced to the infant's physical needs. Horace's odes, as major lyrics, are still a kind of song. Against this background Dryden's songs have more impact than one might expect, especially since one of them is about a girl called Sylvia, named after the book itself. Dryden's contributions thus strengthen the anti-heroic norm of *Sylvae*. *Sylvae* mingles the genres throughout, denying epic finality and suggesting a more emotional perspective on experience. The collection also shows the limits of Epicureanism as a basis for art. The Epicurean artist strives for and possibly achieves order and detachment, but in the long run he can only console himself and restate the persistence of the body's need for expression.

VIRGIL, LUCRETIUS, AND EPICUREANISM

Dryden's fragmentary *Aeneis* is asymmetrical, like the brief narratives of classical literature discussed above. His four selections in *Sylvae* neither condense the *Aeneid* nor foreshadow the themes of his complete *Aeneis*, published in 1697. Nor do they resemble other fragmentary seventeenth-century translations of the *Aeneid*, by writers such as John Denham and John Harrington: they were political, more like Dryden's 1697 version, whereas Dryden's 1685 *Aeneis* is not. The 1697 dedication and *Aeneis* present a multifaceted view of both hero and poem, while the 1685 version is simplified. Though not quite so negative as *Ovid's Epistles*, it is closer to Dido's view than to the later dedication. Only in 1687, in *The Hind and the Panther*, does Dryden begin to shift his views, though even here he presents both sides. The Panther, like Dido, believes in a 'bad' Aeneas:

> Methinks such terms of proferr'd peace you bring
> As once *Æneas* to th' *Italian* King:
> By long possession all the land is mine,
> You strangers come with your intruding line. (III.766–9)

The Hind tries to correct the Panther's view, since her character of the 'Plain good Man' is a composite of James II, Aeneas, Christ, and Chaucer's virtuous knight (III.906–14). The Hind's effort to see good in everyone is a corrective to the Panther's malice, but it does not efface the memory of the Panther's image.

The bad Aeneas of *Sylvae* is not the scoundrel who rejected Dido, the man of destiny who destroyed a peaceful Italian culture, but the hero of a fragmentary Epicurean epic.[18] He is nearly as inaccessible as a god and he remains untouched by normal feeling; not a representative man himself, his mysterious ways cause anxiety and pain to others. Dido does not appear in the poem. None of Dryden's four selections comes from the main narrative action – the Trojan's journey to Italy and establishment there – and none deals with or even seems to recognize Aeneas's inner conflicts or character development, especially his quintessential ability to endure stress. In 1697 Dryden himself recognized Aeneas's concern for his followers,[19] and noted that '*Æneas* was actually wounded ... though he had the same God-Smith to Forge his Arms, as had *Achilles*. It seems he was no War-luck, as the *Scots* commonly call such Men, who they say, are Iron-free, or Lead-free' (K, III, 1022). Nevertheless, *Sylvae* presents the war-luck, a godlike Epicurean who does not experience human conflict and rarely takes an interest in it; like a god, he is unknowable, absent when needed, a bit of a joker.

Aeneas's good humour appears in the games episode, the first poem in *Sylvae* and the high point of the work from the viewpoint of its happy ending. Set in a 'native Theater,' surrounded by a wood (3, 5), the games suggest the artificiality of that type of structured conflict, but without the suggestion that game-playing is a good way to learn about conflict without getting hurt. Aeneas's game is not well-structured and he breaks the rules, making up for the arbitrariness of fortune and of skill, rewarding everyone alike. Nisus trips Salius, enabling his friend Euryalus to win, and the loser understandably objects.[20] Dryden added the last two lines of Aeneas's bland explanation:

let no disputes arise;
Where Fortune plac'd it, I award the Prize.
But give me leave, her Errours to amend,
At least to pity a deserving friend. (81–4)

The race became a game of chance only because Nisus cheated, but this means less to Aeneas than equalizing the conflict. In a game rewards for bad performance or non-performance may cause more uncertainty than no rewards for contestants who deserve to lose. Nisus, the cheater and one of the losers, actually protests over the consolation prize given to Salius, with a witty play on the idea of the *felix culpa*: 'Wou'd fortune make me fall as happily' (94). So Aeneas, 'Th' indulgent Father of the people' (97), gives Nisus a shield 'Of wond'rous art' (99), foreshadowing the armour which

Venus will later give to him. Dryden has coloured this incident to set Aeneas up as a complacent god-figure. By emphasizing the theme of armour, he also shows how much the Trojans valued invulnerability. Aeneas is the channel by which divine invulnerability descends to his men.

The next selection, from Book IX, completes the Nisus and Euryalus episode. It is a night scene. Aeneas has gone to King Evander, leaving in charge Ascanius, who tries to imitate his father. Ascanius lets Nisus and Euryalus try to make their way past enemy troops, promising lavish rewards – some not yet captured – if they bring Aeneas back. Nisus and Euryalus gallantly accept the rule of chance (138, 156) but fail to distinguish between the artificial order of a game and their present undertaking, in which a chance element can be fatal. Euryalus, cheating again, pauses to steal a helmet:

> through the doubtful shade
> His glitt'ring Helm *Euryalus* betray'd;
> On which the Moon with full reflection play'd. (289–91)

Dryden added line 291, emphasizing the moon which betrayed Euryalus. Nisus, who is in both Virgil and Dryden an eclectic about his beliefs, then invokes that very moon, 'Grace of the Stars, and Goddess of the Night' (330). The night scene brings out the emptiness of human belief systems – and the indifference of gods and goddesses to humanity.

Ironically Nisus himself appears to be an invisible god to Volscens, Euryalus's captor, when he throws a javelin at him:

> Fierce *Volscens* foams with rage; and gazing round,
> Descry'd no Author of the Fatal wound,
> Nor where to fix revenge. (348–50)

Volscens's rage is a result of his confusion. In that state he kills Euryalus, and Nisus becomes indirectly responsible for his friend's death. In the symbolic situation represented by this episode each person is isolated in a dark universe and attributes to chance inexplicable events, which are in fact caused by other isolated human beings. The drunken, hedonistic Latins make too little effort to control the world, but the Trojans have a false confidence that everything can be foreseen and controlled. This moral could be deduced from Virgil as well as from Dryden.

Virgil's dark universe, however, is just a limited view of men caught up in a tragic situation; in his role as narrator he conveys a deeper sense of nature's organic unity, which his characters fail to grasp, employing a verbal pattern which Dryden seems to have tried *not* to translate. Dryden thus transforms this selection into an Epicurean poem, although Virgil's original displayed only several imperfect characters as Epicurean and seems to have had the express purpose of showing the limits of Epicureanism.[21] In the first half of the episode in which the two friends persuade Ascanius and his aged counsellors to let him go (IX.176–302), Virgil reiterates the word 'anima' (spirit, soul, mind, heart) and like-sounding words that acquire related meanings through association, such as 'annos' (years) and 'amnem' (river). The idea of the cycle is the basis for this association. The young men have spirits beyond their years: 'pulcher Iulus, / ante annos animumque gerens curamque virilem' (LOEB TRANSLATION 'fair Iülus, with a man's mind and a spirit beyond his years') (IX.310–11). They lack wisdom, however; they have not sufficiently experienced the river of time. Nisus's claim to know the local topography, including the river, thus becomes chillingly ironic:

> vidimus obscuris primam sub vallibus urbem
> venatu adsiduo et totum cognovimus amnem.
> Hic annis gravis atque animi maturus Aletes ... (IX.244–6)

> LOEB TRANSLATION Down the dim valleys in our frequent hunting we have seen the outskirts of the town and have come to know all the river.
> Then Aletes, stricken in years and sage in council ...[22]

The old men, a weak and sentimental lot, are so overwhelmed by Nisus's youthful energy that they fail to use their wisdom to stop him. The aged mind and youthful ardour, two kinds of 'anima,' work at cross purposes. That is one real irony of Aeneas's absence; the middle-aged man could have reconciled them. Virgil's amused contempt for old men is consistent.

What is lost in translation is the idea that some force connects all living things, all 'animalia' (IX.224). Virgil's world is an organism, while Dryden's is soulless as well as godless. Dryden uses the word 'soul' only once, when Ascanius vows friendship to Euryalus (150). In the 1697 *Aeneis* he uses it twice more, to replace 'breasts' in the phrase 'breasts so void of fear' and 'youth' in the line 'My youth so sad a farewel cou'd not bear.'[23] The characters in the 1697 translation at least have souls. Virgil's Nisus also echoes the famous 'mens agitat molem' passage on the world-soul, from *Aeneid*, VI.726–7, which Dryden quoted in the preface to 'Annus Mirabilis' (I, 54). One thus assumes that Dryden saw the point in Nisus's phrase, 'mens agitat mihi' (IX.187).[24] In Virgil the world-soul is expressed in Nisus's character, though it drives him to death, but Dryden makes him an heroic egotist:

Or do the Gods this Warlike warmth inspire,
Or makes Each Man a God of his desire?
A Noble Ardour boils within my Breast,
Eager of Action, Enemy of Rest. (15–18)

Nisus actually combines Absalom's dangerous ardour with Achitophel's restlessness, a satiric overtone that casts doubt even on the sense of responsibility that gives him some dignity when he dies. Virgil uses the word 'anima' only twice in his account of the expedition itself (349, 353), each time for the escape of a man's soul at the moment of death. Dryden translates the more physically explicit reference as 'soul':

purpuream vomit ille animam et cum sanguine mixta
vina refert moriens. (IX.349–50)

The wound a blended stream of wine and blood
Pours out; the purple Soul comes floating in the floud. (252–3)

So we find out what is the essence of man. Dryden's version is consistently materialistic, while Virgil's – in this episode – is about the subjectivity of human beliefs.

The sense of a materialistic, indeed a mechanistic, universe intensifies in the freely translated 'Episode of Mezentius and Lausus' from Book x of the *Aeneid*. Dryden has expanded the descriptions of the tyrant Mezentius in his armour and of weapons and their impact, stressing the reality of things and forces. Thus might a tyrant experience the cosmos, but his perceptions are apparently shared by the narrator, and Mezentius almost gains our sympathy after Aeneas kills Lausus, Mezentius's son. Our normal sympathies are reversed, since we are not shown how Aeneas came to kill a youth like his own son or why Mezentius's death is justifiable.

Dryden's account is more physically detailed than Virgil's and he describes mass and trajectory with uncommon precision. Armour is very important, first when Mezentius tries to kill Aeneas, and later when Aeneas succeeds in killing Lausus:

straight with all his force he [Mezentius] threw
The massie Spear; which, hissing as it flew,
Reach'd the celestial Shield; that stop'd the course:
But glanceing thence, the yet unbroken force,
Took a new bent obliquely, and, betwixt
The Side and Bowels, fam'd *Anthores* fixt. (30–5)

And lifted high, the conquering Sword appears,
Which full descending with a fearful sway,
Thro' Sheild & Cuirasse forc'd th' impetuous way,
And buried deep in his fair bosome lay.
The springing streams thro' the thin Armour strove
And drencht the golden Coat his [Lausus's] careful Mother wove. (87–92)[25]

Aeneas has an unfair advantage because *his* mother is a goddess and thus has provided better armour than Lausus's. Yet Dryden placed the account of Aeneas's '*Vulcanian* Orb' (70), which comes from Book VIII, after the Mezentius selection, reversing Virgil's order and making Aeneas seem impervious to death, a 'War-luck' even before Venus's intervention. This is a universe of random physical activity, where forces merely cancel each other out: 'Thus equal deaths are dealt, and equal chance' (1).

Aeneas is beyond sympathy. He watches Mezentius with 'joyful eyes' (21) and warns Lausus with 'friendly threatning' (79), as if he still were playing a game, while Mezentius learns feeling through his son's death. Dryden's reference to Aeneas 'Collected in himself, and like a Rock / Poiz'd on his base' (22–3) recalls Milton's Satan, who 'Stood in himself collected' while tempting Eve. In 1697 Dryden changed the first line to 'Collected in his Strength,' and 'joyful' (really a literal translation of 'laetus,' which is all wrong in English) to 'dauntless.' The 1685 version is more Miltonic; for Milton even Aeneas's persistence through all his suffering was Satanic. Dryden does not go that far in blackening Aeneas; even if the '*Vulcanian* Orb' recalls the blank shield of Satan in hell, it is Mezentius who speaks 'Of hateful men, and of more hated Light' (152). As both characters have recognizably Satanic elements, the meaning of their conflict remains ambiguous.

Dryden's treatment of Mezentius after Lausus's death is sentimental, almost grotesque. Mezentius's only personal relationship now is with his horse: 'The Horse seem'd sensible,' Dryden adds (161). Mezentius's words of farewell to his horse recall Hector's farewell to Andromache:[26]

For after such a Lord, I rest secure,
Thou wilt no Foreign reins, or *Trojan* load endure.
He said; and straight th' officious Courser kneels
To take his wonted weight. (170–3)

Whether he is considered as lord, load, husband, or sheer body, Mezentius is burden personified, and pure machine when mounted:

His hands he fills
With pointed Javelins; on his head he lac'd
His glittering Helm, which terribly was grac'd
With crested Horsehair, nodding from afar,
Then spurr'd his thundring Steed, amidst the War. (173–7)

Mezentius is virtually indestructible, but Aeneas kills the horse, which falls on its rider, who is trapped 'with his weight opprest' (214); then Mezentius commits suicide. In the original the horse's shoulder is also dislocated as it dies, linking this passage to a motif which becomes irrelevant in the fragmentary version: whose shoulders can bear a weight that would crush anybody else?[27] Could Aeneas be that Atlas figure? The motif is an index to Aeneas's growth, for he leaves Troy weighed down by his father on his back but ends merged with nature's strength, a mountain shaking the oaks on his back. In Dryden's poem Aeneas's development is not in question and the weight of either Mezentius or his horse, a centaur-figure, suggests only body as such.

'The Speech of Venus to Vulcan' now becomes ironic, because the gods help a man who already seems to be a winner. Venus and Vulcan enjoy sex in spite of the darkness covering the world (1) and their gift to Aeneas helps to sustain the war. Moreover, it is only in this section, which is concerned directly with the gods, that the Lucretian boundaries of matter are overcome:

Her soft embraces soon infuse desire,
His bones and marrow suddain warmth inspire;
And all the Godhead feels the wonted fire. (30–2)

However, Vulcan is also an artist (42) and the warmth and energy that Venus infuses into him are transmitted to his shield:

Whatever melting Metals can conspire,
Or breathing bellows, or the forming fire,
I freely promise. (47–9)

This selection has a double effect. With reference to the content of the poem thus far it suggests human limits, but it also reveals art as an activity independent of human conflict, as if art confers a power that may compensate for other kinds of weakness. Some kind of positive force emanates from divinity to man, as the speaker of Lucretius's invocation asks for and perhaps obtains Vulcan's power:

My tuneful Song inspire,
And kindle with thy own productive fire.
('The beginning of the First Book,' 32–3)

The rhyme words, bringing out the continuity between Venus, Vulcan, Virgil, and Lucretius, and another key word, 'infuse,' which appears in both passages, suggest the disappearance of the personal boundaries which characterize the material universe. Art has qualities of the divine.

Dryden never says that the artist's power is illusory, but he does imply that its attraction is that it compensates for certain human deficiencies, especially for man's difficulty in exerting an impact on the world which batters him. The power associated with art contrasts with every other area of life, making artistic activity seem like an extreme case of philosophic detachment. However, there is some irony in artistic detachment. Lucretius's invocation reveals his ignorance of the gods as we have thus far seen them in the *Aeneid* selections, not noticeably interested in peace and quiet. Lucretius is also weary of war, hoping that Venus will so 'fetter' Mars in her body that 'quiet to the weary World' will be restored ('The beginning of the First Book,' 58), but we have seen her occupied with Vulcan. The two passages give such contradictory images of Venus's activities that they appear to demonstrate no more than human confusion about the gods.

Dryden's Lucretius does not sustain his high note for long. Both in his invocation and in 'The beginning of the Second Book' he quickly deteriorates into anxiety, even self-disgust, and a sense of the primacy of the physical. The lovemaking of Venus and Vulcan anticipates that of the human lovers in 'Concerning the Nature of Love': 'While with thy heavenly form he feeds his famish'd eyes: / Sucks in with open lips, thy balmy breath' ('The beginning of the First Book,' 50–1); the 'wretched man' (16) of 'The beginning of the Second Book' 'overfeeds / His cramm'd desires' (18–19), 'craves' to be left alone (21), 'trembles' and 'shakes' with dread (60, 62). It is Dryden's diction that creates these effects; even mental entities, like 'bugbears,' are represented physically (64). This language is sometimes coarse, but the coarseness has a clear direction – to reveal a self-hatred of which Dryden's speaker may be only partly conscious. Lucretius cannot quite believe either in a 'Propitious Queen of Love' ('First Book,' 2) or in the possibility of escape to an ivory tower, 'From thence to look below on humane kind, / Bewilder'd in the Maze of Life, and blind' ('Second Book,' 10–11). In each case, after only a few dozen lines he is immersed in the anxious world again; indeed, the act of contemplating escape contributes to that immersion. In this respect Dryden's Lucretius resembles Dryden himself, who always seems to revert to satire though he may be forced to shift its direction. The parallel between Dryden and the thought processes of his speaker again implies that Dryden is not just letting a pagan philosopher reveal his own limits.

Though the five selections at first seem an epitome of the whole book, Dryden omits everything Lucretius says – a considerable amount – about the perception of beauty; he omits the concept of 'swerve,' and he leaves out the genuine philosophy, like the distinction between primary and secondary qualities, and the account of idols detaching themselves from real objects. The longest sections are 'Against the Fear of Death' and 'Concerning the Nature of Love'; sexual love thus appears to be a form of escapism when seen against the background of anxiety in the selection from Book III. The speaker loses his confident voice, just as Moeris became hoarse when he responded to life, and projects instead a kind of bravado:

> Though Earth in Seas, and Seas in Heav'n were lost,
> We shou'd not move, we only shou'd be tost.
> Nay, ev'n suppose when we have suffer'd Fate,
> The Soul cou'd feel in her divided state,
> What's that to us? for we are only we
> While Souls and bodies in one frame agree. ('Against the Fear of Death,' 13–18)

The speaker is not reassured by the thought that personal identity is transient. But 'soul' disappears altogether in the selection on love. Sometimes parents fail to conceive a child because their bodies are ill-matched and no spiritual force exists to effect blending:

> The too Condens'd, unsould, unwieldly [sic] mass
> Drops short, nor carries to the destin'd place:
> Nor pierces to the parts, nor, though injected home,
> Will mingle with the kindly moisture of the womb.
> ('Concerning the Nature of Love,' 251–4)

There is nothing for human parents to 'infuse' or to 'inspire'; they are no more than their reproductive parts. Mechanistic human sex is a long way from the amorous rolls of the gods.

The shipwrecked child of the eighteen-line coda from Book V is less grotesque than one might expect from a mechanistic union, but one feels that, like Tristram Shandy, it has suffered heroic trials even before birth. All the struggles and self-deceptions of human life have only managed to produce a child who will inevitably die without the elaborate structures of civilization, though civilization will make the child as anxious as its parents. Dryden's arrangement concentrates our interest on the child's fate and on the improbability of a golden age. These lines present the golden age in negative form and in fact refer to the simple needs of animals:

They want no Rattles for their froward mood,
Nor Nurse to reconcile them to their food,
With broken words; nor Winter blasts they fear
Nor change their habits with the changing year:
Nor, for their safety, Citadels prepare;
Nor forge the wicked Instruments of War:
Unlabour'd Earth her bounteous treasure grants,
And Nature's lavish hands supply their common wants. (11–18)

This is the same kind of poetry of illusion as Dryden's 'Pollio.' Aesthetically the lines make a good stopping point; the tempest seems to have hurled the child at the feet of the comfortable philosopher of Book II and forced him to think about it. This time for consideration functions as a caesura between Lucretian love and the next poem, Theocritus's 'Epithalamium of Helen and Menelaus,' whose Spartan maidens seem as fated to disillusionment as the shipwrecked child itself.

THEOCRITUS, HORACE, AND DRYDEN'S SONGS

The three Theocritan idylls are a cycle in themselves, a historical epitome like *Ovid's Epistles*. The first, the 'Epithalamium,' is set in an age of innocence, but it is ironic because every reader knows that this marriage will precipitate the Trojan war. Theocritus, of course, was exploiting this irony,[28] but Dryden is writing so much later that the historical certainties are more depressing. The second idyll, 'The Despairing Lover,' has an urban setting. The third, 'Daphnis,' returns to the country, but the speaker recalls Paris's abduction of Helen as past history (1–4) and refers to Queen Elizabeth as a contemporary. Elizabeth is just enough in the past in Dryden's day to sustain an archaic tone. Despite the historical progress in this group the recurrence of rape (or ravishing, or seduction – it is always ambiguous) creates a fatalistic effect. The poems are also arranged according to the characters' rank. The first treats royalty, the second an anomalous kind of city people, and the third shepherds who proudly compare themselves to royalty. It is a descending pattern, with a witty return to the beginning.

All three poems concern 'inauspicious love' ('The Despairing Lover,' 1), contrasting it with the 'auspicious moment' of Venus and Mars's lovemaking in Dryden's translation of the beginning of the first book of Lucretius. There are several varieties of love, in and outside of marriage, but all have disastrous consequences; in 'The Despairing Lover' Dryden changed a homosexual relationship to a heterosexual one, with strikingly little effect on the quality of the emotions described. (Dryden might not have been reflecting his readers' tastes, but affirming his own. Creech left this poem as it was, and Rochester and Aphra Behn wrote on homosexual themes. There was at least a small audience for homosexuality.) In any case the rejected lover remains male and neither sex invariably victimizes the other. In the first two idylls women are responsible for disaster, though in 'The Despairing Lover' the cruel nymph is punished; in 'Daphnis' a man victimizes a woman and flatters himself that Helen was the lesser figure in *her* story.

The 'Twelve *Spartan* Virgins, noble, young, and fair' (1) who sing the 'Epithalamium' are as innocent of sex differences as of the Trojan war. They recall their own 'manly exercise' (41) and have a non-Lucretian view of sexuality:

> Betwixt two Sheets thou shalt enjoy her bare;
> With whom no *Grecian* Virgin can compare:
> So soft, so sweet, so balmy, and so fair.
> A boy, like thee, would make a Kingly line:
> But oh, a Girl, like her, must be divine. (33–7)

Far from being a return to innocence, this passage just underlines their naïvety. To the maidens Helen and Menelaus are a magical couple, at once children, rulers, and divinities. The maidens' only notion of conflict is that of games and competitions, in all of which Helen's superiority is accepted (54–62). They also delight in Hymen's metaphoric conquest:

> *Hymen*, oh *Hymen*, to thy Triumphs run,
> And view the mighty spoils thou hast in Battle won. (94–5)

This final couplet both recalls Venus's triumph and anticipates the future, the real battle of the Trojan war. The ideal moment expressed in the song lasts no longer than the song itself; the reader is precipitated into the future.

The 'Epithalamium' also suggests how much individuals exist in separate worlds. Not only do the lovers never unite in spirit, but the maidens are enclosed in a private world of their own. Still, their imagery is beautiful and open:

Rise in the morn; but oh before you rise,
Forget not to perform your morning Sacrifice.
We will be with you e're the crowing Cock
Salutes the light, and struts before his feather'd Flock. (90–3)

In contrast, the 'drooping Boy' (11) of 'The Despairing Lover' speaks to his mistress' locked doors (31). He bids farewell to her stony house (53–4), claims that she is descended from the stones out of which Pyrrha and Deucalion recreated the human race (37–8), and hangs himself by throwing 'a weighty Stone' over a beam (90). Theocritus's lover kicked a stone from under his feet; Dryden changes the image slightly to show how two masses will balance each other out. The idea that knowledge comes, if at all, through contact with the irreducibly physical world is borne out by the deaths of both lovers. In the act of hanging himself the lover makes the door fly open:

The bounce burst ope the door; the Scornful Fair
Relentless lookt, and saw him beat his quivering feet in Air. (96–7)

The Fair ignores this dance of death and goes dancing herself, but later, at the bath, a statue of the God of Love falls and crushes her. As in Mezentius's case, death by crushing is reserved for a person who has been removed from feeling.

The dialogue form of 'Daphnis' should, like repartee or rhyme itself, symbolize harmony between Daphnis and Chloris, but the poem also brings out the separation between the lovers, even though they have sexual intercourse during the poem. Chloris resists because she foresees the consequences of marriage and childbearing – 'You kick by day more than you kiss by night' (47) – but her image of the 'deadly pain' (50) of childbirth makes no impact on Daphnis. Chloris is always aware of the future, even when her body takes over, while Daphnis argues that all women are subject to the same fate. Their reactions to their own lovemaking show no emotional contact, although both call upon the gods:

Chlo.
Forgive thy handmaid (Huntress of the wood,)
I see there's no resisting flesh and blood!

Daph.
The noble deed is done; my Herds I'le cull;
Cupid, be thine a Calf, & *Venus*, thine a Bull. (112–15)

The gods themselves have an ambiguous role, since they are apparently willing to support either side; thus Diana, who should help women, is invoked by Daphnis:

> *Diana* cures the wounds *Lucina* made;
> Your Goddess is a Midwife by her Trade. (52–3)

Dryden's poem contains a whole pantheon of indifferent deities. Pan and Cupid are mentioned, and Dryden adds the God of Love, connecting this poem to the previous one. In general, the gods merely embody the characters' fantasies and the God of Love is present only because the poet says so:

> Thus did the happy Pair their love dispence
> With mutual joys, and gratifi'd their sense;
> The God of Love was there a bidden Guest;
> And present at his own Mysterious Feast.
> His azure Mantle underneath he spred,
> And scatter'd Roses on the Nuptial Bed;
> While folded in each others arms they lay,
> He blew the flames, and furnish'd out the play,
> And from their Foreheads wip'd the balmy sweat away.
> First rose the Maid and with a glowing Face,
> Her down cast eyes beheld her print upon the grass;
> Thence to her Herd she sped her self in haste:
> The Bridgroom started from his Trance at last,
> And pipeing homeward jocoundly he past. (120–33)

As in Dryden's other endings, art denies the very reality it describes. This pretty ending simply refuses to take into account Chloris's realistic anxieties about the future.

Dryden's imagery here is more idealized than Theocritus's, but his treatment of the lovers is more ironic; both are prisoners of their illusions. Daphnis, after his trance, no longer seems a conqueror and he was never a bridegroom, while Chloris's empty print recalls Lucretius on the illusory nature of love: Daphnis has loved an idol and not the substantial reality of another person. Dryden also uses political or legalistic words, of which 'Queen *Elizabeth*' (35) is only one example. Daphnis contrasts Paris's use of force with his own wish to get Chloris's 'free consent' (3); Chloris wants a 'jointure' and is offered a 'settlement as good as Law can make' (57, 59). These references localize the Doric, but they also tell us that Chloris is not in fact protected by law, though the letter of the law is on her side. Daphnis rejects force, but one cannot say that Chloris consents 'freely' to sleep with him, since she and her body are at odds. Chloris does not benefit from living in a civilized country, and Daphnis exploits the disjunction between public and private realms. Personal isolation subjects a woman to the rule of force, a theme which Dryden returns to in 'Sylvia the fair.'

The speakers of the Horatian poems all reject the disastrous involvements of Theocritus. Dryden's Horace is a poet of retreat, but that does not always mean of virtue and sincerity. Negative tones, the voice of a petty or a self-deprecating speaker, undermine magnificent images from nature. Dryden shifts key in astonishing ways, not wholly authorized by his original. Even his images present nature as an antagonist to human life, for nature is so violent, or at least indifferent, that retreat seems well-advised. The sublime is no home for man. The fourth poem of the sequence, 'Epod. 2d,' contains the most pleasing and Edenic images of all – 'He joyes to pull the ripen'd Pear, / And clustring Grapes with purple spread' (30–1) – but at the end they turn out to be only a merchant's fantasy which will never be realized because the speaker, Morecraft, is too engrossed in business to change his life. Morecraft's hypocrisy does not entirely undermine the three odes, but it develops out of them surprisingly well. The new perspective of the ending is, as before, ambiguous.

The first poem, 'Ode 3. Lib. I, Inscrib'd to the Earl of Roscomon, on his Intended Voyage to Ireland,' touches most directly upon heroic themes, as one can see by a comparison to *two* models. The Horatian original was addressed to Virgil, who sailed to Greece where he planned to revise the *Aeneid.* Virgil's sea journey is somehow equivalent to Aeneas's; writing, or completing, an epic is itself a heroic act because the poet must in an imaginative sense encounter the same dangers and uncertainties as his hero. Roscommon never went to Ireland and he died soon after Dryden wrote this poem, but his 'Essay on Translated Verse' made him a suitable analogue for Virgil, as both were literary guides and sources of inspiration, sailing into uncharted literary waters.

Dryden's second model is perhaps a surprising one, Andrew Marvell's 'An Horatian Ode,' recently published in the posthumous *Miscellaneous Poems* (1681). Marvell is not usually cited as a model for Dryden's lyrics, though one detects his tone in the garden imagery in 'Epod. 2d' and the theme of celibacy in Eden appears in both 'The Garden' and 'To My Honour'd Kinsman.' Marvell's 'Horatian Ode' was subtitled 'Upon Cromwell's Return from Ireland,' a much closer parallel to Dryden's subtitle than that of Horace's poem.[29] Marvell was primarily concerned with political and military heroism and Dryden with literary heroism, though one can make no rigid distinction: Marvell's poet/speaker questions his own life of retirement and Dryden's alternative to translation would probably have been political poetry. Also, because Cromwell had already demonstrated heroism, Marvell was in a better position than Dryden to explore its destructiveness. These contrasts are subtle, but the central problems of both poems are the same: will heroic action inevitably dehumanize the hero? Dryden writes:

> Sure he, who first the passage try'd,
> In harden'd Oak his heart did hide,
> And ribs of Iron arm'd his side! (13–15)[30]

With its reference to the proverbial British hearts of oak Dryden's poem gains some public significance, without singling out a specific individual as villain. The British character itself has this dubious kind of heroism, reminiscent of the overly daring Aeneas/Achitophel.

It is interesting that Dryden responds positively to Marvell at all, for they had been enemies during the *Rehearsal* controversy, with opposed political and religious allegiances which Marvell channeled into resentment over Dryden's adaptation of *Paradise Lost* as an opera.[31] During the 1670s Dryden would have known Marvell only as the prose satirist who attacked Anglican authoritarianism in *The Rehearsal Transpros'd*, and possibly as the political poet who had celebrated Cromwell on various occasions. Dryden, like everyone else of his time, could have read the lyrics only after Marvell died, reversing the order in which modern readers usually come to know Marvell's work. However, Marvell's lyrics reveal an uncertainty about political engagement that is not essentially different from Dryden's own feelings at this time, for his treatment of the theme transcends political or even religious allegiance. On this level Dryden and Marvell are not hopelessly opposed. A further shift in Dryden's response to Marvell can be found slightly later, in *The Hind and the Panther.* The Hind's attack on King Buzzard, who is usually identified with Gilbert Burnet, contains a cluster of verbal parallels to *The Rehearsal Transpros'd*;[32] these are hard to explain unless we note that Dryden was satirizing an Anglican clergyman on much the same grounds that Marvell had satirized Samuel Parker. Dryden apparently decided that Marvell had been right about the bishops' lust for power and used the device of an allusive cluster to say so.

Marvell found compensation for Cromwell's destructiveness in his civilizing activity. Cromwell's subjects needed him, for they were too frightened to wield the sword themselves; Marvell sees the military man as no worse than the people who can accept butchery when someone else, a leader, a scapegoat, performs it on their behalf. Yet Marvell, like Horace and Dryden, wonders at the hero's ability to endure suffering, since heroic endurance implies a dangerous indifference to feeling. Horace and Marvell withhold judgment. Dryden does not exactly attack the hero, but his suspicions are more in evidence; his hero is just a bit Satanic:

No toyl, no hardship can restrain
Ambitious Man inur'd to pain;
The more confin'd, the more he tries,
And at forbidden quarry flies. (34–7)

Yet Horace, like Dryden, says that the man so ready to confront 'monsters rolling in the deep' (25) will become monstrous himself, a monster of indifference, composed of iron and wood. The poem is consistent with Dido's view of Aeneas's character though it transcends her personal involvement.

Marvell avoids Christian associations in 'An Horatian Ode,' ending with an image of 'The spirits of the shady night' (118), the psychic darkness that Cromwell may not yet have investigated in himself. Dryden's vocabulary is never openly Christian, but 'forbidden quarry' (37) has Christian associations and Nature has the character of a god:

In vain did Natures wise command,
Divide the Waters from the Land,
If daring Ships, and Men prophane,
Invade th' inviolable Main. (28–31)

Dryden's Hercules and Daedalus, exploring the forbidden regions of hell and air, are somewhat frenetic (48–51) and Dryden ignores a pun in the original that moderates Prometheus's aggressiveness. Horace names him 'Iapeti,' linking him to 'Iapyx,' a favourable wind, while Dryden simply writes 'soft *Etesian* Gales' (6) and 'bold *Prometheus*' (38). However, the obscurity of 'Iapeti' could explain Dryden's change, and Dryden's oxymoron, 'soft gales,' shows an effort to avoid simple judgments. Dryden's last couplet blames human beings for provoking divine wrath. The pronoun 'we' once again links poet and hero:

We reach at *Jove*'s Imperial Crown,
And pull the unwilling thunder down. (54–5)

Although 'Ode 3' is thus a warning, it does not quite urge the artist to avoid the unknown. In 'Alexander's Feast,' St Cecilia draws an angel down in nearly the same language. She is hardly Satanic, yet she might be considered Promethean, and the difference may ultimately depend upon the individual artist's character.

'Lib. I. Ode 9' and 'Ode 29. Book 3' both present the pleasures of retreat in terms of a hedonistic Epicureanism. Both poems enact the same degenerative process, spacious images of nature giving way to images of darkness and confinement. In each case the speaker of the poem sees nature as if through a window. The speaker of 'Ode 9,' who declares 'Behold yon' Mountains hoary height / Made higher with new Mounts of Snow' (1–2), admits that the sheer mass of the snow places nature in 'Icy Fetters' (5), while he himself is safely indoors, enjoying the fire, thinking of wine and 'sprightly Wit and Love' (10). 'Ode 29' is addressed to 'the Right Honourable Lawrence Earl of Rochester' (Horace had addressed Maecenas), so the poem cannot be totally ironic; yet the speaker seems bored, asking his friend to leave 'The nauseous pleasures of the Great' (14) and enjoy 'A short vicissitude, and fit of Poverty' (23). Horace offers no precedent for this kind of diction, which foreshadows the hypocrisy of Morecraft. Both poems recapitulate the structure of *Religio Laici*, beginning magnificently, in some of the best poetry Dryden ever wrote, deteriorating to small-minded nastiness. It seems that beauty can exist only if no hard questions are asked about reality.

The impulse to retreat begins relatively well but leads to darkness or self-imposed limitations. 'Ode 9' is about the pleasures of youth, or perhaps an older man's attempt to retrieve 'those golden early joyes, / That Youth unsowr'd with sorrow bears' (25–6). Horace's poem is directed to a young man; Dryden's is coloured by the sour consciousness of maturity. The last stanza retreats to a 'pleasing whisper in the dark' (33) and a sexual encounter. 'Ode 9' makes one question the pleasures available either to youth or to age, for the safe pleasures involve an escape from vision.

There is even a retreat from motion when one moves from one poem to the next. 'Ode 3' at least imagined a real journey, but 'Ode 9' urges a youth to stand still and 'snatch the pleasures passing by' (21), and 'Ode 29' recommends a negative journey, *away* from business, city life, and real activity. The sublimity of the fifth stanza of 'Ode 29' may conceal the fact that even nature undergoes an entropic process:

> The Sun is in the Lion mounted high;
> The *Syrian* Star
> Barks from a far;
> And with his sultry breath infects the Sky;
> The ground below is parch'd, the heav'ns above us fry.

The Shepheard drives his fainting Flock,
Beneath the covert of a Rock;
And seeks refreshing Rivulets nigh:
The *Sylvans* to their shades retire,
Those very shades and streams, new shades and streams require;
And want a cooling breeze of wind to fan the rageing fire. (29–39)

Retreat and contemplation are probably better than the purposeless action of nature itself; at least they can be absorbed into the realm of art. Stanza 7 presents a mechanistic nature in which objects are reduced to masses displaying their own unthinking face – the Epicurean sublime:

And trunks of Trees come rowling down,
Sheep and their Folds together drown:
Both House and Homested into Seas are borne,
And Rocks are from their old foundations torn,
And woods made thin with winds, their scatter'd honours mourn. (60–4)

In context these lines come from an extended metaphor for the 'tide of bus'ness' (52) and not from a description of nature.[33] Horace's simile is shorter and is an image for the river of life. Dryden's expansion helps to make his ode more Pindaric (an intention stated in his subtitle), but the change in the meaning of the simile sustains the theme of his characters' worldliness.

The irony leads inexorably to a small-minded voice at the end who rejects 'malicious' fortune: 'I puff the Prostitute away' (73, 84). The prostitute image looks back to 'Ode 9'; a reference to a 'greedy Merchant' (92) looks ahead to Morecraft. The Pindaric experiment ends with an image of a complacent mariner who refuses to sail:

What is't to me,
Who never sail in her unfaithful Sea,
If Storms arise, and Clouds grow black? (88–90)

In his 'small Pinnace' he turns inward, to 'some little winding Creek' (99, 103) from which he can watch the storm in safety. This conclusion is Dryden's. Horace's sailor remains at sea, for his philosophy has taught him how to survive the inevitable risks of life. I do not see Dryden as revealing Horace's subliminal cowardice, because Horace in fact wants someone, if not himself, to undertake that heroic sea journey, and he tries to show how the moderate man can achieve his own kind of heroism. Dryden's main antagonists were not the ancients, but he is using Horace's poems as a point of reference, from which he can develop his own views of social man. He replaces the sea journey with the dubious risk-taking of merchant and politician, and he constructs throughout an image of the worldly man who cannot respond to the attractions of heroism.

'Epod. 2d.' begins with the familiar rubric: 'How happy in his low degree.' Not till the end is all revealed as Morecraft's fantasy, by which time the reader has probably been induced to share it. This poetic deception need not invalidate the image of a golden age, for almost any philosophy can be threatened by giving it to an inappropriate speaker; in his Chaucer and Boccaccio translations Dryden has several speakers whose ideas are better than their personal characters. The assumption that speech is always a product of a speaker's character does not always work in reading Dryden's poetry, and in the case of 'Epod. 2d.' one can only read the poem both ways, with two possible attitudes towards the life of retreat remaining in suspension.

Of course the effect of the poem changes after one has learned who the speaker is. Morecraft's paradise now seems to fulfill the impulse to entropy in the two preceding poems:

Sometimes beneath an ancient Oak,
    Or on the matted grass he lies;
No God of Sleep he need invoke,
    The stream that o're the pebbles flies
    With gentle slumber crowns his Eyes. (36–40)

The sea imagery of the earlier odes is sustained. Morecraft rejects 'the dangers of the deep' (13), even giving up fish caught during rolling tempests (76); he is protected during winter and enjoys a small-scale nature that he can readily imagine as pleasing. His pleasure in hunting can be seen as a sublimated urge to violence,[34] though hunting is characterized as one of the 'harmless easie joys' (54) that he decides to settle for. The problem in reading this poem, whether in Horace's or in Dryden's version, is like deciding whether Milton's Eden was corrupt before the fall because so many of his images show it as tending to be wild. One does not read descriptions of Eden with an innocent eye but projects one's own assumptions about human evil on to the poet's ambiguous language.

The artistic trickery of 'Epod. 2d.' also links it to Dryden's conclusions to his selections from Virgil, Lucretius, and Theocritus. In all cases an idealized poetic image is demonstrably at odds with the human reality constructed by the group of poems as a whole. It is as if human beings are too petty to live out the ideals they can conceive, while artists compromise by transforming the ideal into an image and deciding to ignore its lack of congruity with real life. The Epicurean artist would accept this lack of congruity, having achieved beauty and order within his own work. Dryden's double endings, however, show that he was disturbed by the conflict between art and life and by the possible hypocrisy of detachment. Two possible responses to the conflict – the pleasures and the anxieties of detachment – are left unresolved by the structure of *Sylvae*.

Dryden's songs work as punctuation marks, closing *Sylvae* by recapitulating its major themes. The full weight of the translations resonates behind them, making them far more effective when read as elements in 'a structure of structures' than when read alone. 'A New Song' ('Sylvia the fair') is about the rape or seduction of a fifteen-year-old girl as seen from her point of view, the feminine viewpoint reversing Theocritus's 'Daphnis.' At the same time Sylvia's youth links her to the Spartan maidens and even to the isolated Lucretian child. She hardly seems to understand what is happening to her and at first experiences men's advances, more or less, as pleasure: Epicurean 'knowledge' has impact only when encountered physically, and it is impact indeed. As in 'Daphnis' there is a contemporary English setting:

Ah she cry'd, ah for a languishing Maid
In a Country of Christians to die without aid!
Not a Whig, or a Tory, or Trimmer at least,
Or a Protestant Parson, or Catholick Priest,
To instruct a young Virgin, that is at a loss
What they meant by their sighing, & kissing so close! (12–17)

The passage is interesting for the range of sects and parties that Dryden condemns alike and for the fact that religious sects are condemned as if they were parties. From Sylvia's point of view their activity might as well be non-activity, since they neither teach her to avoid danger nor rescue her after she has encountered it. Their failure is partly responsible for Sylvia's isolation; it is not just a consequence of her juvenile epistemology. At the end, however, Sylvia obtains what she feels is godlike pleasure and knowledge of the one sort that is available to her.

The second song, 'Go tell Amynta gentle Swain,' offsets the sexual theme with a response to art. This song has a male speaker who asks a musician to use his 'tuneful Voice' to woo Amynta on his behalf. The lovers either have no voice or 'dare not' speak (8), but music may succeed in joining them. Whatever the value of the artist's function here, the poet still uses art to compensate for the deficiencies of life, though contributing to sexual pleasure leaves unresolved the larger problems implied by 'Sylvia the fair.' Art itself may do no more than provide a rarefied sort of sexual pleasure. The two songs in effect leave *Sylvae* unresolved. One is negative but seems to urge the reader, who must be more aware than Sylvia, to consider social problems; the other holds out a promise of happiness, though the lover continues to languish. Both fear and hope are qualified by their opposites.

The frame of *Sylvae* is thus not firmly closed. One feels rather that the energy of the sequence has played itself out, as if Dryden preferred to avoid a decisive ending which would falsify the uncertainties of real life. I return to the point I made before, that Dryden's critique of Epicureanism was not that of a Christian secure in his superiority to struggling pagans like Virgil and Horace. 'Sylvia the fair' alone suggests that the materialistic pagan world was analogous, not opposed, to Dryden's own; history was repeating itself. *Sylvae* provides a multifaceted response to the social and psychological implications of materialism. If Dryden had not felt that his contemporaries were taken in by a lightweight version of Epicureanism, his emotional involvement might have been less.

5

Examen Poeticum: Dryden against His Age

Examen Poeticum (1693) continues to display an interest in Epicureanism, but by now the contributors generally seem conscious of its limits from the Christian point of view, especially its failure to provide consolation for the fear of death. One finds, not so much a critique of Epicureanism, but an effort to absorb it into a Christian perspective; that is, the Christian belief in God and the afterlife are superimposed on an Epicurean sense of awe in reacting to the void. *The Annual Miscellany: For the Year 1694* is far more disorganized than *Examen Poeticum*, but it contains much political poetry (something generally absent in the 1693 volume) all of it Williamite. In *Examen Poeticum*, where the religion of the poets is at issue, one senses how atypical Dryden was with respect to his contemporaries – he seems much less troubled by a fear of emptiness and he displays an interest in miracles, even in the possibility of a miraculous transformation of nature, all of which he expresses through the pieces he selected from Ovid's *Metamorphoses*. Nevertheless, Dryden created a collective poem, a genre that interested his contemporaries. Some of the other poems in both miscellanies also imply that Dryden was under an insidious kind of pressure to go along with, agree with, the majority who felt that William and Mary were sponsoring a major cultural revival. (After the pessimism of the 1680s much could be said for this view: at least the poets display optimism.) Finally, one discovers that Dryden did not have the option of remaining completely silent, even if he had wanted or been able to afford to do so. As the major poet of his age he was expected to write on subjects of public interest, like everyone else, and his failure to do so would have been almost as conspicuous as the expression of an unpopular opinion.

For *Examen Poeticum* Dryden translated Book I of the *Metamorphoses*, 'The Fable of Iphis and Ianthe' from Book IX, and 'The Fable of Acis,

Polyphemus, and Galatea' from Book XIII. These were his first published translations from Ovid's major poem though, as I have said, he had been privately choosing his favourite passages since at least 1666. Dryden did not include his 1693 translations in *Fables.* If nothing else, this shows that he planned his selections for each occasion and they were not random selections from a given poet. Dryden's 1693 translations of Ovid have a positive and glowing tone, like that of a Shakespearean romance, and in some ways recall the good humour of *Love Triumphant.* Acis in particular recalls *The Tempest* because he undergoes a sea-change; Galatea's inhuman detachment (she is a nymph, not a mortal woman) recalls Ariel's; and Isis's role as reconciler in 'Iphis and Ianthe' can be compared either to Hermione's in *The Winter's Tale* or to Ximena's in *Love Triumphant.*

The glowing Ovid is an aberration for Dryden. The preface to 'Annus Mirabilis' shows a taste for the darker, self-destructive passions, and the selections in *Fables*, which include heroic material as well as explorations of the passions, also seem darker than *Examen Poeticum*, with the possible exceptions of 'Pygmalion' and 'Baucis and Philemon,' though even these have ironic overtones. In *Fables* Dryden manages to make even Ovid political; in 1693, however, Ovid seems to have no political relevance whatsoever. In *Fables* the glow of the 1693 Ovid is transferred to Chaucer, who is in turn distorted by Dryden's rejection of the darker or bawdier possibilities among the *Canterbury Tales.* His 1693 Ovid emphasizes the themes of regeneration in nature, beneficent female power, and the possibility of real contact with the divine. One thread in Ovid's *Metamorphoses* is humanity's search for an epiphany; Dryden picked up that, ignoring the heroic or mock-heroic themes. This represents a nobler Ovid than the poet of the elegies and possibly even of *Fables*, since the *Metamorphoses* is epitomized as a religious epic.

Examen Poeticum reprints some of Dryden's earlier poems. In addition to the translations of Ovid, he also contributed the dedication, a translation of 'The Last parting of Hector and Andromache' from the *Iliad*, and three original poems: 'Song to a Fair, Young Lady, Going out of the Town in the Spring,' 'Veni Creator Spiritus, Translated in Paraphrase,' and 'Rondelay.' These three poems do not comprise a real sequence, though they are all concerned with love and death, or with the question of whether love is powerful enough to overcome death. 'Hector and Andromache' is linked not to Dryden's other poems but to two other pieces from the *Iliad*, both concerning Hector's death, translated by Dryden's new friend William Congreve. The 'Song' and 'Veni Creator Spiritus' are related to each other through a few verbal links, and the two shorter Ovid selections clearly belong together.[1] Their relationship to 'The First Book of Ovid's Metamorphoses' is less obvious, but Book I introduces Isis under the guise of Io, and Isis's presence is felt even in 'Acis,' so that she is a linking figure. In so far as all the poems, original and translated, deal with the regenerative power of love, they are related; but this does not quite make them an integrated whole. 'Hector and Andromache,' though, has an ironic connection to the rest, since Andromache's love is not powerful enough to keep Hector from going out to fight and be killed. This is appropriate, since the *Iliad* is a poem of force:

> For *Homer* ... can move rage better than he can pity: He stirs up the irascible appetite, as our Philosophers call it, he provokes to Murther, and the destruction of God's Images; he forms and equips those ungodly Man-killers, whom we Poets, when we flatter them, call Heroes; a race of Men who can never enjoy quiet in themselves, 'till they have taken it from all the World. This is *Homer*'s Commendation, and such as it is, the Lovers of Peace, or at least of more moderate Heroism, will never Envy him. (IV, 374)

Thus Dryden wrote in his dedication. The *tender* Homer, which Dryden and Congreve constructed, was very selective indeed.

Examen Poeticum lacks the unity of tone and concept that makes *Miscellany Poems* and *Sylvae* successful as books. It contains some translations from Catullus, Ovid's *Elegies*, and Horace but has a much higher proportion of original work by new writers – not only Congreve, but also Addison, Prior, Granville, and a few others of lesser note. It is here that Jacob Tonson announced his design to publish an annual miscellany, '*after I have procur'd some Stock to proceed upon*,' and to preserve in print '*ev'ry Choice Copy that appears; whereas I have known several Celebrated Pieces so utterly lost in three or four years time after they were written, as not to be recoverable by all the search I cou'd make after 'em*.'[2] (In fact, only *The Annual Miscellany: For the Year 1694* appeared before Dryden's death.) However, the higher proportion of original work to translation does not in itself produce a better book, and *Examen Poeticum* seems to me disorganized. Tonson's laudable desire to preserve contemporary poetry has produced a corresponding randomness in organization.

Nevertheless, some unity was produced by the similar assumptions and experiences of the other contributors, and Dryden inevitably was excluded from it. If there is any relationship between his contributions and the other poetry in both the miscellanies of this period, it is one of opposition, or of reserved contempt, though the contempt does not show directly: one feels only that Dryden's silence on political subjects proves his utter indifference to political poetry, and his emphasis on love and regeneration his desire to move away from the values ordinarily enforced by epic. It is pertinent here that William's military exploits were considered matter for the national epic that had yet to be written, although there was some doubt about whether anyone could rise to the occasion, and Mary's female virtues and her ability to rule in her husband's absence became the basis for a complementary feminine ideal. Until Mary's death the royal couple were regarded as complementary examples of civilized virtue.

There seems to have been real pressure for poets to write on public themes, even if a national epic (probably centred on a historical figure like Arthur, who could stand for William through an easy process of historical allegory) could not be produced on demand. In the mean time odes had to suffice. No one expected a Tate or a Stepney to write an epic, but Dryden, as the poet uniquely qualified to do so, was conspicuous by his absence from the chorus of praise and by his unwillingness to forget his differences with the new regime. Dryden thus failed in his effort to adopt a strategy of silence, though even his silence was only relative, for the attack on Homer quoted above might well be an indirect blast at the poets who flattered William and not a value-free statement on the merits of epic as a literary form. The pressure to write epic or at least public poetry would account for the hostility that Dryden revealed in the passage and for the tone of irritability that is apparent throughout the dedication, since this pressure had been directed quite unambiguously against Dryden on several occasions for almost a decade. For instance, 'Urania's Temple: or, a Satyr upon the Silent Poets' (1695) comments nastily upon the 'sullen Knot of *Tongue-tied Sons*' who wrote nothing on Mary's death; though Dryden is not named, the satirist uses recognizable images from *MacFlecknoe* (pp 4–5), which suffice to bring Dryden to mind. This type of allusion must have qualified as direct speech in 1695.

Elsewhere it was implied that Dryden was at fault for his stubbornness, that he was responsible for his own exile and would have been received back into the fold if only he had let himself be persuaded. Charles Montagu in 'An Epistle to the Right Honourable Charles, Earl of Dorset' (first published in 1690) sought a poet great enough for the times:

> But who is equal to sustain the Part!
> *D--n* has Numbers: But he wants a Heart;
> Enjoyn'd a Penance (which is too severe
> For playing once the Fool) to Persevere.[3]

In 1697 this poem was republished in a brief collection by Nahum Tate, dedicated to Sir Robert Howard, in which Howard is praised for 'shewing the World, that a Poet can likewise be a *Statesman* and *Patriot* of his Country.'[4] Given the fact that Howard and Dryden were brothers-in-law, Tate's dedication implies some failure on Dryden's part to emulate his brother-in-law and, no doubt, to surpass him, considering Dryden's superior talents. It also shows just how long this suspicion about Dryden's silence endured. (In 1699 he was still being attacked for his failure to write on the death of the Earl of Abingdon, Eleonora's husband. William Pittis accuses Dryden of indifference to the public and wonders that his resentment should have persisted so long.)[5] Tate's collection centres on the Marquis of Normanby's *Essay on Poetry* (first published in 1682), which in some ways reads like a sketch of Pope's *Essay on Criticism*, though it is really a truncated imitation of Boileau's *L'Art poétique*; it is organized around the hierarchy of genres, which culminate at the level of Parnassus in epic.[6] For Pope the poet's difficulties just begin at this point, with the decision to write ambitiously. One can more readily appreciate Pope's conciliatory stance in the *Essay on Criticism* if we see that the general admiration for epic had so recently been exploited both to flatter William and to attack Dryden, who was Pope's model, not only as a great writer, but as a Catholic poet who survived hostile political conditions. In this context Dryden's dedication of the *Aeneis*, addressed to Normanby himself and beginning 'A Heroick Poem, truly such, is undoubtedly the greatest Work which the Soul of Man is capable to perform' (K, III, 1003), appears sardonic, especially since Dryden goes on to explain precisely when and why a poet may not be able to write as he likes. Dryden's opening line virtually paraphrases Normanby's conclusion and the dedication gives a personal dimension to the endlessly repeated clichés about the difficulties of epic composition.

Dryden's quarrel with his age rose to the surface in the *Annual Miscellany: For the Year 1694*, where Joseph Addison tried to conciliate Dryden in his progress piece, 'An Account of the Greatest English Poets.' Addison presents English literary history as culminating in the reign of William and the poetry of Dryden, as if William had somehow made Dryden's writing possible. This is either monumentally tactless, if one could imagine Addison to be ignorant of Dryden's situation, or, more likely, a calculated attempt to portray Dryden as less disaffected than he really was and thus to convince him that he was needed, that his friends would make the first overtures.[7] But Dryden remained stiff-necked. The *Annual Miscellany* also contains his own progress piece, 'To Sir Godfrey Kneller,' in which he dwells upon the failure of their age to appreciate either Kneller or himself (100–1, 115–19).[8]

Addison must have written his poem in response to Dryden's, to imply that it was Dryden's fault if he insisted on being alienated, though it is barely possible that Dryden was reacting to the assumption that he could easily be conciliated.

One may be convinced that pure literary criticism (divorced from political overtones) scarcely existed at this time. The plan for an Arthurian epic that Dryden outlined in the 'Discourse of Satire' is not only (maybe not even primarily) a statement of personal ambition but an outline for a non-Williamite epic on a subject that would be patriotic without forcing the author either to praise or to satirize William's glory. Dryden, trying to redirect the usual emphasis on literature and politics to literature and religion, focuses on the problem of accommodating epic machines to a Christian poem.[9] However, Dryden failed even in this attempt. One can sympathize with his anger when Sir Richard Blackmore stole his Arthurian plan, since Blackmore used Arthur to stand for William. John Dennis, although he was pro-Williamite, also considered Blackmore a miserable writer and insisted that Blackmore's party line did nothing to improve his poetry. Dennis thus held out for what he called a 'poetical criticism,' commentaries based on literary merit only instead of political criticism that sought to detect a thinly disguised allegory and that crudely evaluated literature on the basis of the writer's politics.[10] The other poets of the period either attempted political readings, sought them in the works of others, or felt pressured to take them into account – as even Dryden did when he was trying hardest to avoid politics.

Dryden's emphasis on the feminine in his Ovid translations can be seen as a tactful attempt to stay within the range of interests established by his contemporaries while treating the subject apolitically. Female power was undeniably of interest at this time because of the very existence of the joint rule of William and Mary and because of the fact that Mary indeed helped William to govern England. Isis, however, is a purely religious power, and she not only lacks a corresponding male to complete her, so that there is no easy balance of the two sexes, but she actually transcends masculine power and reveals its inherent defects. The stereotype of complementary ideals appears in George Stepney's 'Poem Dedicated to the Blessed Memory of her late Gracious Majesty Queen Mary' (1695):

Grace and mild Mercy best in Her were shown,
In him the rougher Vertues of the Throne;
Of Justice *She* at home the *Ballance* held,
Abroad, Oppression by *His Sword* was quell'd;

True Emblems of the *Lyon*, and the *Dove*;
The God of Battel, and the Queen of Love
Did in Their happy Nuptials well agree;
Like *Mars*, He led our Armies out, and She
With Smiles presided o're Her Native Sea! (P 4)[11]

One recalls that Dryden's apology to 'the fair Sex' in his argument to Juvenal's sixth satire was published in the same year as *Examen Poeticum*. The ambivalence towards woman expressed in the conflict between the argument and the poem must have been intensified by the fact that Mary was the archetypal strong woman of the 1690s.

Dryden several times uses the masculine-feminine theme in his own poetry and on every occasion but one it implies some failure on the part of William and Mary. That one exception is his praise of Anne Killigrew, who could paint both a 'Martial King' and the 'matchless Grace' of a queen (III, 113). Presumably Anne had the ideal to paint from, and for her the reign of James really was a joint rule. In 1690 Dryden parodied the idea in his prologue to *The Prophetess*, which was considered offensive and not allowed to be spoken a second time. Here, the 'bright Beauties' in the audience of a half-empty theatre mourn the absence of their 'doughty Knights,' fighting with King William in Ireland (III, 255–6, 507n). Obviously the poem appeared to mock the queen's loneliness as well. This prologue undoubtedly showed Dryden what he could not say, but the motif retained a metaphorical value through which he could more subtly reject William and Mary. In 'To my Dear Friend Mr. Congreve' (1693; IV, 432–4) Dryden simply attributes to *The Double-Dealer* the combined virtues usually linked with the two rulers or the two sexes:

Firm *Dorique* Pillars found Your solid Base:
The Fair *Corinthian* Crowns the higher Space;
Thus all below is Strength, and all above is Grace. (17–19)

In other words, who needs William and Mary if one can write and appreciate good literature? Since Congreve was a Whig, Dryden's image has even more point in showing one poet's effort to create a relationship based on literature, not politics.

In the paired panegyrics of *Fables*, 'To Her Grace the Dutchess of Ormond' and 'To my Honour'd Kinsman, John Driden' (K, IV, 1463–7, 1529–35), feminine and masculine are once again made political. The Duchess, for example, is a nearly messianic figure who brings peace to a troubled Ireland (where her husband was lieutenant-governor):

> The Waste of Civil Wars, their Towns destroy'd,
> *Pales* unhonour'd, *Ceres* unemploy'd,
> Were all forgot; and one Triumphant Day
> Wip'd all the Tears of three Campaigns away.
> Blood, Rapines, Massacres, were cheaply bought,
> So might Recompence Your Beauty brought. (64–9)

By implication the Duchess has made up for the harm done by William himself, since William was responsible for the disasters mentioned in these lines. By contrast, Driden of Chesterton is capable of enacting a heroic sort of justice for the sake of protecting his flocks:

> With well-breath'd Beagles, you surround the Wood;
> Ev'n then, industrious of the Common Good:
> And often have you brought the wily Fox
> To suffer for the Firstlings of the Flocks;
> Chas'd ev'n amid the Folds; and made to bleed,
> Like Felons, where they did the murd'rous Deed. (52–7)

The Duchess and Driden thus have qualities much like those associated with Queen Mary and King William: because they are treated as complementary, simultaneously mythic and political in significance, we see the Duchess of Ormonde and Driden as the joint potential saviours of British culture. The conventional vocabulary of praise has simply been transferred to a new subject, in one case to another Mary, since the Duchess's name was in fact Mary Somerset and she seems to exist in a private world, although she may still produce a son to preserve her family's name. Interestingly the isolation of Dryden's two figures – the Duchess is separated from her husband and Driden is celibate – parallels both Mary's loneliness when *her* husband went to Ireland and William's well-attested isolation in the six years after the death of his wife. Courage in isolation was one part of the panegyric convention of complementary masculine and feminine ideals.

The religious poetry of *Examen Poeticum* is striking for its obsession with death and, if we contrast the book to *Miscellany Poems*, its indifference to sexual escapism. Christian poets seem to have succeeded in defining themselves or their situation in contrast to the pagan's inevitable terror of death and the unknown. For instance, Matthew Prior's poem on Dr Sherlock's 'Practical Discourse concerning Death' says that Sherlock had succeeded where Lucretius failed. Readers of Sherlock

> Shall look to Heav'n, and laugh at all beneath,
> Own Riches gather'd Trouble; Fame, a breath;
> And Life an Ill, whose only Cure is Death.[12]

There is 'A Song by *My Ld.* R.' on the theme of being 'lost in endless Night.' 'Lord R.' is probably Edward Radclyffe, certainly not Rochester, but one wonders if the author or the editor felt that the initial would attract attention by suggesting Rochester's name, as it certainly does to the modern reader.[13] *Examen Poeticum* also contains many poems on the deaths of specific persons: John Selden, the Lady Elizabeth Seymour, Hector, King Charles II, and several others. Dryden's ode to Anne Killigrew is reprinted.

Thomas Yalden, an important contributor, was drawn to the combined subjects of death and cosmic awe. He wrote 'A Hymn to Darkness' which superficially resembles Rochester's poem 'Upon Nothing':

> DARKNESS, thou first kind Parent of us all,
> Thou art our great Original:
> Since from thy Universal Womb,
> Does all thou shad'st below, thy numerous Offspring come.[14]

However, Yalden has none of Rochester's irony; this might be a kind of sacred parody. In fact, Yalden's style anticipates Blackmore's creation poems and ultimately the poetry of Pope's dunces. Dryden's 'Song for St. Cecilia's Day,' also reprinted here,[15] is not out of place, since the conception of 'jarring Atoms' producing a 'Universal Frame' is another variation on the idea of Christian Epicureanism. *Examen Poeticum* includes some love poems, but instead of glorifying the self-congratulatory rake they present love as a quasi-religious force, as does Dryden's 'Song to a Fair, Young Lady.' There is also a translation of the section on the force of love from Virgil's third Georgic, where Virgil has imitated Lucretius (Dryden's version appeared the next year). Dryden's Ovid translations sustain the religious theme while ignoring or rejecting the gloom of the other contributors. The Ovidian epic of creation is *not* entropic.

Dryden's Ovid appears to show the operation of grace in nature, grace being channelled through a female deity. Book I in itself traces a complete cosmic cycle from Jove's destruction of the human race in punishment for

Lycaon's sins to humanity's subsequent rebirth; all this is followed by several tales of a god's love for a mortal woman, each of whom is transformed to a higher state. The last of these, Io, first suffers because Jove changes her into a heifer to protect her from Juno, but she ends as a priestess in Egypt. 'Iphis and Ianthe' and 'Acis, Polyphemus, and Galatea' are both love stories in which a goddess effects a hitherto impossible union; in 'Iphis' a human marriage occurs and in 'Acis' a transcendent union between immortals, so that the selections provide a contrast as well as a similarity in theme. The two shorter poems appear to be set in a realm of grace and the reader is brought ever closer to the immortal's point of view, for the last poem is narrated by Galatea, who seems unable even to understand death and thus is not disturbed by it.

'The First Book of Ovid's Metamorphoses' shows Jove's power yielding to a feminine principle and also recapitulates the pattern of Christian history, in which the Old Testament God of wrath yields to a merciful deity who offers the possibility of redemption. Dryden's Jove is a god of power, vengeance, and 'Indignation' (234) who inspires fear even among the other Olympians. Though his vengeance upon the murderer Lycaon is just (Jove changes him into a wolf), his reactions seem overdone, almost absurd, as in his pompous attack on mankind:

Mankind's a Monster, and th' Ungodly times
Confed'rate into guilt, are sworn to Crimes.
All are alike involv'd in ill, and all
Must by the same relentless Fury fall. (322–5)

Dryden's Ovidian puns on 'all' and 'ill' bring out the element of parody and make Jove's ability as divine ruler suspect. Jove's theology – punishing the race for the sin of one man – seems to be a primitive and overly enthusiastic version of the fall. Jove reassures the Olympian sycophants in lofty phrase – 'Mine be the care' (339) – but he is insecure about the limits of his own action: 'And what he durst not burn, resolves to drown' (354). Dryden's phrase 'a Watry Deluge' (353) also suggests a Christian analogy, but the most conspicuous witty anachronism, a comparison of Jove's court to a palace that 'I dare to call the *Loovre* of the Skie' (227) is really a joke at the expense of George Sandys, who had compared the palace to Whitehall.[16] The 'I's of Dryden's translations are often problematic in their reference, deliberately so in some places, but here at least two of the possible men behind the pronoun, Dryden and Ovid, agree that Jove works so hard at his role of tyrant of the skies that he fails to be convincing. Sandys must have found Jove wonderful if he compared him to an English king; Dryden jokingly pretends that a tyrant would have to be French.

Lycaon's sin is that of Thyestes. He murders a legate, cooks the human body, and serves 'the mangl'd Morsels in a Dish' to Jove (300), who has secretly been touring the world. This is not only murder and potential cannibalism but also a blasphemous perversion of the Eucharist. By Dryden's standards Lycaon is so extreme a case of the butcher-hero whom Dryden attacked in his preface, enjoying 'the destruction of God's Images' (IV, 374) and then displaying the result to Jove himself, that he seems almost Satanic. Dryden's intentions are sufficiently clear, for his description of Lycaon as a wolf is expanded from Ovid and recalls one of his own beast descriptions in *The Hind and the Panther*:

> He grows a Wolf, his hoariness remains,
> And the same rage in other Members reigns.
> His eyes still sparkle in a narr'wer space:
> His jaws retain the grin, and violence of face.
> ('The First Book of Ovid's Metamorphoses,' 316–19)

The malevolent grin in the deformed body resembles the Protestant beasts generally and a phrase used earlier, 'famish'd face' (313), is actually repeated from the description of the wolf in *The Hind and the Panther* (I.160). Dryden thus associates Lycaon with Protestantism and once again implies that Protestants and not Catholics are the true cannibals.

Jove promises to restore mankind to 'try [his] skill again' (341), in Dryden's Miltonic phrase. However, his second creation is possible only because of the faith of a pious married couple, Deucalion and Pyrrha. Ovid's account of human history thus diverges from Milton's, in which man and wife turned on each other after the fall; perhaps Dryden linked Milton to the flawed conception of an all-male spiritual principle, as he had earlier done in *MacFlecknoe*. Deucalion and Pyrrha succeed in transforming the world because they have enough faith to obey the goddess Themis, who says: 'Throw each behind your backs, your mighty Mother's bones' (517); Deucalion interprets this to mean: 'This Earth our mighty Mother is, the Stones / In her capacious Body, are her Bones' (528–9). An organic earth, 'teeming' with life (557), produces animals once again through a creative union of heat and moisture, while the stones become human beings – 'a Miracle to Mortal View, / But long Tradition makes it pass for true' (536–7). Miracles may have been possible in this prehistoric setting, though Dryden and Ovid are a bit suspicious. Some amusement at Ovidian science comes out in Dryden's reference to 'mingl'd Atoms' (576), and in his phrase 'the fæces of the Flood' (580), which carries the image of an organic earth to absurd lengths. However, Dryden does not ridicule the Ovidian notion of miracle itself. The second human race, marked by love and piety, is itself a miracle requiring no divine intervention.

Book I proceeds to describe the transformations of Daphne into a laurel and of Io into a heifer. The Io story is interrupted by two more stories, 'The Eyes of *Argus* Transform'd into a Peacock's Train' and 'The Transformation of *Syrinx* into Reeds,' and then at last Io becomes a priestess who bears Jove's son. All these stories except Io's have some connection to art, since the laurel is a reward for victory and reeds are transformed into a musical instrument. Though the stories progress towards spiritual love – Pan enjoys Syrinx as 'the Consort of my Mind' (983) – Apollo still speaks, like Jove, in the pompous tones of a male deity:

> Mine is th' invention of the charming Lyre;
> Sweet notes, and Heav'nly numbers I inspire. (697–8)

Even the story of Io has comic elements: in the image of 'a lovely Cow' (835) who makes pathetic efforts to speak to her father (907), but even more in the contest between two all-powerful deities, Jupiter and Juno, to control her fate. It is absurd to imagine *two* omniscient and omnipotent gods existing at once: how can one keep a secret from the other? how can one act without being immediately forestalled by the other? The effect is to undermine the very notion of godhead as tyrannical omnipotence. Dryden follows Ovid in exaggerating the rapidity of Juno's discovery and Jove's retaliation. Jove indulges in the claptrap of omniscience (809–11) but is soon reduced to the character of an 'Almighty Leacher' (832), while his wife becomes a 'cautious Goddess' (852). These gods cannot sustain the powers that all-powerful deities are supposed to have, though they do manage to make Io and her father miserable. The Io story thus suggests the emptiness of Olympian cosmology and prepares us for a new order.

Io's second transformation creates a new religious environment, for she becomes divine herself:

> A Goddess now, through all th' *Egyptian* State:
> And serv'd by Priests, who in white Linnen wait. (1040–1)

This part of the myth was often seen as showing Io's identity with Isis, an idea that Dryden recalls by identifying Epaphus as the 'Son of *Isis*' (1050), while the role of the cow in the myth was taken as a link between Io and vegetation myths.[17] To Dryden Isis would also have been known from Book v of *The Faerie Queene*, where she represents 'that part of Justice, which is Equity,' as well as embodying a form of female strength that could teach Britomart to moderate Artegall's mechanical rigour and to avoid the excesses of the man-hater Radigund, the kind of strong woman whom Artegall might more readily imagine.[18] Since Plutarch's Isis stood for the reconstruction of truth, Dryden had several precedents for treating Isis as a beneficent power figure and for giving her a creative role within an epic context.

Isis herself appears in 'Iphis and Ianthe,' where she twice responds to the prayers of Telethusa to preserve her daughter's life and happiness. First, after Iphis's birth she helps Telethusa save Iphis from a father who despises girls and would kill his child if he knew her to be female. Lygdus brings Jovian barbarity down to earth, as he speaks in a bumpkin's downright tone:

Girls cost as many throws, in bringing forth:
Besides when born, the Titts are little worth:
Weak puling things, unable to sustain
Their share of Labour, and their Bread to gain. (13–16)

Isis has Telethusa disguise the child as a boy and give her a bisexual name (60–2), which happens also to resemble the goddess's own name. This is a justifiable deception, but not a miracle: 'And Truth was cover'd with a pious Cheat' (65). It shows the same mixed values as Ximena's deception in *Love Triumphant*.

However, Iphis falls in love with another girl, Ianthe, and the two are contracted to marry. Iphis attacks herself in the naturalistic style of 'force of love' poetry, contrasting her situation with that of animals who readily find suitable mates, while Telethusa 'empty'd all her Magazine of lies' (158) and pleads with Isis a second time. Now Isis does perform a miracle, changing Iphis into a man:

Her sparkling Eyes, with Manly Vigour shone,
Big was her Voice, Audacious was her Tone.
The latent Parts, at length reveal'd, began
To shoot, and spread, and burnish into Man. (196–9)

Since Iphis had always been androgynous, the metamorphosis exchanges one potentiality for another rather than effecting a change in basic identity. Isis has demonstrated her power and gained a masculine worshipper (204–5); in a way she has transformed the concept of maleness.

The three characters of 'Acis, Polyphemus, and Galatea' parallel the three figures of the traditional Isis myth: the monster Polyphemus is analogous to Typhon, the destructive force; Acis is analogous to the son/lover Osiris; and Galatea parallels the goddess herself, though reduced to a comic scale. Dryden recast several of Polyphemus's lines in a way that associates Acis's death with the fragmentation of Osiris and recalls Lycaon's meal as well:

> His living Bowels, from his Belly torn,
> And scatter'd Limbs, shall on the Flood be born:
> Thy Flood, ungrateful Nymph, and fate shall find
> That way for thee, and *Acis* to be joyn'd. (181–4)

The phrase 'scatter'd Limbs' and the whole second couplet are Dryden's. Acis is killed by a 'mighty Fragment' (211), a 'Rib' of the living rock, upon which Galatea transforms him into a river. Acis now undergoes his sea-change:

> Up starts a Youth, and Navel high he stood.
> Horns from his Temples rise; and either Horn
> Thick Wreaths of Reeds, (his Native growth) adorn.
> Were not his Stature taller than before,
> His bulk augmented, and his beauty more,
> His colour blue, for *Acis* he might pass:
> And *Acis* chang'd into a Stream he was. (225–31)

The endings of both short poems have the same attractive sensuality, although in the second it is incorporated into a world of the spirit.

This poem consists mostly of Polyphemus's address to Galatea, rendered in a style like that of Dryden's Theocritan poems, and framed by Galatea's account of the story itself. She reveals herself as very sophisticated, feeling an aversion towards Polyphemus, so that her delicacy and his rusticity provide two nicely contrasted versions of comedy. One is still aware that Polyphemus is the Cyclops who would threaten Ulysses (38–9), the cannibal 'who made his bloody Feasts / On mangl'd Members, of his butcher'd Guests' (21–2). Yet he remains a rural fellow, like Lygdus in 'Iphis and Ianthe.' The character types overlap in disturbing, if amusing, ways, while the comic version of the Isis story – for which Dryden, more than Ovid, is responsible – suggests the capacity of myth to be transmuted into ever-new forms and of epic to become a fragment in a story about the gods.

Dryden's approach to myth itself deserves comment. He has chosen fragments or motifs that readily imply a Christian analogy – this sequence is about death and resurrection – and that possibly even have Catholic overtones, since Isis's concern for humanity and for a son in particular might recall Mary's. He has treated the theme seriously; the central images on which the myth revolves have genuine life. This is different from *Ovid's Epistles*, where myth was employed to disorient us: how can Aeolus, Leda, and Jove *really* be the parents of the characters we are reading about? The *Epistles* depend on an essentially modern scepticism. The environment of the stories disintegrates as we read, while the heroines' emotions acquire force and credibility, as if myth ultimately underlines the fact that the heroines live in private worlds. *Examen Poeticum* is different; we do not believe in the historical existence of Isis or Galatea, but we readily accept them as magical beings or as cult figures. The difference is that *Examen Poeticum* is in part about miracles, whereas the *Epistles* were not; miracles may not be possible now (1693 might as well be 'now' in this context), but they were possible at one time and the mythic setting helps to represent that time in literary terms. Dryden's poem thus affirms the possibility of miracles, avoiding both the air of suspicion characteristic of *Ovid's Epistles* and the harsh sense of reality found in *Miscellany Poems* and in *Sylvae*. Worldliness does enter into the poem, but mainly in the pleasingly comic character of Galatea, who is a kind of Popean Belinda of mythology.

It would be easy to say that Dryden's conversion made him more certain of things he could not see or demonstrate with the usual kinds of evidence, and that it gave him a higher vision of human possibilities. For a few years Dryden showed an interest in secular saints (Don Sebastian, Eleanora, Cleomenes), and there is much conviction underlying the providential vision of *Examen Poeticum*, *Love Triumphant*, and the temple imagery of his poem to Congreve. In *Fables*, however, miracles arouse a strain of doubt which is never entirely dispelled, and the few characters who perceive revealed truth are so exceptional that they remain concepts or possibilities. The creation poem of *Fables* is 'Of the Pythagorean Philosophy' (K, IV, 1717–36), part of Book XV of the *Metamorphoses*, which is so immersed in matter, blood, and slime as to give an entirely different image of flux from that of the sea-change:

> But this by sure Experiment we know,
> That living Creatures from Corruption grow:

Hide in a hollow Pit a slaughter'd Steer,
Bees from his putrid Bowels will appear;
...
And Worms, that stretch on Leaves their filmy Loom
Crawl from their Bags, and Butterflies become.
Ev'n Slime begets the Frog's loquacious Race:
Short of their Feet at first, in little space
With Arms and Legs endu'd, long leaps they take,
Rais'd on their hinder part, and swim the Lake,
And Waves repel. (539–42, 551–7)

The poetry is marvellously delicate – even imitating metrically the leap of the frog – but one of its major aims is to create a sense of matter. The Pythagorean philosophy is Dryden's ultimate attempt at an Epicurean poetics, but it is one based on immersion in matter rather than on detachment. The immersion of language in matter underlines the separation of nature from God, or at least it creates the feeling that nature has a kind of reality which grows ever more difficult to relate to the presumed intentions of God. Yet *Fables* resembles *Examen Poeticum* in affirming the self-sustaining power of nature and the reality of language, so that one comes to feel that the poem can supplant nature. *Fables* simply incorporates the darker side of nature into the more restricted, if idealistic, vision of the 1693 Ovid. In *Examen Poeticum*, too, Dryden first used traditional motifs with enormous allegorical potentialities to unify a collective poem. The motifs rise above the narratives in which they are embedded to create a poetic density in the whole poem which might be lacking if the poems were read separately.

There is little more to say about the three short poems in *Examen Poeticum*, which treat three different manifestations of the force of love. The name Chloris, in 'Song to a Fair, Young Lady,' resembles Chloe in 'Rondelay,' which is about a woman's power to arouse a man to repeated orgasms. Chloris's power to inspire love, however, transcends 'all Religions' and can 'change the Laws of ev'ry Land' (15–16); the poem is sometimes read as a Jacobite response to the absence of a beloved monarch. In 'Veni Creator Spiritus,' the creator spirit, if it comes, will free human beings 'From Sin, and Sorrow' (5). The poem is a prayer for faith. In all cases either the speaker or the male figure in the poem experiences the absence of an inspiriting power and requires the agency of an outside force to revive him. In a way Chloris's magical power recalls Isis's:

When *Chloris* to the Temple comes,
  Adoring Crowds before her fall;

She can restore the Dead from Tombs,
    And ev'ry Life but mine recall. (19–22)

In 'Veni Creator Spiritus' Dryden refers to human beings as 'thy Temples,' thus recalling the temple image in the lines just quoted. The metre is nearly the same in the three poems – an emphatic iambic tetrameter in 'Song to a Fair, Young Lady' and in 'Veni Creator Spiritus,' which becomes trochaic in 'Rondelay,' written in alternating eight- and seven-syllable lines. The pulsating effect of all three poems is nearly the same. Though it seems crude to connect 'Rondelay' with 'Veni Creator Spiritus,' Dryden believed that it was honest to remind himself and his readers about the persistence of bodily impulses, and the poems do show how such impulses can be sublimated. The links between 'Song to a Fair, Young Lady' and 'Veni Creator Spiritus' are quite clear, and the songs parallel the selections from Ovid in using a technique of repetition that shows a single pattern of action being re-enacted on several planes of moral experience.

6

Dryden's *Aeneis* and *Fables*

THE LIMITS OF TRANSLATION IN THE *AENEIS*

Examen Poeticum does not really foreshadow *Fables Ancient and Modern*, except when hindsight permits us to detect some minor connections. It is less developed than *Sylvae*, and the spiritual optimism with its emphasis on the miraculous projects an altogether different and more unified mood. Nevertheless, Dryden was now translating more poets who wrote in major forms and this shift is reflected in his translation of Ovid's creation epic, instead of the elegies and epistles, which offer a deliberately off-centre vision of life. From one point of view *Fables* unites Dryden's interest in the varieties of epic with the interest in fragmentary translation that he developed in the 1680s. What made this synthesis possible was quite likely his experience in translating the *Aeneid*, which seems to me to account for the shift to a darker mood and which was in its own right a major accomplishment. Yet from other points of view the *Aeneis* must have been singularly frustrating. It has occurred to me, though this is a small point, that Dryden's decision to follow the labour of translating Virgil with fables was influenced by John Ogilby, who also translated first the *Aeneid*, then two years later a book of Aesopic fables freely rendered, because he wanted both to relax and to demonstrate his originality.[1] Fable translation is thus more original than Virgil translation! Dryden characteristically attacked Ogilby in his preface to *Fables*, protesting too much as so often in his relationships with minor writers, but the coincidence between his progress and Ogilby's cannot be denied. Ogilby showed him what could be done next.[2]

Dryden was uncomfortably aware that the archetypal Virgilian career, in which the poet moved triumphantly from eclogue to georgic to epic, could not serve as a model for him. In any case, his career had been infinitely more diversified; one cannot always regret the products of financial exigency. But at sixty-seven Dryden claimed to feel uneasy about translating the *Georgics.* By the standards set by Virgil, who died at fifty-two, Dryden was too old to write or even to translate an epic. Dryden himself considered epic translation prolonged and tiring. In the preface to *Fables* he complained of the difficulty of translating Homer, whose style appeared to demand sustained rapture: 'The continual Agitations of the Spirits, must needs be a Weakning of any Constitution, especially in Age: and many Pauses are required for Refreshment betwixt the Heats' (K, IV, 1449).[3] *Fables*, however, resolves the problem of age. The whole collection is epic in length, but it is composed of short parts whose effect would have been about the same had Dryden died before translating every one of them or had he lived to translate a few more. His inclusion of Book I of the *Iliad* 'as an Essay to the whole Work' (K, IV, 1444) is a sign of remarkable self-assurance, as if *Fables* itself was simply a resting-place between two major efforts. *Fables* is truly open-ended, though the arrangement that we have is carefully planned.

It is interesting to set *Fables* beside the *Aeneis*, because they suddenly seem to become part of a larger whole comprehending them both, and they certainly illuminate each other by juxtaposition. In an important sense *Fables* is simply a return to themes and stylistic problems that the *Aeneis* resolved inadequately. The translation of a complete long poem was obviously far more limiting than fragmentary translation, where Dryden could ignore whatever did not suit his interests or his views. The Drydenian overlay in the *Aeneis* is awkwardly prominent; some long sections, or even whole books (especially Books IV, XI, and XII) seem to emanate as much from his mind as from Virgil's, while others fail to connect and seem flat by comparison. For instance, Aeneas is often referred to conventionally as the 'pious hero' in passages uncoloured by the overlay, while elsewhere he appears as a butcher or a 'War-luck,' and in Book IV, where Aeneas behaves like a Dorimant, the description 'pious' is ironic.

There was also the political problem that would not go away, or, to put it in more abstract terms, the problem of how to treat military heroism. Dryden continued to link Homer's heroes with brutality at its worst and he brought Ovid's Ajax into *Fables* in 'The Speeches of Ajax and Ulysses.' Ajax is an emblematic union of stupidity and brutality, worse than Alexander or Achilles. As Dryden describes Ajax in the dedication of *Fables*: 'Science distinguishes a Man of Honour from one of those Athletick Brutes whom undeservedly we call Heroes. Curs'd be the Poet, who first honour'd with that Name a meer *Ajax*, a Man-killing Ideot' (K, IV, 1442). Ovid's comic disparagement was thus congenial to Dryden and the real heroes of *Fables* are philosopher-kings or poets, whom I shall discuss in the next chapter. But Dryden's distaste for the active hero extended to Aeneas, who *ends* as a butcher, though elsewhere in the poem he is sensitive and conscientious. In the dedication of the *Aeneis* Dryden even defends his tears: 'Thus he weeps out of Compassion, and tenderness of Nature, when in the Temple of *Carthage* he beholds the Pictures of his Friends, who Sacrific'd their Lives in Defence of their Country' (K, III, 1023). Dryden could have added that Aeneas is a model of control in comparison to Turnus and most of Virgil's old men, whose tears flow in rivers, but he must have wanted this image of the man of feeling to remain in our minds to offset the butcher. These two Aeneases remain in suspension, and the character is further complicated by a picture of the Roman rake, the seducer of Dido:

> I made no such Bargain with you at our Marriage, to live always drudging on at *Carthage*; my business was *Italy*, and I never made a secret of it. If I took my pleasure, had not you your share of it? I leave you free at my departure, to comfort your self with the next Stranger who happens to be Shipwreck'd on your Coast. Be as kind an Hostess as you have been to me, and you can never fail of another Husband. In the mean time, I call the Gods to witness, that I leave your Shore unwillingly; for though *Juno* made the Marriage, yet *Jupiter* Commands me to forsake you. This is the effect of what he saith, when it is dishonour'd out of Latin Verse, into English Prose. If the Poet argued not aright, we must pardon him for a poor blind Heathen, who knew no better Morals. (K, III, 1033)

Dryden casts a whole series of filters over Aeneas's character, each one of which has some truth and is comprehensible by ordinary human psychology. Their very inconsistencies prepare us to read the poem with suspicion, since the partial truths are never reassembled.

Dryden also had to compensate for the desire of his contemporaries to find William III shadowed in the person of Aeneas/Augustus or any plausible substitute. There is an often repeated story of how Tonson had the plates from Ogilby's *Aeneis* retouched, adding a hooked nose to make Aeneas look more like William.[4] A royalist moustache, vaguely like that of Charles I, was also removed, as can be verified in every plate in which Aeneas's face is shown closely enough to reveal facial details, especially when the face is in profile. It is not a subtle change at all. Dryden retaliated by turning the pathetic fugitive into a foreign pirate at every available opportunity, so that Aeneas's enemies are often Dryden's mouthpieces; in general he created an Achillean or Alexander-like Aeneas, whom William's admirers would be reluctant to identify with their king, assuming that they read Dryden's poem closely enough to see the difference. Luke Milbourne attacked Dryden for his treatment of Virgil's politics and Pope seems to have caught the satiric potential in Dryden's style.[5] Still, this highly indirect way of communicating his own principles may have been frustrating enough to move Dryden to write another poem, an anti-*Aeneis* or a continuation of the *Aeneis*, where he presents another version of heroism altogether, attacks military invaders over and over again, and adds stupidity as a new component in his image of the active hero. In such a poem he could choose his own selections and not have to overcome the distorting expectations of a largely Williamite audience.

The self-consciousness that Dryden undoubtedly experienced and which he also projected onto Virgil produced its own kind of distortions. His alleged failure to grasp Virgil's 'atmosphere' or 'subjectivity'[6] is less because of a failure in response than because Virgil's poem was the wrong place for him to be Virgilian. Dryden also emphasizes the surly resentment of the political man, which in turn is based on that kind of man's endlessly frustrated anger. Some of Dryden's *Fables* are more Virgilian than most of the *Aeneis* and a few of them contain important parallels to the *Aeneis* and must have been attractive for that reason. *Fables* is partly the overflow from Virgil. In the later work Dryden separated his aesthetic response to Virgil from his political response and from his reservations about the content of Virgil's poem. An 'innocent *Aeneis*,' unconditioned by anyone's preconceptions, was virtually impossible.

The chronic resentment evident in the *Aeneis* is Dryden's version of Virgilian *furor*, a more elevated and definitely a supernatural force. Resentment is as malevolent and contagious as *furor*, but it is debased, its pettiness and distortion recalling the world of Ovid's rake and satires like *The Medall* (1682), from which I quote a representative passage:

> He cast himself into the Saint-like mould;
> Groan'd, sigh'd and pray'd, while Godliness was gain;
> The lowdest Bagpipe of the squeaking Train.
> But, as 'tis hard to cheat a Juggler's Eyes,
> His open lewdness he cou'd ne'er disguise.
> There split the Saint ... (33–8)[7]

These ugly physical and vocal distortions might be funny in the right context, but they are still evil. In the *Aeneis* Juno (a political person, though a goddess) remains the souce of evil, as she is in the original, but Dryden's vocabulary from the start shifts towards a satiric view of inward impulse:

> O Muse! the Causes and the Crimes relate,
> What Goddess was *provok'd*, and whence her hate:
> For what *Offence* the Queen of Heav'n began
> To *persecute* so brave, so just a Man!
> Involv'd his anxious Life in endless Cares,
> Expos'd to Wants, and hurry'd into Wars!
> Can Heav'nly Minds such *high resentment* show;
> Or exercise their *Spight* in Human Woe? (I.11–18, my italics)

Turnus, more obviously than any other character, catches this disease. By the opening of Book XII Dryden can describe him in almost the same vocabulary used for Juno in Book I. Turnus is 'the Mark of publick Spight' (XII.3) (spite has transcended the personal), 'with Vulgar hate oppress'd' (XII.5) (Turnus is hated by the vulgar, but the hatred he feels is vulgar as well), and 'Fury boil'd' (XII.6) inside him (fury seems to come from unsettled humours, while *furor* comes from the gods). Dryden has a unifying psychology (it is one of his major unifying threads), but it is not quite Virgil's psychology. The boiling cauldron of the emotions can also be found in *Absalom and Achitophel* (136–41), not to mention the Nisus and Euryalus episode in *Sylvae*. One may not be surprised to find this continuity. However, in the *Aeneis* Dryden cannot present boiling emotions from the viewpoint of a king or poet who is immune to them, and he emphasizes, like Virgil, the pain they cause until the individual finds release. The *Aeneis* is actually more disturbing than Dryden's satires for being an epic invaded by the psychology of satire.

That psychology is most dramatically presented in Book XI, which emerges as Dryden's personal attack on the evils of war. In this book the Latins' debate on how to proceed in their war with the Trojans is framed by the deaths of two young people, the funeral of Pallas (the son of Evander, Aeneas's ally) at the beginning and the death in battle of Camilla (a sort of Amazon on whom Turnus is forced to rely) at the end. Both are essentially sympathetic characters in spite of the impulsiveness that leads to their deaths, while their allegiances seem irrelevant since neither has been responsible for planning the war.

We might look at Dryden's treatment of Evander's lament. Virgil's Evander is very emotional, one of the tearful old men I have already mentioned.

Excessive crying is a sign of impotence. But Dryden's Evander is also disgusted, angry at something that he is in no position to describe openly:

I warn'd thee, but in vain; for well I knew
What Perils youthful Ardour wou'd pursue:
That boiling Blood wou'd carry thee too far;
Young as thou wert in Dangers, raw to War!
O curst Essay of Arms, disast'rous Doom,
Prelude of bloody Fields, and Fights to come!
...
Yet will I not my *Trojan* Friend upbraid,
Nor grudge th' Alliance I so gladly made.
'Twas not his Fault my *Pallas* fell so young,
But my own Crime for having liv'd too long. (XI.232–7, 250–3)

Evander now regrets his involvement with such a powerful ally. Virgil's 'nec vos arguerim, Teucri, nec foedera nec quas / iunximus hospitio dextras' (XI.164–5) sounds sincere, if ruefully aware of a tragic political mistake. His Evander still believes in the alliance or 'foedera,' while Dryden's has come to resent it, though he is trapped in a position where he has to suppress his natural antagonism to Aeneas. Evander's attack on war now seems to be a way of evading a direct attack on his Trojan friend. This is not just a matter of Dryden's diction ('curst Essay of Arms,' 'grudge'), but a new tone of voice. Virgil's speech is primarily an agonized lament, though it contains a political warning, while Dryden's is a dissection of the reasons that cause men to wage war in spite of their better judgment. Both speeches arouse compassion and both *imply* the emotions that they leave out; that is, a reader of Virgil should react with Dryden's outrage and a reader of Dryden can take for granted Evander's underlying pain. The versions are complementary. From this point of view Dryden's version is sometimes a *response* to Virgil rather than an attempted equivalent.

Dryden's version of the council scene is effective, not so much because the character of Drances (XI.510–18) recalls that of Zimri in *Absalom and Achitophel*,[8] but because Diomedes' rejection of the Latins' plea for aid conveys the nightmarish guilt of a man who wished he had never engaged in war or in fatal alliances or indeed in Odyssean adventure. For self-revulsion the satires provide only a starting-point. Diomedes' question, 'What Madness has your alter'd Minds possess'd, / To change for War hereditary Rest?' (XI.388–9), recalls the satire but there is a stronger emphasis on madness and even those who know better are touched by it.

Diomedes is horrified that the Latins are repeating his own mistake. Guilt mingled with self-contempt leads naturally to revulsion at the envoy's proposals:

> Out-casts, abandon'd by the Care of Heav'n:
> So worn, so wretched, so despis'd a Crew,
> As ev'n old *Priam* might with Pity view.
> ...
> Such Arms, this Hand shall never more employ;
> No Hate remains with me to ruin'd Troy.
> I war not with its Dust ... (XI.399–401, 429–31)

The reader may get more involved in this passage than in any other in the poem, but Dryden caps it by damning it as a 'cold Excuse' (451), implying a level of calculation neither present in the original or apparent in his own version of the speech yet in keeping with his general sense of the characters' psychology. Their emotions are twisted, they may not understand themselves, and they are so aware of political implications that their speech can never be sincere, even when it is pervaded by deep feeling. Dryden's lack of sympathy for fugitives (so despis'd a Crew') can be explained by the fact that William was a foreigner. Finally, Dryden adds an incongruous element to his version of the tale of Camilla's life:

> The little *Amazon* cou'd scarcely go,
> He loads her with a Quiver and a Bow. (XI.858–9)

One needs some humour at this point in the poem, but the passage also implies that only a child could be as enthusiastic about fighting as Camilla reveals herself to be. The humour does not grow out of the council scene except as comic relief. Dryden seems to fragment the poem, allowing separate sections to elicit whatever response seems appropriate for that section.

Dryden's satire is impartial and disorienting: virtually any character can become either its object or its mouthpiece. He refuses to stabilize himself either for or against his hero, and if we decide that on balance Aeneas is an exploitive bounder, that does not make Dido the focus of our remaining sympathies. They simply display two versions of the conflict between negative inner impulse and an exterior that does not quite hang together because it can never sincerely express the character's secret life. Dryden's courtly treatment of the episode was anticipated in the mid-century translation by Godolphin and Waller, but they shortened Virgil's narrative passages so much, especially his accounts of the characters' inner states, that the lovers seem idealized; they are what they say in their utterances.[9] This approach to character is almost antithetical to Dryden's. Dryden anticipated it in his own early play *Secret Love*, as in the vocabulary of the song from the fourth act (IV.ii.25–6):

> *'Tis such a pleasing smart, and I so love it,*
> *That I had rather die, then once remove it.* (*Works*, IX, 177)

The queen in *Secret Love* is partly based on Dido rejected by her 'false *Æneas*' (III.i.233); she even tries to make her lover her admiral. Yet we can pity the queen and are supposed to admire her decision to sacrifice love, an action that proves her to be superior to Dido both in morality and in political common sense. In *Secret Love* Dryden hints at the unpleasantness of the hidden self but reverts to imaging an ideal clarity of self much like that in Godolphin and Waller. The queen is what Dido could have been.

Dryden's Dido is constantly nursing an unpleasant sort of emotion which is certainly not resentment but appears to be its amatory equivalent. From the beginning she 'fann[s] the secret Fire':

> His Words, his Looks imprinted in the Heart,
> Improve the Passion, and increase the Smart. (IV.5–6)

She lies to herself and to the public about the nature of her relationship with Aeneas: 'But call'd it Marriage, by that specious Name, / To veil the Crime and sanctifie the Shame' (IV.249–50). Virgil provides the same fact – including the fact of Dido's self-deception – but not the sense that Dido is hugging a secret to herself. Her reference to her 'dear perfidious Man' is unpleasantly sentimental (IV.439). Virgil himself presented Dido as a tragedy queen and used a theatrical metaphor, which Dryden expands (IV.469–72), to pinpoint her disintegration, but Dryden's Dido is like a tragedy queen adrift in the wrong kind of play, a Mrs Loveit or a Lady Wishfort.

Aeneas is more unequivocally contemptible in Book IV than in any other part of the poem. Dryden's prose paraphrase of Aeneas's excuses in the dedication prepares us to regard Aeneas with suspicion, and our expectations are not disappointed. Dryden expands Virgil's comparison of Aeneas to Apollo, which in the original can be read as a tribute to Aeneas's essential detachment and a foreshadowing of his survival. However, Dryden's hero contemplating 'The merry Madness of the sacred Show' (211) seems to be planning to have a good time at Dido's expense; we shall learn how a man of detachment, a 'War-luck,' behaves in a love affair. Dryden is sometimes explicit about Aeneas's duplicity and manipulativeness:

He longs to fly, and loaths the charming Land.
What shou'd he say, or how shou'd he begin,
What Course, alas! remains, to steer between
Th' offended Lover, and the Pow'rful Queen!
This way, and that, he turns his anxious Mind,
And all Expedients tries, and none can find:
Fix'd on the Deed, but doubtful of the Means;
After long Thought to this Advice he leans.
Three Chiefs he calls, commands them to repair
The Fleet, and ship their Men with silent Care:
Some plausible Pretence he bids them find,
To colour what in secret he design'd.
Himself, mean time, the softest Hours wou'd chuse,
Before the Love-sick Lady heard the News;
And move her tender Mind, by slow degrees,
To suffer what the Sov'raign Pow'r decrees. (IV.407–22)

Hermes addresses Aeneas in the style of plain invective ('Thou Woman's Property,' IV.390), while Aeneas himself thinks in a style of elegant insult, that of a rake. Some of his seemingly complimentary epithets suggest the way Dido is caught between conflicting roles, and generally phrases like 'the Love-sick Lady' (IV.420) show Aeneas's contempt and his ability to cope with Dido by stereotyping her, thus distancing himself from her feelings. Dryden's vocabulary of contempt demolishes any faith we might have had in the hero's good intentions.

Aeneas's search for 'Expedients' makes him political in the worst sense of the word, while his concern for his fleet *should* have made him Dryden's spokesman at this point. Dryden tends to underline passages where Aeneas (or Virgil) speaks as a navy man, adding a line or two, or making the details concrete. Dryden argued elsewhere that England should maintain her fleet as her source of strength,[10] and it was generally felt that William did not care about the navy. Defence of the navy was one possible response in the standing-army debate. Here we have an example of how Dryden's floating topical satire works. Aeneas cannot possibly stand for William at this point, even a defective William; nor can he be a good navy man like Dryden's friend Samuel Pepys, or like John Driden (as Dryden urged him to be). Instead of allying him with a party, we see Aeneas as the oak-headed Englishman, using his navy as an excuse to leave his nymph on the shore much like the Trojan/English sailors of Purcell's *Dido and Aeneas.* Though Aeneas is not stupid, his limited feelings ally him with the mental defectives of *Fables*, at least in this section of the poem.

The conclusion to Book XII is so ambiguous in the original that Dryden was forced to take some kind of stand about Aeneas's true nature. His is almost the opposite of Virgil's; the two poets have essentially different views of Aeneas's tormenting inhibitions, both here and earlier in the poem. Virgil is almost sympathetic. His Aeneas could not indulge the innate human urge to violence and thus suffers to an unusual degree from his pent-up feelings. He is like Hamlet. When release comes at last, it is purgative, though it takes a horrifying form: he kills Turnus, a defeated suppliant, just as Achilles killed the suppliant Lycaon in Book XXI of the *Iliad.* The Homeric parallel defines the moral realm to which Aeneas has descended. Yet, since Achilles was, like Aeneas, in pain at that point (each recalling the death of a loved friend), one could equally well say that Achilles has grown into a conflict-ridden Virgilian hero, who murders a man to end his own suffering. The Homeric parallel does not resolve the ambiguity; it compounds it by providing another situation where we are asked to accept the rightness of a killing even though its main value is to help the killer understand himself.

Dryden thinks that Aeneas should exercise control. In Book II, during the destruction of Troy, Aeneas seeks an outlet for his horror at seeing the city burn. Unable to do more, he wants to kill Helen, thinking, 'The punish'd Crime shall set my Soul at ease' (II.797). However, Venus – not only Aeneas's mother, but also Helen's protector – appears and attacks Aeneas's 'Madness' or, in Dryden's words, 'unmanly Rage' (II.808, 810). Virgil suggests a tinge of effeminacy in Aeneas's submission to a woman, while Dryden thinks that *rage* is unmanly; Venus is right. His vocabulary in the concluding passage of Book XII is similar:

> In deep Suspence the *Trojan* seem'd to stand;
> And just prepar'd to strike repress'd his Hand.
> He rowl'd his Eyes, and ev'ry Moment felt
> His manly Soul with more Compassion melt.
> When, casting down a casual Glance, he spy'd
> The Golden Belt that glitter'd on his side. (XII.1360–5)

Dryden associates restraint and compassion with manliness, not with effeminacy, and thus shows Aeneas's good impulses being defeated at this point. He also attributes a greater role to chance, here and elsewhere in Book XII. Both poets have Aeneas repeat the name 'Pallas' in a way that imitates his very action of stabbing the enemy:

> Pallas te hoc vulnere, Pallas
> immolat et poenam scelerato ex sanguine sumit. (XII.948–9)

To his sad Soul a grateful Off'ring go;
'Tis *Pallas*, *Pallas* gives this deadly Blow. (XII. 1372–3)

However, Virgil sounds almost pitying, possibly a bit contemptuous, while Dryden makes Aeneas seem almost insane. The line 'Then rowz'd anew to Wrath, he loudly cries' (XII. 1368) tells us how we should hear Aeneas's speech at the end. Virgil's Aeneas is 'furiis accensus et ira / terribilis' (XII. 946–7), but not loud.

In a parallel passage earlier in Book XII Turnus achieves his moment of greatest insight. Dryden expanded the passage, making us aware that Aeneas killed a man who was capable of goodness at last, and introduced his own moral vocabulary:

Stupid he sate, his Eyes on Earth declin'd,
And various Cares revolving in his Mind:
Rage boiling from the bottom of his Breast,
And Sorrow mix'd with Shame, his Soul oppress'd:
And conscious Worth lay lab'ring in his Thought,
And Love by Jealousie to Madness wrought.
By slow degrees his Reason drove away
The Mists of Passion, and resum'd her Sway.
Then, rising on his Car, he turn'd his Look;
And saw the Town involv'd in Fire and Smoke.
...
Sister, the Fates have vanquish'd: Let us go
The way which Heav'n and my hard Fortune show.
The Fight is fix'd: Nor shall the branded Name
Of a base Coward blot your Brother's Fame.
Death is my choice; but suffer me to try
My Force, and vent my Rage before I dye. (XII. 967–76, 981–6)

The dichotomy between reason and passion is, predictably, Dryden's, though both poets present much going on in Turnus's mind and both put an accent on 'conscious Worth' ('conscia virtus,' XII. 668). Dryden adds the image of Turnus elevating his eyes from the earth and changes the meaning of the inward fire which parallels the fire destroying Latium: Dryden associates the fire with boiling rage, in other words, Turnus's weakness, but Virgil's 'ardentis oculorum orbis' (XII. 670) seems to project the new inner light, the consciousness that Turnus has just achieved. Turnus thereupon makes a conscious, almost an inspired, decision to commit himself to his own 'furor' before he dies, while Dryden's Turnus, aware of his limited options, decides to vent his rage. He allows himself to fall ('leaping down,' XII.987), though he falls in a different place from the one where he started. In Dryden's version both heroes appear to sacrifice the potential for self-transcendence that they almost achieve, in fact do achieve for a brief moment in each case.

The *Aeneis*, therefore, has no resolution, no definite sense of an ending that might have been provided by the clear moral superiority of one hero over the other, or by the heroes' achievement of self-control, or even by their unequivocal distintegration. However, two alternative 'endings' to the *Aeneis* appear in *Fables*. In Part II of 'Palamon and Arcite' Theseus controls his own boiling rage, under the influence of his queen and her ladies, and decides against the impulsive punishment of the two young knights:

> He paus'd a while, stood silent in his Mood,
> (For yet, his Rage was boiling in his Blood)
> But soon his tender Mind th' Impression felt,
> (As softest Metals are not slow to melt
> And Pity soonest runs in gentle Minds:)
> Then reasons with himself; and first he finds
> His Passion cast a Mist before his Sense,
> And either made, or magnifi'd th' Offence. (II.328–35)

The vocabulary of inner debate is the same as that in Turnus's recognition scene, while the moment of suspense when 'Compassion' (342) wars against physical impulse recalls the moment when Aeneas almost refrained from murder. Theseus, therefore, is a morally successful version of both of Virgil's heroes. By contrast, Palamon and Arcite fight in a state of 'dumb Surliness,' which here, as in the *Aeneis*, Dryden associates with fury (II.190–2). They are trapped at the level of Virgil's twelfth book until Theseus rescues them from themselves, as if the conflict between Turnus and Aeneas were itself meaningless. Dryden considered Chaucer's poem 'perhaps not much inferiour to the *Ilias* or the *Æneis*' (K, IV, 1460); he turned it into a continuation of the *Aeneis* or a transition into a new moral realm.

In contrast, 'The First Book of Homer's Ilias' shows a regression to a pre-Virgilian moral state. It is a concise epitome of a world of primitive violence which is nevetheless subject to the distortions of political involvement. Everyone burns with fury; even the priest, Chryses, 'Devoutly curs'd his Foes' (56). Puns on 'fury' and 'fire' (not to mention 'fierce') can be found everywhere, as in this description of Agamemnon, another variation on the theme of Aeneas getting ready to act:

Thus answer'd then
Upstarting from his Throne, the King of Men,
His Breast with Fury fill'd, his Eyes with Fire;
Which rowling round, he shot in Sparkles on the Sire. (151–4)

Dryden's Agamemnon pushes some implications further: what happens when the impulsive man actually has royal power instead of merely aspiring to it?

Dryden's Achilles is not just a furious man; he is perceived in republican terms as an insulted lord who considers it servile to let any limits be imposed on his freedom. The curious result is that both tyrant and rebel appear to be dangerously egotistical and prone to violence, inhabitants of the same political order though superficially opposed within the framework of that order. We cannot choose between them any more than we can between Palamon and Arcite or possibly Turnus and Aeneas. Achilles' nervous resentment often recalls that of Dryden's Turnus, as when Achilles looks 'on the King askant' (224), and his attack on Agamemnon replays Drances' on Turnus in Book XI of the *Aeneis*. Drances says:

Mankind, it seems, is made for you alone;
We, but the Slaves who mount you to the Throne:
A base ignoble Crowd, without a Name,
Unwept, unworthy of the Fun'ral Flame:
By Duty bound to forfeit each his Life,
That *Turnus* may possess a Royal Wife. (XI.570–5)

Achilles uses the same rhyme words for the same charge and vigorously rephrases Drances' image in a satiric twelve-syllable line:

O, Impudent, regardful of thy own,
Whose Thoughts are center'd on thy self alone,
Advanc'd to Sovereign Sway, for better Ends
Than thus like abject Slaves to treat thy Friends.
...
Thine is the Triumph; ours the Toil alone:
We bear thee on our Backs, and mount thee on the Throne. (225–8, 238–9)

Generally, Achilles' imagery is more unpleasant, more concrete, and more interesting than Drances', as when he makes Agamemnon seem like an iron man with 'hook'd rapacious Hands' (247). This has several important implications. First, Dryden could be stylistically more free in a fragmentary translation from Homer than in translating a whole poem; also second thoughts may have been best. Moreover, Dryden was capitalizing on the fact that Virgil had obviously been imitating Homer in this section;[11] it was fun to play chronological games, making Homer seem to develop out of Virgil instead of the reverse, and to uncover his predecessors' tracks. Last, Dryden's own politics or anti-politics were somewhat more definite: Achilles speaks with more authority than Drances and makes a just rebellion seem possible, though only in a world where tyrant and subject deserve each other.

VIRGIL AND BOCCACCIO

Virgilian allusions seem most concentrated in the three Boccaccio poems in *Fables*, each of which also parallels some fragment of the plot of the *Aeneis*. The traces of a so-called gothic style in 'Theodore and Honoria' and 'Sigismonda and Guiscardo' might more properly be called a Virgilian style finally imitated in English. Dryden affected to be unaware of Boccaccio's admiration for Virgil,[12] emphasizing Boccaccio's role as founder of a vernacular literature, an Italian Chaucer, and thus in a way an anti-Virgil (K, IV, 1446). My own guess is that mysterious links connected Boccaccio to his Italian predecessor, but Dryden suppressed or ignored them, making Boccaccio seem more an equal of Virgil than an imitator. Boccaccio occupies an intermediate stage between the paganism of Ovid and Homer and Chaucer's cheerful energy and relative moral certainty, thus filling the historical position that Virgil might have occupied. The moral limbo in which Boccaccio's characters function resembles in a general way the existential confusion of Virgil's world. Supernatural influences are ambiguous, not overtly contemptible as in the *Aeneid*, but hell is more forcible than heaven and ultimately the characters are guessing about the after-life. The lack of historical definition in Boccaccio's world contributes to the gothic feeling. Political statements are only occasionally precise (the Norman Tancred does have a standing army: 'Sigismonda and Guiscardo,' 590–605); more often they are amorphous and vaguely universalized, set in a cloudy realm of myth which surely allowed Dryden far greater freedom to criticize the political order.[13]

Dryden's use of the 1620 English translation possibly contributed to his stylistic vagueness, though he certainly knew the original,[14] and the 1620 translator was incapable of even seeing the ironies in Boccaccio that Dryden develops so well. The 1620 translator used an expurgated version of the Italian text (Leonardo Salviati, 1582) from which many Christian references, like the word 'God,' had been left out because Boccaccio seemed frivolous to the Counter-Reformation mind.[15] Dryden does not replace them. Thus, in the original of 'Cymon and Iphigenia' several characters invoke God, while Dryden uses phrases like 'the Bless'd above' or 'the Pow'rs above' (261, 489), making his characters seem less confident of their faith or of whatever supernatural force authorizes their actions. The calculating Lysymachus is the only exception in the 1620 version; he refers to God three times, once more than in Boccaccio.[16] Dryden makes this character into an Achitophel, who invokes the flattering gods who reward *virtu* and who openly disdains religion: 'Let Heav'n be neuter, and the Sword decide' (537). We remain in doubt about where God really stands, if there is a God at all.

In Boccaccio's 'Sigismonda' Tancred, the heroine's tyrannical father, makes four of the five references to God. Dryden's Tancred only exclaims: 'To what has Heav'n reserv'd my Age?' (325); Sigismonda refers three times to heaven and once to hell in her death scene, but uncertainty returns when she refers to Guiscardo as 'Source of my Life, and Lord of my Desires' (651). Boccaccio's Tancred thus emerges as a genuine spokesman for justice despite his cruelty, perhaps having constructed an Old Testament image of God, while Dryden's Tancred appears to speak only in the name of personal power. Sigismonda, by default, seems to speak for God since she defends the oppressed and has a clearer sense of justice. She appears to have faith in an invisible God: 'Or call it Heav'ns Imperial Pow'r alone, / Which moves on Springs of Justice, though unknown' (493–4). Characters who struggle for faith or attempt to find a basis for heroism in a dark universe do seem admirable, just as Virgil's Nisus, or even Turnus, is admirable, though they lack Aeneas's unaccountable certainty: 'Iuppiter hac stat' (XII.565). 'Theodore and Honoria' has a negative kind of certainty. While the knight in the 1620 version says evasively that his lady was sent 'to the same place where I was tormented,'[17] Boccaccio names the inferno, and Dryden mentions it at every opportunity. His visionary knight is 'damn'd in Hell,' an 'infernal Knight,' a 'Fiend,' a 'grisly Spectre,' assisted by 'Hell-hounds' (165, 189, 193, 197, 213).[18] Moral values in this poem are unverifiable and the infernal vision comes like a self-fulfilling expectation.

Dryden's Virgilian tone reinforces this amorphous sense of a supernatural presence and adds levels of uncertainty about the psyches of the main characters. 'Theodore and Honoria' contains a description of nature before each of the infernal knight's two appearances.[19] Nature's mysterious disorders at once project Theodore's anxieties and prepare for the vision, which enacts the punishment of a scornful woman like Theodore's ironically named mistress, Honoria (Dryden invented the name). The passages thus bring Theodore's subconscious hostilities to the surface. The following lines expand upon only one sentence in Boccaccio:

> While list'ning to the murm'ring Leaves he stood,
> More than a Mile immers'd within the Wood,
> At once the Wind was laid; the whisp'ring sound
> Was dumb; a rising Earthquake rock'd the Ground:
> With deeper Brown the Grove was overspred:
> A suddain Horror seiz'd his giddy Head,
> And his Ears tinckled, and his Colour fled.
> Nature was in alarm. (88–95)

> Et essendo già passata presso che la quinta ora del giorno, et esso bene un mezzo miglio per la pigneta entrato, non ricordandosi di mangiare nè d'altra cosa, subitamente gli parve udire un grandissimo pianto e guai altissimi messi da una donna.[20]

Reuben Brower has observed that these lines in 'Theodore and Honoria' recall Hecate's approach in Book VI of the *Aeneid*,[21] but the passage also happens to be much more Virgilian than Dryden's translation of the Hecate scene, which was cheerfully vivid, almost theatrical in style: 'Then Earth began to bellow, Trees to dance; / And howling Dogs in glimm'ring Light advance' (VI.366–7). This is not filtered through Aeneas's psyche as the lines from 'Theodore and Honoria' are filtered through Theodore's, and the philosophical and political material in Book VI of the *Aeneis* tends to overwhelm any potential interest in the hero's subconscious. Yet that essential dimension of Virgil's style, which a reader of the *Aeneis* might assume Dryden failed to understand, is reproduced in *Fables*. The so-called gothic style is actually Virgilian imitation.

The style of 'Sigismonda and Guiscardo' might be called 'political gothic,' a concept that seems appropriate to describe such works as *The Castle of Otranto* and *Caleb Williams*.[22] In political gothic, tyranny and freedom seem inflated to cosmic proportions and the tensions of an oppressed state seem diffused across the landscape. Tyranny becomes an essence that transcends the evils of any specific regime. This style distinguishes Dryden's 'Sigismonda' both from Boccaccio's story and from the other English versions of the tale, none of which Dryden knew, in any case, except for Robert Wilmot's *Tragedy of Tancred and Gismund* (1591–2).[23] These versions and Dryden's could be read in terms of their authors' efforts to rationalize Tancred's double role as cruel father and suffering old man and in turn to rationalize subtle characterization with the folklore element of the tale, Tancred's decision to punish his daughter by sending her Guiscardo's heart in a goblet. Wilmot plays upon the word 'heart' so that the murder of

Guiscardo gives real shape to an accumulating image pattern; Dryden plays on the various implications of the word 'blood,' adding disturbingly carnal overtones to the conception of noble descent.[24] Dryden also emphasizes Tancred's old age, though this is hardly intended to make him sympathetic, since Dryden did not perceive old age as a gentle and virtuous state of being (he even admits to the old man's persisting lust in the *poeta loquitur* introducing 'Cymon and Iphigenia'). Dryden's Tancred shows what can happen if a lustful, self-pitying old man rules a patriarchal state with unlimited power to act out his impulses. Because of his power his very humanity is a negative fact – a perception which Dryden may owe to republican theorists. Tancred's jealousy blights the entire landscape of Salerno, which is like a prison in belonging to him emotionally as well as politically.

Dryden shows Tancred's 'ownership' of Salerno in his account of the cave where the lovers meet, another metaphoric landscape going beyond Boccaccio. On one level he follows the sustained *double entendre* provided by Boccaccio, in which the cave is a gigantic image for Sigismonda's repressed sexuality, 'o'ergrown / With Brambles, choak'd by Time, and now unknown' (113–14).[25] After the relationship has gone on for some time, 'The Cave was now become a common Way, / The Wicket often open'd, knew the Key' (181–2). This reveals what Sigismonda does not know about herself, like the passage in 'Theodore,' though it is more overtly ironic. However, Dryden's cave is also political, suggesting the vague ancestral force lying behind Tancred and showing how a tyrant can become imprisoned by his own malevolence:

> The Work it seem'd of some suspicious Prince,
> Who, when abusing Pow'r with lawless Might,
> From Publick Justice would secure his Flight. (104–6)

Though Tancred commits no public crime, he likes to retreat to this 'Tyrants Den' (119) where his daughter makes love in a 'glimm'ring and malignant Light' (116), thinking that she is free. But tyranny as an essence is inescapable, as Tancred's very presence in the cave seems to demonstrate. He considers himself at home in the realm of his daughter's most private thoughts and actions.

The heroine herself is thus infected by the psychic environment of the poem. But Dryden also translated this story against the background of the Dido episode and gave Sigismonda an equally ambiguous character.[26] The basic parallel is that each is an attractive widow of great intellectual and emotional power, *almost* a political leader but never entirely free from the lurking threat of a male invader; each tries to control her own destiny by embarking on a love affair. Like Dido, Sigismonda is defeated by Fate itself (*Aeneis*, IV.517; 'Sigismonda,' 187, 224).[27] Both heroines try to rationalize their affairs by getting married, though the marriages seem inauthentic because they are so clandestine. Sigismonda's priest 'mutter'd fast the Matrimony o're, / For fear committed Sin should get before' (165–6). In the original story Ghismonda did not marry; her extramarital sex was justified by the conventions of courtly love. Marriage is a rough road in the *Decameron*, few couples having the persistence to work out honest mutual relationships with each other. The hypocritical priest may be designed to satirize Dryden's enemies Collier and Milbourne, and he also recalls the various Parson Smirks of Restoration comedy. Yet, within the context of the poem Dryden's change recalls Dido's self-deception and implies that Sigismonda is not very concerned with respectability.

Both heroines marry in a symbolic cave. Sigismonda's contains a 'conscious Bed' (231) like that on which Dido dies (IV.932); Sigismonda is married by a 'conscious Priest' (151) and Dido is observed by 'conscious' and 'howling Nymphs' (IV.244). All of this consciousness tells us only how much the heroines lack it. Their half-buried guilt is projected onto their environment, which seems to accuse them by uttering their secret thoughts. Their husbands' intentions are never completely known. Boccaccio provides no chance to eavesdrop on Guiscardo's thoughts, but Dryden makes him seem at least as insincere as Aeneas. Boccaccio's Guiscardo speaks only one line, summarized in the first line of the following passage:

> The Faults of Love by Love are justifi'd:
> With unresisted Might the Monarch reigns,
> He levels Mountains, and he raises Plains;
> And not regarding Diff'rence of Degree,
> Abas'd your Daughter, and exalted me. (281–5)

Inevitably Dryden has been accused of ruining the mystery,[28] but he seems to have been interested in making Guiscardo as conscious of and close-mouthed about the subliminal politics of love as Aeneas. Guiscardo's response thus contributes to the ominous atmosphere engulfing Sigismonda. In neither version is the author mainly concerned with mutual, requited love.

'Sigismonda,' like the Dido episode, treats an independent woman in a political context. Dido is at least sporadically aware of her role as a queen and she feels threatened by the rejected suitor Hyarbas, who might invade

Carthage; while Hyarbas in turn recalls that he gave Dido the land on which Carthage was built in the first place. Nevertheless, Dido is a victim in relation to men and is most articulate in expressing feelings. Sigismonda controls her feelings and uses a concrete political vocabulary:

> What have I done in this, deserving Blame?
> State-Laws may alter: Nature's are the same;
> Those are usurp'd on helpless Woman-kind,
> Made without our Consent, and wanting Pow'r to bind. (417–20)

This is the language of Restoration feminism, which had already appeared in the works of Otway and Behn and was, at the very time Dryden wrote this poem, being developed more fully by Mary Astell.[29] It is essentially a Whig argument for just rebellion applied to the condition of women; interestingly, it was *not* automatically rejected by writers who despised the Whigs. Although the argument remains somewhat suspect because of its origins, it pointedly reveals that Whigs and Tories alike have created the conditions for a just rebellion within their own families. Sigismonda, like Achilles, thus presents a genuine attack on tyranny, though like Achilles she is flawed by the dubious impulses that afflict everyone.

In one important way Sigismonda and Dido seem to be opposites. As their stories progress, Dido becomes frenzied, Sigismonda abnormally controlled – masculine, as Dryden perceives it (376, 384). She refuses to cry, while Tancred – like Virgil's old men – cries endlessly and copiously. Sigismonda invokes nature's laws and justice; Dido attacks 'Man's Injustice' and calls Aeneas a traitor to her 'Throne and Bed' (IV.531, 539). However, the apparent contrast conceals an underlying similarity, for both heroines behave theatrically and the logic of their emotions in each case leads to a ritualistic and flamboyant suicide. Each heroine becomes engrossed in dismembered bits of animal flesh. Dido (even early in the book) inspects 'the panting Entrails' of a sacrifice to learn about her own 'bleeding Heart' (IV.88, 90). Later, the wine she pours becomes 'putrid Blood' (IV.659), she engages in 'Rites obscene' (IV.748), and she collects 'hoary Simples' and 'baleful Juices' (IV.743, 745), thoroughly immersed in the world of the flesh. Sigismonda prepares a 'Juice of Simples, friendly to Despair' (624) and 'devoutly glew[s] / Her Lips' to Guiscardo's heart (641–2) before drinking poison from the very goblet containing the heart. Like Dido's behavior, Sigismonda's seems part of a performance, and we wonder if her intellect only serves her inner drives. Still, this does not wholly undermine her self-defence, since no one in her morally obscure world has better grounds for conviction. Aeneas at least got messages from Jove and Venus, however doubtful these gods seemed to Dryden; Dido is a less privileged character in a story where *some* characters benefit from supernatural guidance. In 'Sigismonda,' however, every character exists in uncertainty, a state that reflected Dryden's own feelings more truthfully.

The Virgilian parallels in 'Cymon and Iphigenia' are used quite differently, except that again we feel trapped in a world providing little guidance to truth. 'Cymon' contains parallels both to Virgil and to Homer, since much of its action involves a sea journey and its conclusion is the rape of a city for the sake of abducting two women. These motifs are part of the general epic tradition, which Dryden here uses satirically. Cymon, the son of a country squire, is awakened to consciousness by love, but his new ability to think only teaches him to back up love with violence: 'Love taught me Force, and Force shall Love maintain' (303). This is as ugly a comment on political sex as Guiscardo's retort to Tancred.

Dryden's innocent bumpkin is no *tabula rasa* but a mass of chaotic feelings, and Cymon's easy transition to man of action shows how the ordinary man, the essential 'Man-Child' (216), and the butcher-hero can be seen as one. Dryden's satiric implications appear in the echoes of *Absalom and Achitophel*, one in Lysymachus's speech, which I have already discussed, and the other in the bland introductory lines that link Cymon's Cyprus to David's patriarchal fantasy land:

> In that sweet Isle, where *Venus* keeps her Court,
> And ev'ry Grace, and all the Loves resort;
> Where either Sex is form'd of softer Earth,
> And takes the bent of Pleasure from their Birth;
> There liv'd a *Cyprian* Lord, above the rest,
> Wise, Wealthy, with a num'rous Issue blest. (42–7)

Cymon corresponds to Absalom/Monmouth. Though Dryden would hardly have bothered to satirize Monmouth at this point, the analogy still defines Cymon's character. On very slight suggestion from Boccaccio Dryden created a satiric epyllion or a second-degree mock-epic, since the world of *Absalom and Achitophel* is debased to a still lower degree.

Since Boccaccio gave the Homeric names Iphigenia and Cassandra to the two women in his story, one wonders if Boccaccio himself was attempting an epic parallel that Dryden chose to develop, much as he developed the Virgilian possibilities in 'Palamon and Arcite.' For instance, Dryden compares Cymon's capture of Iphigenia to Paris's rape of Helen (319). However, 'Iphigenia' had comic overtones for Dryden at this time: in 1699 she had been the subject of two bad tragedies. Dryden wrote of these competing plays: 'Both the Iphiginias have been playd with bad Success; & being both acted, one against the other, in the same week, clashd together, like two rotten ships, which cou'd not endure the shock; & sunk to rights.'[30] The name thus belongs to mock-epic and in the context of Dryden's poem suggests mainly the heroine's remarkable willingness to be sacrified to men and to let men sacrificed themselves for her. She is a debased version of the female stereotype, just as Cymon is of the male. The real Iphigenia, Agamemnon's daughter, is mentioned earlier in *Fables* in 'The Speeches of Ajax and Ulysses,' where Ulysses brags of getting Agamemnon to sacrifice his daughter: 'I only durst th' Imperial Pow'r controul, / And undermin'd the Parent in his Soul' (302–3). Though here Iphigenia is truly a victim, both poems show the epic world as dehumanizing.

Cymon's sea journey might at first recall many others. However, Dryden's ominous tone replicates that of the Swallows' disastrous flight in *The Hind and the Panther*; again, without implying that Cymon is a Swallow/Catholic, Dryden makes him seem equally foolhardy. More concretely, Dryden treats the sea journey as a mock epic parallel to Book III of the *Aeneis*. Book III, as part of Aeneas's account of his experiences before reaching Carthage, belongs to the early stages of his development, when he is at least roughly comparable to Cymon. Like Aeneas, Cymon encounters a symbolic storm, heavy with moral implication:

> And Night came on, not by degrees prepar'd,
> But all at once; at once the Winds arise,
> The Thunders roul, the forky Lightning flies:
> In vain the Master issues out Commands,
> In vain the trembling Sailors ply their Hands:
> The Tempest unforeseen prevents their Care,
> And from the first they labour in despair. (332–8)

In the *Aeneis* the pilot Palinurus 'no distinction found / Betwixt the Night and Day' (III.264–5). Both storms are as figurative as the gothic landscapes, symbolizing the heroes' lack of moral direction and more generally the human lack of foresight. For all his flaws, Cymon is universalized much as Aeneas is.

The differences are also important. Aeneas has not at this point recognized his true home, which will be Italy, or detached his will from that of his aged and burdensome father, whereas Cymon has left a comfortable home, to say the least, for an unknown future. He proceeds to degenerate, not to transcend his earlier self. He agrees to Lysymachus's plan for the double rape, and on breaking up the wedding feast, he and his troops are compared to harpies (581–3), the monsters who polluted the Trojans' meal (III.294–6). Dryden's symbolism has so reversed itself that Cymon has become more like Aeneas's enemy than like Aeneas himself, though it is true that Aeneas eventually invades Italy and disrupts the marriage planned between Turnus and Lavinia. A final parallel differentiates Cymon from Aeneas. Cymon at the end of the poem finds refuge in Crete: '*Jove*'s Isle they seek; nor *Jove* denies his Coast' (628). At just this point, and in almost identical words, Aeneas has been forced onwards again: 'Search *Italy*, for *Jove* denies thee *Creet*' (III.228). Cymon is now an anti-Aeneas.

At the very least Cymon is incapable of Aeneas's struggle, remaining in the self-enclosed world of the stupid man and failing to attain to the level of awareness that Aeneas has reached in Book I. The ironic parallel works whether one takes Aeneas as a positive or negative point of reference, though Dryden's meaning becomes far more devastating when one takes the bad Aeneas into account. 'Cymon and Iphigenia' then becomes the commentary on the dark side of Aeneas which Dryden could not have made while translating Virgil without taking far more exorbitant liberties than even he allowed himself. The attack on heroism in *Fables* includes a new component, stupidity. In this final respect 'Cymon and Iphigenia' completes the *Aeneis*. One inevitably asks at this point just what political stand Dryden took in *Fables*, since he gives the arguments against tyranny a hearing without idealizing or even seeming to approve of their proponents. In the next chapter I shall try to define his stand more precisely. Dryden was trying to convince the reader, perhaps even himself, that he was beyond political stands altogether.

7

Fables Ancient and Modern

EPICUREANISM IN OLD AGE

The politics, or anti-politics, of *Fables* are a part of Dryden's effort at detachment, or, rather, part of the struggle between detachment and political involvement that is hardly unique in his last work. I can imagine someone arguing that Dryden's detachment was an aspect of his politics, a stance and no more, perhaps even designed to present himself attractively. However, I think that Dryden's struggle was genuine and that sorting out his feelings for James II – what kind of loyalty remained feasible? – was more of a problem for him than deciding how to satirize William, which, I suspect, came easily.

Dryden certainly strove for a mellow, Christian Epicureanism in his old age, evident in the serenity of his dedications to Virgil's *Eclogues* and *Georgics*, and most of all in the preface to *Fables.* Suggestive of prose eclogues, these essays reveal a wish for greater calm in the last years before he died, even if complete serenity was unattainable. Dryden's late letters – he finally wrote some worth reading as literature – present the same face as the prefaces, turning their English country setting into an image of the life of retirement. Visitors and friends pass by, but Dryden himself is stable and hardly moves. The letters make frequent references to gifts of food, such exchanges becoming symbolic of the private values of hospitality and friendship. In one letter, written to Mrs Steward, Dryden uses a food image to describe the gift of *Fables* itself:

In the mean time, betwixt my intervalls of physique and other remedies which I am useing for my gravell, I am still drudging on: always a Poet, and never a good one. I pass my time sometimes with Ovid, and sometimes with our old English poet, Chaucer; translating such stories as best please my fancy; and intend besides them to add somewhat of my own: so that it is not impossible, but ere the summer be pass'd, I may come down to you with a volume in my hand, like a dog out of the water, with a duck in his mouth.[1]

The dog has hunted down a duck, but seems strikingly harmless, neither a Cerberus nor a cynic satirist. Though in the event it was not entirely true, Dryden wanted to feel that his last work transcended satire, if only for the benefit of his own health.

The preface to *Fables* reveals his limited success: after a good beginning as a harmless old gentleman, he ends by responding to the attacks of Richard Blackmore, Jeremy Collier, and Luke Milbourne. The passage conveys disgust enough, though it is almost entirely cast as an explanation of Dryden's refusal to lose his temper:

If he [Collier] be my Enemy, let him triumph; if he be my Friend, as I have given him no Personal Occasion to be otherwise, he will be glad of my Repentance. It becomes me not to draw my Pen in the Defence of a bad Cause, when I have so often drawn it for a good one. (K, IV, 1462)

This contempt is relatively moderate in tone, but several poems in *Fables* itself reveal old men to be subject to lust, jealousy, impulsive cruelty, and wordiness, not just to harmless flaws like a weak memory. Tancred displays all these dangerous qualities except wordiness, Nestor's claim to fame in 'The Twelfth Book of Ovid,' though he is on the whole conciliatory. Dryden at last admits himself into the poem once again, responding to Collier directly in the introduction to 'Cymon and Iphigenia':

What needs he Paraphrase on what we mean?
We were at worst but Wanton; he's Obscene.
I, nor my Fellows, nor my Self excuse;
But Love's the Subject of the Comick Muse:
Nor can we write without it, nor would you
A Tale of only dry Instruction view ... (21–6)

If Dryden had been rigidly political, he might have identified with Collier, who as a non-juring clergyman was in a position of exile comparable to Dryden's. But Dryden shows no moderating admiration or regret for Collier's misplaced energy; Collier had discredited himself in his attack on the stage, revealing himself as an enemy to literature. He is a foil to Dryden in *Fables*, which shows how two men who refused allegiance to William adapted in opposite ways. Dryden associates himself with Chaucer, who could either satirize or eulogize a priest, whichever was more appropriate, and retain his serenity:

Yet my Resentment has not wrought so far, but that I have follow'd *Chaucer* in his Character of a Holy Man, and have enlarg'd on that Subject with some Pleasure, reserving to my self the Right, if I shall think fit hereafter, to describe another sort of Priests, such as are more easily to be found than the Good Parson; such as have given the last Blow to Christianity in this Age, by a Practice so contrary to their Doctrine. But this will keep cold till another time. (K, IV, 1454–5)

The encomium on Chaucer tends to fill out Dryden's own character, so that we end up feeling that Dryden was the man with a wonderfully comprehensive nature: Apelles is never entirely concealed behind his statue.

The more scientific side of Epicureanism appears in Dryden's imagery. One aspect is atomism, used as an image to show the rule of chance in the physical world, as in the Duchess of Ormonde's illness, caused by 'malignant Atoms' (113).[2] The crone in 'The Wife of Bath Her Tale' says:

Chance gave us being, and by Chance we live.
Such as our Atoms were, ev'n such are we,
Or call it Chance, or strong Necessity.
Thus, loaded with dead weight, the Will is free. (421–4)

Chaucer too had implied that human nature depends partly on accidents of the body, but his Wife of Bath is relatively indefinite about how it works, while Chaucer himself generally emphasized a psychology based on the humours, of which there is no significant trace in *Fables*. Dryden was possibly more interested in the negative connotations of atomism than in matter theory itself. He seems to have conflated atomism with the Lucretian idea of the seeds of things, since he uses 'seeds' in a more positive context to convey the intangibility of matter or the uncertainty of substance at a microscopic level, as when the fairy knights in 'The Flower and the Leaf' light a fire, 'And Seeds of Latent-Fire from Flints provoke' (414). In 'Of the Pythagorean Philosophy' Pythagoras uses a more neutral image in the phrase 'pure Particles of *Æther*' (290). Three different philosophies underlie these images, but Dryden shifts his imagery because the philosophies have different connotations.

Another aspect of matter is its very substantiality. I have already mentioned Dryden's style in 'Of the Pythagorean Philosophy'; in 'Ceyx and

Alcyone' nature seems more real than either the human or the divine characters. This description of a storm at sea lacks the obvious moral overtones of the storm in 'Cymon and Iphigenia':

> Now Waves on Waves ascending scale the Skies,
> And in the Fires above, the Water fries:
> When yellow Sands are sifted from below,
> The glitt'ring Billows give a golden Show:
> And when the fouler bottom spews the Black,
> The *Stygian* Dye the tainted Waters take:
> Then frothy White appear the flatted Seas,
> And change their Colour, changing their Disease. (125–32)

Dryden added some details to Ovid's description, like 'golden Show,' 'fouler bottom,' 'Dye,' 'tainted,' and the whole last line, which connects the disease in nature to whatever malignant force threatened the Duchess of Ormonde's life; Dryden seems to be exaggerating the out-of-season wit that he disapproved of in Ovid (Ceyx dies in this storm).[3] His additions also make nature seem ominous and unstable, not truly impersonal though not precisely evil either: the god Aeolus's indifference to humanity lies behind this storm, but it is an active or conscious sort of indifference. 'Ceyx and Alcyone' intensifies the Epicurean mode of *Sylvae*, while revealing a new poetic strength, a sense of nature's energy, presented in its own terms.

Dryden is here displaying one possible attitude for our judgment. One is not expected so much to share it as, in Epicurean style, to contemplate it momentarily until it is replaced by a better one. 'Ceyx' is followed by 'The Flower and the Leaf,' in which nature's theatre is far more innocent and has a simple meaning contributed by a youthful observer. From the seclusion of her bower she watches a visionary procession consisting of two stylized groups of knights and ladies, a 'Mystique Show' (460), in the same way that we enjoy and interpret works of art without thinking that we are literally 'inside' their worlds. Dryden suggests this kind of aesthetic situation – half in, half outside the world of the work of art – by making his objects seem substantial yet always about to disappear or transform themselves into something else:

> Nine royal Knights in equal Rank succeed,
> Each Warrior mounted on a fiery Steed:
> In golden Armour glorious to behold;
> The Rivets of their Arms were nail'd with Gold.

Their Surcoats of white Ermin-Fur were made;
With Cloth of Gold between that cast a glitt'ring Shade.
The Trappings of their Steeds were of the same;
The golden Fringe ev'n set the Ground on flame;
And drew a precious Trail ... (254–62)

The gold from Ovid's tempest reappears here, as if it were a permanent essence that can be reshaped in ever-changing poetic artefacts. Gold is either unstable like sand or suggestive of intangibility itself.

'The Flower and the Leaf' also includes a moral, which follows the spectacle without intruding on its immediacy. The narrator has thus been detached only for the time of viewing. Her detachment is encouraged by the fact that most of the 'action' is a tournament, recalling Aeneas's ritualized games in *Sylvae*, or Theseus's ordered games in 'Palamon and Arcite' (though Theseus's games deteriorate into chaotic violence). Moreover, a character in the poem, a fairy, actually relates 'The secret meaning of this moral Show' (599), though she soon has to leave, obeying the laws of her own world. The moral is in fact childishly simple – asceticism outlasts sensuality – but we discover a more interesting truth, that a work of art 'talks' to us in some way. The spectator thus benefits from her partial involvement, which was possible in the first place because the human and moral elements in the spectacle gave her something to identify with. In *Sylvae* the human elements contradicted the aesthetic order; here they reinforce each other. The narrator, of course, is a character in Dryden's 'The Flower and the Leaf' and so has the same relationship to us that the fairy had to her. She is both a representative literary character and a representative reader, whose unusual innocence does not separate us from her because we share with her other human qualities, like inexperience with visions. The theory of art in this poem also draws on the use of fairies by some other great English writers. Dryden was trying to define and thus to create an English tradition:

The Master Work-man of the Bow'r was known
Through Fairy-Lands, and built for *Oberon* ... (78–9)

Dryden here foreshadows much in the aesthetics of Pope, Addison, and Collins, and the influence of this poem is still apparent in several of the Romantic writers. Keats wrote a sonnet to it: 'Written on a blank space of a leaf at the end of Chaucer's tale of The Flowre and the Lefe.' One should not be fooled by the archaic spelling of the title into thinking that the original medieval poem was the important one; Keats could have read the original bound in with a collection of Dryden's *Fables*, along with the originals of Dryden's other Chaucerian pieces. Dryden presented 'The Flower and the Leaf' as a synthesis of one aspect of English literature, implying that he could do honour to his native country without descending to political controversy or even to a fable based upon a great military action.

POLITICS IN *FABLES*

The politics of *Fables* involves a more calculated sort of detachment and some topical allusions, though I do not think that an account of these allusions would entirely explain Dryden's stance. *Fables* is anti-Williamite, as one might expect, blatantly so when Dryden early in the sequence contrasts Theseus's gratitude towards artists with the indifference of 'Princes now' ('Palamon and Arcite,' II.661). On this theme Dryden can never be accused of silence. But *Fables* is not decisively Jacobite either, and Dryden just might be saying 'a plague on both your houses' to the rival kings. We should not conclude that because Dryden attacks a whole spectrum of tyrants and warriors he favours James by default. Rival lovers and rival warriors (though traditional in heroic plays) are in fact a prominent motif in *Fables* – for example, Palamon and Arcite, Ajax and Ulysses, Cymon and Pasimond – and in each case the opponents are either too evenly matched or too flawed to permit an easy decision between them, though each may be flawed in a different way. Such conflicts cannot be resolved without the intervention of a figure superior to the conflict itself. However, this occurs only in 'Palamon and Arcite,' when Theseus intervenes, first to transform the knights' conflict into the art of tournament and later, after Arcite's death, to persuade Emily to wed the survivor. The very presence of a king like Theseus reflects an imaginary situation, though the concept of the philosopher-king (Numa is another) may represent utopian politics in *Fables*. In stories without such a transcendent figure, like 'Cymon and Iphigenia,' the rivalries must work themselves out through some combination of force, deception, and chance. Even when the rivals are opposites in character, one may end by rejecting both; for instance, Ajax is an athletic brute, but Ulysses is manipulative and inhumanly cold.

One can find another variation on this theme by turning back to the fourth Georgic, to the battle of the bees or, as Dryden puts it, 'two contending Princes' (121).[4] In Dryden's version, as in Virgil's, the rightful king can easily be distinguished from the usurper. At first, Dryden seems to be showing a preference:

One Monarch wears an honest open Face;
Shap'd to his Size, and Godlike to behold,
His Royal Body shines with specks of Gold,
And ruddy Skales; for Empire he design'd,
Is better born, and of a Nobler Kind.
That other looks like Nature in disgrace,
Gaunt are his sides, and sullen is his face:
And like their grizly Prince appears his gloomy Race:
Grim, ghastly, rugged, like a thirsty train
That long have travel'd through a desart plain,
And spet from their dry Chaps the gather'd dust again. (138–48)

Dryden exaggerates Virgil's contrast between the two kings, associating the false king with William's well-known lack of good looks. The true king seems a bit complacent, but his 'honest open Face' deflects suspicion, especially as it recalls the 'Plain good Man' of *The Hind and the Panther*, who was a composite figure linking James to Aeneas and to Christ.

However, the next lines create suspicion of kingship as such by shifting the perspective to the detached, superior point of view of Aristaeus, the beekeeper, who has no special interest in either rival, beyond the bees' appearance of health. The beekeeper only wants to preserve his swarm and so he clips the wings of their leader or leaders – 'their high-flying Arbitrary Kings' (162) – whoever they are:

At their Command, the People swarm away;
Confine the Tyrant, and the Slaves will stay. (163–4)

Tyrants and slaves have complementary roles within the same closed system, but the tyrant is himself a slave of the beekeeper-god, who like Theseus transcends the rivalry. I think that Dryden, too, came to see the rivalry between William and James as spurious. The hive is very fragile as a model community, and I am not sure than even Virgil saw it as an *ideal* community, marked as it is by an abnormal, asexual devotion to work and indifference to the individual, a flaw that almost destroys the beekeeper, Aristaeus, himself. Aristaeus learns to appreciate the strength of the passions later on in the poem, in the Orpheus and Eurydice episode. Aristaeus's near loss of his bees parallels Orpheus's loss of his wife, and when the hive is reborn, it incorporates a feminine principle, appearing like clusters of grapes, or 'uvam' (*Georgics* IV.558). The beekeeper's detachment reflects a distorted self.

Dryden, like Virgil, displays condescension towards the hive, but he uses his own political vocabulary. All kings are potential tyrants. Perhaps he would have preferred James to William, but after eight or nine years of dissociation from the government he stepped back and saw the dangerous elements in kingship itself. His position was thus ambivalent and bears a striking resemblance to republicanism. He might have been Jacobite if there remained any point in being so, but instead he became a critic of monarchy, even adopting such republican terminology as the tyrant-slave dichotomy. However, Dryden's ambiguous treatment of Sigismonda and Achilles should tell us that he was not a republican either, if it meant supporting dangerous individualists or ambitious great lords. The philosopher-kings are the only characters in political roles about whom Dryden is not ambivalent.

Fables contains numerous references to tyrants and tyranny that sometimes recall William but in context often transcend specific individuals. I have already discussed the hopeless conflict between Achilles and Agamemnon, and the *Ilias* selection ends by carrying the tyrant-slave relationship to the level of Olympian domestic life. Juno tries to wheedle her husband, whom she addresses as 'Tyrant of the Skies' (742), into explaining his intrigue with Thetis, Achilles' mother. Jove responds:

> My Houshold Curse, my lawful Plague, the Spy
> Of *Jove*'s Designs, his other squinting Eye;
> Why this vain prying, and for what avail?
> *Jove* will be Master still and *Juno* fail.
> ...
> Curb that impetuous Tongue, before too late
> The Gods behold, and tremble at thy Fate. (752–5, 760–1)

Homeric burlesque permits Dryden to comment on *two* additional realms, the family and the divine order, by analogy to the politics of tyranny. Jove solves his problem in the easiest way possible, always available to a tyrant – by the threat of force. Juno *is* a meddler, but only because her husband's love life has accustomed her to being suspicious, and her submission is not a sign of contentedness. As in Achilles' case, the rebellious slave is a product of tyranny.

Dryden's mingled acceptance of the present situation and nostalgia for the past appear in 'Of the Pythagorean Philosophy,' where political transformations are seen against the background of cosmic process. Life is characterized by change, not by a stable order of things:

Thus in successive Course the Minutes run,
And urge their Predecessor Minutes on,
Still moving, ever new: For former Things
Are set aside, like abdicated Kings:
And every moment alters what is done,
And innovates some Act till then unknown. (272–7)

The word 'innovates' expresses the major note of resentment, recalling the fact that Dryden called innovation 'the Blow of Fate' in *Absalom and Achitophel* (800). However, the later passage treats time, which is inexorable, as the cause of innovation, not fate, whose sporadic and violent attacks may conceivably be opposed through some kind of defensive strength like that advocated by David/Charles. One cannot oppose time, and if time is on the side of faction or usurpation, one must accept political change. Ironically Dryden discovers an orderly 'successive Course' in the process of time and not where he had once sought for it, in a succession of rulers.

The theme of abdication appears in 'Cymon and Iphigenia' as well. Besides blaming Cymon's militancy for Rhodes' downfall, Dryden points to the fact that Lysymachus, the Rhodian magistrate, has not only helped to kill his king, Pasimond, and his younger brother, Ormisda, but has abandoned his country with Cymon and their mistresses. So far, the two brothers might suggest Charles and James, making Lysymachus a sort of Williamite supporter. But the topical allegory is fairly complex, as Dryden jolts us from one perspective to another. Though Lysymachus is not himself a king, he has a responsible role, and is the obvious person to replace Pasimond and Ormisda:

What should the People do, when left alone?
The Governor, and Government are gone.
The publick Wealth to Foreign Parts convey'd;
Some Troops disbanded, and the rest unpaid.
Rhodes is the Soveraign of the Sea no more ... (615–19)

The first line is pointedly applicable to James, while the reference to the navy identifies Rhodes with England. For a moment Dryden has touched on what ought to have been unthinkable, the possibility that the abdicated king was partly responsible for England's vulnerability and the decline of her naval power.

Dryden's comments on armies also attack two sides of a false dichotomy. 'Palamon and Arcite' satirizes standing armies (which were William's preferred mode of defence), especially in the lines 'Laugh'd all the Pow'rs who favour Tyranny; / And all the Standing Army of the Sky' (III.671–2).[5] Tancred's palace thugs are also a standing army, enacting the tyrant's private will by murdering an inconveniently ambitious subject. But 'Cymon and Iphigenia' contains a long satiric passage on the country militia, an alternative form of defence sometimes preferred by William's opponents because it would be composed of local men, not mercenaries answerable to the king. However, Rhodes' militia is incompetent and dangerous in its own way:[6]

> The Country rings around with loud Alarms,
> And raw in Fields the rude Militia swarms;
> Mouths without Hands; maintain'd at vast Expence,
> In Peace a Charge, in War a weak Defence:
> Stout once a Month they march a blust'ring Band,
> And ever, but in times of Need, at hand ... (399–404)

Rhodes should have depended on her navy, without which the country is open to invasion and cannot even pursue Cymon, much less engage in foreign wars. Rhodes is now especially vulnerable to 'Jove' in Crete, who provides asylum for Cymon and seems an obvious parallel to Louis XIV, who exploited James as a potential invader of England. Cymon is thus like William in one part of the poem, but at the end he turns into James at St Germains, a rather unsettling metaphorical shift, since Dryden moves from a predictable to an unpredictable object of historical satire. There is one consistent thread, however, in so far as Dryden throughout the poem satirizes country squires who pursue their own interests, happily oblivious to their nation's fate. 'Cymon' is an attack on such isolationism, the dark side of Dryden's attempt to urge his cousin to leave his patriarchal isolation and contribute his gifts to the nation as a whole. Cymon is particularly dangerous because stupidity is so often considered harmless or even appealing (as in Roger de Coverley), but Dryden seems to have been trying to teach the less stupid local landowners that they were ultimately responsible for the quality of government, that if they assumed responsibility, the identity of their king might become irrelevant.

One can compare Dryden's stance with one that is undoubtedly Jacobite, though when all is said and done the contrast is not absolutely conclusive. A Jacobite position appears in Sir Roger L'Estrange's 1699 collection of fables, most of which are heavily moralized with political and other kinds of opinions. Occasionally L'Estrange's politics are stated directly:

> SOVEREIGN *Power* is, in it's own Nature, *Inalienable*, and a Prerogative not to be parted with for One Single Hour. It is neither Fair to *Ask* it, nor Reasonable to

Grant it; in respect, both of the Danger, and of the President. ... Crown's are Holy Matters, and not to be play'd withal: for People do not use to *Borrow* Royal Authority, with an Intent to Restore it.[7]

However, L'Estrange's usual, less direct technique in *Fables and Stories Moralized* is to create a moral atmosphere where sudden change seems immoral or evil, a tactic that Aesopic prudence can be used to support. He presents every socially disturbing element as a sign of potential rebellion, not just a subject's desire to change governments, but also his desire to change his station or situation in life, since this will accustom him to accept the principle of change everywhere else.[8] One can see that Dryden's acceptance of Pythagoras already distinguishes him from L'Estrange. L'Estrange thinks that human beings are restless and discontented, wanting change for its own sake: 'WHAT is the whole World now, at This rate of Proceeding, but *a Larger Bear-Garden*? And it is much the same Thing in Camps, Courts of Justice, and great Councels.'[9] It is always 'much the same thing' in this style of thought: L'Estrange makes it seem pointless even to think.

Still, his ideas recall Dryden's in *Absalom and Achitophel*, where 'ease,' the desirable state, is contrasted with 'dis-ease,' which subjects bring upon themselves. Dryden escaped dullness through his wit and through his more subtle treatment of human nature, which permits people to be good, bad, or unstable in a variety of ways. L'Estrange is really in the spirit of the polyglot Aesop – *Aesop's Fables with his Life* (1687) – which might well be called the Catholic Aesop.[10] Here, too, ambition and discontent are linked to rebellion, which in turn comes from the desire for perpetual motion characteristic of youth in general and Monmouth in particular.[11] 'Know your place' is the main theme of this volume; if you are a tortoise, beware of the eagle who offers to lift you above the ground: 'Cette Ambition extravagante de la Tortuë nous apprend à ne nous élever jamais beaucoup au dessus de nôtre condition, si nous ne sommes en mesme temps resolus à une honteuse cheute.'[12] Though Dryden's Cymon recalls Monmouth, he is a landowner's son, not a king's, and he is not a conscious political rebel. Moreover, irresponsible youth is only partly to blame for the troubles of the political order.

There is no doubt that Dryden read and responded to L'Estrange, and that this connection helps to explain what 'fable' and 'Aesop' meant to Dryden in 1700. L'Estrange is a link connecting Dryden to the Grub-Street Aesops of the late 1690s. Since Aesop was a voice capable of exposing the egotism of powerful rulers, he always, even in the Middle Ages, had some generalized political meaning. The traditional life of Aesop emphasized this. Aesop was a slave who protested against his master's injustice, using the prudently oblique genres of fable and of symbolic practical joke. He thus gained fame and confidence before he entered the public realm, where he continued to defend freedom, as in helping his king withstand the threats of Croesus, king of Lydia. The former slave saw the need to exert himself to remain free; though prudent, Aesop believed in resistance, and he was willing to take risks. He was several times imprisoned, though never defeated by this treatment, since imprisonment was clearly the way kings vented their frustration at subjects who were essentially indestructible. In 'To my Honour'd Kinsman' Dyden mentions an ancestor who was imprisoned for refusing to pay an illegal tax to Charles I (188–94). Yet this kinsman remained loyal to the king, and his resistance was ultimately an attempt to teach Charles a lesson: both the values and the symbolic imprisonment could be thought of as Aesopic. The traditional Aesop is loyal, but he combines loyalty with various degrees of courageous resistance, though never with hostility.

The Grub-Street Aesops all have slightly different personas, some deviating from the traditional Aesop. They appeared against the background of a Jacobite plot to assassinate William in 1696, as well as Charles Montagu's fiscal innovations (which were designed to support William's wars, or were so taken) and the backlash against Montagu when he was charged with corruption and various forms of self-interest. References to ambitious, bright young men in this period are more likely to have Montagu in mind than Monmouth.[13] Montagu's importance explains why Aesop was resurrected in the first place: through Aesop writers could allude to the famous beast fable by Montagu and Prior, *The Hind and the Panther Transvers'd*, and thus virtually identify Montagu as their centre of interest. Dryden might also be called to mind, since Montagu's fable parodied Dryden's poem, but his association was irrelevant, though presumably annoying to Dryden. One fable collection identifies Montagu: *Aesop at Epsom ... by a Cit* (1698) is addressed to '*the inimitable Author of the* COUNTRY MOUSE, *and* CITY-MOUSE' and defends Montagu against the Tunbridge Aesop, who '*by* feign'd *and* surreptitious *Fables, seems to bewail the change of the late Gevernment* [sic].' *Aesop in Spain* (1701) and *Bickerstaff's Aesop* (1701) both imitate the Montagu/Prior satire, but they are not a satire on *The Hind and the Panther*:

A Milkwhite Rogue, Immortal and unhang'd,
By Fate and Parliaments severely bang'd,
Without a Saint, A Devil was within;
He sought all Dangers, for he knew all Sin.[14]

One can see how Dryden's indirect involvement would have provoked him to adopt some variation of the Aesopic persona.

Two illustrations by Francis Barlow in the Catholic Aesop, *Aesop's Fables with his Life* (1687), linked Dryden to Aesop on the basis of *The Hind and the Panther*. In one of the illustrations for Aesop's life (reproduced on p 160), Aesop confronts his own statue, erected on his behalf by a grateful king. The caption reads:

Blest be thy name, o King! who thus hast sett,
So just a value on immortall witt,
In this dull age, no statues are allow'd,
But Dryden too must fall i[n]th' undistinguish'd crowd.[15]

The last phase of Aesop's career is referred to here: Aesop died a martyr. First betrayed by his adopted son, Ennus, he began his travels, visiting Egypt, Babylon, and Delphos. However, when he outraged the Delphians by disparaging their character, they tried him unjustly and threw him over a precipice. The last illustration in the Catholic Aesop (plate 31, reproduced on p 161) depicts a shrine to Aesop's memory and links him to the martyr Charles I. Though Dryden tended to see himself as a martyr, he did not go quite this far in glorifying his sufferings. In fact, in 'To my Honour'd Kinsman' he presented his ancestor as a martyr *to* Charles I.

In the Grub-Street Aesops conflict between the old and the young has political meaning: 'old' means politically established and just. There is a persistent war between 'old Aesop' and his sons, the various young Aesops, who all, like Ennus, turn against their stodgy father. Old Aesop lives 'at Whitehall,' meaning that he supports William, and threatens that the lion will summon all the young Aesops to him. In old Aesop's opinion, the Jacobites and the Commonwealthsmen are uniting against the government. Old Aesop is thus not a Jacobite but a defender of the existing monarchy, while the young Aesops stand for a variety of factions or deviant opinions. Aesop's youngest son, at Amsterdam, is particularly unpleasant: '*Now being in this place, Father, and breathing in a free Air, I can talk of nothing but Freedom, Liberty and Property. I hope, if it does offend the Assertors of Tyranny, they'l consider I am in a common Asylum, and out of their reach.*'[16] To the youngest Aesop all English subjects are mice and all kings are tyrants. He is a political atheist.

One would think that a Jacobite could be presented as an *old* Aesop, not a *young* one, since his king was displaced by William. L'Estrange took this tactic, presenting himself as a *very* old Aesop, superior to all controversy.

By permission of the Houghton Library, Harvard University, Department of Printing and Graphic Arts

By permission of the Houghton Library, Harvard University, Department of Printing and Graphic Arts

This is the unstated reason why his Preface emphasizes his old age: 'The Man that puts Pen to Paper on the Wrong side of *Fourscore*, might every jot with as good a Grace, set up for a *Beau*, as for an *Author*.'[17] Since L'Estrange really was eighty-three, this is comically appropriate as a retort to the Whitehall Aesop. L'Estrange leaves himself open to question in his assumption that old men are serene and unthreatened and will always bring peace to the disordered state. As we have seen, Dryden disagreed. Dryden was a relatively youthful sixty-nine when he wrote the preface to *Fables*, in which he in part follows L'Estrange and in part tries to outdo him in drawing attention to his own age, as when he compares himself to 'an old Gentleman, who mounting on Horseback before some Ladies, when I was present, got up somewhat heavily, but desir'd of the Fair Spectators, that they would count Fourscore and eight before they judg'd him' (K, IV, 1446).[18] This is only one of several close parallels between the two prefaces. These parallels certainly link Dryden to the conflict between the young and the old Aesops, but Dryden's precise stand is still a little ambiguous. He may be presenting himself as another old Jacobite through his similarity to L'Estrange, or he may be creating yet another role by means of parody. Dryden as old man is a bit tired out and conscious of the visible limits of the old man's image. He goes out of his way to attack Jeremy Collier, who was a Jacobite. He shows that old men can be tyrants, like Tancred, or liars, like Nestor, who admits his failure to praise Hercules because Hercules had injured him ('The Twelfth Book of Ovid,' 757–60). Since Nestor's pretence that Hercules did not even exist is exactly like Dryden's treatment of William, this is a kind of confession on Dryden's part.

Dryden's stand pre-exists even Jacobitism; he is concerned with the realm of literature itself. He has the courage of the fictive writer, for example, in adding twenty years to his age just to outdo L'Estrange, and in allying himself with a female writer, '*Mademoiselle de Scudery*, who is as old as *Sibyl*' (K, IV, 1459), and who like Dryden is involved in translating Chaucer. He tries to return to the Middle Ages in order to remove himself from the atmosphere of present controversy, and there he finds outspoken models who did not simulate a false detachment: Chaucer sympathized with the Lollards and Boccaccio was compulsively anticlerical. Moreover, in an effort to be disarming L'Estrange had warned in *Fables and Stories Moralized* 'that the *Reader* is not to expect *Order* out of Confusion; or that such a *Rhapsody* as This is, of *Independent Tales*, and *Whimsies*; *Broken Thoughts*, and *Scatter'd Fragments*, should be *all of a Piece*.'[19] Dryden, however, goes out of his way to integrate his collection, and his fables are genuine poems, not the worn-out anecdotes that L'Estrange collected. Aesopic simplicity is not Dryden's mode, though he uses an Aesopic fable in 'The Character of A Good Parson' (34–7). The persona of Aesop is thus absorbed and blended into Dryden's larger sense of form.

Another apparent response to the Aesop controversy is Dryden's letter to his former enemy Montagu in October 1699, concerning 'To My Honour'd Kinsman.' Dryden hopes that 'there is nothing which can justly give offence,' and informs Montagu of his plan to translate Homer 'for my Country's honour as well as for my own.'[20] Montagu was out of favour between May and November of that year and Dryden may have felt that they at last had something in common. But the letter certainly shows that Dryden did not want a role in the Aesop controversy to be imposed on him, and I think that he was also refusing to perform as an instant Jacobite. The subtle differences between Dryden and L'Estrange are at least as important as the similarities, and Dryden's imitation or parody of L'Estrange becomes another attack on the limits of detachment. Finally, my conclusions about Dryden's politics have only begun to touch on the influence of his Catholicism on *Fables*. *Fables* also takes a stand on matters of Catholic controversy, as I shall try to show in chapter 8.

THE STRUCTURE OF *FABLES* AND THE MEANINGS OF 'FABLE'

Fables makes a very different impression from Dryden's earlier collections. The whole book is Dryden's, with its antecedents in the miscellany lost or relatively unimportant. The superficially casual arrangement might be justified by L'Estrange's idea of a whimsical rhapsody: a fable collection, unlike a collection of odes or elegies, does not have to *appear* carefully structured. Also, by mingling the translations from his four authors Dryden ensures that the reader will not respond to 'poems from Boccaccio,' and so on, without making a special effort to extract them. 'Palamon and Arcite' and 'The Character of A Good Parson' are the only selections whose position seems to be based on their original source. Dryden's actual arrangement here follows:

'The Dedication'
'Preface'
'To Her Grace the Dutchess of Ormond' (original)
'Palamon and Arcite ... In Three Books' (Chaucer)
'To my Honour'd Kinsman' (original)
'Meleager and Atalanta' (Ovid)
'Sigismonda and Guiscardo' (Boccaccio)

'Baucis and Philemon' (Ovid)
'Pygmalion and the Statue' (Ovid)
'Cinyras and Myrrha' (Ovid)
'The First Book of Homer's Ilias'
'The Cock and the Fox' (Chaucer)
'Theodore and Honoria' (Boccaccio)
'Ceyx and Alcyone' (Ovid)
'The Flower and the Leaf' (considered to be Chaucer's until Skeat's edition, 1894–7)
['Alexander's Feast' – original; never included with *Fables* in modern editions]
'The Twelfth Book of Ovid'
'The Speeches of Ajax and Ulysses' (Ovid)
'The Wife of Bath Her Tale' (Chaucer)
'Of the Pythagorean Philosophy' (Ovid)
'The Character of A Good Parson; Imitated from Chaucer, and Inlarg'd' (a far looser imitation than the poems discussed by Weinbrot, yet clearly inspired by Chaucer)
'The Monument of A Fair Maiden Lady' (original)
'Cymon and Iphigenia' (Boccaccio)

Ironically, some eighteenth-century collections did extract poems by a single author; Samuel Garth's communal translation of the *Metamorphoses* used all of Dryden's translations from Ovid's work, not just those in *Fables*, and Sir Walter Scott separated out the poems from different original sources and gave Boccaccio and Chaucer more conspicuous place than the translations from Ovid and Homer, which he seems to have considered less original.[21] Many people had translated the ancients. The first edition of *Fables* included the Chaucer originals, from Speght's edition, bound in at the end. There may have been no rational reason for this, but it does draw extra attention to Chaucer. The tendency to separate the poems from different sources persists to this day ultimately, I suppose, because many critics are unable to cope with all of Dryden's foreign languages, and are, thus, reluctant to discuss a poem that they cannot compare to its original. However, Dryden's arrangement deliberately plays down the identity of the original author, in complete contrast to the first miscellany. He substitutes links between poems for links between individual poems and their originals. Obviously this flatters the monolingual reader by giving him something to study; Dryden may have had his own achievement in mind just as much as his readers' comfort.

With the exception of the *Iliad*, Dryden's sources are again arranged books, this time collections of stories or of myths. It is risky to suggest definitive interpretations of the *Canterbury Tales* since the collection *may* be unfinished and the poem exists in fragments, but it is clear that at least some parts of the whole, like the marriage group, are interdependent and that the collection as a whole moves from a secular ideal (the knight) to a religious ideal (the parson). The reader becomes a kind of pilgrim, sharing the Canterbury pilgrims' search for religious truth. Dryden's placement of his Chaucer poems implies that he responded to this aspect of the *Canterbury Tales*, and it would be easy to discover a 'marriage group' in *Fables*. The *Decameron* is obviously ordered, if for no other reason than the fact that the ten storytellers are assigned a new subject every day. Sometimes the subject borders on a literary type, such as 'love stories that end happily' or stories involving trickery. In addition, the *Decameron*, like the *Canterbury Tales*, seems to move from worldly to spiritual values (Ser Ciapelletto to Griselda), though with many apparent digressions and much ambiguity about what 'worldly' and 'spiritual' really mean: Dryden thus had *two* models for treating the ends of his work as spiritual polarities, with a complex middle that seems to be a struggle to move from one polarity to the other. The *Metamorphoses* is an integrated collection, or at least modern readers so understand it. As I read it, it enacts on a large scale what the first book enacts on a small scale, a search for an epiphany, for a divine force in harmony with nature and humanity, not a force that is indifferent or hostile, like Olympian Jove. Ultimately Ovid seems to recognize the divine *in* human nature. It is possible that Caesar, who concludes the *Metamorphoses*, is an ironic manifestation of the divine, but this does not entirely undermine the total movement of the poem; one notes that *Fables* ends pessimistically with 'Cymon and Iphigenia' after an apparent shift of direction towards positive spiritual values. The *Canterbury Tales*, *Decameron*, and *Metamorphoses* all have some bearing upon the structure and meaning of *Fables*. Only the *Iliad* is out of key except as comic contrast. It is too much to call it Dryden's 'Sir Thopas,' but one is certainly struck by the inadequacy of epic; Dryden, like Ovid, reduces epic to a peripheral role in the totality of experience. As in the *Metamorphoses*, epic is valuable mainly for its mythic content and as an illustration of one kind of limited human perception.

The original poems in *Fables* are much stronger than the songs in *Sylvae* or *Examen Poeticum*. Dryden felt, with some justice, that they would survive criticism: 'whether they are equal or inferiour to my other Poems, an Author is the most improper Judge; and therefore I leave them wholly to the Mercy of the Reader' (K, IV, 1446). They are carefully placed to create a frame and they are not mere songs. The two panegyrics, 'To the Dutchess of Ormond' and 'To my Honour'd Kinsman,' appear as the first and third poems, just before and just after 'Palamon and Arcite,' the brief epic with which Dryden begins, following Chaucer's placement of 'The Knight's Tale.' The panegyrics are clearly linked to 'Palamon and Arcite,' since the Duchess is compared to Chaucer's Emily and John Driden is urged to become a national leader, a kind of referee between disputing parties, much as Theseus functions as a referee between Palamon and Arcite. They take an active role in balancing opposed forces and are not mere trimmers. These devices give a heroic status to the Duchess of Ormonde and Driden. The image of an impartial judge or jury runs through the preface as well, bringing the preface into Dryden's frame. He constantly asks the reader to judge his poetry or to compare 'competing' poems like 'Sigismonda' and 'The Wife of Bath Her Tale.' The dedication of *Fables*, addressed to the Duke of Ormonde, presents him as a Christian hero whose fortitude is as important as his military valour. This essay is set off against the poem to the Duchess, so that there is no rigid distinction between the poems and Dryden's two works written in 'the other Harmony of Prose' (K, IV, 1446). Since both dedication and preface generate some central images sustained throughout *Fables*, they may be read as part of the total work.

'The Character of a Good Parson,' though nominally based on Chaucer's 'General Prologue,' has so much new material that it seems to be Dryden's poem. Dryden claimed that Chaucer was so much a kindred spirit that he could freely add or omit material, especially when 'I thought my Author was deficient, and had not given his Thoughts their true Lustre, for want of Words in the Beginning of our Language' (K, IV, 1457). Thus, Dryden's Parson uses no smutty language, but he can preach hell-fire (27). The epitaph the 'Monument of a Fair Maiden Lady' is also original, making with 'The Character of a Good Parson' a second pair of poems on a masculine-feminine couple, placed almost but not quite at the end, where Chaucer placed the parson's prose tale. In *Fables* the two appear next to each other, not separated by a long poem. However, 'Cymon and Iphigenia' breaks the frame. Dryden ends with an ironic poem, sceptical about human improvement. If the frame had been unbroken, *Fables* would have closed with a couple standing for purity and religion, balancing or even supplanting the couple at the beginning who are urged to change the world. As it is, Dryden ends with political realities and a doubtful future. His last original poem, 'Alexander's Feast,' was originally written in 1697. Subtitled 'the Power of Musick,' it appropriately follows 'The Flower and the Leaf,' which is about the affective nature of art. Both poems also revolve around saintly woman artists, though the narrator of 'The Flower and the Leaf' lacks confidence in her 'homely Verse' (616), while the 'Inventress of the Vocal Frame' (172) has Orphic power. St Cecilia thus fulfils the promise inherent in the previous poem. As is true throughout *Fables*, juxtaposition provides at the very least affective contrast and variations on a theme, and usually more – a meaningful relationship between themes and a sense that the later poems develop out of the earlier ones through a dialectical progression. Dryden's seemingly arbitrary inclusions ('Alexander's Feast') and omissions (the 1693 Ovid) show that *Fables* was not a random hodge-podge of poems that for some reason he suddenly decided he liked.

The theme of art is more important than ever before, but Dryden's emphasis shifts from detachment to the moral implications of an art that has power to move. He ends, Janus-like, in two not quite consistent positions. Dryden defends the comic muse against Jeremy Collier on the grounds that love

> oft to virtuous Acts inflames the Mind.
> Awakes the sleepy Vigour of the Soul,
> And, brushing o'er, adds Motion to the Pool. ('Cymon and Iphigenia,' 28–30)

Even the narrator of 'The Flower and the Leaf' had felt some gentle waves (30–1). But the truly ideal artist may be the Good Parson, who combines the 'Eloquence innate' (17) of the orator, the musical power of David, and the prophetic role of Moses. The Parson uses Aesop's fable-making ability for gentle persuasion:

> To Threats, the stubborn Sinner oft is hard:
> Wrap'd in his Crimes, against the Storm prepar'd;
> But, when the milder Beams of Mercy play,
> He melts, and throws his cumb'rous Cloak away. (34–7)

This reverts back to Dryden's own ideas about fables. They are effective because simple and familiar, religious because Christ spoke in parables (and may be multi-leveled, because Christ's parables are open to higher interpretations), and erotic, since Dryden makes no claim to the Parson's superior perfections.

The meaning of 'fable' itself is open to question, as Dryden has clearly not restricted himself to Aesopic fables and no single meaning of 'fable' applies to all the poems. Dryden really plays upon the equivocal meaning of the word, which brings to mind works by writers as different as Aesop, La

Fontaine, Ogilby, and L'Estrange, not to mention Homer and Virgil, since 'fable' also means the unifying action of an epic or tragedy. Dryden himself used the word in this latter sense: ''Tis the moral that directs the whole action of the play to one centre; and that action or fable is the example built upon the moral, which confirms the truth of it to our experience: when the fable is designed, then, and not before, the persons are to be introduced with their manners, characters, and passions.'[22] Technically there is a difference between a fable, meaning the whole, and an episode: 'For the fable itself, 'tis in the English more adorned with episodes, and larger than in the Greek poets.'[23] But in *Fables*, written twenty years after the works from which these quotations are taken, Dryden sometimes made a fable out of an episode or fragment, sustaining the kind of structural asymmetry that marked *Sylvae* or Ovid's *Metamorphoses*. The complex meanings of 'fable' let Dryden bring together epics and epic fragments, a beast fable, stories about human relationships, and stories resembling myth or fairy tales ('Meleager and Atalanta,' 'The Wife of Bath Her Tale'), not to mention the satiric epyllion 'Cymon and Iphigenia.' Two or three concepts of fable may overlap in one selection, as 'Meleager' is an epic narrative edging towards parody, as well as a myth and a unified action; or as the battle of the Centaurs and Lapiths (part of 'The Twelfth Book of Ovid') is mock-epic combat and obviously feigned, since centaurs are imaginary. Fable obviously can mean 'feigned narrative,' in Sir Philip Sidney's sense of fictive literature, but Dryden also uses the range of meanings that Sidney rejected – 'lie,' 'superstition,' 'myths that sensible people no longer believe in.' Thus, Pythagoras attacks obsolete images of heaven and hell:

> Why thus affrighted at an empty Name,
> A Dream of Darkness, and fictitious Flame?
> Vain Themes of Wit, which but in Poems pass,
> And Fables of a World, that never was!
>
> ('Of the Pythagorean Philosophy,' 223–6)

This is a Lucretian Pythagoras, recalling the selection on the fear of death in *Sylvae*. Pythagoras, however, seems intended to be read without irony. In a religious or philosophical poem 'fable' retains its derogatory meaning; appropriately the metamorphoses that Pythagoras uses as examples of universal change are given a 'scientific' dimension that makes them plausible commentaries on the way nature functions.

The multiple meanings of 'fable' allow Dryden to cut across the hierarchy of genres once again, since 'fable' can describe so many aspects of literature.

One could argue that epic is still normative,[24] but odes and sermons penetrate everywhere. 'Of the Pythagorean Philosophy' is almost all sermon, 'The Wife of Bath Her Tale' contains a 'long Sermon' by the crone (509), and 'The Character of a Good Parson' includes an account of the ideal sermon style, full of awe like Pythagoras's, but gentler.[25] While in a general way the Parson's style may be related to ideals of simple, affective preaching that had been developing throughout the century, it has equally pertinent similarities to the style of St Francis Xavier, a baroque saint whose life Dryden had translated from the original by Dominique Bouhours.[26] As a missionary in southeast Asia, St Francis had had to rely on techniques that transcended mere verbal discourse:

> Father *Xavier* follow'd them [the sick], and with the assistance of his two Companions, undertook to attend them all. The undertaking was beyond his Strength; but the Soul sustains the Body of Apostolical Men, and Charity can do all things.
>
> Animated with this new fervour, he went from Chamber to Chamber, and from Bed to Bed, giving remedies to some, and administring the last Sacrament to others. Every one desir'd to have him by him, and all acknowlodg'd that the only sight of his Countenance, avail'd them more than a thousand Medicines. (XIX, 53)

> The holy Spirit, who had inspir'd his Tongue, gave efficacy to his Words, by touching the Hearts of those who heard them. (XIX, 86)

Like the Good Parson, whose 'Eyes diffus'd a venerable Grace' (3) St Francis appears himself to be an image of God and the very impact of his presence seems additional proof of his sanctity. Bouhours treated sainthood as a mode of aesthetic existence in which the grace beyond the reach of art exerted itself for its ideal purpose – to make converts. The sermon, as it is treated in *Fables*, may not be essentially different from the ode, both being literary forms designed to ravish the auditors and bring their spirits closer to heaven.

Dryden's spectrum of genres in *Fables* has itself shifted upwards, perhaps going beyond epic at its upper end, as in 'Palamon and Arcite,' 'The Twelfth Book of Ovid,' and several other poems which subordinate action narrative to understanding the universe, in some sense making converts to a higher vision of life. Dryden's range includes prose as well as poetry, since no definition of fable makes any stipulation about metre. But he turns Boccaccio's stories into the same kind of poetry he uses elsewhere, and in part of the dialogue in 'The Flower and the Leaf' Dryden produces the effect of conversational prose through enjambment, caesuras placed near the beginning of a line, and alliteration emphasizing the beginning of the line:

and I who much desir'd to know
Of whence she [the 'Lady all in White'] was, yet fearful how to break
My Mind, adventur'd humbly thus to speak.
Madam, Might I presume and not offend,
So may the Stars and shining Moon attend
Your Nightly Sports, as you vouchsafe to tell,
What Nymphs they were who mortal Forms excel,
And what the Knights who fought in listed Fields so well. (472–9)

Dryden had once thought it slightly absurd that rhyme should seem out of place in conversation while other equally artificial devices do not, and here he writes a kind of 'homely Verse' which is all the more artificial in order to distinguish it from the surrounding passages of mere 'poetry.'[27]

Some of Dryden's ideas about fable come from René Le Bossu (including a conception of 'prose' as metrically shaped lines, lacking only the quality of song). More important, Le Bossu, writing in 1675, associated beast fable and epic, possibly in an effort to do justice to La Fontaine's achievement, though he does not discuss him; he discusses Aesop instead. Aesop and Homer are said to have similar didactic goals and they both chose to illustrate the same morals. The *kind* of characters they invented is less important than the fact that both invented characters to act out a theme which had been formulated in advance:

Il n'y a donc plus que les noms à donner à ces personnes feintes. Il importe peu pour la nature de la Fable, que l'on prenne des noms de Bêtes ou des noms d'Hommes. Homére a choisi ces derniers; Il a donné la qualité de Rois à ses personnages. Il les a appellez Achilles, Agamemnon, Hector, Patrocle, & a exprimé par le nom de Grecs, le bien que les confédérez vouloient conserver. Esope à sa façon, a donné à tous des noms de Bêtes: les Chiens sont unis ensemble, le Loup est leur ennemi, & il a nommé Moutons ce que le Poëte a appellé Grecs.[28]

Dryden's juxtaposition of Homer and 'The Cock and the Fox' thus has a basis in Le Bossu, though Dryden was far more ironic.

La Fontaine's fables must have influenced Dryden in some basic way. Since La Fontaine took the form quite seriously, he regarded some of his poems as little epics (possibly responding in turn to Le Bossu's glorification of the beast fable), and he treated Aesop as an Orphic figure, a theological poet. In his epilogue to Book XI of his fables, published in 1679, he thus describes his own art:

C'est ainsi que ma Muse, aux bords d'une onde pure,
Traduisait en langue des Dieux
Tout ce que disent sous les cieux
Tant d'êtres empruntants la voix de la nature.
Trucheman de peuples divers,
Je les faisais servir d'Acteurs en mon ouvrage;
Car tout parle dans l'Univers;
Il n'est rien qui n'ait son langage.[29]

This aspect of fable is evident in *The Hind and the Panther*, where the Hind is inspired like Christ, a narrator of fable, and is also an admirer of Homer's ability to speak the language of the sky (III.821). However, there are no specific parallels between La Fontaine's fables and Dryden's. In fact, La Fontaine is more like Ogilby, odd as this may sound, since both wrote brief poems in varied line lengths using the traditional Aesopic stories. Authorial tone is very important to both and permits constant expansion and digression, while both try to be precise in their diction, relying often on the single colloquialism or idiom to create a sense of character. Their relative quality is not my point here, though a few people feel that Ogilby's fables are underrated.

La Fontaine's *Contes et Nouvelles* are another matter. They are stories in verse, new versions of stories from various ancient, medieval, and Renaissance sources, including Boccaccio, Ariosto, Machiavelli, Rabelais, and the *Cent Nouvelles Nouvelles*. In some cases La Fontaine's exact source is unknown, but enough analogues exist to make the story seem part of a popular European tradition. Like Dryden, La Fontaine overcomes the difference between high and low sources. In each case the stories are assimilated to one level, defined by the poet's very distinctive voice and attitudes; the author's personal voice and not his invention reveals his individuality and his merits as a poet. The original authors are diminished in importance and the 'translations' have a far different meaning than they had in their original contexts.

A story from La Fontaine's first group of *Contes* (1665), the tale of 'la Joconde' from Ariosto, aroused some controversy because La Fontaine deviated so much from his epic original (no one cared how a less respected source was treated). La Fontaine and his style of free translation were defended in 'La Dissertation sur la Joconde,' which was published in editions of the *Contes* from 1669 on and is often thought to be by Boileau, though this attribution is not definite. The author of the essay emphasizes the pleasing qualities of La Fontaine's version, as opposed to a cold narration ('une traduction seche et triste'); La Fontaine's narrative style is not only better than that of a literal translator who had recently published a competing version, but possibly better than that of Ariosto himself.[30] Even if Ariosto has 'toute la gloire de l'invention,' La Fontaine must be granted 'le prix qui luy est justement dû pour l'elegance, la netteté, et la brieveté inimitable avec laquelle il dit tant de choses en si peu de mots.' La Fontaine has taken only his subject from Ariosto; he has made himself 'maître de sa matiere' and written an essentially original poem based only on Ariosto's story.[31]

This is more than the old distinction between servile and free translation, or paraphrase and imitation, since 'La Dissertation' implies that a poem is made new if the second poet completely rethinks his material, retaining little more than the story as narrative base. I think La Fontaine goes much further than Dryden in adding commentary, especially of a wry, sophisticated sort, on his material. But Dryden works in the same direction and the preface to *Fables* makes similar distinctions between story and treatment, such as his not bothering to follow Chaucer literally, his reorganization of the material on the Good Parson, the extensive changes that make 'The Flower and the Leaf' and 'Cymon and Iphigenia' so different in tone, structure, and meaning from their originals, and his very free use of Boccaccio's introduction to the fourth day, which, strictly speaking, Dryden does not translate at all (see below). Dryden and La Fontaine both assume that a modern writer's style and narrative technique may be better than those of even the great writers of the past and both feel that a story is the property of no single author but rather belongs to a culture. Dryden says:

> I had thought for the Honour of our Nation, and more particularly for his, whose Laurel, tho' unworthy, I have worn after him, that this Story was of *English* Growth, and *Chaucer*'s own: But I was undeceiv'd by *Boccace* ... [I]t appears that this Story was written before the time of *Boccace*; but the Name of its Author being wholly lost, *Chaucer* is now become an Original; and I question not but the Poem has receiv'd many Beauties by passing through his Noble Hands. (K, IV, 1460–1)

Stories are endlessly recast. The authors who do the recasting have a talent for discovery rather than for invention, or, like Dryden, a talent for opening an old book in the right place to see a great subject leap into view. The author of 'La Dissertation' even uses the image of the writer's hands in the same way as Dryden; with a bad translator, 'les plus belles fleurs qu' Arioste luy fournit deviennent seches entre ses mains.'[32] Dryness, and not literary theft, is the ultimate sin.

The *Decameron* is one of La Fontaine's most important sources; he does not use the Greek or Latin classics at all and his work thus has an obvious affinity to the medieval and Renaissance collections of novels that Dryden's *Fables* do not immediately bring to mind, though Boccaccio's collection is surely relevant. But two of La Fontaine's Boccaccio selections are in *Fables* as well. One is 'Les Oies de Frère Philippe,' from the introduction to the fourth day, which defends frivolous or erotic literature on the grounds that it is futile to protect young people from their own sexuality. Dryden omits Boccaccio's bawdy anecdote, in which an adolescent is attracted to some women, confusing them with beautiful geese, but he retains the basic idea in his introduction to 'Cymon and Iphigenia,' which defends eroticism in literature and argues that literature is obscene only if a Collier-reader is looking for obscenity. La Fontaine's story 'le Fleuve Scamandre' *is* the story of Cymon falling in love, though it may have been drawn from another version than the *Decameron*. On a more general level La Fontaine expresses much anti-clericalism, a minor but persistent theme in *Fables*, and he constantly defends the overpowering force of natural love: 'Hommes & dieux tout est sous sa tutelle, / Tout obéit, tout cède à cet enfant.'[33] Dryden concedes the force of love in 'To the Dutchess of Ormond' (7–10) as well as in the introduction to 'Cymon,' and this force is illustrated in many other selections, including 'Palamon and Arcite,' 'Cinyras and Myrrha,' and 'Sigismonda and Guiscardo.' Neither poet vindicates promiscuous sex – La Fontaine thought it funny and Dryden thought it sinful – but both want to show that eroticism can be sublimated into affective literature and that literature requires these feelings at its base. Any of these parallels might be coincidental though the Boccaccio selections Dryden chose suggest to me that he probably knew La Fontaine's *Contes* and may have used them as a model for loosening the kind of linked poem he had developed in *Sylvae*, as well as going beyond the predictable ancients of the early miscellanies for his originals. In their awareness of literary types La Fontaine and Dryden both range from epic down to the nameless writers of prose novels (the level at which L'Estrange was fixed), and La Fontaine provides a model for translating upwards from a prose original, Boccaccio, or from a badly written poem, like the original of 'The Flower and the Leaf.' An altogether different notion of the sources of literature is now involved; its matter is found in popular culture, and the epic model is rather a joke. Dryden also needed Catholic models. St Francis Xavier had limited usefulness, since not only was Dryden not a saint, but he could count on his audience hating a Jesuit missionary; and Dryden never managed to assimilate Dante, as I have indicated in chapter 2 (except for the important theme of cannibalism). Boccaccio was a good compromise and, as far as I can tell, Dryden's interest in Boccaccio and the idea of versifying him came from La Fontaine's *Contes*.

8

Dryden's Theological Poets

CATHOLICISM AND THE LANGUAGE OF THE GODS

The link between animal fable and epic and the aspiration of La Fontaine and Dryden to write serious poetry in the form of fable have further significance. The modern poets were aspiring to imitate the ancient theological poets like Aesop, Orpheus, and Pythagoras, or, in Dryden's case, to present them as an ideal which the non-visionary poet might observe and record, assuming the role of a kind of apostle. Theological poets were the original law-givers, who were thought to have used the language of fable to transmit divine wisdom to primitive man. Even Le Bossu was not just an Aristotelian but a critic trying to reconcile Aristotelian criticism with the concept of the theological poet. In the second chapter of his treatise he points out that the style of the ancients 'étoit pleine de mystéres & d'allégories' and that fables 'furent emploiées pour parler de la Nature divine en la maniere qu'on la concevoit alors. Cette grande matiere donna aux prémiers Poëtes, le nom de Théologiens, & fit appeller la Poësie le Langage des Dieux.'[1] La Fontaine uses this last phrase in the epilogue to Book XI of his *Fables*, already quoted in chapter 7:

C'est ainsi que ma Muse, aux bords d'une onde pure,
  Traduisait en langue des Dieux
  Tout ce que disent sous les cieux
Tant d'êtres empruntants la voix de la nature.[2]

The concept of the 'language of the gods' is a key phrase here. As it was explicated by Giambattista Vico in the next century, the phrase means the language used by the theological poets in discourse concerning the gods, not language used by the gods themselves, which is unknowable.[3] Originally language was mute, both human and divine, and the gods communicated with man by means of signs, like thunder, which were also symbolic actions arousing responses such as fear and awe. The theological poets interpreted these signs, producing a natural language comprised of metaphor and fable and turning themselves into priestly law-givers because of their role as mediators between man and the divine.

Dryden's variation of the idea (appearing in *The Hind and the Panther*) suggests that these poets might almost claim to know God's language. The Hind says:

> *Homer*, who learn'd the language of the sky,
> The seeming *Gordian* knot wou'd soon unty;
> Immortal pow'rs the term of conscience know,
> But int'rest is her name with men below. (III.821–4)[4]

The Gordian knot is both thing and metaphor, while Homer's (or Alexander's) violent action in cutting it is the sort of action/sign that the language of the gods is supposed to consist of. Since the Hind is inspired, she just may know this language, but the passage is also satiric, contrasting the gods' truthful use of a word with men's use of the same word to conceal their self-interest. The 'language of the sky' may be double-talk. Dryden's use of the phrase is ambiguous. The Hind also alludes obliquely to an absurd debate over a confusing formula in Homer's writings, exemplified by a passage in Book XIV of the *Iliad*, which says that the gods call a certain mysterious bird 'chalcis' and men 'cymindis.' Homer seems to be saying that the gods and men have two sets of names for the same things. The reader's problem is to make sense of Homer's two untranslatable foreign words, although Homer appears to have known what he was talking about. This passage aroused considerable interest: Plato discussed it in the *Cratylus* and Pope wrote an important and explicit note on it, wherein he concludes that the language of the gods is poetical diction, or what he and we call periphrasis. Pope translates Homer's mysterious bird as a 'bird of night' and solves the problem of clarity by quoting in his note Thomas Hobbes's translation, which plainly names it an owl.[5]

Dryden seems closer to Vico than to Pope (he is indifferent to periphrasis in this context), though their positions are not identical. The Hind, who is the theological poet of *The Hind and the Panther*, exasperated with human dishonesty, attacks the human race in a form that will expose them to themselves. This form of attack can be fable, which is like a thing or action, not just a collection of words, in that it does something to the listener. In fact, each of Dryden's animal protagonists tells a fable that changes the other. Each becomes a little frightened, a little less sure of her ground, and the two beasts approach each other out of a common desire to avoid violence. God's voice creates uncertainty, but the listener is moved in the direction of a more realistic image of her own limits.

Some of these implications are less evident in Dryden's *Fables* than in certain eighteenth-century poems like Mandeville's *Grumbling Hive*, the fables of John Gay, and some fable-like poems of Jonathan Swift, in which a satirical and angry god performs a decisive action to expose the folly of the little people below. For instance, Mandeville's Jove decides to make the bees honest and then he watches their prosperous economy disintegrate, or rather we do, since Jove, having initiated the change, disappears from the poem. Such a god-figure is like a scientist experimenting in a laboratory; also, *he* is the satirist, while the poet claims only to report his 'speech.' Satire thus has an affinity with vision, as is also the case in Swift's poem 'The Day of Judgment,' which culminates in the utterance of a satirical god: 'I to such blockheads set my wit! / I damn such fools! – Go, go, you're *bit*' (21–2). The structure of such fables may be no more than a contrast between the situation before Jove appears, in which the little people are shown in their happy foolishness, and the situation after they have been exposed to him and forced to come to terms with their real selves. Dryden avoided this denunciatory style in *Fables*, but it is implicit in *The Hind and the Panther*, and also in the theory which held that the central images of fable were originally uttered by the gods and designed to teach men of the existence of a superior power.

Associations between Aesopic fable and primal myth appear in Ogilby's parallels between his fables and the myths of the ancients, which place him in the mythographers' tradition. Sir William Davenant thus praises Ogilby's recovery of ancient wisdom:

> Accurs't be *Ægypt*'s Priests, who first through Pride
> And Avarice this common light did hide:
> To Temples did this morall Text confine,
> And made it hard, to make it seem Divine ...
> This clouded Text, which but to few was known,

In time grew darker, and was read by none;
So weak of Wing is soaring Mystery;
And Learning's Light goes out, when held too high:
But blest be *Æsop*, whom the wise adore,
Who this dark Science did to light restore ...
Blest be our Poet too! whose fire hath made
Grave *Æsop* warm in Death's detested shade ...[6]

This poem seems to have influenced Dryden's 'To My Honored Friend, Dr. Charleton' (1663; I, 43–4). Dryden's Aristotle, who limits access to learning, corresponds to Davenant's priests, and Charleton, who rediscovers a truth that has never really been lost but only concealed, corresponds to Aesop, though Dryden rejects the Egyptian theme with his more stimulating references to English history and tradition, especially to Stonehenge, a monument that competes with the pyramids in its capacity to fascinate.

Davenant was responding to Ogilby's method. Ogilby's fables draw parallels or make allusions to classical myth, as the Hands in Fable 47, 'Of the Rebellion of the Hands and Feet,' brag of building the pyramids, the tower of Babel, and Daedalus's wings, or the poet in Fable 58, 'Of the Fox and the Goat,' describes a hot day by saying, 'Scarce would *Deucalion's* Flood restore the Grass.'[7] The parallels are witty and not especially inflated. Ogilby's marginal annotations also draw parallels to classical sources, some quoted both in the original language and in Ogilby's translation. Annotations include references to the halcyons, to the origin of the centaurs, to Ajax's shield, and to the transmigration of Pythagoras's soul, all of which figure in Dryden's *Fables*.[8] I do not think that Dryden chose his subjects because Ogilby had annotated them, but we can be fairly sure that some of Dryden's readers knew that physical (scientific) or moral allegories had been attached to these myths, even if Dryden broke with tradition by not burdening his book with annotations. He might have chosen to omit the annotations because the material was familiar, not because it failed to interest him. Ogilby wanted to be a mythographer, like George Sandys, and he succeeds in re-creating Aesop as an Orphic figure.

Dryden's imitation of a writer he professed to despise may prepare us for parallels between his work and Sir Richard Blackmore's. Blackmore first stole from Dryden, taking his ideas for an Arthurian epic and for the use of guardian angels as supernatural machines,[9] but Blackmore thereupon gave the epic a turn of his own. First, he treated the writer of epic as a theological poet; he writes in the preface to *Prince Arthur* (1695):

> *The word* Fable *at first signified indifferently a true or false Story, therefore* Cicero *for distinction, uses* Fictas Fabulas *in his Book* de Finibus. *But afterwards Custom obtain'd to use the word always for a feign'd Discourse. And in the first Ages, especially in the Eastern World, great use was made by Learned and Wise Men of these* feign'd Discourses, Fables *or* Apologues, *to teach the ruder and more unpolish'd Part of Mankind.* Theologians, Philosophers, *and great Law-givers, every where fell into this way of instructing and cultivating the People in the Knowledge of Religion, Natural Philosophy, and Moral and Political Virtues. So* Thales, Orpheus, Solon, Homer, *and the rest of the great Men in those Ages have done, and the famous Philosopher* Socrates *is by some affirm'd to be the Author of many of the Fables that pass under* Æsop's *name ... Now the first Wise Men that undertook to* civilize *and* polish *the barbarous World, found this way of* Fables, *especially in Verse, to be mighty* Acceptable *to the People.*[10]

We may notice the conventional list of great names brought together under the rubric 'Theologians, Philosophers, *and great Law-givers.*' Everyone concerned with the subject tended to provide a range of such figures, all inspired in the same way and conscious of similar goals, rather than using one isolated example like Christ, who is different from every other prophet. The duplication of the law-givers, in character and experience, seems to lend authenticity to each one, although it may make them seem mythic rather than historical. There is no reason why new figures cannot be added to such a list; it seems designed to encourage optimism in looking for new examples. Dryden's wide range of inspired figures in *Fables* fits in with Ogilby's and Blackmore's tendency to notice a common purpose instead of emphasizing differences.

Blackmore's addition is Arthur himself, whom he conceives of as a poet-visionary as much as a military hero or historical British king. Prince Arthur is an inspired teacher, while King Arthur, the hero of the sequel which Blackmore published in 1697, actually enters the action by having a dream. The language of the following passage from *Prince Arthur*, which turns a feast into a banquet of sense, has some likenesses to Dryden's descriptions of Nestor and the Good Parson:

> But what more chear'd them than their Meats and Wine,
> Was wise Instruction, and Discourse Divine,
> From God-like *Arthur*'s Mouth, by Heav'n inspir'd;
> Which all their Breasts with sacred Passions fir'd.
> Great were his Thoughts, strong and sublime his Sense

Of Heav'n's Decrees, Foreknowledge, Providence.
He reason'd deep of Heav'n's mysterious Ends,
And made stern Justice, and fair Mercy Friends.
How high he soar'd, how noble was his Flight,
Speaking of Truth divine, and Wisdom infinite!
He opens all the Magazins above,
Of boundless Goodness and Eternal Love,
From these rich Stores of Heav'n, these sacred Springs
Of everlasting Joy and Peace, he brings
Ambrosial Food, and rich Nectarean Wine,
Which chear pure Souls, and nourish Life Divine.[11]

I think that Dryden returned Blackmore's compliment by making Blackmore's type of hero central to *Fables*. Blackmore's Arthur is also a transparent allegory for William, and his epic may have been an effort to compete with Dryden's *Aeneis*, since Arthur is throughout presented as an improvement on Virgil's hero. For instance, Arthur treats the defeated Gauls with mercy, in contrast to Aeneas's butchery of Turnus.[12] Blackmore's poems are a strange pastiche of incidents from Milton and Virgil, usually revised with a kind of positive irony, so that a defect in the earlier hero becomes a good quality in Blackmore's. Aeneas, like Milton's Satan, is a negative point of reference. Blackmore's Arthur is what Aeneas should have been, fighting for a good cause and exercising Christian virtue whenever possible.

Dryden takes the Duke of Ormonde as his Christian hero, setting him off against the Ajaxes, and in another way balancing him against his own cousin Driden, who has not yet become active:

For this Reason, my Lord, though you have Courage in a heroical Degree, yet I ascribe it to you, but as your second Attribute: Mercy, Beneficence, and Compassion, claim Precedence, as they are first in the divine Nature. An intrepid Courage, which is inherent in your Grace, is at best but a Holiday-kind of Virtue, to be seldom exercis'd, and never but in Cases of Necessity: Affability, Mildness, Tenderness, and ... good Nature, are of daily use: They are the Bread of Mankind, and Staff of Life: Neither Sighs, nor Tears, nor Groans, nor Curses of the vanquish'd, follow Acts of Compassion, and of Charity: But a sincere Pleasure, and Serenity of Mind, in him who performs an Action of Mercy, which cannot suffer the Misfortunes of another, without redress; least they should bring a kind of Contagion along with them, and pollute the Happiness which he enjoys. (K, IV, 1440–1)

'Heroical' in part suggests transport, the intense energy that motivates the duke when he leads his men in action (IV, 1442), but it also suggests Dryden's own feelings in describing him. A similar link exists in 'To My Honour'd Kinsman'; that is, the poet and his cousin are complementary figures:

> Nor think the Kindred-Muses thy Disgrace;
> A Poet is not born in ev'ry Race.
> Two of a House, few Ages can afford;
> One to perform, another to record.
> Praise-worthy Actions are by thee embrac'd;
> And 'tis my Praise, to make thy Praises last. (201–6)

Such parallels and complementary relationships provide a structure for *Fables.* Arthur appears only around the edges, though he is given a positive role. In 'The Wife of Bath Her Tale' he yields to the influence of a parliament of women and pardons a rapist, much as Theseus pardons Palamon and Arcite. The women are influenced by the man's attractiveness (78), but Genevra's speech implies a higher motive, a reluctance to repay blood with blood (90–2). Whatever her reasons, she and, through her influence, Arthur in fact transcend the *lex talionis.* Chaucer does not describe the ladies of Arthur's court as a parliament, though he, too, uses the episode to show an ideal relationship between king and subject, in which the subject introduces the element of transcendent grace. In 'The Flower and the Leaf' twelve Arthurian knights appear in the visionary procession. Arthur thus becomes an ideal British monarch, a native Theseus, and a representative of the realm of grace, in contrast to the tyrants, brutes, and misogynists of the other poems.

Dryden's Catholicism, however, underlies his use of theological poets as central figures, though the idea may have been catalysed by a desire to put down Blackmore. As I have said above, it was in his Catholic poem, *The Hind and the Panther*, that the problem of channelling God's word through this kind of intermediary to a general audience became important to Dryden, though he also showed his suspicions of mythological claptrap and his fear of having his readers link it to to his new religion. The theological poets are essentially literary figures, associated with the realms of art, history, and fable, and thus more acceptable on the grounds of familiarity than a specifically Catholic hero. One can imagine the effect of St Francis Xavier, the Jesuit missionary, as the hero of an English poem, though both Bouhours and Dryden went out of their way to make him fascinating and comprehensible to a sceptical modern audience: *The Life of St. Francis Xavier* is astonishingly sophisticated for a saint's life. Nevertheless, Dryden had to appear to be less concerned with Catholicism as such than with the general facts of human nature.

In *The Hind and the Panther* Dryden was very concerned with depicting Catholics as normal people and showing that their religious practices, which of necessity had been performed in secret until 1685, were neither perverse nor unusually esoteric. The Hind thus retaliates against her enemies:

An hideous Figure of their Foes they drew,
Nor Lines, nor Looks, nor Shades, nor Colours true;
And this Grotesque design, expos'd to Publick view.
One would have thought it some *Ægyptian* Piece,
With Garden-Gods, and barking Deities,
More thick than *Ptolomey* has stuck the Skies.
All so perverse a Draught, so far unlike,
It was no Libell where it meant to strike. (III. 1042–9)

As in *The Hind and the Panther*, Dryden is concerned in *Fables* with specific polemical issues relating to Catholicism, one of which is the Catholic's public image. His defence of the essential normality of the religious individual, never specified as Catholic, continues, as in the appealing narrator of 'The Flower and the Leaf' and the charitable Good Parson. In addition, by introducing a series of poet-prophets who form a kind of mystical succession if only through the temporal succession of writing *Fables* itself, Dryden provides an idealized image of a series of apostles, again without defending the Roman Catholic Church in itself. Dryden merely shows the oral delivery of a story or sermon exerting a direct impact to humanize an audience. Finally, through his attacks on cannibalism and ultimately on violence itself Dryden defines the true nature of the Eucharist as a banquet of sense and retaliates against the Anglican efforts to represent the Catholic as a weird mixture of cannibal and naïf for his insistence on taking Christ's phrase, 'This is my body', literally.[13] Dryden's defence of Catholicism or Catholic practices is never stated directly. His technique of indirection is designed to present the Catholic prophet as really a prophet of enlightenment.

Dryden's emphasis on Pythagoras (whose sermon occupied half of Ovid's concluding book) is part of his silent polemic, for Pythagoras, in addition to being the archetype of the whole range of theological poets, was also an exemplar of Catholic humanism. What he is not is as important as what he is, and the same is true for his student Numa, a philosopher-king, whose story is told in the passages framing Pythagoras's sermon. The story of Numa's life descends to us by 'sure Tradition' (76), a phrase which catholicizes him, and Pythagoras, Numa, and Numa's successors become an apostolic sequence linking up to the church itself:

> These Precepts by the *Samian* Sage were taught,
> Which Godlike *Numa* to the *Sabines* brought,
> And thence transferr'd to *Rome*, by Gift his own:
> A willing People, and an offer'd Throne.
> O happy Monarch, sent by Heav'n to bless
> A Salvage Nation with soft Arts of Peace,
> To teach Religion, Rapine to restrain,
> Give Laws to Lust, and Sacrifice ordain:
> Himself a Saint, a Goddess was his Bride,
> And all the Muses o'er his Acts preside.
>
> ('Of the Pythagorean Philosophy,' 711–20)

Ovid's poem thus reads like a model of the oral tradition linking the Catholic popes, and Dryden emphasizes Numa's apostolic role in the phrase 'transferr'd to *Rome*' (for Ovid's 'populi Latialis'), since Rome did not yet exist in Numa's lifetime. There was an alternative image of Numa available in Plutarch and Livy, where Numa is described as introducing a long list of very specific ceremonies which were used to manipulate and control his people. Dryden (like Ovid) understates Numa's interest in ceremony and does not make him seem calculating. Both Plutarch and Livy considered Numa's marriage to Egeria (Dryden's 'Goddess') to be a myth invented to hoax the people, and Plutarch especially dwelt on the element of terror in some of the customs that Numa introduced, like the punishment of burial alive imposed on unchaste vestal virgins. Neither historian believed that Numa was Pythagoras's student, and Dryden's headnote to this poem shows his knowledge of alternative possibilities: '*On this Occasion*, Ovid *following the Opinion of some Authors, makes* Numa *the Schollar of* Pythagoras.' Dryden was perfectly aware that he was providing a selective view of Numa.[14]

In Dryden's time the ceremonial Numa was usually linked to the concept of a state church, whatever church was relevant in a given context. He could stand for the pope or be taken as the historical source of popish ceremonies. In the latter role he figured in an attack on Catholic superstition made by one French Protestant:

> Y a-t-il de l'apparence que Iesus Christ nous ait delivrez de dessous le joug de Moyse pour nous mettre sous celui de Numa Pompilius, ou plutost de l'esprit malin avec qui ce Magicien avoit des communications.[15]

However, to at least some important Anglicans, anxious to defend their own ceremonies and their state church, Numa was a positive figure and his purported manipulativeness went unnoticed: 'This care had monarchy of religion,' said Sir Robert Filmer, treating Numa primarily as a king, but one who allowed himself to be troubled with ecclesiastical matters.[16] Obviously, Dryden would want to dissociate himself from both the positive Anglican image and the negative anti-Catholic image of Numa. Dryden's Numa links Catholic leadership (he is still an apostle) with simple teaching, peacemaking, and tradition. Numa is more like Theseus, Nestor, and the Good Parson than like an Anglican bishop.

The images of Pythagoras fall into similar, though not identical, polarities. Pythagoras was sometimes glorified as a student of Egyptian mysteries, as by Sandys in his essentially conventional commentary on Book xv of the *Metamorphoses*: 'and that he might more freely participate of [the Egyptians'] mysteries, [Pythagoras was] initiated in their orders, and withall circumcised: a custome derived belike from their ill intreated Guests, the *Hebrews*; which even the *Copties* [sic], the reliques of the ancient *Aegyptians*, observe at this day, although they be Christians.'[17] Here, the exoticism of circumcision undermines the potentially apostolic links both to Old Testament Hebrews, especially Moses, and to Christianity by way of the Copts. One can see that Dryden did not automatically follow the Ovidian commentaries available to him, although he probably knew Sandys by heart. Of course, Pythagoras is first of all important because of his fame as a forerunner of Christianity; he also has a central role in the primitive oral tradition because he failed to commit his ideas to writing. But as late as 1699 the Anglican Bishop of Worcester felt that he had to attack the association of Pythagoras with natural religion and reject his '*impudent Diabolical Fictions.*' The bishop was disgusted with the readiness to confuse Pythagoras's theory of transmigration with the Christian belief in personal immortality.[18] The Anglicans had a stake in intelligent distinctions between apparently similar versions of faith. None of these writers mentions the Pythagoras of the Hermetic tradition who discovered the arcane numerical relationships holding together the cosmic frame. Number theory must have been important to Dryden, who wrote his first ode for St Cecilia's Day on heavenly harmony (1687), but there is no trace of the subject in *Fables.* The mathematical Pythagoras and the Pythagoras of Egyptian studies were both so commonplace in the Renaissance and later that Dryden's silence on these points is itself notable.

A homelier image of Pythagoras was, however, current in Dryden's time, emphasizing his role as a practical moralist and his attack on meat-eating, based, of course, on transmigration theory. The so-called golden verses of Pythagoras, uninspired collections of maxims with little interest except for their association with Pythagoras's name, were published in translations by J. Hall in 1657, John Norris (a Cambridge Platonist and commentator on Locke) in 1682, and Nicholas Rowe, with a life of Pythagoras by André Dacier, in 1707, by which time no doubt Dryden's *Fables* had itself contributed to a revived interest in the subject.[19] All of these translators or commentators assume a link between the golden verses and Moses' commandments and they all published their verses with a commentary by a Christian, Hierocles, who was thought to have recovered the original resemblance between Pythagoras's beliefs and the Jewish faith.[20] A new interest in chronology, an effort to make definite historical links between pagan and biblical events, may account in part for the Pythagorean revival. Pythagoras was no longer shrouded in the prehistoric past but was thought once again to be accessible. Since Dryden shows no special concern with matters of chronology, he apparently expected readers to place Pythagoras somewhere on the boundary between history and myth.

Dryden's Pythagoras is important for his attack on cannibalism. He seems to have no ceremonial importance whatsoever, but gives this sort of advice:

> Thy Friend, thy Brother, any of thy Kin,
> If none of these, yet there's a Man within:
> O spare to make a *Thyestæan* Meal,
> T'inclose his Body, and his Soul expel. (678–81)

The reference to Thyestes, who unwittingly ate his own son, is in Ovid (xv.462) and recalls various other episodes in the *Metamorphoses*, like Lycaon's cannibalism and Procne's murder of her son, whom she fed to her husband to avenge his rape of Philomela. These episodes are not in *Fables*, but Dryden included several which are comparable, like the deaths of the spiteful '*Thestyan* Brethren' in 'Meleager and Atalanta' (222), Sigismonda's death scene – 'and oft (her Mouth apply'd / To the cold Heart) she kiss'd at once, and cry'd' (689–90) – and the sadopornographic vision in 'Theodore and Honoria':

I pierce her open'd Back or tender Side,
And tear that harden'd Heart from out her Breast,
Which, with her Entrails, makes my hungry Hounds a Feast. (183–5)

The strange, almost perverse, vividness of some of this imagery can be explained by the likelihood that Dryden wanted to distinguish between cannibalism and the Catholic belief that Christ's blood and body were present in the Eucharist.

These images are negative and cannibalistic, but they do show that Dryden could appreciate the implications of 'real presence'; body and blood are living metaphors for him. Yet, in the 'feasts' at which true spiritual communion takes place, some of which I shall mention later, Dryden leans over backward to show that more is going on than just eating and drinking. The feast becomes an occasion for some kind of ennobling experience, though sometimes it is limited by the capacities of participants who still like their meat and drink. The good feasts are always communal events, unlike Sigismonda's private ritual with Guiscardo's heart, and they seem to represent a universal cultural need, as is shown by their distribution over time, from Homer's 'Blood of Oxen, Goats, and ruddy Wine, / And Larded Thighs on loaded Altars laid' ('The First Book of Homer's Ilias,' 62–3) to the present, whether we think of 'Alexander's Feast,' written in honour of St Cecilia's Day, or the Good Parson's charity: 'Yet, of his little, he had some to spare, / To feed the Famish'd, and to cloath the Bare' (50–1). Dryden's various feasts suggest that Catholicism is a universal or 'catholic' religion, without blurring the meaning of the Eucharist into mere symbolism with no sense of physical intensity.

It would have been self-defeating for Dryden to defend ceremonies or any other aspect of Catholicism in a way that set Catholics apart from other Englishmen. Instead his approach makes Catholicism seem to be the only religion, a natural religion grounded in human need and instinct. Even an imperfect version of the Eucharist, like Sigismonda's, can be read as showing a spiritual need which, although it cannot be satisfied adequately in her world of anxious tyrants and muttering priests, is nevertheless genuine. Although *Fables* is too varied to be reduced to one moment in Catholic polemic, it does take a stand on certain issues involving Catholicism, and some of Dryden's central images are grounded in Catholicism. It is a long way from *The Hind and the Panther*, with which Dryden managed to alienate an astonishing number of readers, miscalculating how little his readers could tolerate a straightforward statement of Catholic belief. In *Fables* he takes a far more cautious and ecumenical approach, introduced too briefly in his earlier poem to save it from misunderstanding: he tries to make the apostle seem human.

DRYDEN'S THEOLOGICAL POETS AND THE LIMITED VISION

The characteristic speeches of Dryden's theological poets – those in which their wisdom and their moral advice are conveyed – read more like utterances, clearly set off from and thus transcending the action (which may be relatively slight) of the rest of the poem. However, the speeches are also connected to each other and to similar speeches in other literary works by their formulaic quality, which makes each speech seem to announce itself as an utterance, and which of course universalizes it. An utterance of this kind does not have to be entirely in character in the ordinary sense, nor need it be considered primarily as flowing from or advancing the action, like a fragment of dialogue in a play or a modern novel. Its function is to present one speaker's perspective on universal wisdom; its content is partly cosmological and partly moral, showing the implications of that cosmology in the speaker's particular situation, which usually represents some aspect of the human condition. Dryden's use of a formula – similar introductory lines, recurrent cosmic images – invites comparison among the various speeches, although no two are alike. The theological poets in *Fables* conduct an unresolved dialogue on the problems of moral action in a dark universe. Though their wisdom seems to come from God, the poets are in fact the sources of light.

Dryden takes over an already conventional formula from Virgil's sixth eclogue, in which Silenus – a mock-poet, a drunken rustic bard – describes '*The Formation of the Universe, and the Original of Animals, according to the* Epicurean *Philosophy*' (K, II, 894–7):

> He sung the secret Seeds of Nature's Frame;
> How Seas, and Earth, and Air, and active Flame,
> Fell through the mighty Void; and in their fall
> Were blindly gather'd in this goodly Ball.
> The tender Soil then stiffning by degrees,
> Shut from the bounded Earth, the bounding Seas.
> Then Earth and Ocean various Forms disclose;
> And a new Sun to the new World arose. (49–56)

As Silenus gets carried away, he lists the stories he would like to tell – 'the double *Scylla*'s Fate' (105), the 'ravish'd *Philomel*' (111). They are all metamorphoses; in other words, Silenus's stories are generated by his philosophy of change and would be concrete expressions of it. Silenus might have become an Ovid, recasting ancient myths as philosophical tales whose power comes from the way in which cosmic forces are shown to be operating in individual lives. In the *Aeneis* Iopas, Dido's singer, is described in much the same formula (I.1038–46). Iopas sings his song during a banquet, right after Dido has fallen in love with Aeneas and just before Aeneas embarks on his own story. Because of his structural position in the action, either Dido's love story (which has just begun) or the narrative of Aeneas's past troubles (which is about to begin) can affect us as one of Iopas's philosophical tales. This is appropriate, since both characters, Aeneas as well as Dido at that point, are letting themselves be controlled by cosmic forces and cannot be fully understood without reference to the gods and to the material turbulence of nature. But ultimately Virgil's characters have considerable independence as 'persons,' while Dryden's universe is not deterministic. Somehow freedom of action and freedom of reflection are possible.

Dryden's inspired speakers often start from Epicureanism – they are materialist, or even atomist – and they experience revelation without rejecting their materialist philosophy. They do not leap from the physical to the spiritual but incorporate their sense of physical truth into their higher vision, adopting a kind of 'double truth' since the reality of matter and the possibility of revelation must both be accepted. Dryden himself must have accepted this double truth, since nothing in the structure of *Fables* undermines it, while the structure does imply more specific differences in the speakers' world-views or in their ability to make moral applications to their own lives. The speakers are groping towards the truth, like the rapist-knight in 'The Wife of Bath Her Tale,' who travels through a setting that recalls *Religio Laici*:

> Lonely the Vale, and full of Horror stood
> Brown with the shade of a religious Wood. (211–12)

Occasionally they find that truth transcends their 'environments,' or the stories which are the metaphorical expression of their environments. The moments of transcendence have as much in common with each other as with other parts of the same story.

Fables is almost a theodicy, although it tends to emphasize the absence of God and the rarity of illumination. The theological poets are moralists rather than discoverers of a new wisdom, and their rhetorical intentions, especially the difference between trying to threaten and trying to console, are almost as important as the content of their speeches, which is essentially predictable except for details. Unmoderated awe is the second-class technique in *Fables*, a symptom of anxiety on the speakers' part, which causes them to employ unduly terrifying or vivid imagery in order to compensate for their own distance from God. Some of the inspired speakers also seem to be finding words for the first time; at first glance inspired speech is out of character for Sigismonda and for several others. However, the very notion of speaking in character is inappropriate here. The speakers should be seen in terms of Silenus, the comic figure who is nevertheless inspired and a traditional image for a figure with an ugly exterior that conceals goodness or wisdom. Socrates and Aesop were others of the type.[21]

Such characters can be seen as wise fools. The *Canterbury Tales* and the *Decameron* are filled with wise fools, from the Summoner to patient Griselda, not to mention characters who really are fools, though their words may contain some truth that they do not understand themselves. The whole idea is parodied, both by Chaucer and by Dryden, in the tale of the Cock and the Fox, in which the Cock defends the truthfulness of visions against his wife's suspicious materialism. According to Madam Partlet, 'All Dreams, as in old *Gallen* I have read / Are from Repletion and Complexion bred' (140–1). Much of 'The Cock and the Fox' is a philosophical debate between one speaker who believes in visions, revelation, and miracles and another who comically associates things of the spirit with husbandly pretentiousness and does a fairly good job of undermining spiritual belief on that basis, since Partlet is right about her husband's character. In the long run one does not know whether to take each philosophical stance as just an expression of character and dismiss the controversy as absurd or to separate the issues from the speakers' characters and take them seriously. The very conception of the story helps to define some of the problems of belief, showing how ideas are hopelessly tangled up in the circumstances of the imperfect characters who conceive them. In the *Decameron* Boccaccio's opening story, about the false confession of the sinner, Ser Ciappelletto, has the same function of creating doubt about the human sources of wisdom, because we are never sure if Ciappelletto is a plain liar or a penitent in spite of himself, making a genuine deathbed confession. Boccaccio moves from Ser Ciappelletto, who is completely disorienting, to Griselda, the heroine of his last tale, whom we are certain to trust, though one accustomed to the stereotyped submissive wife may be startled that Griselda should stand up for herself at all, sardonically warning Gualtieri not to put his second wife through the sort of trials that he imposed upon her. In fact, Griselda's acquired worldly wisdom helps to make her seem trustworthy. Chaucer and Boccaccio and Dryden all warn us not to sentimentalize innocence, and they include parodies of their most important ideas because they are concerned with the doubts that may trouble believers of complex understanding.

In the opening story of *Fables* Theseus's speech, designed to persuade his subjects to accept Arcite's death, recalls the Silenus formula very closely. He arises 'with awful Grace' and says:

> The Cause and Spring of Motion, from above
> Hung down on Earth the Golden Chain of Love:
> Great was th'Effect, and high was his Intent,
> When Peace among the jarring Seeds he sent.
> Fire, Flood, and Earth, and Air by this were bound,
> And Love, the common Link, the new Creation crown'd.
> The Chain still holds; for though the Forms decay,
> Eternal Matter never wears away. ('Palamon and Arcite,' III. 1024–31)

Theseus relates a human event to the nature of the cosmos; he arouses awe by describing the cosmos though he emphasizes peace and love; and he anticipates Pythagoras in affirming the eternity of matter. Though Theseus believes in a first cause and in the possibility of cosmic harmony, he remains a materialist, even in his characterization of humanity. However, his style is ultimately affectionate. Within the context of his materialism Theseus conveys a sense of personal intimacy:

> So Man, at first a Drop, dilates with Heat,
> Then form'd, the little Heart begins to beat;
> Secret he feeds, unknowing in the Cell;
> At length, for Hatching ripe, he breaks the Shell,
> And struggles into Breath, and cries for Aid;
> Then, helpless, in his Mothers Lap is laid. (III. 1066–71)

Theseus's hatching image is repeated in 'Ceyx and Alcyone' in the dubious miracle of the halcyons' birth (dubious because of Aeolus's timing, since he calms the sea only after letting Ceyx die) and mocked in Chantecleer's exclamation, 'And ev'n this Day, in more delight abound, / Than since I was an Egg, I ever found' (465–6). Each variation of the idea has a different impact, though the vocabulary of inspiration remains constant, suggesting the ultimate unity of truth. The image of man as a 'Drop' also recurs in Orpheus's lines on Adonis's birth:

> The Drop, the Thing which late the Tree inclos'd,
> And late the yawning Bark to Life expos'd;

A Babe, a Boy, a beauteous Youth appears,
And lovelier than himself at riper Years. ('Cinyras and Myrrha,' 384–7)

Matter thus provides delight for Chantecleer (amusingly, in spite of his belief in visions) and is a source of beauty for Orpheus, who has declared his hatred for women. Theseus's human baby also recalls Lucretius's shipwrecked child, but the difference is possibly more important in showing Dryden's development since 1685. Lucretius is appalled at the human situation, while Theseus is in the process of becoming reconciled to it, and, since he is trying to promote a marriage, he can envision an archetypal child being delivered to a mother's care and not to a wasteland. 'The Cock and the Fox' and 'Ceyx and Alcyone' qualify or add to Theseus's vision, which does not tell us everything about life, but the most limited vision provides the most bliss. Chantecleer's dream really does predict disaster, though he cannot convince Partlet of its truth and he himself forgets it quickly. He could not have felt animal delight if his dream had truly changed him or if it had made him constantly prone to anxiety, like Theodore, Alcyone, or Myrrha, several of Dryden's more tension-ridden characters, whose imaginings or dreams contribute to their inner stress. Chantecleer is lucky to be such an imperfect blend of matter and spirit.

Orpheus, though famed among theological poets, is a flawed character in *Fables*, as he is in Ovid. He appears as the narrator of 'Cinyras and Myrrha,' a story of moral confusion and incest, redeemed at last by Adonis's birth. He narrates 'Pygmalion and the Statue' as well; it precedes 'Cinyras,' but Dryden does not say so until the headnote to the latter poem, so that at first we do not read 'Pygmalion' as an expression of Orpheus's character, and the effect of the story is distinctly more cheerful than in the *Metamorphoses*. In 'Cinyras and Myrrha' Orpheus arouses awe because he is thoroughly caught up in his own tale, an imperfect speaker experiencing an unusual degree of personal involvement:

I sing of Horrour; and could I prevail,
You shou'd not hear, or not believe my Tale.
Yet if the Pleasure of my Song be such,
That you will hear, and credit me too much,
Attentive listen to the last Event,
And with the Sin believe the Punishment. (5–10)

Ironically his rigid morality goes along with a willingness to titillate himself and his audience; he is a pagan Jeremy Collier. And even Myrrha (who is

Orpheus's idea of a 'normal' woman) understands the meaning of sin, though she tries to convince herself that either a deviant culture or her own mind has created it:

> But is it Sin? Or makes my Mind alone
> Th' imagin'd Sin? For Nature makes it none.
> What Tyrant then these envious Laws began,
> Made not for any other Beast, but Man! (39–42)

To some extent Myrrha is not an independent character; rather she reflects the problems of her narrator, who sang this song during his misogynist period after Eurydice's death, when he could not bear women's presence. Unable to deal with his own frustrated love and his responsibility for Eurydice's return to hell, Orpheus created a character whom a male moralist could enjoy hating. The language of Myrrha's inner debate revolves around precise distinctions between the meanings of sin, law, and crime, recalling the opening lines of *Absalom and Achitophel*, in which the sin of polygamy is reduced to the level of social custom. But her attempt to excuse her impulses by the promiscuity of the animal world (a common libertine motif) can only arouse disgust, since she lacks the innocence of the beasts. Myrrha is a scapegoat for Orpheus's misogyny, but her father is truly repulsive when she finds him 'Easie with Wine, and deep in Pleasures drown'd, / Prepar'd for Love' (249–50). Orpheus seems gradually to be admitting that men provide the occasions for female deviations, but his moral confusion still appears in his use of his best imagery to describe the act that nauseates him: 'The Sire, unknowing of the Crime, admits / His Bowels, and profanes the hallow'd Sheets' (295–6). This is almost an image of ingestion and excretion, one of the anti-symposia.

'Pygmalion and the Statue' recounts the story of a woman-hater turned artist. Though the poem might be read as containing an ideal aesthetic in Pygmalion's creation of a living work of art, I consider Pygmalion's aesthetic flawed by its absurdly literal-minded sublimation: he creates a statue of his ideal woman, caresses it, and so on. In general, I do not think that any poem in *Fables* should be read one-sidedly; Dryden created a moral labyrinth, not a series of virtues and vices. Thus, Pygmalion may genuinely try to create a work of art that is superior to living women, but he fails to understand the extent of his own physical involvement with art. The poem proceeds to a kind of reverse sublimation – Venus turns the statue whom Pygmalion has come to love into a real woman – and surely admits that the artist cannot involve himself in art unless it provides an outlet for his real physical desires, which Dryden admitted more forthrightly in the introduction to 'Cymon and Iphigenia.' The two-part sequence composed of 'Pygmalion' and 'Cinyras and Myrrha' shows Orpheus progressively revealing, though never admitting, his sexual disgust, while trying somewhat dishonestly to detach himself by emphasizing women's desires instead of men's. The complications of sex-reversal and authorial detachment are developed even more fully in the original sequence in the *Metamorphoses*, which ends with the love story of Venus and Adonis and Adonis's death. Orpheus *is* Venus at last: both endure hopeless suffering after a lover's death, and the aggressive goddess projects a rather ambiguous male sexuality in addition to revealing a guilty feminine principle in Orpheus himself. Dryden translated only enough to show how Orpheus's disgust influences the nature of his art. Dryden does not explore the ramifications of gender identity and, perhaps more important, he cannot have taken Venus's inner conflicts seriously, even if she is only a mask for the poet. Dryden does not treat Venus, Diana, and Mars as persons in *Fables*.

Some of the old men in *Fables* are sermonizers, but all are coloured by Dryden's various confessions about himself – his bad memory and his tendency to ramble, his obstinate resentment of his enemies, and his continued attraction to women, however sublimated into admiration for 'Beauty.' When we read in 'The Twelfth Book of Ovid' that Nestor decided not to praise Hercules because Hercules was his personal enemy (711–22), we quickly recognize the parallel with Dryden's treatment of William and note that Dryden is admitting a possible error in judgment. Yet Nestor as a genial storyteller is able to create a banquet of sense:

> The mellow Harp did not their Ears employ:
> And mute was all the Warlike Symphony:
> Discourse, the Food of Souls, was their Delight,
> And pleasing Chat, prolong'd the Summers-night. (218–21)

Dryden had outlined a more ascetic symposium in *The Hind and the Panther*, when the normally carnivorous Panther accepts the Hind's hospitality:

> Mean while she quench'd her fury at the floud,
> And with a Lenten sallad cool'd her bloud.
> Their commons, though but course, were nothing scant,
> Nor did their minds an equal banquet want. (III.26–9)

This is a communion in the sense of a meeting of minds, and it is most emphatically not cannibalistic. Conversation as a higher level of gratification actually seems to distract the Panther from her normal preoccupations. At the same time the Hind is somewhat idealistic to offer the Panther such a radically restricted diet, and Nestor, who has to entertain a whole army of meat-eating predators, is more accommodating; he does not ask his audience to give up their usual pleasures. Nestor is doing well to elevate their minds at all and he suggests a more realistic kind of model for the poet who wants to survive in real life.

Nestor's story, the battle of the Centaurs and Lapiths, works because it is so well suited to its audience. The Centaurs are man-beasts, perhaps parodies of the Greek heroes themselves, and the human Lapiths quickly degenerate to the Centaurs' level. The story is an action narrative, filled with violence as ingeniously contrived and comic as a barroom brawl in a traditional western, and certainly all parties have had enough to drink. Yet the action is distanced in that half the characters are not human but mythical creatures, Centaurs, and there is even a female Centaur, the 'fair *Hylonome*' (539). The very concept is hilarious, though eminently logical. Theseus reappears here as an ordinary warrior, since the battle occurs at the marriage of his friend Perithous to a Lapith woman, the 'fair *Hippodame*' (293); thus, Nestor's symposium frames a story of a *disrupted* feast, or an anti-symposium, in which an unstable community is achieved and quickly lost because it is based on the wrong values. The anti-symposia in *Fables* are acceptable when they are framed in an aesthetic construct, and dangerous only when the boundaries between art and life are unclear. In this case one may assume that Nestor's story teaches the warriors to laugh at and possibly to understand themselves, and it certainly provides something better to do than eating, drinking, and fighting.

However, distinctions between art and life are confused in 'Theodore and Honoria,' where the hero first reacts to, then exploits in his turn, the affective power of a diabolic vision. It is likely that Dryden wanted this story to be a comment on art and morality, since he changed the name of the infernal knight to that of the medieval poet Guido Cavalcanti (Boccaccio has 'Guido degli Anastagi'), linking the knight to his other theological poets, who all carry messages from supernatural realms. Dante had put Cavalcanti in hell; Boccaccio apparently objected because in a later story in the *Decameron* he treats Cavalcanti as a witty and moral Epicurean who accuses some boisterous men of being no better than living corpses.[22] Cavalcanti is thus like Nestor, able to control violent men through wit, but less amiable, since his episode takes place in a cemetery and the environment has symbolic force. Dryden has thus combined Dante's Guido with Boccaccio's, leaning somewhat to Dante's, since the Epicurean is outwitted at last when we find that he is damned.

Dryden's poets cannot transcend their moral limits in the uses to which they put their art. We do not know who arranged the vision in which Guido appears, but we can hazard a guess. It is a kind of work of art – theatrical, a too lively spectacle – and it certainly possesses Theodore's mind. To browbeat his own scornful mistress he arranges a repeat performance at 'A Feast prepar'd with riotous Expence' (253); this anti-symposium is real within the terms of the story and Honoria too gets to watch the hell-hounds eating a woman's entrails, a still worse variation on the theme of the feast. She is afflicted with nightmares and soon yields, revealing a female inconsistency like Althea's and Iphigenia's, 'Resistless in her Love, as in her Hate' (424). But Honoria's reasons for yielding are disturbing in themselves, since the excessive *liveliness* of what she has seen has made her ill:

> This dreadful Image so possess'd her Mind,
> That desp'rate any Succour else to find,
> She ceas'd all farther hope ... (380–2)

Whether Guido's performance is read in aesthetic or in religious terms, his (or Theodore's) success in making a convert is not justified by his method. And his very success is doubtful, since Honoria will presumably be vulnerable to future influences and anxious to repress the awful imagery that changed her in the first place.[23]

The problem is that real images, approximating as closely as possible the material world itself, are the only ones that seem to have impact on a world without clear evidence for faith. Perhaps one should not qualify the statements; in one case only reality has impact. In 'Ceyx and Alcyone' the heroine learns twice about her husband's death, which is an unpleasant truth. The first message comes in a dream-vision whose uncertain validity is emphasized by a long digression on Morpheus and several other inhabitants of Morpheus's cave. Morpheus, the 'Player-God,' pretends to be Ceyx, 'and adding Art / Of Voice and Gesture, so perform'd his part' (375–6) that Alcyone seems convinced and becomes hysterical. However, we sense that she does not really absorb the fact of her husband's death until she sees the corpse itself:

> for now the flowing Tide
> Had brought the Body nearer to the side:
> The more she looks, the more her Fears increase,
> At nearer Sight; and she's her self the less:
> Now driv'n ashore, and at her Feet it lies,
> She knows too much, in knowing whom she sees. (458–63)

That is, Alcyone does not commit suicide until this point, suggesting that she had some reservations before, since she took no decisive action. Dryden's emphasis on 'knowing' underlines the idea. Body alone is truly real to most people, who are like Samuel Johnson in wanting a rock to kick, and sight is the only source of information that we actually trust, whatever we claim about our higher beliefs. Alcyone has faith, but sight has an impact that revelation even when supported by faith cannot fully compete with. Nevertheless, immediacy is dangerous. Alcyone is moved too quickly and too violently in her effort to blot out her knowledge. Her response parallels Honoria's, but it is even more self-destructive.

'Sigismonda and Guiscardo' also occurs in this dubious moral region where images have impact but are too physical and too affective in their consequences. Sigismonda's account of human nature recalls Theseus's, at least in her use of the formula of inspired utterance, but her vocabulary is more immersed in the physical:

> Search we the secret Springs,
> And backward trace the Principles of Things;
> There shall we find, that when the World began,
> One common Mass compos'd the Mould of Man;
> One Paste of Flesh on all Degrees bestow'd,
> And kneaded up alike with moistning Blood. (499–504)

Dryden's language here recalls his account of primal man and the fall in *The Hind and the Panther* (1.251–90). Man at his creation was 'kneaded up with milk' (1.274), but he became soured and bloody as he gradually (as part of a natural process) became capable of the first act of violence. Dryden associates violence with male sexuality – 'The murth'rer *Cain* was latent in his loins' (1.279); Sigismonda's effort to become masculine is thus somewhat ironic, since primal femininity is associated with the absence of violent impulses. Like many aspiring women in a patriarchal culture, she can imagine power only in terms of masculine imagery.

Sigismonda also has a limited, postlapsarian vision. She imagines a bloody origin for humankind, for she lives in a world of human carnivores and has some carnivorous qualities herself. Dryden makes it clear that both her perceptions and Tancred's are limited, possibly by their physical nature: 'Gorge with my Blood thy barb'rous Appetite,' Sigismonda says ironically (570).

Dryden uses the word 'blood' twelve times in this poem – not an inordinate repetition, but enough to suggest a certain obsession with the subject on his characters' part. Seven of these references occur in Sigismonda's defence of her marriage and include the meaning 'noble blood' (489, 546); nobility is thus defined concretely, in terms of physical substance. Dryden also uses images of physical violence or dismemberment that foreshadow Guiscardo's death: 'So was she torn, as from a Lover's Side' (Tancred is Sigismonda's Adam); 'At length their twisted Rays together met'; 'the blind Grot'; 'the choak'd Entry of the Cave'; 'Amazement ty'd his Tongue' (23, 64, 112, 146, 238). These body metaphors acquire unusual vividness as they accumulate. Several of them have to do with distorted vision, as if the characters, especially Tancred, are unable to see the truth because some barrier, possibly the confused sexual images in their minds or possibly their physical nature itself, stands between their perceptions and the real world, in so far as an objective world exists in this poem. As William Blake was to say again, the organic eye is a barrier to perception. Dryden uses the Lucretian word 'Idol' to describe Tancred's obsession with his daughter – 'The worshipp'd Idol of her Father's Eyes' (31) – while Sigismonda says that 'Int'rest made a Jaundice in thy Sight' (542), as if a sort of blood disease were to blame for Tancred's false perceptions. Thus, Guiscardo's heart will 'glut the Tyrant's Eyes' (595), though it is an object of lust to Sigismonda too:

> Then, to the Heart ador'd, [she] devoutly glew'd
> Her Lips, and raising it, her Speech renew'd. (641–2)

Sigismonda's final speech is literally in contact with the physical stuff of life.

Nevertheless, Sigismonda has definite political and moral concerns. She analyses the nature of justice and personal worth and refuses to judge men on the basis of their 'blood.' In Boccaccio her defence of the low-born seems a characteristically medieval defence of the 'little people,' the sort of feeling that made Aesop popular in earlier times because slaves, animals, children, and the poor were all 'little' in some sense. Dryden's Sigismonda, however, upholds a feminized republicanism, imagining a natural aristocracy that would single out the exceptional man of low birth for high reward. (She, of course, has done the singling out in this poem.) Such exceptional men transcend the realm of chance:

> Ev'n mighty Monarchs oft are meanly born,
> And Kings by Birth, to lowest Rank return;
> All subject to the Pow'r of giddy Chance,
> For Fortune can depress, or can advance:
> But true Nobility, is of the Mind,
> Not giv'n by Chance, and not to Chance resign'd. (557–62)

She also informs Tancred that men's self-determination should be shared by women because of their similar physical natures; indeed, women's confined way of life, without physical outlets, is likely to intensify their sexual urges. Seventeenth-century republicans tended to be misogynist and they projected an obsession with the physical onto women and pampered monarchs. Sigismonda seems to agree, but at the same time she is honest, refusing to imagine either herself or her father as superior to their bodies; both characters try to achieve insight in spite of their flaws. The poem, therefore, has both republican and monarchist components, for the irredeemably sinful nature of humanity is usually a monarchist argument. It reflects a genuine dialectic, once again unresolved, in which Dryden appears to be asking what would happen if a republican condescended to think about the dark side of human nature.

The crone's sermon in 'The Wife of Bath Her Tale,' like Sigismonda's speech, defends both women and low-born men against aristocratic contempt, if not worse: the story begins with a knight's rape of an anonymous countrywoman. The crone, like Sigismonda, has more concrete political views than the same character in the original poem. Chaucer's speech was an extended and somewhat repetitive definition of true 'gentilesse,' seen as a matter of personal worth and not just descent; Dryden translates it and clarifies it. A scion of a noble family has to justify his nobility through personal merit:

> Nobility of Blood is but Renown
> Of thy great Fathers by their Virtue known,
> And a long trail of Light, to thee descending down.
> If in thy Smoke it ends ... (439–42)

However, Dryden seems more concerned with the failure of the noble houses in his time than with the defence of low-born replacements. He implies that the nobility were self-interested, adding some disparaging comments on 'Pow'r, and Place' and 'vast Estates to mighty Titles ty'd,' and accuses them of indifference to responsibility (379, 393). The modern representatives of such houses appear unworthy of the power that they have amassed over the generations. The crone's speech, I think, should be read along with 'To my Honour'd Kinsman' and 'Cymon and Iphigenia,' in which Dryden also reflects on the implications of the power vacuum left by an absent king and worries about the landowners' capacity to fill it. Royal power has only a distant connection with the crone and her knight, though the early part of 'The Wife of Bath Her Tale' glorifies a benign relationship between king and parliament, in which the king has nominal power but is willing to yield to parliament, especially when he recognizes that personal impulse may be dominating him. The king-parliament relationship is modelled on the idealized marriage of Arthur and Genevra; it is repeated, with the sexes reversed, when the crone yields to her husband at the very moment when she has won power over him.

The problems of marriage are concretely related to the unfulfilled role of the noble houses, which Dryden says are weak in part because they have degraded themselves through ill-considered marriages. Dryden's crone says more about women's influence than Chaucer's, though it seems to do her sex very little credit. Mothers as well as fathers influence their children's characters, whether for good or for ill, and the mothers seem to contribute more than their share of the ill. Even the statement that Christ 'took his Earth but from an humble Maid' (387) reads like a left-handed compliment to Mary. Nobility descends through the male line (the simple truth under the system of primogeniture), but 'No Father can infuse, or Wit, or Grace, / A Mother comes across, and marrs the Race' (400–1). This is beginning to sound like the house of Shandy, except that Sterne's completely degenerate system was afflicted with a pattern of role reversal and his noble women tended to run off with the coachman. Dryden's emphasis on women underlines the fact that a political system founded on kinship networks is basing itself on the body; it cannot idealize itself but must take account of the many absurd reasons that people have for marrying. Marriage is part of the rule of chance:

> Chance gave us being, and by Chance we live.
> Such as our Atoms were, ev'n such are we,
> Or call it Chance, or strong Necessity.
> Thus, loaded with dead weight, the Will is free. (421–4)

Dryden may have been influenced by Locke's view that parents in the act of conception are not worried about their children's well-being; Congreve also satirized the lunatic impulsiveness often displayed by the members of great houses in choosing their mates. All three writers advocate caution and forethought to make up for the ridiculous fact that the political system is based on marriage. Yet even the virtuous and almost saintly wife Mary, Duchess of Ormonde, is subject to the rule of chance on another level, that of disease, and the 'precious Mould' (142) responsible for her family's future was saved only by a medical miracle.

In those *Fables* with a relatively benign view of life matter is objectively present, neither good nor evil, but still perceived as powerful and vital. The narrator of 'Baucis and Philemon,' Lelex ('an old experienc'd Man,' 11), tells his story to convince Perithous of the truth of miracles, as we learn from Dryden's headnote. Perithous, Theseus's friend, appears in various roles in four different selections; now he is revealed as an atheist. Lelex's miracle ostensibly shows the gods rewarding a pious couple for their hospitality, but it is ambiguous because Baucis is clearly able to perform household miracles of her own, making ordinary, inanimate objects come alive:

The Trivet-Table of a Foot was lame,
A Blot which prudent *Baucis* overcame,
Who thrusts beneath the limping Leg, a Sherd,
So was the mended Board exactly rear'd.
...
A Garden-Sallad was the third Supply,
Of Endive, Radishes, and Succory:
Then Curds and Cream, the Flow'r of Country-Fare,
And new-laid Eggs, which *Baucis* busie Care
Turn'd by a gentle Fire, and roasted rear. (84–8, 94–8)

Yet it is the gods who ensure that the wine bowls 'Fill'd without Hands, and of their own accord / Ran without Feet, and danc'd about the Board' (124–5), so that some mysterious co-operation between divine and human seems to have transformed the 'Country-Banquet' (117). Baucis's meal of dairy and vegetables is in the Pythagorean spirit, but her menu is a lot more varied than the dull salad which the Hind offered the Panther. Baucis at least provides three separate and physically distinct ingredients.

Materialism in *Fables* tends to support the idea that poetry should be allowed to make an impact on its own account; the 'morality' of Epicurean art inheres in the fact that matter transposed into vision is beyond good and evil and vision is almost a paradigm for art. In 'The Flower and the Leaf' the virtuous and sensuous knights and ladies alike please the narrator, though she (or Dryden) makes it possible for us to distinguish the two groups. The following lines describe the overdressed, sensuous people of the Flower:

The Ladies dress'd in rich Symarrs were seen
Of *Florence* Satten, flow'r'd with White and Green,
And for a Shade betwixt the bloomy Gridelin.
The Borders of their Petticoats below

Were guarded thick with Rubies on a-row;
And ev'ry Damsel wore upon her Head
Of Flow'rs a Garland blended White and Red.
Attir'd in Mantles all the Knights were seen,
That gratify'd the View with chearful Green. (341–9)

At first, only the word 'thick' is a bad sign, since both groups are well dressed and heavily jeweled. A more subtle detail, apparent if one contrasts this passage with the description of the ascetic group, is the tendency towards 'blending,' a loss of distinctions of various sorts, among the Flower people. Men and women arrive together instead of in separate parties, white and red are blended in their garlands, suggesting a vague third colour, and even the pattern of the ladies' 'Symarrs,' perceived in our minds and at a distance, seems indistinct.

The narrator at this point responds only on the level of sight, which is 'gratify'd.' This is not complete aesthetic perception, however, since aesthetic *comprehension* comes only when the spectacle is over and the narrator has understood 'The secret Moral of the Mystique Show' (460). Dryden thus separates two levels or stages of the aesthetic experience so that the poem becomes an analysis and a representation of those stages. His ideal picture involves mixing the various components of the show without allowing them to lose their separate identities. The symposium in 'The Flower and the Leaf,' at which the people of the Leaf invite the people of the Flower to join them, and which thus reconciles the conflict by transcending it, may be the ideal image for the aesthetic order in *Fables*:

The Ladies sat, with each a Knight between
Distinguish'd by their Colours White and Green:
The vanquish'd Party with the Victors join'd,
Nor wanted sweet Discourse, the Banquet of the Mind. (429–32)

It is also important that the narrator is not personally involved in the action of the show, though she has admitted to an ability to feel passion (24–32). The action is so transmuted into pure symbolic event – tournament, storm, reconciliation – that no one could here get involved in the naïve, empathetic way that Honoria does when she so quickly recognizes herself in Theodore's show. The narrator of 'The Flower and the Leaf,' enclosed in a bower, 'Single, and conscious to my Self alone' (142), and apparently unseen, thus becomes a kind of mean between the extremes of Lucretian detachment and Honoria's total identification with a character whose experience duplicates her own.

In 'Alexander's Feast' (K, III, 1428–33) St Cecilia's artistic nature borders even more closely on that of the saint or visionary. She displaces, though only at the very end, the pagan musician Timotheus, whose cheerfully amoral art provokes Alexander into behaving ridiculously and at last dangerously, when, aroused by the excessive vividness of Timotheus's music, he burns down his palace:

See the Furies arise!
See the Snakes that they rear,
How they hiss in their Hair,
And the Sparkles that flash from their Eyes! (132–5)

The urgent command to *see* and to hear produces a kind of mental procession by an image which in turn leads to impulsive action, much like Honoria's, as a result of Alexander's need to free himself from a nightmare. Though the artist is not unduly involved, his audience is, and if we judge by Dryden's treatment of his other seemingly good-humoured artists (Nestor, Dryden himself), we may guess that some unstated hostility towards Alexander may underlie Timotheus's comic exposure of the 'joyless Victor' (84). The artist wants the monarch's power.

Once again the feast represents a failed symposium, though, like 'The Flower and the Leaf,' the poem itself is also a genuine symposium, since it contains so much on the nature of art. Both Timotheus and St Cecilia are vehicles linking man and the supernatural, Timotheus even being placed symbolically between earth and heaven:

Timotheus plac'd on high
Amid the tuneful Quire,
With flying Fingers touch'd the Lyre:
The trembling Notes ascend the Sky,
And Heav'nly Joys inspire. (20–4)

A kind of witchcraft seems to operate in which Timotheus's music literally activates the gods' song, although we are told that 'The Song began from *Jove*' (25). As in 'Baucis,' the miracle of art involves a collaboration between men or women and God. However, Timotheus works within the traditional system of modes and some of his techniques are amusingly predictable, like his transitions between related but contrasting passions and his attempt in the style of his work to imitate the passions – though Dryden here has none of the thundering drums of his first St Cecilia's Day ode.[24] Dryden may have considered these conventions limiting, because Cecilia not only completes but also breaks the system. She is an '*Inventress*' (a quality that Dryden felt that he himself lacked) and an '*Enthusiast*,' whose saintliness reinforces her inventiveness because drawing on her own inner resources is the same as reaching up to God. Dryden's final irony is not the cliché that pagan art is fulfilled by Christianity, but the paradox that faith brings an artistic freedom that makes Timotheus's art passé. Since Timotheus is another one of Dryden's masks, one may conclude that Dryden would be better off were he less obsessed with heroism and with his hostilities to particular heroes, like William.

'Alexander's Feast' has a baroque structure, with its apparently spacious environment opening up at the end to reveal the limits of Timotheus's world. *Fables* likewise has an ambiguous shape in several respects; even its beginning and ending are not absolutely rigid. For instance, are the dedication and preface inside or outside the work? Dryden's reference in the preface to 'the other Harmony of Prose' (K, IV, 1446) suggests that we should not ignore the prefatory material simply because it is not metrical. Is 'To the Dutchess of Ormond' a separate poem or an introduction to 'Palamon and Arcite'? Should we read *The Secular Masque* as part of *Fables*, even though it was written for an altogether distinct purpose, since it nevertheless revolves around the Venus-Diana-Mars triad from 'Palamon and Arcite,' which is one of the recurrent motifs of *Fables*? The very boundaries of *Fables* are indistinct, more like parentheses than a rigid frame.[25]

All this is most important in considering how to take the ending of *Fables*, which is ambiguous without being entirely liberating. The neatly paired poems on the Good Parson and the Maiden Lady have a deceptive finality, since Dryden follows them only with a piece of a new frame, the introduction or *poeta loquitur* to 'Cymon and Iphigenia,' which returns us to the familiar political order and not to God. However, 'The Character of a Good Parson' and 'Cymon' are alike in that Dryden seems to emerge from behind the poems that have so far concealed him. On one level the Parson can be seen as the last of Dryden's idealized selves, a benevolent man of sixty who 'well might last / To Sixty more' (8–9) and thus is a little more removed from the immediacy of death than Dryden himself. Perhaps the Parson would not experience death as a boundary. He also is free of Dryden's well-known flaw of sullenness:

> Nothing reserv'd or sullen was to see:
> But sweet Regards; and pleasing Sanctity. (14–15)

The Parson is a non-juring clergyman who has lost his benefice; in that respect, too, he is like Dryden, who no longer has an official role connecting him to the court. However, the Parson abandoned his benefice voluntarily (126) and he seems to have been freed by his lack of position, not made resentful by it:

Now, through the Land, his Cure of Souls he stretch'd:
And like a Primitive Apostle preach'd.
Still Chearful; ever Constant to his Call;
By many follow'd; Lov'd by most, Admir'd by All. (127–30)

No longer restricted by time and place, the Parson has found that he has access to a universal audience. This is not isolation but boundlessness, which may be frightening in itself – since it also suggests proximity to death – but, as it is presented here, it is an experience that Dryden can come to terms with.

Dryden compares the Parson to so many biblical precursors that his individuality blends into a composite figure based on the biblical prophetic tradition, emphasizing Moses, David, Job, and St Peter, the various types and post-types of Christ. There are no references to the theological poets like Orpheus and Pythagoras, whose tradition has been entirely supplanted by the biblical. Curiously enough, Dryden's references take the poem back to the real world. James Kinsley has argued that the figure of the Parson was based on Thomas Ken, the non-juring Bishop of Bath[26] – the same city where the Fair Maiden Lady was buried – as if Dryden wanted to redeem Bath by associating it with two figures superior to Chaucer's Wife! Kinsley mentions Ken's fame as a preacher and author of hymns, but Ken also wrote a Jacobite text, linking James II to Job: 'There is at this Day an Illustrious Instance in the World, that has well near Equaliz'd *Job* in his Afflictions.'[27] One may ask if Dryden's own reference to the sufferings of Job is a vestigial remnant of his Jacobitism; strictly speaking, however, Dryden directs his sympathy to those who suffered because of their loyalty to James II, and not to James II himself. 'The Character of a Good Parson' may be Jacobite, and it is certainly nostalgic in mood, but in *Fables* poets and parsons are Dryden's centre of interest. Dryden may even have sensed the falsity of the efforts to make a Job-figure out of the king who was in fact responsible for the sufferings of such men as Dryden and Thomas Ken himself.[28]

The Fair Maiden Lady was Mary Frampton, who had died in 1698 at the age of twenty-one, and Dryden's poem was in fact her epitaph. In its origins the poem thus points outward to the real world though in itself it is abstracted beyond any personal reference, as epitaphs so often are. The poem, however, does bring another Mary into *Fables*, offsetting both the Duchess of Ormonde and the queen whose death Dryden had refused to commemorate. By implication he is willing to pay tribute to a genuine saint, though her virtues made her earthly existence nearly imperceptible:

> All white, a Virgin-Saint, she sought the Skies:
> For Marriage, tho' it sullies not, it dies. (19–20)

As the Maiden Lady has crossed the boundary between poet and saint, she utters nothing except in so far as she herself is God's message:[29]

> Each Thought was visible that rowl'd within:
> As through a Crystal Case, the figur'd Hours are seen.
> And Heav'n did this transparent Veil provide,
> Because she had no guilty Thought to hide. (15–18)

Dryden's cosmic image of the watch, used to describe the Lady's inner self, is actually based on the image of Momus's glass, which Sterne also delighted in: what if everyone had a glass window through which his or her thoughts were displayed for the world's amusement? Momus figures as a satirist in *The Secular Masque*, but he can find nothing to attack in the Lady.

In 'Cymon and Iphigenia' Dryden virtually announces himself to be personally present. This is partly through the phrase '*poeta loquitur*,' which Dryden had used only once before, in *The Hind and the Panther* (marginal gloss to II.658), a poem whose openness was distinctly ill-considered. In *The Hind and the Panther* Dryden claimed to have seen a divine messenger, while in *Fables* he attacks a false priest, Jeremy Collier. Apparently Dryden felt impelled to sign his name to a particular passage when he took on the role of witness or apostle, which seems to have required sorting out the false from the true messengers of God. Because Dryden introduces visionaries and saints into *Fables*, his application of the role of theological poet changes slightly. Dryden never identifies himself with the visionary or saint, nor does he present himself as a direct interpreter of God's messages; rather, he mediates between the saints themselves and the public, since the saint may be so indifferent to his or her fame as to require an extra link in the chain to ensure the survival of God's word. In 'Cymon and Iphigenia' Dryden then seems to let out all the stops in showing us what he is uniquely qualified to do as a poet. This poem is dense in allusions to Dryden's earlier poems – *The Hind and the Panther*, *Absalom and Achitophel*, *MacFlecknoe*

(Cymon's chaotic mind), and the *Aeneis* – as well as earlier poems in *Fables* and heroic poetry in general. Dryden's personal style and opinions almost bury the original story, at which point we see that translation has indeed lost its name and become a complicated form of literary concealment and oblique self-revelation.

At the end, then, Pythagoras, the Parson, and the satirist are all foils for each other. They have in common the desire to use not just language but forcible imagery to effect changes on some imagined auditor: first, Numa and through him his people; second, all Engand, conceived of as a great parish; and finally, England conceived of as a kingdom in process of disintegration. All three speakers use vivid cosmic imagery, but they differ in the precise kind of moral and emotional involvement anticipated from both the speaker and his auditors. Pythagoras uses imagery of the body perceived with extreme immediacy:

> For whether Earth's an Animal, and Air
> Imbibes, her Lungs with coolness to repair,
> And what she sucks remits; she still requires
> Inlets for Air, and Outlets for her Fires;
> When tortur'd with convulsive Fits she shakes,
> That motion choaks the vent till other vent she makes. (513–18)

The Parson's imagery is more abstracted but not removed from things of this world:

> For Priests, he said, are Patterns for the rest:
> (The Gold of Heav'n, who bear the God Impress'd:)
> But when the precious Coin is kept unclean,
> The Soveraign's Image is no longer seen. (81–4)

And 'Cymon' returns to satiric fable, at every stage infusing cosmic imagery with a sense of tension over lost human possibilities:

> Sigh'd to herself the fair unhappy Maid,
> While stormy *Cymon* thus in secret said:
> The time is come for *Iphigene* to find
> The Miracle she wrought upon my Mind:
> Her Charms have made me Man, her ravish'd Love
> In rank shall place me with the Bless'd above.
> For mine by Love, by Force she shall be mine,
> Or Death, if Force should fail, shall finish my Design. (256–63)

The Parson's image may be the most central. If the image on the sovereign, or *of* the sovereign, is lost, it is all the more important for Dryden to construct human models. 'Cymon and Iphigenia' conveys an unmistakable sense of disappointment in humankind, but *Fables* as a whole contains a range of models in the moral conflicts of the series of poets and occasionally in the structured insights of the saints. Dryden perceived sainthood in aesthetic terms – the saint was an idealized human microcosm, able to convey an image of God, whether he or she spoke or not. However, the saint could not be relied on to speak. His or her perfection itself created a deficiency, and Dryden, who tries to record or to reconstruct the saint's visions, serves as another mediator between the individuals closest to God and the rest of the world. He himself has become part of an apostolic chain.

9

The Use of Hieroglyphs in *Fables*

Fables as a whole is obviously not a single unified narrative, though it contains many shorter narratives, and to a large extent it works by creating an illusion of narrative with a collection so well integrated that we experience it as a tightly constructed sequence. From one point of view *Fables* recalls the long, sometimes nearly endless, poems of the mid-century, like William Davenant's *Gondibert* and William Chamberlayne's *Pharonnida*, whose authors seem to have made use of every possible opportunity for digression and imagistic development and which have a similar combination of serious meaning and frequently homely tone. *Fables* is the kind of 'epic' that a writer who grew up in the 1640s and 1650s might have chosen to write. Love, valour, political loyalty, and religious experience were major elements in these poems as well. However, *Fables* is more closely organized than the earlier works, following a model that includes something like the relationship between type and anti-type. That is, Dryden provides a range of examples of a given character, some of them only prefiguring an ideal, like Sigismonda or Pythagoras, others seeming to complete it because they appear chronologically later in the poem, like the Good Parson, who may be the only unadulterated example. They are distributed over a work so wide-ranging that it seems to represent the history of culture itself. There is no steady movement upwards but rather an apparent high point near the beginning in Theseus, a relative falling away (one index for which is Theseus's reappearance as an ordinary warrior with an atheist for his best friend), and then a new high point in the Good Parson, from which Dryden falls away again in 'Cymon and Iphigenia.' Whatever precise shape the reader gives to the whole poem, and some aspects of its structure are highly ambiguous, it is certainly given coherence through Dryden's systematic use of a relatively small vocabulary of representative characters and experiences. They are 'typical' in our sense as well as 'types' in the older meaning of the word.

Narrative seems to become less important, too, as one moves towards the end of *Fables*; this is logical because physical heroism, which displays itself best in action, becomes less important. However, even in the earlier poems story often seems to work as a frame for a dialogue or a vision, as in 'Sigismonda' or 'Ceyx and Alcyone.' There is a kind of spiritual turning-point – I feel the major turning-point – in moving from the questionable miracle of 'Ceyx' to the green world of 'The Flower and the Leaf,' after which none of the poems is narrative except incidentally. 'The Flower and the Leaf' itself is a vision framed by the narrator's account of her own experience, which made the vision possible. Although events occur during the course of 'Alexander's Feast,' which follows 'The Flower and the Leaf,' it is an ode. 'The Twelfth Book of Ovid' frames Nestor's adventure story (the battle of the Centaurs and Lapiths) within a radically condensed version of the story of the Trojan war; structurally it thus resembles 'The Flower and the Leaf,' improbable as the comparison between these two poems may otherwise seem. 'The Speeches of Ajax and Ulysses' consists of just those two speeches, subsuming narrative into the two contestants' recollections, as Ajax tells the story of Philoctetes to illustrate Ulysses' inhumanity (63–8). This is precisely the kind of structural asymmetry that was important in *Sylvae*, though here it appears more subtly. Ajax knows that his stories are subject to the charge of being lies:

> That this is not a Fable forg'd by me,
> Like one of his, an *Ulyssean* Lie,
> I vouch ev'n *Diomede*, who tho' his Friend
> Cannot that Act excuse, much less defend. (99–102)

Dryden thus tends to frame his narratives or to make their existence hinge on some more 'truthful' element in the poem. A narrative may enclose the truth or be enclosed by it or be juxtaposed to it, but it does not stand alone.

In 'The Wife of Bath Her Tale' the structure of 'The Flower and the Leaf' and 'The Twelfth Book of Ovid' is reversed. The story of the rape is over in a few lines (46–60), the rapist's search for truth takes longer, and the crone's sermon becomes the centre and climax of the tale. This structure could be explained by the Wife's rambling and self-involved style if we were considering the poem as part of the *Canterbury Tales*, but here it shows an ascent from pure action, rape being the archetypal action mingling sex and violence, to a search which is both physically active and intellectual, and then to an account of truth itself. 'Of the Pythagorean Philosophy' is almost all sermon, framed by the brief historical account of Numa. 'The Character of a Good Parson' and 'The Monument of a Fair Maiden Lady' are characters of idealized individuals, and the second poem is an epitaph. 'Cymon and Iphigenia' accumulates not *narrative* tension but *moral* tension, because Dryden creates so many significant parallels to other poems and to real events outside the poem. I do not think that any of these poems is primarily a narrative, though we may be persuaded otherwise because they do contain so many narrative elements deployed in a peculiar way. We can look at a passage from 'The Character of a Good Parson':

> The Tempter saw him too, with envious Eye;
> And, as on *Job*, demanded leave to try.
> He took the time when *Richard* was depos'd:
> And High and Low, with happy *Harry* clos'd.
> This Prince, tho' great in Arms, the Priest withstood:
> Near tho' he was, yet not the next of Blood.
> Had *Richard* unconstrain'd, resign'd the Throne:
> A King can give no more than is his own:
> The Title stood entail'd, had *Richard* had a Son. (106–14)

This passage *seems* to be narrative because it seems to deal with a sequence of events in time, and it is in part about time, history, and matters related to sequential events like royal succession and entail. Yet most of the passage is composed of biblical, historical, and topical allusions which force the reader to think in terms of parallels, between Richard and James II, for instance, or Richard and Job. The first allusions, to the tempter and to Job, are transparent enough not to confuse the essential development of the passage, but the possibility of seeing William as 'happy *Harry*' is more complex (all allusions converge on the present), and the bare suggestion of 'happy *Harry*' looks ahead to the next poem and a potential comparison to Cymon. Also, the last three lines, the triplet, concern hypothetical alternatives to what happened, even though they are about succession in time. Since an orderly succession as Dryden saw it had in fact been disrupted, perhaps non-narrative method was inevitable.

Dryden is thus as likely to provide truncated, fragmentary narratives or reminiscences of narrative as to provide a plain story, the main structure of which is its plot. A narrative reminiscence (my term) is a reference to a character like Helen or Job, whose stories we know so well that we feel as if they have been retold even though Dryden has given us only one or two details. Frequent references to legendary characters like Arthur, Ajax, or Theseus, who usually figure in action narrative, or to groups of characters like the knights and ladies of 'The Flower and the Leaf,' who belong to the age of chivalry and action, make us feel that much more is happening than a vision or a dialogue. Dryden's stage setting is heroic, but not the spiritual action, which is what really matters. Finally, the more we read of *Fables*, the more we see that the most literally active characters are both dangerous and contemptible: rapists, Centaurs, and finally Cymon, the 'Man-Beast' (147).

The primacy of narrative in *Fables*, therefore, is to a great extent illusory, a product of Dryden's ability both to suggest that more is happening than he need bother relate and to be crisp when something is in fact going on. An amusing perspective on narrative action appears in the passage from 'The Twelfth Book of Ovid' that describes the deaths of Cyllarus and Hylonome. Every couplet, sometimes every phrase, adds another detail to what seems to be a clearly defined sequence of events:

> Uncertain from what Hand, a flying Dart
> At *Cyllarus* was sent; which pierc'd his Heart.
> The Javelin drawn from out the mortal Wound,
> He faints with staggring Steps; and seeks the Ground:
> The Fair, within her Arms receiv'd his fall,
> And strove his wandring Spirits to recal:
> And while her Hand the streaming Blood oppos'd,
> Join'd Face to Face, his Lips with hers she clos'd.
> Stiffled with Kisses, a sweet Death he dies;
> She fills the Fields with undistinguish'd Cries:
> At least her Words, were in her Clamour drown'd;
> For my stun'd Ears receiv'd no vocal Sound.
> In madness of her Grief, she seiz'd the Dart
> New-drawn, and reeking from her Lover's Heart;
> To her bare Bosom the sharp Point apply'd;
> And wounded fell; and falling by his Side,
> Embrac'd him in her Arms; and thus embracing, dy'd. (560–76)

Relationships between events and the events themselves have an almost object-like clarity. One may even enjoy the sentimentality in this union of idealized Love and Death. Still, one should recall that these lovers are Centaurs; all the narrative clarity displayed above is calculated to make the reader or listener forget the one fact that would almost certainly limit involvement, although it is fascinating to see how we get involved in any case when we read the whole poem, forgetting what we already know, repressing inconvenient details in our passion to enjoy or identify where we can. The whole incident is Ovid's joke on what narrative poets can do with words. Nestor, who turns out to be a liar on the theme of his enemy, defends his reliability:

> A Stump too heavy for a Team to draw,
> (It seems a Fable, tho' the Fact I saw;)
> He threw at *Pholon*. (583–5)

> The Javelin wounded me; (behold the Skar.) (595)

Nestor's affirmations of truth seem to increase with the improbability of the tale.

Dryden knew what he was doing when he selected the Cyllarus and Hylonome episode. Though credit for the joke must be granted to Ovid, Dryden underlined it by intensifying the appallingly sentimental diction – phrases like 'The Fair,' 'Stiffled with Kisses,' and 'In madness of her Grief' – though Ovid's tone of voice is sentimental enough. The passage is ten lines long in Ovid,[1] and seventeen in Dryden, mainly because Dryden elaborates the precise sequence of detailed subevents. He added the action, 'He faints with staggring Steps; and seeks the Ground,' and made Hylonome *receive* Cyllarus, instead of only embracing him, so that her embrace seems to complete Cyllarus's fall and to become part of the action. Dryden emphasized the detailed events expressed in the triplet and he added Nestor's later witticism contrasting fable and fact, though 'behold the Skar' simply translates 'signa vides' (XII.444). For all his changes, Dryden has a remarkable grasp of Ovid's aesthetic effect and the frequent inadequacies of simple moralizing. Dryden presumably wanted a selection that called attention to the illusory aspects of narrative and not just one that helped to sustain his theme. He does not isolate the Centaur episode from the context that makes it witty (in contrast to Sandys' commentaries, which separate the myths from each other, thus fragmenting or really ignoring Ovid's structure).[2] The Centaurs remain as background to the bestial man Cymon and thus keep their traditional meaning as symbols of violence or bestiality, while their ultimate non-existence helps to characterize one of Dryden's important storytellers.

Dryden's most important technique for achieving structural unity could be called the 'recurrent motif,' though the term is completely empty of connotation. Perhaps it should be called the 'recurrent hieroglyph,' even though 'hieroglyph' connotes an enigmatic mode that Dryden avoided, indeed had to avoid in order to preserve the catholicity of his central characters, the theological poets, and his poem as well. Nevertheless, the theological poets were thought to have communicated their wisdom in the form of fables which were also hieroglyphs, as in the Hind's image of the Gordian knot which could either be untied with due respect for its complexity or cut apart with one penetrating slash of a knife, if one were, like Homer, an Alexander of interpretation. Dryden's important motifs do in fact have antecedents in the hieroglyphs of Renaissance thought and art, and although they are relatively simple stylistically in any given appearance in *Fables*, they acquire complexity in part just because of their recurrence and also because they are multifaceted, revealing lighter or darker sides, spiritual or earthly meanings, depending on the perspective of an individual poem.[3] They are also complex simply because of the traditions lying behind them. One can hardly suppose that Dryden was ignorant of the meanings attributed to Centaurs, Venus-Diana, the symposium, and so on, and it seems too much of a coincidence to imagine him placing so much structural emphasis on these once enigmatic motifs if he did not want to suggest something of their traditional importance. Dryden grants much more to the common reader than Spenser does, but, once again, I think that this was not because he considered his readers more stupid than Spenser's, but because Catholics were isolated enough as it was without presenting a Medusa-face of esoteric wisdom, Spenser's image for virtue in the *Epithalamium*. Otherwise, Dryden uses his motifs – or hieroglyphics – much as Spenser would have, to give a comprehensible structure to what on the surface appears a complex and meaningless narrative. The meaning of *Fables*, if one worked it out in every detail, would in large measure be a commentary on a vocabulary of a controlled group of hieroglyphs.

I have already discussed several instances of the symposium and shown that it can represent at one extreme (or in one of its manifestations) cannibalism and at the other the banquet of the mind, which in turn can be either a religious or an aesthetic experience. Dryden does not disparage the aesthetic, as he had in *Religio Laici.* The symposium embodies a universal need for communal pleasure, but that need can be satisfied on a variety of moral levels. I have also mentioned two occurrences of the Centaurs, one literal, in Nestor's story, and the other figurative, in Dryden's account of Cymon. On a very general level all the hieroglyphics bear out the implications of the symposium and the Centaur theme – the idea that human nature is an unhappy compound of soul and body. Even the compound words that Dryden uses to describe Cymon suggest this. Not only is he a 'Man-Beast' (147), but also a 'Man-Child' (216), and he is constantly trying to juggle two incompatible impulses. Dryden is quite explicit about what is wrong with Cymon and this passage might almost be read as a conclusive statement of what *Fables* is about:

> Fair, Tall, his Limbs with due Proportion join'd,
> But of a heavy, dull, degenerate Mind.
> His Soul bely'd the Features of his Face;
> Beauty was there, but Beauty in disgrace.
> A clownish Mien, a Voice with rustick sound,
> And stupid Eyes, that ever lov'd the Ground.
> He look'd like Nature's Error; as the Mind
> And Body were not of a Piece design'd,
> But made for two, and by mistake in one were join'd. (52–60)

The phrase 'Nature's Error' universalizes Cymon and the whole triplet presents him as an instance, though perhaps a strikingly absurd instance, of humanity's essential flaw. Dryden's next couplet after this passage – 'The ruling Rod, the Father's forming Care, / Were exercis'd in vain, on Wit's despair' – presents Cymon's unnamed father in terms appropriate to a frustrated deity. (Boccaccio names the father Aristippo, limiting him to a human identity.) At the beginning the father is a '*Cyprian* Lord' (46), who perhaps deserves the son he gets if he is a servant of Venus, but he is an Old Testament God shortly afterwards, and then almost invisible in the rest of the poem. These fluctuating meanings are Dryden's equivalent for Spenser's enigmatic technique. One need not overstate their difficulty, but it does help to be attuned to them. For instance, if 'god' in this poem is ineffectual, though he may have good intentions, one can infer something of Dryden's ideas about how little God can do to stimulate moral action, even if God really exists and wished humanity well at the outset of creation.

Another important hieroglyph in *Fables* is the androgyne, a figure who combines masculine and feminine identities, or who changes from one sex to the other, or, on a more figurative level, a man and woman so deeply united that they can be considered one person.[4] The second version, the person who changes sex, would not today be considered androgynous, but it still belongs in Dryden's metaphoric system because in his day such distinctions were generally overlooked or ignored. Dryden, like many others, also chose to ignore the fact that the original myth of androgyny, as told by Aristophanes in Plato's *Symposium*, included homosexual couples of both sexes who yearned to be reunited just as much as the heterosexual couples; accurate or not, the union of complementary qualities linked to both sexes is the essence of the myth of androgyny. Dryden's primal man in *The Hind and the Panther*, kneaded up with milk, was androgynous.[5] The androgyne is comparable to the Centaur, since both unite two identities which are separated in nature, but the androgyne is more closely associated with primal harmony, while the Centaur represents a failure in harmony. These two images of humanity's double nature are themselves a complementary pair.

An emphasis on doubles, twins, and double-natured creatures ('biformis') can be found throughout Ovid's *Metamorphoses*, and especially in 'Meleager and Atalanta.' Many of the heroes engaged in hunting the Caledonian boar are paired – Theseus and Perithous, Castor and Pollux, the Thestyan brethren. Dryden's translation draws attention to the theme. Theseus and Perithous are 'A single Concord in a double Name' (51); Ovid says 'Perithoo, felix concordia, Theseus' (VIII.303), joining the friends' names by the relevant phrase. Dryden's Castor and Pollux are 'Fair *Leda*'s Twins' (46); the description of 'twice old *Iolas*, and *Nestor* then but young' (60) shows that even aging produces a double identity in characters who might normally be thought of as composed of one nature only. Dryden repeated Ovid's idea in the Good Parson:

> Of Sixty Years he seem'd; and well might last
> To Sixty more, but that he liv'd too fast. (8–9)

By repeating the interval of sixty years Dryden doubles the Parson's life, instead of merely extending it, although he still envisions continuity in the Parson's identity, instead of Ovid's disturbing and surreal changes. 'Meleager' thus contains both harmonious pairs – though we find that Theseus and Perithous will be divided later (by Perithous's marriage) – and incongruous pairs, like the image of the youthful Nestor superimposed upon our conventional image of the old man.

All these twin figures prepare for an androgynous Atalanta, who takes part in the hunt like 'A fair fierce Boy' (75) and thereby arouses a male warrior's jealousy; ultimately even Atalanta becomes a foil for Althea's purely human conflict of identity. After Althea's son, Meleager, kills her brothers, she suffers from divided loyalties:

> The Sister and the Mother long contest
> Two doubtful Titles in one tender Breast. (268–9)

Althea burns the brand that is fated to cause her son's death. In this story any sort of double identity means that the self is endangered by its own complexity. Dryden's interest in the kind of conflict that Althea experiences dates back to his earlier plays (especially Antony in *All for Love*), but it intensified in the 1690s (*Amphitryon*), as I have shown. He had personal reasons for choosing a poem about twins, doubles, and an androgyne, and one notes that the first half of the poem – the hunt – shifts the emphasis away from Althea's human problem to the hieroglyphic which places it in an intellectual context. The poem itself is split in two (the hunt, then Althea's conflict), its structure becoming an image of its theme.

Another important character in 'Meleager' is the androgynous warrior '*Ceneus*, once a Woman, now a Man' (53), whose story is told more fully by Nestor in 'The Twelfth Book of Ovid.' As a woman, Caenis, she was raped by Neptune, who allowed her to choose her own reward:

> The haughty Fair
> Who not the Rape, ev'n of a God cou'd bear,
> This Answer, proud, return'd: To mighty Wrongs
> A mighty Recompence, of right, belongs.
> Give me no more to suffer such a Shame;
> But change the Woman, for a better Name,
> One Gift for all: She said; and while she spoke,
> A stern, majestick, manly Tone she took.
> A Man she was. ('The Twelfth Book of Ovid,' 278–86)

Neptune in addition makes Ceneus invulnerable to wounds, but the Centaurs kill him by heaping weights upon him; the ideal androgyne is defeated by 'The united Force, / Of two the strongest Creatures, Man and Horse' (665–6). Ceneus's death scene is reminiscent of Mezentius's in *Sylvae*, both in pictorial effect (a man-body tangle) and in meaning (the poetic justice of a warrior's defeat by pure mass). Dryden's treatment of Caenis/Ceneus is noticeably more sardonic than Ovid's.[6] Though condemning the rapist god, Dryden calls the victim a 'haughty Fair' who appears rather self-important, a heroine like Sigismonda in her demand for a 'mighty Recompence.' Ovid did not call manhood 'a better Name'; his Caenis simply changed from an ideal woman to an ideal man. Yet in Dryden's version Caenis's wish for manhood is ironic since the eternal masculine in *Fables* is chronically prone to rape and violence. Therefore, her metamorphosis and her immediate desire to fight (290) prefigure Cymon's doubtful transformation from country rustic to butcher-hero.

Not all the androgynes in *Fables* are Ovidian. Sigismonda, another doubtful union of two conflicting selves, suppresses her female identity in order to meet her father courageously. Tancred does most of the crying in the poem. However, Dryden suggests that Sigismonda's self-control is somehow inauthentic; a 'heroine' cannot also be womanly:

> But in-born Worth, that Fortune can controul,
> New strung, and stiffer bent her softer Soul;
> The *Heroine* assum'd the Womans Place,
> Confirm'd her Mind, and fortifi'd her Face. (374–7)

The word 'heroine' is not complimentary in Dryden's vocabulary, suggesting at best the extravagance of Ovid's *Heroides* or of Dido and at worst the erotic lust for power revealed in characters like Nourmahal and Lyndaraxa from the heroic plays. Sigismonda is a fiery character like Nourmahal (the villain of *Aureng-Zebe*), and her very rhyme words recall Lyndaraxa's in *The Conquest of Granada*:

> Why wou'd I be a Queen? because my Face
> Wou'd wear the Title with a better grace.
> If I became it not, yet it wou'd be
> Part of your duty, then, to Flatter me.
> These are not half the Charms of being great:
> I wou'd be somewhat – that I know not yet:
> Yes; I avowe th' ambition of my Soul,
> To be that one, to live without controul.[7]

Ironically Sigismonda does not need or desire the kind of power that Lyndaraxa wants, but even her more reasonable demands are slightly discoloured by her 'heroical' language and its concomitant suppression of femininity. Dryden's ambivalence is undoubtedly a challenge to female readers. Susannah Centlivre, in her tragicomedy *The Cruel Gift*, reworked the Sigismonda story in an effort to portray a woman who was at once heroic (courageous, capable of fortitude and political thought) and feminine (emotional though not to excess, interested in marriage). Centlivre also ignores the vocabulary of androgyny, which seems to equate an unusual woman with a masculine woman or even with an Ovidian freak.

Dryden is also ambivalent about marriage as an image of ideal harmony. Baucis and Philemon are the only happy couple in *Fables* whose unity remains unthreatened, even after death: Ceyx and Alcyone, for example, are abnormally dependent on each other; Emily marries Palamon as a second choice; and Pygmalion loves a statue of his own creating, a nice comment on the sort of mistress who would be likely to satisfy a misogynist. In 'To my Honour'd Kinsman' Dryden connects the physical union of marriage with fragmentation of the self:

> Minds are so hardly match'd, that ev'n the first,
> Though pair'd by Heav'n, in Paradise, were curs'd.
> For Man and Woman, though in one they grow,
> Yet, first or last, return again to Two.
> He to God's Image, She to His was made;
> So, farther from the Fount, the Stream at Random stray'd. (21–6)

Marriage leads to fragmentation of loyalties, too, since Driden would not be able to devote himself to his larger family, the people on his estate, if he were not celibate. Dryden does, however, idealize masculine-feminine harmony in the realms of the spirit and of art. He links his cousin Driden with the goddess of agriculture, Ceres, and calls him '*Rebecca*'s Heir' (43, 46), as if, having sacrificed an earthly marriage, he is free to incorporate within himself a feminine principle. Similarly, Numa is married to the goddess Egeria, and Theseus, though he is literally married to Hippolita, the Amazon queen – not a very important figure in the poem – is figuratively linked to Hippolita's sister, Emily:

> she blush'd; and as o'eraw'd by Might,
> Seem'd to give *Theseus*, what she gave the Knight.
> ('Palamon and Arcite,' III.1135–6)

On the frankly political level Emily's 'marriage' to Theseus, the superior male, will protect her from the dangers posed by a husband's 'sensual Gust' and 'surly Pride' (III.231). These are her words, in her prayer to Diana. Chaucer's Emily worried more about childbirth and less, if at all, about the husband's opportunity for unjust assumptions of power.[8] The line 'Man, the Tyrant of our Sex, I hate' (III.228) reflects Dryden's perception of marital politics; his Emily is also more of a huntress than Chaucer's (III.247). This is completely appropriate to her faith in Diana's guardianship, but it makes Emily, like Caenis and Sigismonda, prone to violence within the framework of her feminine identity, even a type of Atalanta.

Dryden's pictorially attractive mingling of knights and ladies in 'The Flower and the Leaf' is one sort of aesthetic marriage; the use of two sets of paired poems on two idealized couples is another. Once again Dryden provides a double set of twins. The Duchess of Ormonde is structurally linked to two men, just as Emily is, though she is presented as living with neither. Her link to Driden is completely symbolic and structural; the Duchess and Driden are the subjects of two closely related poems, with a very long poem, 'Palamon and Arcite,' intervening between them. The Duchess is also isolated from her husband, as Dryden emphasizes:

All is Your Lord's alone; ev'n absent, He
Employs the Care of Chast *Penelope*.
For him You waste in Tears Your Widow'd Hours,
For him Your curious Needle paints the Flow'rs:
Such Works of Old Imperial Dames were taught;
Such for *Ascanius*, fair *Elisa* wrought. (157–62)

The Duchess becomes a synthesis of women who have experienced every kind of isolation, like all Ovid's abandoned heroines combined into one, experiencing at once widowhood, the prolonged though partly accidental separation of Penelope and Ulysses, and the outright rejection of Dido by Aeneas. Her embroidery is a symbol of her limited world, a little wooden hoop replacing the cosmic circles of Dryden's opening lines: 'As when the Stars, in their Etherial Race, / At length have roll'd around the Liquid Space, / At certain Periods they resume their Place' (21–3). Yet at the same time her embroidery is a little aesthetic universe, a garden of the mind that she has created by herself, and her husband, who displayed his 'Heroick Charity' when he was in prison (K, IV, 1443), was not much better off than a woman limited by social convention and biological destiny. Both of them demonstrate their best qualities within a limited space.

Because Dryden has placed his paired poems symmetrically, one pair at each end (almost) of *Fables*, it is hard to decide whether the two pairs are meant to be read as equally important, or if the second pair, about a more spiritualized couple, is meant to replace the first. The first pair are greater poems, I think, if they are read without regard for their place in *Fables*; the ideas and the imagery are more dense, and the two poems complement each other in a variety of interesting details. The second pair complement each other only in their general subject, and our conventional response, to set the religious order above the political, may be misplaced. In any case the first paired poems have religious implications in their cosmic imagery and in their references to the fall, and 'The Character of a Good Parson' has political implications; the two orders are thus mixed in all but 'The Monument of A Fair Maiden Lady,' which is too simple to be a better poem.

Dryden's structure in *Fables* may be explained by reference to a final twin-figure, Janus, the god of thresholds, who was yet another representation of man's double nature, looking both ways, one face towards the physical and the other towards the spiritual.[9] The structure of *Fables* is Janus-faced and appropriately Dryden shows his face by speaking in his own person at the beginning and at the end of the work, though not in the middle. Janus is never mentioned in *Fables*, but he is important in the late work *The Secular Masque*, from which I feel it is legitimate to import the image. *The Secular Masque* looks two ways in time, satirically towards the century just past and with some kind of relief, though with no special optimism, towards the unknown future. Janus introduces the masque itself, calling on Chronos, the god of time, and Momus, the satirist, to appear on stage. These three constitute a superior triad of gods, who reduce Mars, Venus, and Diana to the level of time-bound and deceptive goals which, with any luck, the new century will leave behind. Some of this comes from 'Palamon and Arcite,' where Chronos, or Saturn, represents a higher order on which the differences between Mars, Venus, and Diana are reconciled. However, Dryden was not inclined to idealize the figure of Time:

> Though sparing of his Grace, to Mischief bent,
> He seldom does a Good with good Intent.
> Wayward, but wise; by long Experience taught
> To please both Parties, for ill Ends, he sought:
> For this Advantage Age from Youth has won,
> As not to be outridden, though outrun. (III.383–8)

In *The Secular Masque* Janus is master of ceremonies, controlling even the god who thinks he effortlessly controls everyone else. His role is something like that of Timotheus in 'Alexander's Feast,' but no one supplants him. He is a brilliant figure for Dryden himself, the perfect symbol of control at the limit of life. Janus epitomizes the best in the long series of theological poets in *Fables*, and he really stands on the boundaries between life and death, or heaven and earth. He makes the world his stage and thus makes himself superior to it. The appearance of Janus almost persuades me that Dryden made his own decision to die (as an Epicurean he ought to have been able to do so); in any case Dryden takes full literary advantage of his personal situation, which was almost but not quite removed from the flux of seventeenth-century history.

Epilogue

It does not seem surprising that Dryden should have sought images of benign control in his late poems, but what is impressive is the multiple reference of these images. From one point of view figures like Timotheus, Janus, Nestor, and the Good Parson seem to be idealized images of Dryden himself, expressing not always the way he saw himself in fact, but hypothetical selves. Dryden is less interested in apologizing for such flaws as sullenness or an unduly prolonged hostility to his political enemies than in exhibiting with some pride his own potentialities, at least some of which had been fulfilled over the years, indeed in *Fables* itself. I am not reducing *Fables* to sublimated autobiography. Dryden said that Homer and Virgil put their characteristic energies into their respective heroes; he did the same, providing a tantalizing range of heroes, no two the same, yet all obviously sharing common qualities, which the reader will ultimately find grounded in the preface to *Fables*. Dryden's artist-heroes have supreme control over their art, and through their art over the more conventional figures of power, kings and men of action. Dryden no longer regarded such heroes as mere butchers. By the time of 'Alexander's Feast,' 'The Speeches of Ajax and Ulysses,' and the dedication to the Duke of Ormonde he saw them as mindless idiots, not worth taking seriously except for the disruption they caused to everyone else. Probably such men were beyond redemptive influence (though they could be manipulated with pathetic ease), but Dryden also wanted to affect general readers who had the option of supporting them or not; even more he wanted to persuade men and women like his cousin Driden, the Duke and Duchess of Ormonde, and the unnamed equivalents of Cymon's father and the nobility of 'The Wife of Bath Her Tale' that a power vacuum existed that they could effectively fill. Dryden looked to the country party to save

England, but his approach was to jolt them out of their inertia and self-interest into taking responsibility for England as a whole.

Dryden did not doubt the power of his writing; if anything, he worried that art (because of its liveliness) might too easily influence others. His solution was never restraint, but the combination of terror and benevolence. His power figures also suggest his sublime confidence in himself in relation to the poets he translated. He never claimed to be the equal of Homer or Virgil, but no other poets elicited from Dryden more than a reluctant decision to confine his genius to that of his original (in itself a sly reminder of his presence in the poem). Between 1685 and 1700 Dryden came to regard his originals as kindred spirits, so that the sense of confinement vanished. He knew the difference between translation and original composition, though he also showed how hard it was to distinguish between them in cases like Ovid's *Metamorphoses* and Chaucer's 'The Knight's Tale' and he exploited this ambiguity for all it was worth. Dryden's self-assurance went even further. As a translator/re-creator picking and choosing among the stories of the past, he was in a sense rescuing his poems from limbo, so that the original poets owed their immortality in part to him. Stories undergo metempsychosis, but Dryden was the Pythagoras in whom they are reborn. The element of self-deception here may be forgiven in a man who knew he was about to die, or at least be understood an an effort to interpret and judge his own life by the standards of the immortals and not by those of his own time. Dryden was an Epicurean who wanted to control the psychological conditions under which he encountered death.

If I seem to be speculating too much about Dryden's personality and about motives that he may not always have admitted to himself, let me say that Dryden himself invited such speculation, never consenting to invisibility in his poems, again and again insisting on revealing himself, if only in part. No doubt the secondary role of translator impelled him to compensate by drawing inordinate attention to himself; he seemed to like masks that were shadowy indeed. I would not accept an analysis of these poems, especially of *Fables*, that treated them as purely objective works of art or as unremittingly public statements on some religious or political issue, and certainly not as inspired hack work. Nevertheless, Dryden was involved to the end in both religious and political argument and I think had fairly precise things to say. To some extent his works were utopian. He idealized philosopher-kings and poet-priests, imagining them in idealized personal relationships with their subjects, uninterested in self-aggrandizement, and in control of their own passions, though their subjects might have to offer some guidance, a timely word of warning on the need for restraint. The concept of the philosopher-king enabled Dryden to transcend the tedious and pointless rivalry between James and William.

The philosopher-king also fit in very well with Dryden's Catholicism, because these priestly legislators were also apostolic. The very presence of several such characters in *Fables* creates the image of a series of witnesses to an essentially unified truth, persisting through time by means of an oral tradition and occasionally renewed revelation, though revelation never seems to come whole. Like *The Hind and the Panther*, *Fables* is a propaganda statement on behalf of the Catholic's essential humanity and benevolence, though *Fables* is far more cautious in design, avoiding the risks (direct self-defence, the use of animals as narrators) of the earlier poem. Dryden also defended (still obliquely) the humaneness of that most controversial of Catholic beliefs, belief in the real presence of Christ in the Eucharist. He insisted upon the social and spiritual implications of the feast, while deriding cannibalism as an extension of the violence of primitive and unenlightened souls; yet at the same time he used the imagery of cannibalism and of the body to show that he had not reduced the meaning of the feast to mere symbol. Dryden got the real presence of words into his poetry. He could do so before his conversion, too, but in *Fables* his talents were concentrated on giving heightened reality to accounts of sacramental occasions.

Dryden's attitude towards translation was always re-creative and he tended to integrate groups of short poems into a whole, to such an extent that in *Sylvae* and *Fables* he constructed major works out of what could have been random collections. The conceptions underlying *Sylvae* and *Fables* are not, however, identical; *Fables* achieves much greater subtlety and much more extensively subordinates the original poets to Dryden's design. The principles underlying these poems have seemed worth exploring in detail; I do not claim to have discovered all the relevant models, but I remain convinced that we should understand the integrated nature of these collections so that we are free to read Dryden's poems as true poems.

Notes

CHAPTER 1

1 One admires, however, the response of Vinton A. Dearing, textual editor of *Sylvae*, who paused in the midst of his commentary to say that Dryden's translations of Horace were his finest work: *The Works of John Dryden* (Berkeley and Los Angeles: University of California Press 1969), III, 533. References to this edition will henceforth be cited in the text by volume and page number. As neither Dryden's Virgil nor his *Fables* have yet been published in the California edition, for these works I shall use James Kinsley's four-volume edition of *The Poems of John Dryden* (Oxford: Clarendon 1958).
Admiration for Dryden's *Fables* was characteristic of the Romantic poets; this is interesting in the light of Wordsworth's declaration that the poet need no longer feel himself 'in the situation of a translator, who deems himself justified when he substitutes excellences of another kind for those which are unattainable by him': 'Preface to Lyrical Ballads (1802),' *Literary Criticism of William Wordsworth*, ed Paul M. Zall (Lincoln: University of Nebraska Press 1966), p 50. Yet Wordsworth did try to translate Chaucer, and his sister Dorothy emulated the narrator of 'The Flower and the Leaf,' seeking contact with the earth in order to reach God and the muse. See 'The Grasmere Journal,' *Journals of Dorothy Wordsworth*, ed Ernest de Selincourt (London: Macmillan 1952), I, 86–7. According to Dorothy, William translated some of 'The Manciple's Tale' at this time. Three other translations of Chaucer have survived; they are included in the Cambridge edition of Wordsworth's works.
Sir Walter Scott's is one of the primary responses. Some of *Fables* are so effective, he says, 'as almost to claim the merit of originality. Many passages might be shown in which this praise may be carried still higher, and the merit of invention added to that of imitation.' Yet Dryden, Scott says, coarsens

the female character, like that of Sigismonda. See Scott's *The Life of John Dryden*, ed Bernard Kreissman (1834; rpt Lincoln: University of Nebraska Press 1963), pp 421–2. Scott's charge of coarseness stuck for a long time, though many female readers have been unconvinced by it. Mary Wollstonecraft makes some positive allusions to *Fables*, especially to 'Sigismonda' and 'The Flower and the Leaf.' For a modern response similar to Scott's see Mark van Doren, *John Dryden: A Study of His Poetry*, 3rd ed (New York: Holt 1946), p 215.

2 I shall say more in ch 3 about the interconnectedness of Dryden's classical sources and in ch 7 about the interconnectedness of the sources for *Fables*.

3 Earl Miner, *Dryden's Poetry* (Bloomington: Indiana University Press 1967), p 301.

4 Norman Austin, 'Translation as Baptism: Dryden's Lucretius,' *Arion*, 7 (1968), 576–602.

5 Wordsworth to Scott, 18 Jan 1808, *The Letters of William and Dorothy Wordsworth*, ed Ernest de Selincourt, 2nd ed rev Mary Moorman (Oxford: Clarendon 1969), vol II, Part I, p 191.

6 Wolfgang Jünemann, *Drydens Fabeln und ihre Quellen* (Hamburg: Friederichsen, de Gruyter 1932).

7 William Frost, *Dryden and the Art of Translation* (New Haven: Yale University Press 1955), p 63. See also Michael West, 'Dryden's Ambivalence as a Translator of Heroic Themes,' *Huntington Library Quarterly*, 36 (1973), 347–66. Frost has elsewhere taken a different approach, well suited for dealing with translations from a single author – the study of seventeenth-century editions and commentaries available to Dryden and of earlier English translations of the work in question. See Frost's article 'English Persius: The Golden Age,' *Eighteenth-Century Studies*, 2 (1968/9), 77–101. Austin uses this approach in his article 'Translation as Baptism.' Another student who used the 'subtraction method' to good effect is Antoine Culioli, 'Dryden, traducteur et adapteur de Chaucer et de Boccace,' diss. Paris, 1960. As can be seen from his title, Culioli does not deal with *Fables* as a whole, but he does emphasize the poet's ability to express his own genius as much in a translation as in an original poem (pp 2–3, 37, 91).

8 I have gone over these ideas in my earlier work: 'An Interpretation of Dryden's *Fables*,' *Eighteenth-Century Studies*, 4 (1970/1), 199–211; and 'The Structure of Dryden's *Fables*,' diss. Minnesota, 1968.

9 Frost calls 'Iphis and Ianthe' and 'Acis and Galatea' 'companion pieces,' but observes no relationship between them and Book I, which Dryden translated in its entirety (*Works*, IV, 729).

10 Dryden's activities during this period have not yet been seen coherently. Arthur W. Hoffman represents the period by 'To Mr. Oldham' (1684) and 'To Mrs. Anne Killigrew' (1685) in *John Dryden's Imagery* (Gainesville: University of

Florida Press 1962). Steven Zwicker, *Dryden's Political Poetry* (Providence: Brown University Press 1972), p 117, discusses 'Threnodia Augustalis' (1685) and 'Britannia Rediviva' (1688); he says: 'By 1688 not only had the political and religious climate changed but the poet himself was a different man.' Certain cut-off points in Dryden's life are generally recognized, whether 1685, the year of Charles II's death, or 1688, that of James II's abdication, is emphasized more. The period, of course, included Dryden's conversion. Victor M. Hamm, 'Dryden's *The Hind and the Panther* and Roman Catholic Apologetics,' *PMLA*, 83 (1968), 401, argues that Dryden had a great deal of spare time to read the Catholic apologists: 'Miscellaneous prose, translations, a poor opera, and a few occasional poems – this is not very much to show for more than four years in the life of a professional man-of-letters in his prime.' However much time Dryden managed to devote to each of his activities, he was undoubtedly developing not only in his attitudes towards politics and religion but in his role as a poet. Dryden's translations should not be rendered invisible.

11 T.R. Steiner, *English Translation Theory, 1650–1800* (Amsterdam: Van Gorcum, Assen 1975), pp 29–30. Steiner observes that Dryden's 1680 statement was his most conservative, that he subsequently shifted his emphasis 'from the sense of a work to its spirit, from faithfulness of imitation to the production of pleasure, from the curbing of license to freedom' (p 30). Nevertheless, the metaphrase-paraphrase-imitation theme is endlessly cited, as if it were self-explanatory and made further discussions superfluous.

12 Harold F. Brooks, 'The "Imitation" in English Poetry, Especially in Formal Satire, Before the Age of Pope,' *Review of English Studies*, os 25 (1949), 138.

13 Leonard A. Moskovit, 'Pope and the Tradition of the Neoclassical Imitation,' *Studies in English Literature*, 8 (1968), 446, 449.

14 Howard D. Weinbrot, *The Formal Strain: Studies in Augustan Imitation and Satire* (Chicago: University of Chicago Press 1969), p 4. Weinbrot follows Brooks in seeing the Elizabethan concept of free translation as one of imitation (pp 15–17); see Brooks, 'The "Imitation" in English Poetry,' p 125.

15 The Juvenal and Persius translations are in *Works*, vol IV. Their editor, A.B. Chambers, concludes that Dryden's translations of the satires are basically 'paraphrastic,' especially in filling out obscurities: 'Not everything, however, can be explained in this way. Some of the local details, for example, are peculiarly Dryden's own, including some topical allusions unwarranted by the Latin texts' (*Works*, IV, 595). The 'Character of a Good Parson, Imitated from Chaucer' in *Fables* is another poem that does not readily fit the categories established in 1680. Weinbrot does not discuss it because he is more interested in imitations that border on satire. Other articles on the subject are R. Selden, 'Juvenal and Restoration Modes of Translation,' *Modern Language Review*, 68 (1973), 481–93;

and L.R. Burrows, 'Juvenal in Translation,' *Australasian Universities Language and Literature Association*, Proceedings and Papers of the 12th Congress held at the University of Western Australia, 1970, pp 193–201.

16 John Denham, preface to 'The Destruction of Troy' [1656], in *Poetical Works*, ed Theodore Howard Banks, 2nd ed (1928; rpt [Hampden, Conn:] Archon 1969), p 159. See also Denham, '*To Sir* Richard Fanshaw *upon his Translation of* Pastor Fido [1643 or 1644],' pp 143–44.

17 Chambers notes Dryden's 'obvious delight' in translating Juvenal's bawdy, and comments that Dryden's arguments to the Juvenal satires are original, while those to the Persius satires depend heavily on Casaubon (*Works*, IV, 589, 595).

18 Kinsley, ed, *The Poems of John Dryden*, II, 913. Henceforth references to Kinsley's edition will be cited in the text as K, followed by volume and page numbers.

19 Charles E. Ward, *The Life of John Dryden* (Chapel Hill: University of North Carolina Press 1961), p 271.

20 See Virgil's third Georgic, 95–100. The Loeb translation has: 'Yet even such a steed, when, worn with disease or sluggish through years, he begins to fail, shut up indoors and pity not his inglorious age. Cold is his passion when old, vainly he strives at a thankless toil, and whenever he comes to the fray his ardour is futile, as in the stubble a great fire rages at times without strength': *Virgil: Eclogues, Georgics, Aeneid I–VI*, trans H. Rushton Fairclough (Cambridge, Mass: Harvard University Press, 1924), p 161.

21 Miner, *Dryden's Poetry*, comments on these lines to establish the link between the Ormonde poem and 'Palamon and Arcite' (pp 292–4). See also Hoffman, *John Dryden's Imagery*, pp 141–2, for a discussion of the Platonist imagery in this poem.

22 Murray Cohen, *Sensible Words: Linguistic Practice in England, 1640–1785* (Baltimore: Johns Hopkins University Press 1977), pp 2–4. He makes some interesting comments on *Absalom and Achitophel* (pp 23–5), but says little else on Dryden directly. Background may also be found in D.C. Allen, 'Some Theories of the Growth and Origin of Language in Milton's Age,' *Philological Quarterly*, 28 (1949), 5–16.

23 Richard Simon, *A Critical History of the Old Testament* (London 1682). Book III is entirely about translation. On learning as a process of reconstruction see III, 133. Phillip Harth, in *Contexts of Dryden's Thought* (Chicago: University of Chicago Press 1968), makes extensive and sympathetic comments on Simon (pp 176–7).

24 The Babel myth persisted into the eighteenth century, gaining more, not less, currency with the growth of naturalistic or evolutionary conceptions of language development. *The Hind and the Panther* is an early attempt to reconcile a belief that language can develop historically with a belief in the primal unity of man based on a common language. See William Wotton, *A Discourse Concerning the*

Confusion of Languages at Babel (London 1730), p 12. His discourse is dated 25 November 1713. Wotton believed that the *multiplicity* of languages, though not necessarily speech itself, must have had a miraculous origin.

25 Jean Leclerc, *Five Letters Concerning the Inspiration of the Holy Scriptures*, trans from the French (London 1690). See also William Lowth, *A Vindication of the Divine Authority and Inspiration of the Writings of the Old and New Testament* (Oxford 1692); and Jean Leclerc, *Free and Important Disquisitions Concerning the Inspiration of the Holy Scriptures* (London 1750).

26 Alexander Pope, 'An Essay on the Life, Writings, and Learning of Homer [1715],' *The Iliad of Homer, Books I–IX*, ed Maynard Mack, 2 vols, vol. VII of *The Twickenham Edition of the Poems of Alexander Pope* (New Haven: Yale University Press 1967), pp 27–8.

27 Sir Roger L'Estrange, *Fables of Aesop, and other Eminent Mythologists: with Morals and Reflections* (London 1692), pp 1–2.

28 Charles Boyle, *Dissertations on the Epistles of Phalaris and the Fables of Aesop, Examin'd*, 2nd ed (London 1698), p 235; see also pp 120–1. Paul J. Korshin discusses analogies between Aesop and Jesus current during this period in 'The Development of Abstracted Typology in England, 1650–1820,' in *Literary Uses of Typology from the Late Middle Ages to the Present*, ed Earl Miner (Princeton: Princeton University Press 1977), pp 176–7.

29 Boyle, *Dissertations*, compares Bentley to Spinoza and others like him who threatened to undermine the authority of Moses' writings, yet he agrees that Planudes' life is mostly a fiction. It seems to have occurred to no one that an essentially truthful life story or history might have been cast in a conventionalized form that made it read like fable only to a modern (pp 268–9).

30 Mary Pritchard describes this material in 'Fables Moral and Political: The Adaptation of the Aesopian Fable Collection to English Social and Political Life, 1651–1722,' diss. Western Ontario, 1976, pp 180–96.

31 *Aesop at Tunbridge* (London 1698) was the first. It is bound together with a collection including *Aesop Return'd from Tunbridge*, *Aesop at Epsom*, *Aesop at Amsterdam*, *Aesop at White-Hall*, and *Aesop at Bathe*, but this kind of title was used for yet more pamphlets, after 1699, on other matters of topical interest. 'Tunbridge' seems to be a reference to Rochester's poem 'Tunbridge Wells,' which includes an attack on Samuel Parker ('Pert Bays') who trampled on religion and liberty (pp 60–2). That is why the collections are at first set in watering places.

Samuel Parker, a frantically authoritarian Anglican, is not relevant to the Aesop collections, but the defence of liberty, as opposed to monolithic authoritarianism, is. Rochester, in the tradition of the 'happy beast,' also praised his horse's wisdom, and Aesop, of course, wrote beast fables. On watering places see *Aesop from Islington* (1699), preface. The lines '*Seven wealthy Towns contend for* HOMER *Dead, / Through which* the Living HOMER *begg'd his Bread*' appear in 'Poetry its Cure,' *Aesop at Tunbridge*, p 16. The 'Aesop at' satires are also considered by Thomas Noel in *Theories of the Fable in the Eighteenth Century* (New York: Columbia University Press 1975), pp 30–2, but I do not agree with Noel that Aesopic fable plays absolutely no part in Dryden's *Fables* or that 'the fable enjoyed scant literary status in the seventeenth century' (p 36).

32 Stephen Yenser, *Circle to Circle: The Poetry of Robert Lowell* (Berkeley and Los Angeles: University of California Press 1975), p 6.

33 Robert Lowell, *Imitations* (London: Faber 1961), pp xi–xii.

34 Irvin Ehrenpreis, 'The Growth of a Poet,' in *Critics on Robert Lowell: Readings in Literary Criticism*, ed Jonathan Price (Coral Gables: University of Miami Press 1972), p 31.

35 Yenser, *Circle to Circle*, p 171.

36 Jorge Luis Borges, *Labyrinths*, ed Donald A. Yates and James E. Irby (New York: New Directions 1964). Menard's 'admirable intention was to produce a few pages which would coincide – word for word and line for line – with those of Miguel de Cervantes' (p 39).

CHAPTER 2

1 Dryden refers to himself this way in the dedication of the *Aeneis* (K, III, 1016).

2 *The Letters of John Dryden, With Letters Addressed to Him*, ed Charles E. Ward (1942; rpt New York: AMS Press 1965), p 77.

3 Dryden, *Letters*, pp 80, 82.

4 Henry Horwitz, *Parliament, Policy and Politics in the Reign of William III* (Manchester: Manchester University Press 1977), pp 134, 167.

5 *Critical and Miscellaneous Prose Works*, ed Edmund Malone, 4 vols in 3 (London 1800), III, 387–8. The lives of Lucian and Polybius are available in this edition.

6 'The Added Artificer,' in *On Translation*, ed Reuben A. Brower (New York: Oxford University Press 1966), pp 140–1.

7 Stanley Fish, *Self-Consuming Artifacts: The Experience of Seventeenth-Century Literature* (Berkeley and Los Angeles: University of California Press 1972). See especially ch 3 on Herbert; for example: 'the unacceptability of each of his resolutions leads finally to silence and inaction .. and thus to an involuntary admission that the solution of the dilemma is beyond him. In short, he *gives up*. This prepares the way for the revelation from without, the revelation that the solution, and indeed all else, is beyond him, but that it is well within the capacity and inclination of another' (p 175). One could no doubt trace Dryden's concern with his identity back to an earlier period, especially to the attack on Mr Bayes in *The*

Rehearsal: see George McFadden, *Dryden: The Public Writer (1660–1685)* (Princeton: Princeton University Press 1978), pp 105–7. In that case *MacFlecknoe* – where Dryden casts the Bayes image back at his enemies – would show Dryden exorcising the past before proceeding to a new stage in his career.

8 On the Dickinson lines see Phillip Harth, *Contexts of Dryden's Thought* (Chicago: University of Chicago Press 1968), pp 174, 185–94. Harth counters the view that Dryden inserted the passage to help Tonson raise sales for Dickinson's book.

9 Dryden, *Letters*, III, 123.

10 Malone, ed, III, 255.

11 Malone, ed, III, 248.

12 Malone, ed, III, 362.

13 Malone, ed, III, 371.

14 Robert D. Hume, *Dryden's Criticism* (Ithaca: Cornell University Press 1970), pp 17–18, points out that Dryden increasingly regarded literature as the expression of an individual writer's character and became more interested in the writers' lives.

15 Malone, ed, III, 362.

16 *Works*, XVII, 264 and 440n.

17 See Samuel H. Monk's editorial note, *Works*, XVII, 454–6.

18 Jonathan Swift, 'On Poetry: A Rapsody,' 117–42; Frances Burney, *Early Diary, 1768–1778*, ed Annie Raine Ellis (1889; rpt Freeport, NY: Books for Libraries Press 1971), II, 161–4, 216.

19 Howard Weinbrot, 'History, Horace, and Augustus Caesar: Some Implications for Eighteenth-Century Satire,' *Eighteenth-Century Studies*, 7 (1974), 393, 406, argues that Virgil and the *Aeneid* 'lost esteem' during the eighteenth century because it was felt that Virgil had a political purpose in writing his poem. The antagonism to time-serving poets was in part influenced by Dryden's preference for Juvenal, who had 'more of the commonwealth genius,' over Horace. See also M.M. Kelsall, 'What God, What Mortal? The *Aeneid* and English Mock-Heroic,' *Arion*, 8 (1969), 359–79; and T.W. Harrison, 'English Virgil: The *Aeneid* in the XVIII Century,' *Philologica Pragensia*, 10 (1967), 1–11.

20 *Works*, XV, 406. Citations from *Don Sebastian* and *Amphitryon* are taken from this volume of the California edition of Dryden, edited by Earl Miner (1976).

21 *Works*, XV, 387–8, for Dryden's sources for Almeyda's character.

22 *Works*, XV, 479–80, for parallel passages in Molière.

23 John Dryden, *The Dramatic Works of John Dryden with a Life of the Author*, ed Sir Walter Scott and George Saintsbury (Edinburgh: William Paterson 1882), VIII, 34. See also the note in *Works*, XV, 480.

24 Charles E. Ward, *The Life of John Dryden* (Chapel Hill: University of North

Carolina Press 1961), pp 253–4; Scott and Saintsbury, eds, *Dramatic Works*, VIII, 221–2. Henceforth references to *Cleomenes* and *Love Triumphant*, taken from this volume, will be cited in the text as SS, followed by the volume and page numbers.

25 Saintsbury says that Dryden included this scene 'to gratify the more barbarous part of his audience' (SS, VIII, 209). Its apparent weakness, however, well expresses Dryden's contempt for subjects too cowardly to take risks. 'Egyptians' can be identified with 'Englishmen' because of their attraction to slogans using the word 'liberty.'

26 An excellent article by George Watson, 'Dryden and the Jacobites,' *Times Literary Supplement*, 16 March 1973, pp 301–2, presents reasons why Dryden's Jacobitism would likely have paled during the 1690s. Watson's evidence is different from mine, his conclusions similar.

27 Francesca calls both the book of Lancelot and its author panders, a hypocritical escape from responsibility that shows that she may deserve her punishment. Victoria has not yielded and so cannot be called a hypocrite. There is a chapter on 'The book as *Galeotto*' (i.e., Galahad or pander) in Robert Hollander, *Boccaccio's Two Venuses* (New York: Columbia University Press 1977), pp 92–116.

28 For an analysis of this type of incest in real life see Judith Herman and Lisa Hirschman, 'Father-Daughter Incest,' *Signs*, 2 (1977), 735–56. The authors found that over 90 per cent of the instances of parent-child incest involved fathers and daughters. The rest were about equally divided between fathers and sons, and mothers and sons. Oedipal relationships are thus extremely rare.

29 The Shylock story was also a model for the subplot of *Don Sebastian*, where the Mufti, father of the comic heroine, is outwitted much as Jessica outwits her father. The Mufti is treated with no sympathy at all, and he is more like an Anglican than a Jew.

CHAPTER 3

1 Harry M. Geduld, *Prince of Publishers: A Study of the Work and Career of Jacob Tonson* (Bloomington: Indiana University Press 1969), pp 91–6, says of the first miscellany: 'Compared with the later volumes, [it] is narrow in scope, poor in its choice of subjects, and restricted in form.' He means that long stretches of translation are unbroken by song and that the material seems to be gathered accidentally. I think Geduld has missed some lines of thematic continuity, though the fact that some translations appear twice might support his impression. Geduld feels that Dryden merely advised Tonson on what to include but did not influence the arrangement. Richard C. Boys, 'Some Problems of Dryden's Miscellany,' *ELH*, 7 (1940), 131, is unsure whether Dryden chose the poems. Actually, this sort of work lends itself to co-operation between two or three people. Raymond D.

Havens, 'Changing Taste in the Eighteenth Century,' *PMLA*, 44 (1929), 502–3, 520, 532, notes the decreasing amount of translation after Tonson's first two miscellanies and its near absence from Dodsley's (1748); of Dodsley's he says: 'Indeed, it is doubtful if a better anthology of contemporary poetry was ever made.'

2 Dryden could have been influenced by his friend Roscommon's *Essay on Translated Verse* (1684), though he was already applying Roscommon's principles by 1684 and Roscommon could as easily have been the follower.

3 See Alastair Fowler, *Triumphal Forms: Structural Patterns in Elizabethan Poetry* (Cambridge: Cambridge University Press 1970), pp 113–15. 'The Speech of Venus and Vulcan' is from Dryden's 1685 *Aeneis*, which consists of fragments. In the 1697 *Aeneis* the word 'conquer' replaces 'triumph.'

4 N.E. Collinge, *The Structure of Horace's Odes* (London: Oxford University Press 1961), p 129. Eduard Fraenkel, *Horace* (Oxford: Clarendon 1957), passim, assumes the interconnectedness of Horace's odes not only with each other but with poems by other writers as well, especially Virgil.

5 Collinge, *The Structure of Horace's Odes*, p 36.

6 Gilbert Lawall, *Theocritus' Coan Pastorals: A Poetry Book* (Washington: The Center for Hellenic Studies 1967), p 5. Compare Eleanor Winsor Leach, *Vergil's Eclogues: Landscapes of Experience* (Ithaca: Cornell University Press 1974), p 248, on Virgil: 'the role of the Eclogue Poet develops progressively throughout the book and must be understood as a facet of its order and design.' Brooks Otis, *Virgil: A Study in Civilized Poetry* (Oxford: Clarendon 1963), makes some very elaborate applications of these concepts of structure and shows how what could have been a collection of fragments becomes a continuous narrative.

7 Strictly speaking, the term 'collective poem' means no more than what it says, but it has value in showing that a poem like the *Metamorphoses* is something other than a failed or deviant epic. See G. Karl Galinsky, *Ovid's Metamorphoses: An Introduction to the Basic Aspects* (Berkeley and Los Angeles: University of California Press 1975), p 2.

8 Otis, *Virgil*, p 28.

9 'A HEROICK Poem, truly such, is undoubtedly the greatest Work which the Soul of Man is capable to perform ... This is the *Æneas* of our Author: this is that Idea of perfection in an Epick Poem, which Painters and Statuaries have only in their minds; and which no hands are able to express. These are the Beauties of a God in a Humane Body' (K, III, 1003, 1006).

10 Lawall, *Theocritus' Coan Pastorals*, p 2.

11 See James D. Garrison, *Dryden and the Tradition of Panegyric* (Berkeley and Los Angeles: University of California Press 1975), p 198ff, on the way in which panegyric, a short form, could absorb some aspects of a major form like epic.

12 On Lucretian and Hobbesian dogmatism see the preface to *Sylvae*, *Works*, III, 10.
13 For Dryden's contributions to *Ovid's Epistles* see *Works*, I, 109–38.
14 Real letters by women were very different from the imaginary letters by women created by male writers like Ovid, Pope, and Richardson. Men saw women's letters as expressions of the subconscious, hence as inferior to speech, which is a public act. Richardson's Clarissa writes shorter and fewer letters as she grows more religious, while her friend Anna Howe starts to write more. Real women, however, used letter writing to create a public self and imaginary letters by men gave them some impetus.
15 In the Loeb edition, *Heroides and Amores*, ed Grant Showerman (Cambridge, Mass: Harvard University Press 1947), 'Dido to Aeneas' is the seventh letter in the *Heroides*, 'Canace to Macareus' the eleventh, and 'Helen to Paris' the seventeenth. It is now thought that the paired letters, where both the man and the woman write to each other, were written later than the ones by women alone, assuming that they were written by Ovid at all. Their authorship is still being debated. 'Helen to Paris' is a response to Paris's letter. The paired letters are discussed by W.S. Anderson, 'The *Heroides*,' in *Ovid*, ed J.W. Binns (London: Routledge & Kegan Paul 1973), pp 49–83. Dryden makes no distinction between the paired and the unpaired letters.
16 For Dryden's new contributions to *Miscellany Poems* see *Works*, vol II. *Absalom and Achitophel*, *The Medall*, and *MacFlecknoe* appear in the same volume.
17 *Miscellany Poems* (London 1684), pp 104–5.
18 *Miscellany Poems*, p 153.
19 *Miscellany Poems*, pp 138–9.
20 *Miscellany Poems*, pp 217–18.
21 *Miscellany Poems*, p 263. 'What *Greece*, when Learning flourish'd, onely Knew, / (*Athenian* Judges,) you this day renew': *Works*, I, 146.
22 *Miscellany Poems*, p 269; *Works*, I, 153.
23 *Miscellany Poems*, p 300.
24 Ernest I. Robson, 'Virgil, *Eclogue* 4.18–20,' *Classical Review*, 42 (1928) 123–4, discovers humorous poetic exaggeration. William Berg, *Early Virgil* (London: Athlone Press 1974), p 167, sees the poem as 'less of a studied politico-religious oracle than as a vision from the dreamworld of poetry.'
25 See Berg, *Early Virgil*, p 169.
26 Leach, *Vergil's Eclogues*, p 231.

CHAPTER 4

1 The pagination of *Sylvae* is very peculiar. It jumps from page 168 to page 353, omitting therefore 185 pages. The whole book is really 309 pages long, not 494. In addition, pages 128–45 are confusingly misnumbered (127, 128, 141, 126, 127,

etc). I have used the Scolar Press facsimile edition (London 1973) and have also consulted a first edition in the Clark Library.

2 The word *Sylvae* means forests or thickets. The title belongs to the same genre as that of Ben Jonson's *Underwoods*, a collection or anthology of small pieces. Bacon produced a book called *Sylva Sylvarum*, consisting of one thousand ideas for scientific experiments. A connection between Bacon and Dryden seems forced, but their books share an interest in the implications of materialism, so that a possible link is not out of the question. *Sylva Sylvarum* was published after Bacon's death; the 6th edition came out in 1651.

3 *Sylvae*, pp 406–17.

4 *Sylvae*, pp 475–80.

5 *Sylvae*, pp 452–6.

6 *Sylvae*, p 393.

7 *Works*, III, 10. Quotations from Dryden's contributions to *Sylvae* and from other poems published between 1685 and 1692 are taken from this volume of the California edition of Dryden, ed Earl Miner (1969).

8 Norman Austin, 'Translation as Baptism: Dryden's Lucretius,' *Arion*, 7 (1968), 600. See also Miner on Horace, *Works*, III, 294. Miriam Leranbaum, *Alexander Pope's 'Opus Magnum.' 1729–1744* (Oxford: Clarendon 1977), pp 40–63, has an interesting section on Pope's use of Lucretius in *An Essay on Man*, which in large degree involved undoing Dryden's emphasis.
This part of ch 4, through the discussion of Virgil, is a revised version of my paper 'Aeneas Absconditus: Dryden's First *Aeneis* (1685),' read at the 1978 meeting of the Northeast American Society for Eighteenth-Century Studies.

9 I have a more sympathetic view of Anne, or of Dryden's view of Anne, than some critics do, and thus I do not feel that the 'strange Concourse' was meant to be patronizing. See my note 'The Opening and Closing Lines of "To ... Mrs. Anne Killigrew": Tradition and Allusion,' *Notes and Queries*, ns 26, no. 1 (February 1979), 12–13.

10 *The Odes, Satyrs, and Epistles of Horace*, trans Thomas Creech (London 1684). Creech writes of 'the Encouragement You are ready to give any tolerable attempts, and reach out a helping hand to all those who endeavour to climb that height where You are already seated: E'en this own [sic] its completion to those smiles which You condescended to bestow upon some parts of it' (A4r). See also *Works*, III, 293.

11 I have used T. Lucretius Carus, *Of the Nature of Things*, trans Thomas Creech (London 1714), I, a^{v}.

12 Lucretius, *Of the Nature of Things*, trans Creech, I, a3r.

13 I am using the Loeb edition, trans W.H.D. Rouse (Cambridge, Mass: Harvard University Press 1937).

14 Lucretius, *Of the Nature of Things*, trans Creech, I, 403.

15 David Hume in particular was aware of the fact that the most disastrous events can become pleasurable when presented on stage, and Samuel Johnson insisted that members of an audience never, except in moments of a sort of insanity, believed that they were anywhere but in a theatre. A recurrent eighteenth-century joke involved the rustic theatre-goer who rose up in the middle of a play to demand that Othello not murder his wife, or some such thing. Ironically this emphasis on the audience's lack of involvement must have made stage tragedy seem flat, because there is a corresponding development of interest in discovering tragic themes in history, past or present. Inevitably there is more involvement in events that really happened. Burke treats the French Revolution as a tragedy; with events occurring just over the channel a little bit of the necessary detachment could be retained. I doubt if contemporary English history could have been discussed as tragedy.

16 Miner's notes to *Works*, vol III, discuss Dryden's poetic experiments in *Sylvae*.

17 Miner compares this passage to 'A Song for St. Cecilia's Day,' 3–9 (*Works*, III, 283).

18 The image of the 'bad Aeneas' (because overly self-controlled) has been countered by recent criticism which sees Aeneas's tragedy in the very fact that he had to sacrifice all emotional relationships in order to bear the burden of history. For example, see Steele Commager's introduction to *Virgil: A Collection of Critical Essays* (Englewood Cliffs: Prentice-Hall 1966), p 11; and even more Adam Parry, 'The Two Voices of Virgil's *Aeneid*,' reprinted in the same collection, pp 107–23. Dryden's *Aeneis* of 1697 is consistent with this modern reading, but the 1685 selections are not.

19 K, III, 1023: 'the tears of *Æneas* were always on a laudable Occasion.' Piety, as Dryden defines it, includes 'not only Devotion to the Gods, but Filial Love and tender affection to Relations of all sorts' (III, 1018).

20 The race between Nisus and Euryalus figures in 'To the Memory of Mr. Oldham' (1684), where they stand for Dryden and Oldham respectively. The pair in *Sylvae*, however, do not represent artists, even though the art of armour is elsewhere a theme.

21 Critics debate the extent of Virgil's Epicureanism and question what his real philosophy was. Epicureanism was perhaps the philosophy of his youth, before he began to write seriously. See L.P. Wilkinson, *The Georgics of Virgil: A Critical Survey* (Cambridge: Cambridge University Press 1969), pp 20, 64; Kenneth Quinn, *Virgil's Aeneid: A Critical Description* (Ann Arbor: University of Michigan Press 1968), p 304. Quinn says that 'his own beliefs really matter little; for Virgil is not, I am sure, aiming at serious or creative philosophical or theological exposition.' Virgil seems to me to resemble Shakespeare in using philosophies in part to characterize persons or situations; the 'better' character might not have the

better or the truer philosophy. One ends with a sense of the relativity of belief, while Aeneas's heroism, centred in a conviction of his own strength and the certainty that Jove is on his side, becomes more impressive.

22 *Virgil: Aeneid VII–XII, The Minor Poems*, trans H. Rushton Fairclough (Cambridge, Mass: Harvard University Press 1934), pp 128–9.

23 Lines 112 and 170 in the *Sylvae* version; lines 329 and 387 in the 1697 *Aeneis* (K, III, 1298–9). See *Aeneid*, IX.249–50 ('animos' and 'pectora') and IX.289.

24 'An Account of the Ensuing Poem ["Annus Mirabilis"],' in *Works*, I, 54: 'We see the Soul of the Poet, like that universal one of which he speaks, informing and moving through all his Pictures.'

25 dixit stridentemque eminus hastam
iecit; at illa volans clipeo est excussa proculque
egregium Antoren latus inter et ilia figit ... (X.776–8)

LOEB TRANSLATION He spoke, and threw from far his whistling spear; on it flies, glanced from the shield, and hard by pierces noble Antores betwixt side and flank ...

validum namque exigit ensem
per medium Aeneas iuvenum totumque recondit.
transiit et parmam mucro, levia arma minacis,
et tunicam, molli mater quam neverat auro,
implevitque sinum sanguis; tum vita per auras
concessit maesta ad Manis corpusque reliquit. (X.815–20)

LOEB TRANSLATION ... for Aeneas drives the sword sheer through the youth's [Lausus's] body, and buries it within to the hilt. The point pierced the targe – frail arms for one so threatening – and the tunic his mother had woven him of pliant gold; blood filled his breast, then through the air the life fled sorrowing to the Shades, and left the body.

26 So does Virgil's passage. But Virgil returns to this scene from the *Iliad*, imitating Hector's farewell to his son Astyanax, in Book XII, when the helmeted Aeneas sardonically tells Ascanius to learn how to struggle from him, to rely on fortune from others. This comes right after Aeneas has been wounded. He is shut off from feeling because he has been hurt.

27 Commager discusses the Atlas image in the introduction to *Virgil: A Collection of Critical Essays*, p 8.

28 On Theocritus's sophistication and various definitions of pastoral see Thomas G. Rosenmeyer, *The Green Cabinet: Theocritus and the European Pastoral Lyric* (Berkeley and Los Angeles: University of California Press 1969), ch 1.

29 Marvell's ode is written in four-line stanzas, but Dryden's octosyllabic couplets recall other lyrics by Marvell. See *Works*, III, 291.

30 Horace's tone is less apprehensive:

illi robur et aes triplex
circa pectus erat, qui fragilem truci
commisit pelago ratem
primus. (*Odes*, I.iii.9–12)

Oak and triple bronze must have girt the breast of him who first committed his frail bark to the angry sea, and who feared not the furious south-west wind battling with the blasts of the north.' (*Horace: The Odes and Epodes*, trans C.E. Bennett [Cambridge, Mass: Harvard University Press 1952], p 13)

31 Dryden's response can be found in *MacFlecknoe*, which contains satiric verbal parallels to Marvell's 'First Anniversary.' Dryden's 'Shadwell alone' recalls Marvell's '*Cromwell* alone with greater Vigour runs, / (Sun-like) the Stages of succeeding Suns' (7–8); line 11 also begins '*Cromwell* alone.' Both poems make use of typology, Dryden satirically, especially in lines 29–30. Marvell uses the image of heavy monarchs (15) and refers to Amphion's lute (49, 73–74). Dryden's lute-player is Arion. For Marvell's poems I have used the edition of H.M. Margoliouth, 3rd ed (Oxford: Clarendon 1971).
MacFlecknoe expresses a more general reaction against mid-century poetry than is indicated by A.L. Korn in '*MacFlecknoe* and Cowley's *Davideis*,' reprinted in *Essential Articles for the Study of John Dryden*, ed H.T. Swedenberg, Jr (Hamden, Conn: Archon 1966), pp 170–200. Several poets, good and bad, come under Dryden's attack, Marvell being one of them.

32 *The Rehearsal Transpos'd and The Rehearsal Transpros'd, The Second Part*, ed D.I.B. Smith (Oxford: Clarendon 1971). Most strikingly see p 27 ('Mr. *Bayes* his Allegorical Eloquence'); p 28 ('runs a *Mucke*' and a 'Pissing-place of his Grave'); p 30 (the amorous Parker as 'the *Cock-Divine* and the *Cock Wit* of the Family'); pp 33–4 (note the cluster of names with the initial B); p 39 (chickens 'cramb'd with Spiders').
Dryden's line 'Two *Czars*, are one too many for a Throne' (*The Hind and the Panther*, III.1278) recalls the two kings of Brentford in *The Rehearsal* itself. For the idea that the original Brentford kings stood for Charles and James Stuart see George McFadden, *Dryden: The Public Writer, 1660–1685* (Princeton: Princeton University Press 1978), p 95. Dryden was giving a new political application to an old joke. Why should he have bothered with *The Rehearsal* at this late date? Coincidentally the author of the play, the Duke of Buckingham, died just as Dryden was finishing his poem. My guess is that the last lines of *The Hind and the Panther* were written or revised after Buckingham died and that Dryden's 'Colledge of the Bees' (1286) includes Buckingham as well as Burnet. This would explain the rancour of Dryden's (or the Hind's) conclusion, which envisions the death of King Buzzard and his flock and their descent to hell (1288).

33 The lines might be compared to Swift's 'A Description of a City Shower' (53–63), which overtly makes the change to an urban consciousness and carries Dryden's imagery of inertia to an extreme.

34 See 'To my Honour'd Kinsman' (60–70), where the hunter becomes the hunted; and 'The Secular Masque' (87). Pope's *Windsor-Forest* makes the point more explicitly: hunting animals is tolerable only because it may keep the hunters from murdering each other.

CHAPTER 5

1 See the note by the editors, A.B. Chambers and William Frost, *Works*, IV, 729. References to Dryden's contributions to *Examen Poeticum* and to *The Annual Miscellany: For the Year 1694* will be to this volume of the California edition and will henceforth appear in the text.

2 'The Bookseller to the Reader,' *Examen Poeticum* (London 1693).

3 This passage is reprinted in Hugh Macdonald, *John Dryden: A Bibliography of Early Editions and of Drydeniana* (Oxford: Clarendon 1939), no 264.

4 *An Essay on Poetry* [and other poems], p 3. See Macdonald, *John Dryden: A Bibliography*, pp 217–18, n 7.

5 'An Epistolary Poem to John Dryden, Esq.; occasion'd by the much lamented Death of the Right Honourable James, Earl of Abingdon' (1699), pp 2–3.

6 Boileau's poem appeared in 1674. Dryden and Sir William Soames collaborated on a translation, which was published in 1683. There is more to Boileau than genre criticism, but much of his poem is arranged around a hierarchical account of the main genres, leading up to epic, 'A Poem, where we all perfections find' (736). See *Works*, ed H.T. Swedenberg, Jr, II, 123–56.

7 *Annual Miscellany*, pp 325–6. Addison might also have been trying to get Dryden to write an epic, since he praises Dryden's heroic strains, but more generally he expresses concern at the loss of Dryden's work.

8 In addition, Dryden makes a reference to 'Jacob,' which presumably means Tonson's desire to profit from this publication: 'For oh, the Painter Muse; though last in place, / Has seiz'd the Blessing first, like Jacob's Race' (95–6). One assumes that Tonson was a sensible man and capable of putting up with all this.

9 *Works*, IV, 16–21.

10 John Dennis, *Remarks on a book entituled, Prince Arthur, an heroick poem* (London 1696), b6r–v: '*if he* [Boileau] *who is a Slave could discover by the force of his Reason that he might make so free with his Master, I am confident that no man can take it amiss, that an* Englishman *who Writes to his Fellow Subjects should take the old honest English Liberty of publickly reprehending what he*

disapproves.' Luke Milbourne's *Notes on Dryden's Virgil* (1698; rpt New York: Garland 1974) exemplifies political criticism. He objects most strongly to Dryden's vocabulary of republicanism, which he takes to be a pretence, and to Dryden's argument that Virgil himself was a secret republican (pp 8, 195).

11 Aphra Behn contributed to the development of the theme in the 1680s, since she sometimes praised the queen along with the king even when one could hardly speak of 'joint rule.' See 'A Poem Humbly Dedicated to the Great Patern of Piety and Virtue Catherine Queen Dowager on the Death of her dear lord and husband King Charles II' (1685) and her 'Pindarick Poem on the Happy Coronation of his most sacred Majesty James II, and his illustrious consort Queen Mary' (1685). Behn's 'Congratulatory Poem to her Sacred Majesty Queen Mary' (1689) is more pertinent to Dryden, since she does not mention William at all and links Mary instead to her father James to create the androgyny motif. This is much like Dryden's technique of not only making William invisible but including a provocative replacement as well.

12 *Examen Poeticum*, (1693), p 446.

13 *Examen Poeticum*, (1693), p 258. See David M. Vieth, 'Poems by "My Lord R.": Rochester versus Radclyffe,' *PMLA*, 72 (1957), 612–19.

14 *Examen Poeticum*, (1693), p 132.

15 *Examen Poeticum*, (1693), p 242.

16 'This glorious Roofe I would not doubt to call, / Had I but boldnesse lent mee, Heauen's *White-Hall*': *Ovid's Metamorphosis. Englished, Mythologized, and Represented in Figures*, ed Karl K. Hulley and Stanley T. Vandersall (1632; rpt Lincoln: University of Nebraska Press 1970), p 30.

17 The connection between Io and Isis comes from one of Cnipping's notes (*Works*, IV, 727). Sandys identifies Io with Isis also, or rather he reports that the Egyptians identified them (p 74). On vegetation myths Sandys cites Diodorus: 'She [Io] teaching the *Aegyptians* husbandry & many usefull knowledges, was after deified by them, and honoured with Temples and Altars. Most certaine it is that they worshipped *Osyris* in the likenesse of an Oxe, (and why not *Isis* in the forme of a Cow?) expressing agriculture (as they did) by the one; and the soyle of *Aegypt* by the other' (p 75). One could make further citations, to texts irrelevant here. The point is that Io was generally taken as Isis, and that Io/Isis was a major goddess associated with Egyptian wisdom; Dryden's juxtaposition of Book I with 'Iphis and Ianthe' makes Io's role in Book I even more important than it already is.

18 *Faerie Queene*, V.vii.2–34.

CHAPTER 6

1 Ogilby's Virgil was first published without 'ornament of Sculpture and Annotations' in 1649. The 'Epistle Dedicatory' of his 1651 collection, *The Fables of*

Aesop Paraphras'd in Verse, contains his remark on descending from Virgil to Aesop.

2 Dryden says of Milbourne: 'For 'tis agreed on all hands, that he writes even below *Ogilby*: That, you will say, is not easily to be done; but what cannot M-- bring about?' (K, IV, 1461).

3 Quotations from Dryden's *Aeneis* are taken from K, vol III, and are indicated in the text by book and line numbers. Quotations from *Fables* are taken from K, vol IV.

4 *The Letters of John Dryden, With Letters Addressed to Him*, ed Charles E. Ward (1942; rpt New York: AMS Press 1965), p 93. A theory of how the plates might have been passed from Ogilby to Tonson can be found in Margaret P. Boddy, 'Dryden-Lauderdale Relationships, Some Bibliographical Notes and a Suggestion,' *Philological Quarterly*, 42 (1963), 269–70; but see the objections in John Barnard, 'The Dates of Six Dryden Letters,' *Philological Quarterly*, 42 (1963), 403.

5 Pope's use of the *Aeneis* in *The Rape of the Lock* shows that he saw the satire implicit in Dryden's style. Pope says nothing about what Dryden might have been satirizing, but he does imply that the Catholic nobility should try to be conciliatory.

6 L. Proudfoot, *Dryden's 'Aeneid' and Its Seventeenth Century Predecessors* (Manchester: Manchester University Press 1960), passim, is obsessed with the subject.

7 *Works*, II, 44.

8 Proudfoot, *Dryden's 'Aeneid,'* thinks that Virgil's treatment of Drances may have inspired Dryden's satiric method (p 204). He has a point, though it is overstated in imagining just *one* source for the character technique.

9 Parallels between Virgil's *Aeneid* and Dryden's works, including *Fables*, have been noted by Reuben Brower in 'Dryden's Epic Manner and Virgil,' in *Mirror on Mirror: Translation, Imitation, Parody* (Cambridge, Mass: Harvard University Press 1974), pp 103–22, originally published in *PMLA*, 55 (1940), 119–38. Brower does not distinguish between Dryden's early and late allusions to Virgil or discuss any new meaning that his allusions might have acquired after he translated Virgil, although he feels that Dryden's translation liberated his Virgilian strain.

10 See 'To my Honour'd Kinsman,' 142–9.

11 In the dedication of the *Aeneis* Dryden defends Virgil against the charge of being derivative: '*Scaliger* hath made out, saith Segrais, that the History of *Troy* was no more the Invention of *Homer*, than of *Virgil.* There was not an Old Woman, or almost a child, but had it in their Mouths, before the Greek Poet or his Friends digested it into this admirable order in which we read it' (K, III, 1033). In the preface to *Fables* Dryden admits 'that the *Roman* Poem is but the Second Part of the *Ilias*; a Continuation of the same Story,' but he uses an argument much

like Scaliger's – the existence of an oral or popular culture antedating the great writers – to suggest the precise degree of Chaucer's and Boccaccio's originality (K, IV, 1448, 1461).

12 The legend that living near Virgil's tomb inspired Boccaccio to write is repeated by Thomas Caldecot Chubb, *The Life of Giovanni Boccaccio* (Port Washington, NY: Kennikat 1930), pp 96, 99.

13 See Rachel A. Miller, 'Regal Hunting: Dryden's Influence on *Windsor-Forest*,' *Eighteenth-Century Studies*, 13 (1979/80), 169–88, which shows in detail where Dryden attacked William in *Fables*.

14 See Kinsley's note, K, IV, 2072–4.

15 The relationship between Salviati's text and the 1620 translation are treated at length by Herbert G. Wright, *The First English Translation of the 'Decameron' (1620)* (Upsala: English Institute 1953), pp 146–64, especially pp 151–5. Wright is largely concerned with arguing that John Florio was the early translator. A recent translator of the *Decameron* disagrees; see G.H. McWilliam, trans, *The Decameron* (Harmondsworth: Penguin 1972), p 27. McWilliam also disagrees with Wright's view that the 1620 translator used the original Italian text (pp 34–5).

16 *The Decameron ... translated into English Anno 1620*, introd Edward Hutton, Tudor Translations, 1st series, vol 41 (1909; rpt New York: AMS Press 1967), III, 13–14; *Il Decamerone*, ed Angelo Ottolini (Milan: Ulrico Hoepli 1965), p 319.

17 Hutton, ed, *The Decameron*, III, 72.

18 Hutton, ed, *The Decameron*, III, 71, has 'Bloodhounds.'

19 The passages were admired by Sir Walter Scott, *The Life of John Dryden*, ed Bernard Kreissman (1834; rpt Lincoln: University of Nebraska Press 1963), p 422, for their 'beauties of the terrific order.'

20 Ottolini, ed, *Il Decamerone*, p 356.

21 Brower, 'Dryden's Epic Manner and Virgil,' p 121.

22 *Fables* directly influenced *The Castle of Otranto*. Walpole took the names of two of his characters, Theodore and Hippolita, from Dryden. The fact that Walpole's Hippolita is anything but Amazonian is surely intended ironically, and in fact Dryden's Hippolita, like Chaucer's, exerts a softening, 'feminine' influence on Theseus. On a more provocative level Walpole's complex account of the 'source' of his story – supposedly a sixteenth-century version of a medieval tale, edited, translated, and published in the eighteenth century in an ostentatiously modern style – parallels Dryden's involuted relationship to *his* various originals.

23 K, IV, 2072–4.

24 In Wilmot, *The Tragedy of Tancred and Gismund (1591–92)*, ed W.W. Greg, Malone Society reprints (Oxford: Oxford University Press 1914), all the characters have overflowing hearts or desire to possess the heart of another. The heart is

the person (396–402, 425, 704–6, 1004–7, 1180, and elsewhere). Herbert G. Wright, *Boccaccio in England from Chaucer to Tennyson* (London: Athlone 1957), pp 122–5, argues that the tendency to idealize Tancred makes it harder to explain his cruelty.

Boccaccio's Ghismonda several times refers to herself as 'carne,' so that the physical heart is an ironic response to what she herself has claimed to be her true nature. 'Carne' is usually weakened by translation as 'flesh and blood,' in English a cliché. See Hutton, ed, *The Decameron*, II, 149; McWilliam, trans, *The Decameron*, p 337; *The Decameron of Giovanni Boccaccio*, trans John Payne (New York: Triangle 1940), p 197; *The Decameron*, ed and trans Mark Musa and Peter E. Bondanella (New York: Norton 1979), p 83. Dryden says 'flesh and blood.'

25 Ottolini, ed, *Il Decamerone*, pp 250–1.

26 The popularity of the tale may owe something to its resemblance to Virgil, to which various readers may have responded independently. William Walter's *Guystarde and Sygysmonde* (1532) includes Dido in a roll-call of heroines. This version is reprinted in *Early English Versions of the Tales of 'Guiscardo and Ghismondi' and 'Titus and Gisippus,'* ed Herbert G. Wright, Early English Text Society, no 205 (London: Humphrey Milford 1937), p 111. An Italian play, *Didone* (1547), influenced Wilmot, according to John W. Cunliffe, 'Gismond of Salerne,' *PMLA*, 21 (1906), 442.

27 Boccaccio's heroine blames fortune: 'Ma la Fortuna, invidiosa di così lungo e di così gran diletto' (Ottolini, ed, *Il Decamerone*, p 251).

28 In the original Guiscardo says, 'Amor può troppo più che nè voi nè io possiamo' (Ottolini, ed, *Il Decamerone*, p 252), a speech much admired for its brevity. Scott, *The Life of John Dryden*, objects to Dryden's expansion (p 422). The 1620 version says, 'Alas my Lord! Love is able to do much more, then either you, or I' (Hutton, ed, *The Decameron*, II, 147).

29 See Otway, *The Atheist* (1684), in *The Works of Thomas Otway*, ed J.C. Ghosh (Oxford: Clarendon 1968), II, 379: *Porcia*: [Liberty] is an English Woman's natural Right. Do not our Fathers, Brothers and Kinsmen often, upon pretence of it, bid fair for Rebellion against their Soveraign; And why ought not we, by their Example, to rebel as plausibly against them? *Sylv[ia]*: Most edifying Doctrine this is, truly' (V.430–5). Aphra Behn's complaint occurs in 'The Fair Vow-Breaker' (1689), in *The Works of Aphra Behn*, ed Montague Summers (1915; rpt New York: Phaeton 1967), V, 265: 'since I cannot alter Custom, nor shall ever be allow'd to make new Laws, or rectify the old ones, I must leave the Young Nuns inclos'd to their best Endeavours, of making a Virtue of Necessity; and the young Wives, to make the best of a bad Market.' Sigismonda's antipatriarchal vocabulary also resembles Mary Astell's *Reflections on Marriage*, published in 1700, the same year as *Fables*. In all of these cases a generally Tory orientation does not

preclude sympathy for women on Whig grounds. The authors' sense of irony in fact encourages it.

30 Dryden, *Letters*, p 131.

CHAPTER 7

1 Dated 'Candlemass-Day,' 1698/9: Dryden, *Letters*, ed Charles E. Ward (1942; rpt New York: AMS Press 1965), p 109.

2 E.N. Hooker, 'Dryden and the Atoms of Epicurus,' *ELH*, 24 (1957), 177–90, rpt in *Essential Articles for the Study of John Dryden*, ed H.T. Swedenberg, Jr (Hamden, Conn: Archon 1966), pp 232–44, studies some implications of atomistic imagery. In his *Life of Dryden* Samuel Johnson draws some less ominous implications in his recurrent use of atomistic imagery to suggest the way Dryden's mind worked.

3 See *Metamorphoses*, XI.494–501. Ovid 'would certainly have made *Arcite* witty on his Death-bed. He had complain'd he was farther off from Possession, by being so near, and a thousand such Boyisms, which *Chaucer* rejected as below the Dignity of the Subject' (K, IV, 1451). The last line of Dryden's passage also recalls Althea's response to her brother's death: 'Pale at the sudden Sight, she chang'd her Cheer, / And with her Cheer her Robes' ('Meleager and Atalanta,' 246–7). Ovid has this detail, though expressed with less antithetical wit (*Metamorphoses*, VIII.48).

4 The *Georgics* are in volume II of Kinsley's edition. See Virgil, *Georgics*, IV.92–8. Virgil may or may not have known that bees were ruled by a queen. L.P. Wilkinson, *The Georgics of Virgil: A Critical Survey* (Cambridge: Cambridge University Press 1969), p 264, says that 'The ancients [except for Aristotle] generally referred to the most conspicuous bee in the masculine.' Pope treats Dulness as a queen bee in the *Dunciad* (IV.79–80).

5 See also I.135–40, attacking armies in general.

6 The comic elements of this passage were noted in a discussion of Sir Walter Scott by Herbert G. Wright, 'Some Sidelights on the Reputation and Influence of Dryden's *Fables*,' *Review of English Studies*, 21 (1945), 29.

7 *Fables and Stories Moralized. Being a Second Part of the Fables of Aesop, and Other Eminent Mythologists* (1699), p 135.

8 *Fables and Stories Moralized*, pp 67, 84.

9 *Fables and Stories Moralized*, p 52.

10 Published by the king's printer, Henry Hills, concurrently with *The Hind and the Panther*. An interesting connection between the 1687 Aesop and L'Estrange's first collection, *Fables of Aesop, and Other Eminent Mythologists* (1692), is that both have a picture of Aesop/Adam communing with the beasts. The plates are

different but similar in their general import. By 1699 L'Estrange conceived of Aesop in less mystical terms.

11 The point is apparent in many of the English verses in the polyglot Aesop, written by Aphra Behn, some of which are fairly concrete in their topical reference. For example, see the captions to the fables numbered 30, 43, 46, 67, and 72. Number 67 reads:

The Crow with laden beak the tree retires,
The Fox to gett her prey her forme admires,
While she to show her gratitude not small,
Offering to give her thanks, her prize lets fall.
Morall
Shun faithless flatterers, Harlots jilting tears
They are fooles hopes, and youths deceitfull snares.

12 *Aesop's Fables with his Life*, p 220.

13 Montagu was acquitted. See Henry Horwitz, *Parliament, Policy and Politics in the Reign of William III* (Manchester: Manchester University Press 1977), pp 229–30. An interesting satiric attack on Montagu appears in the anonymous 'Advice to a Painter' (December 1697), lines 80–101, in *Anthology of Poems on Affairs of State: Augustan Satirical Verse, 1660–1714*, ed George de F. Lord (New Haven: Yale University Press 1975), pp 572–3. Macaulay, *The History of England from the Accession of James the Second*, ed Charles Harding Firth (London: Macmillan 1915), VI, 2872–3, is very sympathetic to Montagu; he describes the role of Grub-Street 'fables' in intensifying Montagu's loss of popularity in 1698 and attributes the writers' resentment to their own failure to merit recognition. In his own time Montagu was reputed to have got jobs for several literary friends, especially Congreve and Addison. See Curll's life of Montagu, in Charles Montagu, *The Poetical Works*, 2nd ed (1716), p 49.

14 *Aesop in Spain*, p 14. See also 'Aesop's Thanks,' *Bickerstaff*' s *Aesop*, p 4. Curll relates an incident where the Earl of Dorset introduced Montagu to William: '*May it please your Majesty, I have brought a* MOUSE *to have the Honour of kissing your Hand;* at which the King smil'd, and being told the Reason of his being so call'd, from the Pamphlet before-mentioned, reply'd with an Air of Gayety, *You will do well to put me in a way of making a* MAN *of him*, and order'd him an immediate Pension of 500 *l. per Annum*, out of the Privy Purse' (p 17). Such was Montagu's image.

15 Plate 28. There are 31 illustrating the life, 112 more for the fables themselves.

16 See *Old Aesop at White-Hall*, and *Aesop at Amsterdam* (1698) by Ludlow Redivivus ('Epistle Dedicatory'), as well as the later *Aesop at Court, or State Fables* (1702), in which Aesop addresses the King: 'O fam'd for Arms! and matchless in Renown! / Permit old AESOP to approach thy Throne' (p 5).

17 *Fables and Stories Moralized*, sig. A2.

18 These parallels have been precisely noted in Reginald John Berry, 'Chaucer Transformed, 1700–1721,' diss. University of Toronto, 1978, pp 146–8.

19 Sig. A5.

20 *Letters*, pp 120–1.

21 Scott's discussion of Dryden's *Fables* in *The Life of John Dryden*, ed Bernard Kreissman (1834; rpt Lincoln: University of Nebraska Press 1963), pp 420–7, is entirely concerned with the Boccaccio and the Chaucer selections. Scott may not have considered the Homer and Ovid selections to be 'fables'; his remark that 'When Dryden did translate the First Book of Homer, which he published *with the Fables* [my italics], he rendered it into rhyme' (p 351) suggests that he did not read the fragment of epic as a fable.

22 From 'The Grounds of Criticism in Tragedy' (1679), in *Of Dramatic Poesy and Other Critical Essays*, ed George Watson (London: Dent 1962), I, 248.

23 'Heads of an Answer to Rymer' (1677), in Watson, ed, *Of Dramatic Poesy*, I, 215.

24 H.T. Swedenberg, Jr, 'Dryden's Obsessive Concern with the Heroic,' *Studies in Philology*, extra series 4 (1967), 12–26. Swedenberg stresses earlier poems but concludes that 'in [Dryden's] splendid volume of fables he could indulge his fancy for the heroic to the very end' (p 26).

25 Though Chaucer's young knight uses 'sermon' rather disparagingly, the word also has its Horatian meaning, a discourse in a familiar or plain style. See the preface to *Religio Laici*: 'if he has not read *Horace*, I have studied him, and hope the style of his Epistles is not ill imitated here. The Expressions of a Poem, design'd purely for Instruction, ought to be Plain and Natural, and yet Majestick: for here the Poet is presum'd to be a kind of Law-giver, and those three qualities which I have nam'd are proper to the Legislative style' (*Works*, II, 109).

26 *The Life of St. Francis Xavier* (1688), in *Works*, vol XIX.

27 'As for the question as he states it, whether rhyme be nearest the nature of what it represents, I wonder he should think me so ridiculous as to dispute whether prose or verse be nearest to ordinary conversation': from 'A Defense of "An Essay of Dramatic Poesy"' (1688), in Watson, ed, *Of Dramatic Poesy*, I, 113.

28 *Traité du poëme epique* (Paris 1675), pp 52–3.

29 *Fables de Jean de la Fontaine*, ed Antoine Adam (Paris: Garnier-Flammarion 1966), p 301

30 *Contes et Nouvelles*, ed Jacqueline Zeugschmitt (Paris: Nouvelle Librairie de France 1958), I, 210.

31 *Contes et Nouvelles*, I, 223, 210.

32 *Contes et Nouvelles*, I, 210.

33 *Contes et Nouvelles*, II, 266.

CHAPTER 8

1 Le Bossu, *Traité du poëme epique* (Paris 1675), pp 5–6.
2 There is a subchapter entitled 'The Language of the Gods' in Margaret Guiton, *La Fontaine: Poet and Counterpoet* (New Brunswick, NJ: Rutgers University Press 1961), pp 155–67: 'La Fontaine claims not to have *transcribed* but to have *translated* the voice of nature, as it is expressed by all living things, into the language of the gods, or poetry' (p 155).
3 *The New Science of Giambattista Vico* (1744), ed and trans Thomas Goddard Bergin and Max Harold Fisch (Ithaca: Cornell University Press 1970), p 78. See also p 31 on theological poets and pp 101–2. Fables were hieroglyphs or emblems. Though Vico's work was published much later than Dryden's, the extensiveness of his commentary makes him indispensable for a comprehension of the subject.
4 *Works*, III, 119–200.
5 Pope, *The Iliad of Homer*, ed Maynard Mack (New Haven: Yale University Press 1967), II, 178–9, translates the passage:

Dark in embow'ring Shade, conceal'd from Sight,
Sate *Sleep*, in Likeness of the Bird of Night,
(*Chalcis* his Name with those of heav'nly Birth,
But call'd *Cymindis* by the Race of Earth.) (XIV, 327–30)

Pope may well be ironic in calling the Cratylus a 'Discourse of great Subtility.'
6 '*To my Friend Mr.* Ogilby,' in John Ogilby, *The Fables of Aesop Paraphras'd in Verse* (1651).
7 John Ogilby, *The Fables of Aesop Paraphras'd in Verse* (1668), introd Earl Miner (Los Angeles: William Andrews Clark Memorial Library 1965), pp 114, 144. This edition leaves out the prefatory material cited above.
8 Ogilby, *The Fables of Aesop* (1668), pp 3, 4, 14, 15.
9 On machines see preface to *Fables*, K, IV, 1462; and 'Discourse of Satire,' *Works*, IV, 19–21. For Arthur see IV, 22–3. As Dryden would 'have taken occasion to represent my living Friends and Patrons of the Noblest Families,' he is not entirely opposed to Blackmore's representation of the hero *he* admired.
10 *Prince Arthur*, 2nd ed (London 1695), sig. a2v–b.
11 *Prince Arthur*, p 13. In *Fables* see 'The Twelfth Book of Ovid,' 218 ff, and 'The Character of a Good Parson,' 1–29.
12 *King Arthur* (1697), Book XII, p 343.
13 The Bishop of Winchester, Richard Willis, in *An Address to those of the Roman Communion in England* (1700), pp 58–60, seems to find the literal believers somewhat absurd rather than dangerous. However, it is interesting to find Anthony Horneck, *The Crucified Jesus: or, a full Account of the Nature, End,*

Design, and Benefits of the Sacrament of the Lord's Supper, 4th ed (London 1700), defending the symbolic interpretation of the mass on the grounds of its imagistic vividness.

14 Plutarch, 'Life of Numa,' in *Lives*, trans Bernadotte Perrin (Cambridge, Mass: Harvard University Press 1959), I, 307, 333, 343–5; Livy, *The Early History of Rome*, trans Aubrey de Sélincourt (Harmondsworth: Penguin 1960), pp 52–6. John Milner discusses the problems of dating the lives of these individuals in *A View of the Dissertation upon the Epistles of Phalaris, Themistocles, &c ... in order to the manifesting the incertitude of Heathen Chronology* (1698), pp 6–7. Richard Bentley had based his arguments on the dates provided by ancient sources. Dryden's acceptance of the Pythagoras-Numa relationship despite its historical uncertainty suggests his stand in the ancients-moderns controversy.

15 Pierre Mussard, in *Les Conformitez des Ceremonies modernes avec les Anciennes* (Leyden 1667), p 307; see also p 2. Mussard was minister at Lyon until foreigners were forbidden to preach, and then became minister of the French church in London, where he died ca 1680. His work was translated into English.

16 Sir Robert Filmer, 'Observations upon Aristotle's Politiques Touching Forms of Government,' in *Patriarcha and Other Political Works*, ed Peter Laslett (Oxford: Basil Blackwell 1949), p 207. See also the statement of Robert South, *Sermons Preached upon Several Occasions* (Oxford 1823), I, 113–14: 'And in our judicatures, take away the trumpet, the scarlet, the attendance, and the lordship, which would be to make justice naked as well as blind, and the law would lose much of its terror, and consequently of its authority. Let the ministers be abject and low, his interest inconsiderable, the word will suffer for his sake.' I would like to thank Professor Gerard Reedy for sharing some of his information on Numa with me.

17 *Ovid's Metamorphosis: Englished, Mythologized, and Represented in Figures*, ed Karl K. Hulley and Stanley T. Vandersall (1632; rpt Lincoln: University of Nebraska Press 1970), pp 692–3.

18 William Lloyd, *A Chronological Account of the Life of Pythagoras, and of Other Famous Men his Contemporaries* (1699), pp vi, ix. Lloyd's preface is an epistle to Bentley debunking the traditional lives of Pythagoras. Possibly Lloyd was responding to a work such as Whitelocke Bulstrode's *An Essay of Transmigration, in Defence of Pythagoras* (London 1692).

19 André Dacier, *The Life of Pythagoras, with his Symbols and Golden Verses, together with the Life of Hierocles ...* (1707). Pythagoras, like Numa, was involved in the conflict over ceremony. One French Catholic writer, a member of the oppressed sect at Port-Royal, used Pythagoras as a mask to argue that differences in ceremonies between sects should be considered unimportant: 'The Spirit of Wisdom leads all her Children in the Universal Temple, where there is no Controversie nor Contention about Words and Naked Forms.' See P. Grinau,

Being a Transcript of several letters from Averroes to Metrodorus ... also several letters from Pythagoras to the King of India (1695), pp 128–9; the preface is dated 1687.

20 Dacier, *The Life of Pythagoras*, p xx.

21 In the 'Discourse of Satire' Dryden refers to the '*Sileni*, that is the young Satyrs and the old,' who sang at Bacchus's celebrations. Despite their ugly appearance they contributed to the origins of poetry, apparently in religious ritual (*Works*, IV, 28–30).

22 Guido appears in *Decameron*, Day 6, novella ix; and in Dante's *Inferno*, canto x, which also contains the description of Farinata 'erecting himself,' like Dryden's Corah. Dryden got the name 'Theodore' from Day 5, novella vii, which immediately precedes the story.

23 It is interesting that in the dedication to the *Aeneis* Dryden had criticized tragedy for a related reason: 'The effects of Tragedy ... are too violent to be lasting. If it be answer'd that for this Reason Tragedies are often to be seen, and the Dose to be repeated; this is tacitely to confess, that there is more Virtue in one Heroick Poem than in many Tragedies' (K, III, 1005).

24 There is a useful article on the modes by Douglas Murray, 'The Musical Structure of Dryden's "Song for St. Cecilia's Day",' *Eighteenth-Century Studies*, 10 (1977), 326–34. Pope identified Timotheus with Dryden on a slightly different basis than I do.

25 Dryden himself used the parenthesis as a trope:

> Yet this I Prophesy; Thou shalt be seen,
> (Tho' with some short Parenthesis between:)
> High on the Throne of Wit; and seated there,
> Not mine (that's little) but thy Lawrel wear.

('To my Dear Friend Mr. Congreve,' 51–4)

The parenthesis seems to mean the space occupied by an individual self, Dryden's smaller than Congreve's. It may also be the period of time remaining before self-fulfilment, or the extent of time remaining to each poet in which he will be able to fulfil himself.

26 K, IV, 2080; James Kinsley, 'Dryden's *Character of a Good Parson* and Bishop Ken,' *Review of English Studies*, ns 3 (1952), 155–8.

27 *The Royal Sufferer. A Manual of Meditations and Devotions. Written for the Use of a Royal, tho' Afflicted Family* (1699), p 37. John Caryll's version of *The Psalms of David* (St Germains 1700) contains dozens of headnotes suggesting a parallel between David (endlessly persecuted by his enemies) and James II. A more attractive new version of the psalms, however, was that adopted by the Scottish kirk, *The Psalms of David in Metre newly Translated* (Edinburgh 1699). In ballad metre, or English metre, like the versions of Sternhold, they are poetically far

superior, more like Isaac Watts or even William Blake. Dryden could without distortion replace Orpheus with David at this point.

28 Job was a controversial enough figure to elicit Blackmore's third epic, *A Paraphrase on the Book of Job, as likewise on the Songs of Moses, Deborah, David: On four select Psalms: some chapters of Isaiah, and the third chapter of Habbakuk* (1700). Blackmore's preface includes a thinly disguised attack on Dryden in the context of an attack on the Christian use of pagan mythology: '*We have no* Originals, *but all* Copiers *and* Transcribers *of* Homer, Pindar, *and* Theocritus, Virgil, Horace, *and* Ovid' (sig. br). Dryden retaliated in his virulent prologue to *The Pilgrim*, 'Job's a Bog.' The prologue is one of Dryden's most brilliant satiric pieces, itself an answer to the attack on Dryden's originality, but it is also a little too harsh in its judgment both of Blackmore's poetry and of his literary opinions. Blackmore also shows Job, David, and the rest in their triumphant moments, in contrast to the miseries of the Job of St Germains, from which one concludes that Williamites, Jacobites, and men of detachment all constructed different images of the same biblical figures.

29 Earl Miner, *Dryden's Poetry* (Bloomington: Indiana University Press 1967), pp 219–21, discussing *Eleonora*, shows how this woman at once functions as a pattern *of* God and *for* man. The Maiden Lady is similarly conceived.

CHAPTER 9

1 (auctor in incerto est) iaculum de parte sinistra
venit et inferius, quam collo pectora subsunt,
Cyllare, te fixit; parvo cor vulnere laesum
corpore cum toto post tela educta refrixit.
protinus Hylonome morientes excipit artus
impositaque manu vulnus fovet oraque ad ora
admovet atque animae fugienti obsistere temptat;
ut videt exstinctum, dictis, quae clamor ad aures
arcuit ire meas, telo, quod inhaeserat illi,
incubuit moriensque suum conplexa maritum est. (XII.419–28)

Metamorphoses, ed Frank Justus Miller (Cambridge: Harvard University Press 1968), II, 210.

2 George Sandys, *Ovid's Metamorphosis: Englished, Mythologized, and Represented in Figures*, ed Karl K. Hulley and Stanley T. Vandersall (Lincoln: University of Nebraska Press 1970), p 565, writes that the Centaurs 'were a cruell and libidinous people injurious to strangers; and therefore the Poets invested their beastly mindes with such monstrous bodies; which is not obscurely expressed in their names. For *Aphidas* (as observed by *Delreus*) signifies contentious, *Anti-*

machus an enimy, *Bromus* a railer, *Bianor* [*Bienor*] violent, *Craneus* [*Cranaos* (?)] obdure, *Brialus* [*Briaros* (?)] a theefe; and so in most of the other.' Only Hylonome's role seems out of keeping with all this. Simple romantic love, like brute force, is uncivilized and impulsive. Aphra Behn's heroic couple Oroonoko and Imoinda fight and die together, much like Ovid's Centaurs.

3 On attempts 'to read the riddles hidden beneath the surface of fable,' see Jean Seznec, *The Survival of the Pagan Gods: The Mythological Tradition and Its Place in Renaissance Humanism and Art*, trans Barbara F. Sessions, Bollingen Series 38 (New York: Pantheon 1953), pp 97–8.

4 A useful article on the symbolic meanings of the hermaphrodite, though it concerns Spenser, is Donald Cheney, 'Spenser's Hermaphrodite and the 1590 *Faerie Queene*,' *PMLA*, 87 (1972), 193. Modern distinctions between hermaphrodites, androgynes, transsexuals, etc are useless here. The myths treat them as variations of the same thing, distinguishing primarily between higher and lower forms of the union of two in one, or possibly between stable and unstable unions.

5 Edgar Wind, *Pagan Mysteries in the Renaissance*, rev ed (New York: Norton 1968), pp 212–13, describes the Renaissance Neoplatonists' use of the androgyne to symbolize both Adam and primal man.

6 'magnum' Caenis ait 'facit haec iniuria votum,
tale pati nil posse; mihi da, femina ne sim:
omnia praestiteris.' graviore novissima dixit
verba sono poteratque viri vox illa videri,
sicut erat. (XII.201–5)

LOEB TRANSLATION Then Caenis said: 'The wrong that you have done me calls for a mighty prayer, the prayer that I may never again be able to suffer so. Grant me that I be not woman: then you will have granted all.' She spoke the last words with a deeper tone which could well seem to be uttered by a man. And so it was ...

Note Ovid's imitation of her voice change, which Dryden has to describe with three adjectives ('stern, majestick, manly') and which has no thematic importance that I can see. *Heroides*, ed Grant Showerman (Cambridge, Mass: Harvard University Press 1947).

7 Part I, II.i.141–8, in *Works*, XI, 40.

8 'The Knight's Tale,' 2310. Mary Wollstonecraft quoted Dryden's version of Emily's prayer to support her own views in *A Vindication of the Rights of Woman*, ed Charles W. Hagelman, Jr (New York: Norton 1967), p 208.

9 Wind, *Pagan Mysteries in the Renaissance*, pp 201, 212.

General Index

A separate index of Dryden's works appears on pages 262–5. References to Dryden's letters, however, are included in the General Index.

abdication, theme of 155. *See also* James II

Abingdon, countess of. *See* Eleanora, countess of Abingdon

Abingdon, earl of 112

Addison, Joseph 151; contributor to *Examen Poeticum* 110

– 'An Account of the Greatest English Poets' (*Annual Miscellany … 1694*) 112–13

– *Cato* 37

Aeneas 126–46 passim; and Achilles 30–1, 127; Aeneas-Christ-James II 87, 153; and Alexander 127; and Augustus 35–6, 127; and Blackmore's Arthur 179; as duplicitous 132–3; as hero of Epicurean epic (*Sylvae*) 88–93; as military hero 126–7; as navy man 133; compared to Cymon 145–6; Dryden's contrasted with Virgil's 134–6; 'innocent' 128; Williamite 127. *See also* Dido and Aeneas

Aesop 32, 157–63, 174, 188, 196; 'Aesop the man' 21–2; and fable form 22, 157, 167, 176; and politics 22, 157–63; as Orphic figure 170, 177; as persona for Dryden 159, 163; Grub-Street Aesops 22, 157–9; old and young 159–62; traditional life of 21, 157–8

Aesop at Amsterdam 159

Aesop at Bathe 22, 158

Aesop at Epsom 22, 158

Aesop at Tunbridge 22, 158

Aesop at Whitehall 159, 162

Aesop in Spain 158

Aesop's Fables with his Life (1687) 157, 159, 160–1

age. *See* old age

Ajax 177, 179, 209. *See also* 'The Speeches of Ajax and Ulysses' (*Fables*)

Alexias, St 66

allusion 10, 101; biblical and historical 209; topical 5, 36, 209

androgyny 121, 213–16

Anglicanism 101, 181, 182–3
anti-Augustanism 35
anti-Catholicism 182–3
anti-clericalism 162, 173
anti-symposium 191, 193, 194, 201. *See also* symposium
Apelles 30, 34–5, 149
apostle 174, 183, 186, 204
apostolic succession 181, 182, 183, 206, 222
Ariosto 16, 171, 172
Aristotle 174, 177
armour 88–9, 91–2
art 73, 76, 85, 94, 106–7, 119, 166–7, 180, 199–201, 202, 217, 220–1; and life 77, 99, 106, 193; and morality 193; theory of 151; work of 28, 35, 150–1, 191, 194
Arthur 38, 111, 113, 178, 179, 180, 209
Arthurian epic 113, 177
artist 83, 103; as hero 220; as saint 166–7, 201; concealed 35; quasi-divine 80. *See also* poet
Astell, Mary 143
atomism 149, 187
Augustus 31, 34, 35, 36, 37; and Aeneas 35–6, 127
Austin, Norman, 'Translation as Baptism: Dryden's Lucretius' 4, 79–80, 81

Babel 17–20, 78
banquet of sense 181, 192
Barlow, Francis 159
Bath 203
Behn, Aphra 81, 97, 143
– 'Oenone to Paris' (*Ovid's Epistles*) 56
Bentley, Richard 21, 22
biblical criticism 18, 20
biblical tradition 203
Bickerstaff's Aesop 158
biography 20, 21, 31–4, 73
Blackmore, Sir Richard 113, 116, 148, 180
– *Prince Arthur* 177–9
– *King Arthur* 178, 179
Blake, William 196
blood 141, 195–6
Boccaccio, Giovanni 4, 6, 15, 16, 50, 162, 163, 164, 169, 171; and Virgil 138
– *Decameron* 4, 138–41, 165, 172, 188, 193, 213. *See also Fables*
Boileau, Nicolas 171
– *L'Art poétique* 112
Borges, Jorge Luis, 'Pierre Menard, Author of the *Quixote*' 24
Bouhours, Dominique 169, 180
Bowles, William, contributor to *Sylvae* 78
Boyle, Charles 22
Brower, Reuben, *Mirror on Mirror* 140
Burnet, Gilbert 101
Busby, Richard 13

Cambridge 67
Cambridge Platonists 184
cannibalism 49–50, 118, 173, 181, 184–5, 192, 212, 222
Catholicism 22, 31, 34, 38, 45, 49–50, 118, 122, 163, 174, 180–6, 222
Catullus 78; translations from in *Examen Poeticum* 110
– *Peleus and Thetis* 54
Cent Nouvelles Nouvelles 171
centaur 93, 168, 177, 193, 210–12, 214, 215
Centlivre, Susannah, *The Cruel Gift* 216
Cervantes, Miguel de, *Don Quixote* 24

Chamberlayne, William, *Pharonnida* 207
Charles I 127, 158, 159
Charles II 30, 116, 155
Chaucer 4, 6, 11, 15–17 passim, 20, 21, 50, 109, 138, 149, 152, 162–4 passim, 172
– *Canterbury Tales* 4, 109, 165, 188, 208; 'General Prologue' 166; 'The Knight's Tale' 6, 16, 87, 166, 217, 221; 'The Wife of Bath's Tale' 149, 180, 197, 198; the Summoner 188; Griselda ('The Clerk's Tale') 188; 'Sir Thopas' 165; 'marriage group' 165. *See also Fables*
Christ 87, 153, 167, 171, 178, 181, 185, 198, 222
collective poem 10, 23, 51–63, 123, 222. *See also* translation, collective
Collier, Jeremy 142, 148, 162, 167, 173, 190, 204
Collinge, N.E., *The Structure of Horace's Odes* 53
Collins, William 151
Comenius 17, 20
complements: Dryden and John Driden 180; Duchess of Ormonde and John Driden (*Fables*) 115. *See also* androgyny; centaur; doubles; masculine-feminine couple; old age, and youth; split identity; twins; William and Mary
concealed author 30–7
Congreve, William 198; contributor to *Examen Poeticum* 109, 110
controversy 20, 29, 67, 152, 162, 163. *See also* politics
converts 169, 194
Counter-Reformation 138
Coverley, Roger de 156
Creech, Thomas 68; contributor to *Miscellany Poems* 65
– translation of Lucretius 79, 81, 82
– translation of Horace 81
– translation of Theocritus 81, 97
Croesus 158
Cromwell, Oliver 100, 101–2

Dacier, André 184
dance 84–7 passim
Dante Alighieri 17, 173
– *Inferno* 46, 49, 50, 193
Davenant, Sir William
– '*To my Friend Mr.* Ogilby' 176–7
– *Gondibert* 207
death 78, 108, 115–16, 202, 203, 219; and love 109, 210
Denham, John 17, 87
Dennis, John 113
– 'The Passion of Byblis' 10
Dickinson, Henry 28, 29, 52, 76, 78
Dido and Aeneas (episode) 35, 132–3; compared with 'Sigismonda and Guiscardo' (*Fables*) 141–4
disguise 48–9
'La Dissertation sur la Joconde' 171–2
doubles 25, 41, 214–15, 219
Driden, John 115, 133, 166, 179, 218, 220
Dryden, Charles, contributor to *Sylvae* 77, 78
Dryden, John: and creative role-playing 8, 30; and public affairs 7 (*see also* politics); and religious uncertainty 70; as Catholic poet 50, 112, 173; as old man 14–5 (*see also* old age); confessions about himself 162, 192; conversion to Roman Catholicism 7, 19, 29, 34, 37, 122, 222; idealized selves and

masks 45, 202, 220; mid-life crisis 29; persona in *Fables* 22; political 'exile' 29, 148; self-awareness as translator 10–14; split identity as translator 13, 37
– letters: to Tonson 26; to Mrs Steward 31, 147–8
Duke, Richard, contributor to *Miscellany Poems* 66, 67

eclogue 125
elegy 30, 64, 66, 163
Eleanora, countess of Abingdon 112, 122
Elizabeth I 96
endings 55, 136, 202–6
epic 6, 54, 55, 59, 84, 87, 88, 100, 109, 111, 112, 120, 122, 125–6, 129, 144, 145, 165, 168, 170, 171, 173, 174, 177, 207
Epicureanism 77–107 passim, 147–52, 187, 193, 219, 221; Christian Epicureanism 108, 116, 147; Epicurean art 83–4, 87, 199; Epicurean epic 88; Epicurean poetics 123; limits of 87, 90
epiphany 109, 165
Eucharist 49–50, 118, 181, 185, 222
Examen Poeticum (1693): selections not by Dryden in 110; unity of 110–11
exclusion crisis 63

fable 6, 20–3, 125, 157, 158, 163, 167–71, 175, 176, 180, 212; and parable 20, 167; beast 158, 168, 170, 174; translation of 125
Fairfax, Edward 16, 17
faith 22, 194, 195, 202
father 57, 58, 139, 140
feminism 81, 143
Fielding, Henry, *Tom Jones* 5
Filmer, Sir Robert 183
food imagery 68, 147
fools, wise 188
'force of love' 120, 123, 173
Frampton, Mary 203–4
Frost, William 6, 7
– *Dryden and the Art of Translation* 6

Garth, Samuel, *Metamorphoses* (communal translation) 164
Gay, John, *Fables* 176
georgic 125
Godolphin, Sidney 131, 132
Godwin, William, *Caleb Williams* 140
golden age 96, 105
Good Parson (as ideal) 169, 202–3, 207, 208–9, 220. *See also Fables*
gothic style 138, 140
Granville, George, contributor to *Examen Poeticum* 110

Hall, J. 184
Harrington, John 87
Herbert, George, 'The Collar' 28
Hermetic tradition 183
hero: as artist 220; as brute 180, 210, 211; as butcher 118, 127, 144, 179, 215, 220; as man of action 101, 127–8, 220; as rake 68, 69, 75; as saint 39; Catholic or Christian 166, 179, 180. *See also* heroism
heroism, versions of 104, 126–8, 139, 202; ambivalence towards 6; and endurance 102; and femininity 216; compared with literary activity 14, 23; failure of 45; false 39; military 14, 23, 100, 101, 126–7; physical 208; political 100; private 45

Hierocles 184
hieroglyph 211–18
history 34, 38, 56, 63, 66, 138, 180, 184, 209, 219; and myth 178
Hobbes, Thomas 83, 175; and Lucretius 79–80
Homer 3, 11, 16, 20, 31, 32, 47, 55, 111, 138, 163, 164, 168, 220, 221; as a person 21
– *Iliad* 4, 11, 16, 23, 55, 84, 109, 110, 165, 174. *See also Fables*; Dryden's contributions to *Examen Poeticum*
homosexuality 97
Horace 11, 12, 77, 78, 83, 84; selections from in *Examen Poeticum* 110; selections from in *Miscellany Poems* 65; selections from in *Sylvae* 100, 102–5
– *Odes* 4, 53, 87, 101–25
Howard, Sir Robert 112
humanism, Catholic 181
Hume, Robert 32

identity, development of 58, 59
idyll 66
imitation 8, 10, 24, 172
imprisonment 141, 158
incest 10, 39, 40, 46, 47, 48, 55, 190
inner multiplicity 50. *See also* split identity
Ireland 114, 115
Isis 32–3, 109, 120, 122, 123
isolation 28, 29, 78, 100, 106, 115, 156, 203, 218

Jacobitism 38, 39, 40, 50, 123, 152, 154, 156, 158, 159, 162, 163, 203
James II 30, 38, 45, 87, 147, 152, 154, 155, 156, 203, 209, 222; abdication of 7, 40; exile of 44, 156
Janus 167, 219, 220; Janus-Chronos-Momus 219
Job 203, 209
Johnson, Samuel 9, 10, 195
– 'The Vanity of Human Wishes' 10
Jünemann, Wolfgang, *Drydens Fabeln und Ihre Quellen* 5, 6
Juvenal 11. *See also* Dryden's contributions to the *Satires* of Juvenal and Persius

Keats, John, 'Written on a blank space of a leaf at the end of Chaucer's tale of The Flowre and the Lefe' 151–2
Ken, Thomas 203
king-parliament relationship 198
Kinsley, James 203

La Fontaine, Jean de 167–8, 174
– *Fables* 170–1
– *Contes et Nouvelles* 171–3
language: fragmentation of 18, 19, 20; 'language of the gods' 174–5; power of 123; theory of 17–18
law-givers 178
Leach, Eleanor Winsor, *Vergil's Eclogues* 73
Le Bossu, René, *Traité du poëme epique* 170, 174
Leclerc, Jean 20, 21, 22
Lee, Nathaniel 56, 65
legal vocabulary 60, 99
L'Estrange, Roger 21, 168, 173
– *Fables of Aesop, with Other Eminent Mythologists* (1692) 21, 22
– *Fables and Stories Moralized* (1699) 156–7, 159–63
liar 162, 188, 211
lie 41, 208
Livy 182

Locke, John 20, 198
Lollards 162
Longinus 21, 31
Louis XIV 156
love 14, 64, 65, 117, 207; and death 109, 210; as a quasi-religious force 116; regenerative power of 110, 111; spiritual 119
Loveit, Mrs 132
Lowell, Robert, *Imitations* 23–4
Lucian 31, 32, 50
Lucretius 4, 12, 14, 55, 93, 94, 95, 116, 149, 196, 200; and atheism 12; in *Sylvae* 4, 77–83, 84, 85–7, 93–6, 99, 105, 190; love and sexuality in 14, 81–3

Machiavelli, Niccolo 34, 171
Mallarmé, Stéphane 24
Mandeville, Bernard, *The Grumbling Hive* 176
marriage 97, 142, 196, 198, 216–18
Marvell, Andrew
– 'An Horatian Ode' 100–2
– 'The Garden' 100
– 'To my Honour'd Kinsman' 100
– *The Rehearsal Transpros'd* 101
Mary II 111, 114, 204; and female power 113. *See also* William and Mary
Mary, Virgin 122, 198
masculine ideal 143
masculine-feminine couple 114, 166, 213, 217
materialism 5, 17, 79, 80, 91, 107, 187, 188, 189, 199; Christianity and 80; critique of 83
matter 149, 190; and spirit 190; boundaries of 93–4; sense of 123
mediator 22, 180, 186, 204, 206. *See also* poet
metamorphosis 119, 121, 168, 215
metaphrase 8, 24
Milbourne, Luke 128, 142, 148
military action 152
Milton, John 6, 16, 17, 49, 118, 179
– *Paradise Lost* 5, 92, 105, 179; Dryden's adaptation of as opera 101
– *Lycidas* 75
– *Areopagitica* 33
Miner, Earl 4, 6, 38
miracles 108, 118–19, 120, 122, 125, 188, 199, 201
miscellanies 54; lack of political substance in 77; Tonson's fourth 13
Miscellany Poems, selections not by Dryden in 64–7
misogyny 180, 190, 197, 217
mock-epic 144, 145
mock-heroic 109, 168
models 206; Catholic 49, 173; Christian 6; for translating 173; non-authoritarian 81; Roman 6
Molière, *Amphitryon* 42, 43
Momus, glass of 204. *See also* Janus-Chronos-Momus
monarch, ideal 180
Monmouth, James, duke of 144, 157, 158
Montagu, Charles 22, 158, 163
– 'An Epistle to the Right Honourable Charles, Earl of Dorset' (1690) 111–12
Montagu, Charles, and Matthew Prior, *The Hind and the Panther Transvers'd* 158
Montaigne, Michel Eyquem de 36, 37
Moses 20, 167, 183, 184, 203
mothers 198
Mulgrave, earl of (John Sheffield; later first duke of Buckingham and Normanby) 34–5

– 'Essay on Poetry' 34, 112
mysteries, Egyptian 183
myth 6, 21, 32–3, 56, 59, 62, 120, 122, 138, 165, 180, 182, 192; myth-making 26; mythographers 176–7

narrative, fragmentary 209
narrative reminiscence 209
nature 100, 102, 103–4, 108, 150
Nestor. *See* 'The Twelfth Book of Ovid' (*Fables*)
Normanby, marquis of. *See* Mulgrave, earl of
Norris, John 184
Numa 182–3, 205, 208, 217
number theory 183

ode 111, 163, 168
'Of Natures Changes from Lucretius, Book the 5th. by a Person of Quality' (*Sylvae*) 78
Ogilby, John
– *Aeneis* 125, 126
– *The Fables of Aesop Paraphras'd in Verse* 125, 168, 171, 176–7
old age 5, 8, 13–14, 29–30, 41, 126, 127, 129, 140–1, 143, 147, 148, 162, 192; and youth 14–15, 83, 90, 103, 159–62, 214
Oldham, John, translation of Juvenal's third satire 8
Old Testament 117, 139, 183, 213
'On the Death of *Mr. Oldham*' (*Sylvae*) 78
'On the Kings-House Now Building at Winchester' (*Sylvae*) 78
oral tradition 20, 22
Ormonde, duchess of 115, 149, 150, 166, 198, 204, 217–18, 220
Ormonde, duke of 166, 179, 220
Orpheus 174; as narrator in *Fables* 190–2
Orphic power 167
Otis, Brooks 54
Otway, Thomas 56, 143
– *Venice Preserved* 69
Ovid 6, 7, 10, 11, 15, 46, 47, 138, 163, 164, 187
– *Elegies* (*Amores*) 64, 68–9, 78, 79, 109, 125; translations from in *Examen Poeticum* 110. *See also* Dryden's contributions to *Miscellany Poems*
– *Epistles* (*Heroides*) 53, 54, 56, 58–9, 60–2, 125, 216, 218. *See also Ovid's Epistles*
– *Metamorphoses* 4, 33, 55, 109, 125, 150, 165, 168, 181, 183, 190, 192, 211, 214, 221; selections from in *Examen Poeticum* ('the 1693 Ovid') 108–9, 110, 113, 116–24 (*see also Fables*); as religious epic 109
Ovid's Epistles (1680), selections not by Dryden in 56
Oxford 66

papacy 182
parable. *See* fable
paraphrase 8, 10, 23, 132, 172
Parker, Samuel 101
pastoral 75
patriarchy 57, 141, 195
Pepys, Samuel 133
periphrasis 175
Persius 11. *See also* Dryden's contributions to the *Satires* of Juvenal and Persius
Peter, St 203
Petronius, Arbiter, translation from in *Miscellany Poems* 65–6
Phalaris controversy 22
philosopher-king 127, 154, 182, 221, 222

Pittis, William 112
Planudes 21
Plato
– *Cratylus* 175
– *Symposium* 213
Platonic imagery 16
Plautus, *Amphitruo* 42, 43
Plutarch 31, 34, 44, 80, 182
– *Isis and Osiris* 32–3, 120
– life of Cleomenes 44, 45
poet 127; and king 37, 45; and saint 204, 206; as apostle 174; as law-giver 175; as mediator 175, 204; as mock-poet 186; as outcast 74; as priest 175, 221; as prophet 181; as theological poet 170, 174, 176, 177, 180, 181, 186, 187, 193, 203, 204, 212, 219; as visionary 178
poetry: and Christianity 113, 115–16; as substitute for military heroism 23; heroic 6, 100, 109, 205, 210; political 101, 108, 111, 138; public 30; religious 65
Poggioli, Renato 27
political vocabulary 9, 26, 99, 143, 154
politics 36, 37, 42, 46, 62–3, 69, 77, 101, 128, 130, 137, 140, 159, 166, 196, 207, 218; and anti-politics 146, 147; and literature 29, 109, 113, 114; avoidance of 65; in *Fables* 141, 146, 152–63; in *Don Sebastian* 40; in L'Estrange 156–7; in Virgil 128; marital and sexual 142, 144, 217. *See also* Aesop; heroism; James II; William III
Polybius 31
Pope, Alexander 116, 122, 128, 151
– 'Life of Homer' 21
– 'Essay on Criticism' 112
power 141, 221; beneficent 120; familial 47; female 109, 114, 120, 216; god of 117; masculine 113, 195; of artist 94; of love 110; personal 139; political 47; religious 113; royal 137, 197, 201, 220
primal man 18, 19, 195, 214
primary and secondary qualities 95
print, invention of 18
Prior, Matthew: contributor to *Examen Poeticum* 116. *See also* Montagu, Charles, and Matthew Prior
Prometheus 102–3
Protestantism 33, 118
psychology 131; humour 149; unifying 129
public life 37, 39, 158; themes and issues of 65, 108, 111. *See also* politics
Pythagoras 33, 123, 157, 168, 169, 174, 177, 181–4, 203, 205, 221; golden verses of 184
Pyrrhonism 33

Rabelais 171
Radclyffe, Edward 116
rake 128, 133. *See also* hero, as rake
rape 144, 146, 197, 208, 215
rebellion 137, 143, 157
Reformation 18
The Rehearsal 101
religion 42, 70, 71, 119, 165, 166, 185, 194, 207, 212, 218; religious allegiance 101; religious language 60; religious theme 116; religious unity 18
republicanism 26, 36, 137, 141, 154, 196–7
Restoration comedy 142
retreat 100, 103, 104, 105; to love (in *Miscellany Poems*) 64
revelation 22, 122, 186, 188, 195
revolution of 1688 28

Richard II 209
Rochester, John Wilmot, second earl of 69, 97
– 'Upon Nothing' 116
– 'An Allusion to Horace' 8
Rochester, Lawrence, earl of 103
Roscommon, earl of (Wentworth Dillon), 'Essay on Translated Verse' 100
Rowe, Nicholas 184
royal succession 209
Rymer, Thomas 68
– 'Book 3, Elegy the Sixth' (*Miscellany Poems*) 64–5

St Germains 45, 156
saints 39, 66, 169, 173, 181, 200, 202, 204, 206; and conversion 169; secular 122
Saintsbury, George 43
Sandys, George 117–18, 177
– commentary on Ovid 183, 211
'Sappho to Phaon' (in *Ovid's Epistles*) 56
Satanic figures 102, 103, 118
satire 6, 22, 42, 46, 50, 64, 75, 77, 95, 101, 129, 130, 131, 133, 144, 148, 175, 176
Scott, Sir Walter 164
Sebastian, St 39
sects 19
Segrais, Jean Regnault de 37
Selden, John 116
self: deception of 142; fragmentation of 217; revelation, direct 38; revelation, indirect 30, 205. *See also* translation
sequence (of poems) 53–4
sermon 168, 181, 182, 192, 197, 208
sexual escape 67, 78, 103, 115
Seymour, Lady Elizabeth 116
Shadwell, Thomas 28, 43
Shakespeare 30
– *Hamlet* 39
– *The Merchant of Venice* 49
– *The Tempest* 109
– *The Winter's Tale* 47, 109
Sherlock, Dr, 'Practical Discourse concerning Death' 116
Sidney, Sir Philip 168
Simon, Richard, *Critical History of the Old Testament* 18, 20, 28, 29, 78
Skeat, Walter William 164
Socrates 188
Solomon, judgment of 42
'A Song by *My Ld.* R.' (*Examen Poeticum*) 116
soul and body 212, 219
Speght, Thomas 5, 164
Spenser, Edmund 6, 16, 17, 213
– 'Epithalamium' 212
– *Faerie Queene* 120
split identity 37–50. *See also* Dryden, split identity as translator
Stafford, Mr, 'The Episode of the Death of Camilla' (*Sylvae*) 78
standing armies 5, 133, 138, 155–6
Steiner, T.R. 8
Stepney, George 111
– 'Poem Dedicated to the Blessed Memory of her late Gracious Majesty Queen Mary' (1695) 113–14
Sterne, Laurence, *Tristram Shandy* 95, 198, 204
Steward, Mrs 147; Dryden's letters to 31, 147–8
'structure of structures' 53
stupidity 133, 146, 156, 220
suicide 41, 143, 194
supernatural 128, 139, 144, 193, 201
superstition 31, 62, 69, 182
Swift, Jonathan, 'The Day of Judgment' 176

Sylvae, selections not by Dryden in 77–8
symposium 192, 200, 201, 212. *See also* anti-symposium

Tate, Nahum 7, 28, 81, 111, 112
temple imagery 67, 78, 122, 124
Theocritus 12, 69, 75, 77, 78, 121
– *Idylls* 4, 53; in *Miscellany Poems* 65, 66; in *Sylvae* 83, 84, 85, 96–100, 105
Thyestes 118
Tibullus 78
Timotheus 86, 201–2, 219, 220
Tonson, Jacob 13, 26, 30, 36, 62, 63, 110, 127; Dryden's letters to 26
Tories 143
tragedy 132, 168; theory of 84
translation 3–25, 43–4, 46, 50, 90, 101, 173, 221; and Bible 27, 28; and personal identity 26–50; as oblique self-expression 7, 25, 27, 30, 205, 221; as re-creation 3, 16, 17, 172, 221–2; collective 4, 6, 17, 22, 32, 33, 51–76, 222; creative 5, 7; fragmentary 125; inaccurate 82; limits of in *Aeneis* 125–38; *logos* theory of 17; of epic 126; subject of 'To the Earl of Roscomon' 30
translator: bad 172; integrity of the 27. *See also* Dryden
transmigration 177, 183, 184
Trojan war 56, 62, 96, 97, 208
truth: religious 165; unity of 23, 32
twins 25, 214–15, 217, 219
typology 66, 203, 207
tyranny 119, 154; and freedom 140; arguments against 146; attack on 143
tyrant 57, 117–18, 137, 139, 141, 154, 156, 180, 185; king as 159; tyrant-slave or tyrant-subject relationship 48, 138, 153

universal language 17–19
'Urania's Temple: or, a Satyr upon the Silent Poets' (1695) 111

Valéry, Paul 24
Venus-Diana-Mars triad 202, 219
Vico, Giambattista 174, 175
Virgil 11, 12, 13, 14, 16, 17, 20, 26, 30, 31, 34, 35, 36, 37, 71, 74, 75, 77, 78, 84, 85, 89, 94, 100, 105, 126, 152–4, 168, 179, 220, 221; Boccaccio's admiration for 138; 'Virgil the man' 20
– *Aeneid* 4, 17, 20, 24, 35, 36, 55, 62, 78, 83, 84, 94, 100; and Dryden's translations in *Sylvae* 84, 87–93; and Dryden's *Aeneis* (1697) 125–46; pre-Dryden translations of 8
– *Georgics* 69; fourth georgic compared with Dryden's translation 152–4
– *Eclogues* 53, 54, 64, 72; Christian reading of fourth 71; sixth 186; versions in *Miscellany Poems* 67
– *See also* Dryden's *Aeneis*, *Georgics*, and *Pastorals* in *The Works of Virgil* (1697)
Virgilian career pattern 125
vision 208, 210
visionary *See* saints; poet

Waller, Edmund 16, 17, 131, 132
Walpole, Horace, *The Castle of Otranto* 140
war, evils of 128–30
Weinbrot, Howard 8, 35, 164
Whigs 114, 143
Wilkins, John 17–18
William the Conqueror 5
William III 9, 14, 36, 37, 38, 44, 50, 111, 112, 113, 115, 127, 131, 133, 147, 148,

Index of Dryden's Works

In this index Dryden's contributions to collective poems and translations are listed under the title of the collection. See the General Index for references to Dryden's letters.

Absalom and Achitophel 46, 62–3, 64, 91, 129, 130, 144, 155, 157, 190, 204; reprinted in *Miscellany Poems* 63

Aeneis (*The Works of Virgil*, 1697) 4, 5, 6, 11, 24, 34, 87, 125–46, 179, 187, 205; as response to Virgil 130; compared with fragmentary *Aeneis* in *Sylvae* 90; limits of translation in 125–38

– dedication 6, 12, 20, 31, 34–7, 49, 54, 87, 88, 112, 127, 132

'Alexander's Feast' 4, 86, 102–3, 185, 201–2, 208, 219, 220; as part of *Fables* 164, 166–7

All for Love 215

Amphitryon, or The Two Sosias 37, 41–4, 46, 48–9, 215

– dedication 43–4

– prologue 50

Annual Miscellany: For the Year 1694 108, 110, 112

– 'To Sir Godfrey Kneller' 112

'Annus Mirabilis' 11

– preface 10, 17, 90, 109

Aureng-Zebe 61, 216

'The Character of Polybius and His Writings' 31

Cleomenes 37, 44–6, 49, 122

The Conquest of Granada 216

Don Sebastian 37–41, 42, 122

– prologue 38, 50

Examen Poeticum (1693) 7, 51, 108–24, 125, 165, 167; emphasis on feminine in 113, 167; regenerative power of love in 110–11

– dedication 109, 110, 111

– 'The First Book of Ovid's Metamorphoses' 108, 110, 117–20

– 'The Fable of Iphis and Ianthe. From the Ninth Book of the Metamorphoses' 108, 109–10, 117, 120–1

– 'The Fable of Acis, Polyphemus, and

153, 154, 158, 159, 162, 179, 192, 202, 209, 222
William and Mary 108, 113, 114, 115; as ideal complements 111, 113
Wilmot, Robert, *The Tragedy of Tancred and Gismund* (1591–2) 140–1
Wishfort, Lady 132
Wolsey, Thomas, Cardinal 9
women and heroism, ambivalence towards 216
Worcester, Bishop of 183
Wordsworth, William 4

Xavier, St Francis 169, 173, 180

Yalden, Thomas, 'A Hymn to Darkness' (*Examen Poeticum*) 116
Yenser, Stephen 23
youth 29–30, 81, 157. *See also* old age

Galatea. From the Thirteenth Book of the Metamorphoses' 108–10, 117, 121–2
– 'Song to a Fair, Young Lady, Going out of the Town in the Spring' 109, 116, 123–4
– 'Veni Creator Spiritus, Translated in Paraphrase' 109, 123, 124
– 'Rondelay' 109, 123, 124
– 'The Last Parting of Hector and Andromache. From the Sixth Book of Homer's Iliads' 109, 110

Fables Ancient and Modern (1700) 4, 5, 6, 7, 10, 11, 22, 23, 24, 46, 47, 51, 55, 64, 109, 122–3, 125–46 passim, 147–73, 184–206, 207–19, 220–2; as anti-*Aeneis* 128; as anti-Williamite 152; ending of 202–6; 'marriage group' in 165; revelation in 23; unity of 6–7, 22–3, and passim
– dedication 126, 163, 179, 202, 220
– preface 3, 10, 15, 17, 21, 24, 51–2, 125, 126, 147–9, 162, 163, 165–6, 172, 202, 220; Aeneas and Achilles in 30–1; compared with L'Estrange's preface to *Fables and Stories Moralized* 162; synthetic 'author' of 21
– 'To Her Grace the Dutchess of Ormond' 16–17, 114–15, 163, 166, 173, 198, 202, 218
– 'Palamon and Arcite' (Chaucer) 6, 11, 144, 151, 152, 155–6, 163, 166, 169, 173, 180, 189, 202, 207, 216, 217, 218, 219; as 'ending' to *Aeneis* 136
– 'To my Honour'd Kinsman' 114–15, 158, 159, 163, 166, 180, 197, 217
– 'Meleager and Atalanta' (Ovid) 10, 163, 168, 184, 194, 214–15
– 'Sigismonda and Guiscardo' (Boccaccio) 5, 47, 48, 52, 138, 139, 140–4, 148, 156, 163, 166, 173, 184, 188, 195–7, 207, 208, 215–16
– 'Baucis and Philemon' (Ovid) 109, 164, 199, 201, 216
– 'Pygmalion and the Statue' (Ovid) 109, 164, 190, 191, 192, 216–17
– 'Cinyras and Myrrha' (Ovid) 10, 48, 164, 173, 189–91, 192
– 'The First Book of Homer's Ilias' 47, 126, 154, 164, 185; as 'ending' to *Aeneis* 136
– 'The Cock and the Fox' (Chaucer) 11, 47, 164, 170, 188, 189, 190
– 'Theodore and Honoria' (Boccaccio) 138, 139, 141, 164, 184–5, 190, 193–4, 200, 201; compared with Boccaccio's version 139–40
– 'Ceyx and Alcyone' (Ovid) 47–8, 149–50, 164, 189, 190, 194–5, 208, 216
– 'The Flower and the Leaf' 5, 149, 150–2, 164, 166–7, 169–70, 172, 173, 180, 181, 199–200, 208, 210, 217
– 'The Twelfth Book of Ovid' 148, 162, 164, 168, 169, 192–3, 208, 210–11, 215
– 'The Speeches of Ajax and Ulysses' (Ovid) 15, 126, 152, 164, 208, 220
– 'The Wife of Bath Her Tale' (Chaucer) 16, 52, 149, 164, 166, 168, 169, 180, 187, 197–8, 203, 208, 220
– 'Of the Pythagorean Philosophy' (Ovid) 122–3, 148, 154–5, 164, 168, 169, 181–2, 189, 205, 207, 208
– 'The Character of a Good Parson' (based on Chaucer) 163, 164, 166, 169, 172, 178, 181, 185, 202–3, 205, 207, 208–9, 214, 218, 220

– 'The Monument of A Fair Maiden Lady' 164, 166, 202, 203–4, 209, 218
– 'Cymon and Iphigenia' (Boccaccio) 139, 141, 144–6, 148, 150, 152, 155–6, 164, 165, 166, 168, 172, 173, 192, 194, 197, 202, 204–6, 207, 209, 210, 212–13, 220

Georgics (*The Works of Virgil*, 1697)
– dedication 13, 147
– 'The Third Book of the Georgics' 13–15
– 'The Fourth Book of the Georgics' compared with Virgil 152–4
'The Grounds of Criticism in Tragedy' 168

The Hind and the Panther 7, 18–20, 49, 87, 101, 118, 145, 153, 158–9, 171, 174–5, 180, 181, 185, 192–3, 195, 199, 204, 212, 214, 222

'The Life of Lucian: A Discourse of His Writings' (1696) 26–7, 31–2
'The Life of Plutarch' 31, 32–4
The Life of St Francis Xavier 169, 181
Love Triumphant 37, 46–7, 48–9, 109, 120, 122

MacFlecknoe 111, 118, 204; reprinted in *Miscellany Poems* 63
The Medall. A Satyre against Sedition 64, 128; reprinted in *Miscellany Poems* 63
Miscellany Poems 7, 34, 51–4, 63–76, 78, 100, 115, 122
– prologues and epilogues 66–7
– 'Ovid's Elegies, Book II. Elegy the Nineteenth' 63, 64, 67–9, 71, 72, 73, 80
– 'Amaryllis, or the Third Idyllium of Theocritus, Paraphras'd' 63, 66, 69–70, 75
– 'The Tears of Amynta, for the Death of Damon. Song' 54, 63, 66, 70–1
– Virgil's Eclogues: 'The Fourth Eclogue. Pollio' 64, 71–3, 75, 96; 'The Ninth Eclogue' 64, 71, 73–5

Ovid's Epistles (1680) 7, 51, 52, 53, 55–63, 64, 78, 87, 96, 122
– preface 8, 11; metaphrase, paraphrase, and imitation in 8
– 'Canace to Macareus' 55, 56, 57–9, 60; in *Love Triumphant* 46, 47
– 'Helen to Paris' 56, 59–60
– 'Dido to Aeneas' 56, 60–3

Pastorals (*The Works of Virgil*, 1697)
– dedication 147
– 'The Sixth Pastoral. Or, Silenus' 186–7, 188, 189. *See also Miscellany Poems*
'Prologue and Epilogue to the University of Oxon. Spoken at the Acting of the *Silent Woman*' 1673; reprinted in *Miscellany Poems* 66
'Prologue and Epilogue to the University of Oxford, 1674,' reprinted in *Miscellany Poems* 66
Prologue to *The Prophetess* (Fletcher) 50, 114
'Prologue to the University of Oxford' 1676 43
'Prologue to the University of Oxford' 1680, reprinted in *Miscellany Poems* 66

Religio Laici or A Laymans Faith 7, 18, 27, 28–9, 33, 74, 76, 77, 187, 212

The Satires of Decimus Junius Juvenalis Together with the Satires of Aulus Persius Flaccus 13
– 'Discourse concerning the Original and Progress of Satire' 6, 11, 12–13, 113
– 'The Sixth Satyr of Juvenal,' argument to 13, 114
– 'The Tenth Satyr of Juvenal,' compared with Johnson's 'The Vanity of Human Wishes' 9–10
– 'The Fifth Satyr of Persius,' argument to 13
The Second Part of Absalom and Achitophel 7, 28
Secret Love 132
The Secular Masque, from *the Pilgrim* 202, 204, 219
'A Song for St Cecilia's Day' 183, 202; reprinted in *Examen Poeticum* 116
Sylvae (1685) 4, 5, 7, 12, 34, 51, 53, 55, 67, 73, 76, 77–107, 110, 122, 150, 151, 165, 168, 173, 208, 222; *Aeneid* translation in 87–93; as fragmentary Epicurean epic 88
– preface 11–12, 52, 55
– 'The entire Episode of Nisus and Euryalus, translated from the 5th and 9th Books of *Virgils Æneids*' 85, 88–9, 125, 129, 151
– 'The entire Episode of Mezentius and Lausus, translated out of the 10th Book of *Virgils Æneids*' 78, 85, 91–3, 215
– 'The Speech of Venus to Vulcan' 53, 84, 85, 93–4
– 'Lucretius: The beginning of the First Book' 85–6, 93–4, 97
– 'Lucretius: The beginning of the Second Book' 84, 86, 94
– 'Translation of the Latter Part of the Third Book of Lucretius; Against the Fear of Death' 84, 86, 95, 168
– 'Lucretius: The Fourth Book. Concerning the Nature of Love' 14, 81, 87, 94, 95
– 'From Lucretius, Book the Fifth' 87, 95–6, 190
– 'Theocritus, Idyllium the 18th. The Epithalamium of Helen and Menelaus' 84, 96, 97–8
– 'Idyllium the 23d. The Despairing Lover' 84, 85, 96, 97, 98
– 'Daphnis. From Theocritus Idyll. 27' 84, 85, 96, 97, 98–100, 106
– 'Horace. Ode 3. Lib. 1' 100–2
– 'Horace. Lib. 1. Ode 9' 103, 104
– 'Horace. Ode 29. Book 3' 103–4
– 'From Horace, Epod. 2d.' 100, 105
– 'A New Song' ('Sylvia the fair') 77–8, 87, 100, 106, 107
– 'Song' ('Go tell Amynta gentle Swain') 106–7

'Threnodia Augustalis' 30
'To the Earl of Roscomon' 30
'To the Memory of Mr. Oldham' 29, 30
'To my Dear Friend Mr. Congreve, on His Comedy, call'd, *The Double-Dealer*' 29, 67, 114, 122
'To My Honored Friend, Dr. Charleton' 177
'To the Pious Memory of … Mrs Anne Killigrew' 29, 80, 114, 116